FAMILIES:

A Multigenerational Approach

FAMILIES:
A Multigenerational Approach

MARVIN R. KOLLER
Professor of Sociology
Kent State University

McGraw-Hill Book Company

New York   St. Louis   San Francisco   Düsseldorf   Johannesburg

Kuala Lumpur   London   Mexico   Montreal   New Delhi   Panama

Paris   São Paulo   Singapore   Sydney   Tokyo   Toronto

PHOTO CREDITS: Pp. 24–25 courtesy of the State Historical Society of Wisconsin; p. 24 Culver Pictures; p. 25 courtesy of the Library of Congress; pp. 146–147 Wide World Photos; p. 146 AP Newsfeatures Photo; p. 147 E. Trina Lipton; p. 299 courtesy of the Carnegie Institution of Washington.

FAMILIES: A Multigenerational Approach

1234567890 KPKP 7987654

This book was set in Times Roman and Vega by Black Dot, Inc. The editors were David Edwards and Helen Greenberg; the designer was Mort Perry; and the production supervisor was Bill Greenwood. The drawings were done by B. Handelman Associates, Inc.
Kingsport Press, Inc., was printer and binder.

Library of Congress Cataloging in Publication Data

Koller, Marvin R
    Families: a multigenerational approach.

    1. Family—United States. 2. Family life educa-
tion. I. Title.
HQ535.K65   301.42′0973   73-13932
ISBN 0-07-035331-X

To my parents, Julius G. and Margaret C. Koller,
representatives of past generations to which we are indebted

To my wife, Pauline, life companion and partner,
representative of present generations which enrich life

To our son, Robert Lee, idealist and realist,
representative of the promise of future generations

Contents

Preface

In this text, students and teachers should anticipate a unique treatment of such basic subjects as love, sex, marriage, and family. Traditionally, these topics are treated as two distinctive themes. One is *family life education,* in which the practical problems of understanding oneself and others, finding a mate, marrying, working to establish and maintain a home, building a family, and finding fulfillment in family life are stressed. The second theme is *family theory and research,* which examines family life for its intrinsic worth, its professional applications, and its disciplinary lessons. Most courses in family study offer some blend of the two themes. This text, in part, does the same by offering pragmatic answers to specific questions as well as including materials for those who wish to increase their professional skills or insights.

What is different about this text is the use of a multigenerational approach to organize marriage and family data. The basic details of this approach are outlined in the introductory chapter. Its usefulness and applications are demonstrated in subsequent chapters on love, sex, marriage, and family in past, present, and future generations.

Generational influences, while important to students of family life, have rarely been accorded the prominence they deserve. This theme is particularly relevant to those who are contemplating marriage or who are building young families. They are in the strategic position of discarding or acting upon traditions from past and contemporary generations, and deciding which values they wish to pass on to future generations. What they think and do will deeply mark their own lives, the lives of those closest to them, and, directly or indirectly, many others.

Chapters 1 to 6 are concerned primarily with background data derived from past generations. These include a working vocabulary to describe and analyze family-life variations throughout the world; a discussion of the origin and development of families in Hebrew, Greek, Roman, and early Western Christian cultures; a cross-cultural comparison between preliterate and literate societies; and considerations of sex, age, and race as particularly sensitive areas in family life.

Chapters 7 to 14 concentrate on contemporary American family life. White, urban, middle-class Protestant families are viewed as the norm toward which all other types of families tend. However, since ours is a pluralistic society, equal attention is given to nontypical families—blacks, Spanish-, Japanese-, and Jewish-Americans, the very poor, and the very rich. The problems of generational dissension and consensus, considered in Chapters 9 and 10, illustrate the nature of generation gaps, discontent, or alienation and the chances that exist to bridge them.

Chapters 11, 12, and 13 focus on the creation of the family unit—spouse selection, the husband-wife relationship, and the birth and socialization of children. Chapter 14, which concludes our study of modern American families, traces the changing relationships between and among children, parents, and grandparents as each generation matures, changes its functions, and, to a certain extent, goes its own way.

Multigenerational study of the family does not stop here. Chapters 15 and 16 consider alternate life-styles and forms of families, with education, research, and counseling seen as the resources upon which future generations may rely.

How should value judgments be treated in a field as sensitive as marriage and family? Neutrality, of course, is both a safe and a valid stance. It allows the reader to examine various theories and research objectively and to select whatever set of values pleases him. Further, it allows the author to play the role of educator, exposing every side of the issue for the edification of all. When this seemed to serve the best interests of readers, I chose to remain neutral.

However, as students and teachers know, values are inescapable. They show through every effort to conceal them. Further, the new generations of sociologists no longer feel guilty over expressing opinions. Their values need to be suppressed only if they deny or interfere with the consideration of contrary ideas. While some favor a monolithic society with a single set of values, I recognize a pluralistic society in which opposing values coexist. Accordingly, I have at many points expressed my own views. At least, those who disagree will know where I stand and that I, like they, am also human.

This text, then, attempts a unique multigenerational approach to family life. It does not, of course, pretend to be all things to all people. I hope that it will stimulate further study in the literature on family life, sharpen the skills and insights of teachers, and invite young scholars to bring their zest to bear upon what families mean to their generation and those to come. At best, it can help young men and women deal with human frailties. At worst, it will exposes the shortcomings of the author as he "thinks out loud" with unseen, unknown, and properly critical readers.

Marvin R. Koller

Multigenerational Families: An Introduction

Many parents and grandparents recall little, if any, *formal* study of subjects such as love, sex, marriage, and family. Either these topics were not discussed openly, or it was assumed that all that was necessary was to copy the actions of previous generations. Informal study in which the lessons of family life were "caught, not taught" was held to be sufficient.

Today, well into the seventies, love, sex, marriage, and family are topics of *public* concern and are discussed, investigated, debated, and widely and frankly interpreted. One no longer simply repeats the patterns of his or her parents and grandparents in falling in love, establishing sexual identity, marrying, and creating a family. Students of contemporary family life are keenly aware that rapid social change has made possible a far greater range of alternatives to fulfill the lives of family members than ever before. This text is designed to provide an organizing theme that should pull together what might otherwise become a welter of confusing data concerning marriage and family.

To achieve this end, this text examines two great social complexities: *families* and *generations.* Families are viewed from the perspective of multiple generations, or multigenerations. Families are examined as the context within which multigenerations make repetitive and reinforcing contacts. These contacts vary from empathy, warmth, respect, and admiration to rejection, overt hostility, exploitation, and assault or homicide. Both the internal and external details of contemporary family life have been shaped and stamped by previous generations. By looking at modern families multigenerationally, we can add a valuable dimension to marriage and family life that has often been overlooked—a dimension that young generations of men and women who are about to make adult decisions concerning marriage and family should take into account.

FAMILIES

It would be relatively easy to deal with family if it were a unique, simple social form. But such is not the case. Instead, an almost endless variety of *families* exists. There are families composed of single parents and their dependent offspring; childless couples; both parents with one to a dozen or more children; unmarried brothers and sisters trying to make a home for themselves in the absence of both parents; and young, middle-aged, or elderly couples struggling for existence.

There are other qualities that bring about variations in families. Some families are rural and some are urban. Some are deeply immersed in ethnic, religious, or racial experiences and others are not. Some are impoverished and others live at the peak of prestige and opulence, with myriad variations in between. Some have members who have been educated at the highest formal levels, while others have members who are illiterate. Some families are happy and content with their circumstances. Others are frustrated by conditions beyond their control. Some are at peace, others at odds with the current social order.

For which family variant are we preparing, or should we be preparing, in family life study? In this text, we will emphasize that no ideal family, satisfactory to all, has yet been found or devised. Instead, there are *families* that have both strengths and weaknesses, abilities and disabilities, while individual family members try to follow some dimly defined model. Whatever models we choose, families of almost infinite variety will emerge, and these remain our central concern.

Is Family Universal?

Confronted by the many variations, some students of family life have questioned the thesis that the family is found in every human society.

Attempts have been made to provide some blanket of abstraction that would cover all possible variations of families. Careful definitions are devised and tested against the realities of the tremendous range of family systems found throughout the world. In almost every case, a particular definition of family has been found inadequate or unacceptable. For example, Murdock's definition of family as ". . . a social group characterized by common residence, economic cooperation, and reproduction"[1] is challenged by such notable exceptions as the kibbutzim of Israel[2] and the Navar in Kerala State, India.[3]

Depending upon the approach, family has been defined in many different ways. E. W. Burgess described it as "a unity of interacting personalities."[4] Harold T. Christensen called it "a set of statuses and roles acquired through marriage and procreation."[5] Morris Zelditch discusses the problems involved in reducing family phenomena to some common or universally recognized mold, but he concludes that calling a social institution "family" is more a matter of academic intuition than scientific evidence.

As we have already noted, the academic quest to validate the universality of *family* is hampered by the seemingly endless variations of *families*. In this text we shall examine families as systems in their own right and leave the continuing search for universality to family theorists.

The work of family theorists, however, has yielded one significant point. Family can best be understood through some organizing theme or conceptual approach. Every framework reveals an important facet of family life. Taken together, these approaches may, sometime in the future, elucidate fully the complicated phenomena we have chosen to call family.

The conceptual approach that has been most used to understand families is probably the structural-functional. Because of the way in which families are put together, certain operations, or "functions," occur. A brief discussion of some of these functions can illustrate how our multigenerational approach is connected with them.

Some Vital Functions of Families

Reproduction New generations must be biologically conceived and sustained to some point of independence. In most societies thus far known to scholars, families or familylike units are generally assigned this function; little is left to chance. Normally, parental generations or older generations of adult men and women are committed to each other through some socially approved form of marriage to stay together long enough to reproduce.

Marriage differs from family in that the relationships between men and women are legitimatized to provide for the ultimate goal of establishing some form of family life. Marriage, then, refers to acceptable ways to bring men and women together, to sustain and regulate their mutual affairs, and to provide for the termination of their relationship as circumstances warrant. One basic function of the marital state is procreation, the passage of life from one generation to another.

Socialization   Once present, children need to learn the written and unwritten rules of their society. To neglect this function, even in part, is to socially handicap, cripple, or maladjust them for life. This is no small task to ask of parental generations because all the rules of society may not be known or available for transmission to younger generations. Typically, consciously or unconsciously, parents select from among these rules, which may then be over- or underemphasized, interpreted in different ways, or rendered in some distorted fashion. Further, new generations do not merely absorb what is offered to them by their elders. They also determine for themselves what facets of society they will adopt, modify, or reject.[6] Nevertheless, families, as the first human agency new generations encounter, are charged with the primary responsibilities of socialization. At first informally and unconsciously, and later formally and consciously, the traditions of both past and present generations are passed on to the young.

We would err seriously, however, if we defined socialization as a process reserved exclusively for the young; it is much more inclusive than that. In its broadest sense, socialization occupies entire lifetimes and so applies to middle-aged and older generations as well as to the young.[7] Each generation not only experiences changes but must also constantly modify its behavior according to the limitations imposed upon its age rank. In this larger framework, families play determining roles in whether training and retraining are possible.

Social Placement   Status, or position in society, is basic. By reason of birth in a particular caste, clan, tribe, or family, children are initially placed within the social order. Thereafter, depending upon the degree of openness of their society, children may either rise or fall from the status of their families, or they may spend most of their lives in the same social stratum. If this happens, they remain much as their parents and grandparents before them, neither improving nor losing their original social status.

Production of Goods and Services   As the basic unit of most societies, families provide a wide variety of services. Among the most basic are housing, food, clothing, protection, and socialization. Other services are entertainment, rest, storage of property, and nursing of the sick, injured, or elderly. However, we should note that contemporary families, particularly in modern urban centers, often rely heavily on nonfamily, generally commercial, sources for production and consumption. For those families living in poverty, goods and services may be provided through community-supported welfare agencies.

One cannot place a price tag on all services rendered by families. Devotion and loyalty among family members cannot be reduced to dollars and cents. Dedication under the most trying conditions is far too often held to be an automatic, expected privilege bestowed on persons simply because they are part of a recognized kinship. This type of service is more an unearned, undeserved privilege that many take for granted, except for sentimental occasions such as birthdays or anniversaries.

Emotional Release   This is a priceless boon in an often coldly impersonal world. Secure in the strength of family ties, individuals can safely release the tensions and inhibitions imposed by strangers and associates and still find acceptability. Anger, for example, is a powerful emotion and, if thoughtlessly expressed while engaged in employment, military service, or while working with classmates or teachers, can have dire consequences. Friends and associates are not obliged to absorb anger vented without regard to their feelings. Only in the midst of understanding and sympathetic family members can emotional outbursts occur with little fear of reprisal. By serving as emotional safety valves, families perform a most valuable function.

Of course there is always the possibility that families may be just as emotionally stifling as nonfamily groups. If this is the case, the chances of familial disintegration are excellent. Many individuals can recite how they fled from their families because of personality-damaging or personality-thwarting conditions.

MULTIGENERATIONS

The term *multigenerations*, unlike *families*, is not in common usage. Literature on families is abundant and generally organized.[8] Literature on generations is minimal and scattered.[9] *Generations are defined as cohorts or thousands of persons who share similar, but not identical, experiences because they are born, live, and die within a common historical period.* They may or may not live within the same society or locale. They may or may not experience the same socioeconomic environment. But their times provide common points of reference and are central to their lives. Hence, one of their hallmarks is their temporocentrism; all other periods pale into insignificance when weighed against theirs.[10] After all, it is within their own lifetimes that generations must make their mark in the affairs of humankind.

It is difficult to designate a precise generation span. Usually, however, new generations may be said to appear approximately every twenty to thirty years, time enough for one generation to reproduce and rear the next one to physical and social maturity. If, however, social conditions are rapidly changing, as they are in urbanized, industrialized, and technologically based societies, differences *between* generations may appear more marked. Socialization is geared to meet the increased tempo of events and can differentiate generations within less than five years.

There still remain a number of societies in which the social conventions are slow to change or in which change is resisted to preserve cultural traditions. In such societies, generations that succeed each other are not noticeably distinct. The appearance of contrasting generations in such traditional societies may, thus, take more than the anticipated thirty-odd years.

Lillian E. Troll has ably analyzed the various concept of generations in five different settings.[11]

1 Generation as a developmental stage
Primarily concerned with the individual as he or she moves through the life cycle, this definition of generation can be divided into five developmental stages: childhood, adolescence, maturity, middle age, and old age. In this sense, generation takes on new meaning: the attempt of individuals to satisfy the biological, social, and psychological demands of their chronological age category as well as to develop acceptable ways for making a smooth transition to the next age grade. Childhood occupies approximately the first twelve years of life, adolescence another twelve years or so. Maturity or young adulthood covers approximately fifteen years. Middle age spans some twenty-five years, and old age can extend over thirty years depending on the individual's tendency to longevity and the society's technological sophistication in the field of geriatrics.

2 Generation as ranked descent
In the second conceptualization of generation, ranked descent, chronological age is of little consequence. In this context, generation refers to one's rank in relation to other family members. The oldest living family member is usually said to be of the first generation. Sons and daughters of this person are considered members of the second generation. Grandchildren of the elder are members of the third generation. Great grandchildren of the elder are of the fourth generation, and, great, great grandchildren are said to be of the fifth generation.

3 Generation as an age-homogeneous group or age cohort
The third conceptualization of generation stems from the idea that age

groups occupy a subcultural status and maintains that age cohorts have, indeed, been marked by historical events. Examples of such age cohorts are those belonging to the Depression generation, the post-World War II generation, the Vietnam protest generation, and the like. Such, however, may not be the case. As Troll notes, historical events strike individuals at different points in their own life cycles. Those who are children or adolescents during major social upheavals do not experience the same treatment or have the same perspective as those who are young adults, middle-aged, or elderly.

4 Generation as time span

Generational theorists in Germany, France, and Spain have established the concept of generation as a time span of approximately thirty years. However, the acceleration of social change in more recent times would seem to lend support to a shorter interval—approximately twenty years. In addition, there are those observers of social change who say that three or four years is a more realistic generational time span than the conservative estimate of twenty or thirty years. If such is the case, brothers and sisters with only a few years difference in age could conceivably belong to two different generations, and parents and their children could be separated by as many as five or more generations.

5 Generation as *Zeitgeist*, "Spirit of the Age"

The final conceptualization of generation, *Zeitgeist*, or "spirit of the age," suggests that each generation adopts a moralistic style of its own and acts out this style as best it can. This theory offers an explanation for alienation and conflict between generations or, in more popular terms, "generation gaps." Persons not of the same generation look at the same phenomenon, but the "lenses" they use may be quite different.

The following table summarizes the five different settings or shades of meaning commonly applied to the conceptualization of generations.

Generational Concepts Illustrated

Developmental stage	Ranked descent	Age group	Time span	Zeitgeist (in the United States)
Old age	1. Man(woman)	65(aging)	30 years	Horatio Alger
Middle age	2. Son(daughter)	40–65(adults)	or	Gray flannel suit
Maturity	3. Grandchild	25–40	25 years	Affluence
Adolescence	4. Greatgrand-child	14–25(youth)	or 4 years	Activism and hippies
Childhood	5. Great great-grandchild	0–14		

Source: Adopted from Lillian E. Troll, "The 'Generation Gap' in Later Life: An Introductory Discussion and Some Preliminary Findings," *Sociological Focus*, Ohio Valley Sociological Society, vol. 5, no. 1, p. 20; Autumn 1971. Used with permission of the author and the publisher.

Generational Linkage

Generations are tied to each other in a number of ways. One of the most obvious linkages is that between parental generations and child generations. These are the living generations with whom much of family-life study is concerned. However, past generations, those that have died over the centuries, are also linked with living generations. One would think that with removal by death, past generations could not possibly affect those of the present. Past events do, however, cast long, historical shadows. Ideas set in motion by past generations influence present generations. The linkages are *symbolic*, but this characterizes much of human ways. We are all creatures highly attuned to imagery and symbolization.

Future generations, those yet to be born, are also linked to past and present generations because projections of their lives serve as incentives to those who precede them. The final chapter of this book is devoted to these anticipated generations of the future. Suffice to say here that current family-centered movements such as planned parenthood or birth control are examples of efforts to improve the lives of those who will carry on in the distant future.

Most of those using this text will have the experience of living in both the twentieth and twenty-first centuries. In the early 2000s, these middle-aged generations will become much more conscious of generational linkages than they were as adolescent or mature generations in the mid-1970s. At that point in their lives, these generations may come to know what so many who have gone before them have come to know— that preceding generations labor diligently in behalf of future generations.

Generational Linkage in the Context of Families

Within families, all the symbolic input of past generations, all the give and take of present generations, and all the potentials for future generations come into play. The transmission of symbolic heritages or influences between and among generations is not a smooth, uninterrupted process. Rather, in the midst of family life, struggle and strain are evident and determine which way the fortunes of families and their members will go. Parents, who are the products of their parents, value at least some of the symbolic estates passed on to them. They tend to make moves calculated to preserve elements of this background for their dependent children. To the young, however, particularly when they feel they are on the threshold of independent adulthood, the ideas and wishes of their parents and grandparents no longer appear to be viable. Adolescent refrains familiar to many families are "Times have changed" and "New ways are 'in'; old ways are 'out.' "

In infancy and in highly dependent childhood, young generations are in no position to rebel against parents' wishes, although they may try. Daily family routines may seem to accomplish little, other than meeting physical needs, but these day-to-day activities do leave their mark on impressionable youngsters, who later testify to this fact.

Generational linkages seem to be most sorely tested or challenged as youthful generations reach adolescence. It is during the adolescent period, when age group members have left their childhood somewhat behind and have not yet achieved adult status, that an opportunity is provided to contrast expressed ideals and real behavior in the nonfamily world. Under such circumstances, adolescents can be quick to criticize an adult world that is not of their making, that restrains them from participating, and that so obviously works at cross-purposes from its own ideals. As this oncoming generation moves along, control, influence, and power ebb slowly away from older generations. With their emergence and increasing freedom, younger generations may leave at least a portion of older heritages in disarray.

In numerous American homes, what we have called "breaks in generational linkages" are better labeled "generational clashes" or "credibility gaps." Representatives of youthful generations have pointed out that the words of older generations are simply not matched by their deeds. The perennial idealism of American youth may not be the catalyst of outright rebellion as much as it is the agent of disenchantment toward systems such as democracy or values such as individualism that hold no meaning or promise for coming generations.

Love—that mysterious complex of factors that almost defies definition—has been credited as being the moving force that brings people together and keeps them working harmoniously. To Americans, love is considered to be the reason for getting married. On the other hand, it is instructive to note that romantic love has been treated as being extremely disruptive in traditional societies in other times and other places. In such societies, families have exercised great care to remove the threat of instability that love can produce in order to preserve established systems. To that end, early betrothal, child marriages, and kin-arranged marriages have dampened unwanted exclusiveness and possible family divisiveness. Elaborate precautions, including controls such as chaperonage, veiling, and separation of the sexes, were frequently taken in traditional societies. Many of these same practices, or their remnants, are found in present-day traditional societies throughout the world.

By contrast, in contemporary American society, young men and women are confident that their love can overcome any differences in religious backgrounds, ethnic heritages, education, socioeconomic life-styles, or loyalties to families and friends. It is a confidence that is sorely tested in the crucible of actual experiences. It is also a confidence that plays havoc with some of the heritages of past and present generations.

Change and challenge go hand in hand and are observable on the macrolevel of families around the world moving toward the common model of a conjugal family system and on the microlevel of American families trying to incorporate love, freedom, and individuality into their systems.[12] On the world scene, the ideologies and values of Western democracies have sharply altered the traditional family life as past generations shaped it. In the United States, the posture of democracy in family life has been one of flexibility, tolerance, and encouragement.[13] Democratic family life, based upon inner, freely given controls, has been alleged to be far superior to a system of external, imposed, fairly rigid family controls often inherited from past generations.

This idealistic portrayal of democratic family life, in America at least, has fallen short of the real experience of many young people. Depending upon personal circumstances and the personalities involved, environmental and peer influences, and the existence of opportunities to express reactions, young individuals in their teens or early twenties have disagreed with their elders. Some young persons adopt a relatively mild, but significant, stance by identifying their problems as stemming from communication gaps. Others believe the schism between generations is wider and deeper, and speak of alienation as a more honest description of their feelings toward their parents. A few fanatics have not hesitated to express their contempt for repressive family life by urging mass audiences to "kill" their parents as the first step in achieving personal freedom. Such rhetoric, no longer in vogue, was, of course, symbolic protestation designed to sway audiences. It did, however, indicate the despair of some young generational representatives.

Intergenerational and Intragenerational Relationships

It is important not only to note discontinuities *between* generations but also to observe that there is disassociation *within* each generation. Young, college-age Americans do not totally agree with each other. There is probably no monolithic youth bloc of complete solidarity. Rather, there are factions that range from nonmilitant conservatives to militant radicals. Whereas some young persons are well-adapted to their families, others make a shambles of family traditions. Furthermore, parental expectations concerning friendships, use of leisure time, dating, sexual conduct, drug use, and attitudes toward marriage may or may not be supported by younger generations. Thus, whatever values are held, they rally only segments of youthful generations who stand opposed to others of their own peer group.

Intergenerationally, there is one pattern that appears with enough regularity to be recognized and studied: one generation may depart from the aspirations and cherished ways of its forebears, but the children of the second generation may rediscover the heritage of their grandparents. This third generation conscientiously restores the older generation's ways in order to preserve a distinctive style that could be lost forever. This *three-generational effect* is best documented among immigrant families in the United States, but it can be seen in other settings as well. Among families marked by religious orientations, the faith of the fathers may seem anachronistic to their children, but the children's children see something of worth in their grandparents' lives and do not hesitate to revive it. By reactivating these traditions, their own lives are affirmed.

Cultural marginality plays an important role in producing this three-generational effect. Stonequist's ideal-typical "marginal man" is constructed from the cases of minorities whose representatives try to join the larger society.[14] When these minorities experience rejection, they retreat into marginality—a status of having an interest in both minority and majority societies but lacking acceptance in either. Failing even in marginality because it is a most uncomfortable posture to maintain, many invest their lives heavily where they will find acceptance, namely, among their own people who cling to the ways of their ancestors. American Indians, Spanish-Americans, Chinese- and Japanese-Americans, American Jews, and American blacks provide examples in their patterned generational lives. Numerous families from such backgrounds can report how many of their members departed the older ways and how some came back shaken by their inacceptability to strangers.

Family Loyalty Versus Generational Loyalty

Choices may have to be made between standards acquired through the family and those acquired outside the home. When these two sets of standards are closely aligned, there is minimal stress. But when standards are widely disparate, decisions to go one way or the other can prove heartbreaking. In identifying with their families, youngsters may cut themselves off from some of their own age mates, frequently saying, "I cannot bear to hurt my parents or grandparents." On the other hand, others conclude, "I must live my own life," and become attuned to the life-style of their own generation.

Reisman's characterization of American generations as wavering between "tradition, inner-, and other-directed" philosophies was noted some twenty years ago.[15] In the present, popularity with one's own generation may have to be purchased at a price. That price may mean separation from one's family, or it may mean becoming captive to the tyranny of one's own age group. This price is paid in becoming "other-directed" since others set the directions in which one must move. In such a case, a person keeps his social radar working to avoid colliding with the directions in which others are traveling.

Cross-generational Loyalties

Intergenerational and intragenerational tensions constitute only one set of family-associated problems. There are also cross-generational loyalties that find elders quite sympathetic with the causes of youth. Parents and children may present a united front before the criticisms of grandparents. Doting grandparents who protect, defend, and encourage their grandchildren to follow their predilections to the utter dismay of parental generations are familiar stereotypes. Hypocritical grandparents who are shocked by what they call the crudities, discourtesies, and excesses of their grandchildren often find themselves effectively bypassed by the alliance of parents and children. On college campuses, some middle-aged professors who had long thought of themselves as liberals find themselves viewed as defenders of the establishment, complicit in fomenting generational strife and resistance among the young. But other middle-aged professors have taken the opposite tack, identifying with their young students to condemn the so-called violence brought on by their own middle-aged generation.

Dominant Generations

Americans are accustomed to conferring power upon the middle-aged, those generations that are neither young nor old. The elderly are generally asked, by implication, to relinquish many of their privileges and so are effectively nullified. The young are generally seen as not yet ready to assume responsibilities. Parental power is thus wielded in the family and is extended to every other social institution.

An extension of parental power was found on many college campuses in the not-so-distant past. The policy was known as *in loco parentis*, "acting in the place of the parents," and has not entirely disappeared even in the present. Contemporary American college students, however, no longer meekly accept rulings made by professors, deans, departments, or trustees. They continue to seek much more direct control over their scholastic destinies than did their predecessors. Lewis Feuer has documented this phenomenon as "a rebellion against the fathers" and found that it has occurred in European and Asian countries for many generations.[16] *Mesoarchy*, rule of the middle-aged generations, has thus been challenged not only within the family but wherever it spills over into other contexts that affect the living conditions of the young.

If parental generations are not to be authorities in families or in familylike systems, then there are two other possible ways to distribute generational power. One of these has its roots in antiquity and is termed *gerontocracy*, rule of the elders. As with mesoarchy, gerontocracy has survived through the ages—again, originating in families and extending to religious, educational, economic, and political organizations. Gerontocracy is predicatably prevalent in preindustrial, preliterate societies in which change is slow and time-honored wisdom can be acquired only through seniority. In the 1970s, gerontocracies are passing from the world scene, but they are certainly not totally absent from contemporary life.

A relatively new phenomenon *seems* to be taking root in the United States. It would appear that it is the young or the young-in-heart who set the tone of society. If such a thesis is correct, we observe a unique form of generational dominance, *juvenocracy*. In portions of this text, we examine some of the available evidence that juvenocracy does exist within American family life and, by extension, we can examine how this emphasis on youth diffuses into nonfamily social structures or functions. While adults are ostensibly "in charge," they appear to take their cues from the generation they are attempting to socialize.

In the United States, parents or grandparents may be the nominal heads of families. But, quite frankly, many of them proudly proclaim that the well-being of their children takes precedence over much of what they are trying to achieve. Such families cannot be said to be patriarchies, matriarchies, mesoarchies, or gerontocracies. Instead, they are variously dubbed child-centered, permissive, or filiocentric. When such is the case, parents and elders follow the lead of their children or grandchildren.

In many ways, the United States can be singled out as the prototype of a society that, for the first time in human history, is essentially and forthrightly youth-oriented or youth-dominated. Perhaps another appropriate term would be "youth-intoxicated." To be young in America is often called good. As those growing older can testify, being old is bad.

The Intrinsic Worth of Each Generation

In this text, then, we will concentrate upon families and place particular emphasis upon how generations have shaped them. Just as generations are conceived and given their earliest experiences in families, so, in a larger sense, we can begin to see just how much this familial socialization spreads out over an entire society and colors that society with its own distinctive ways.

Modern American youth has been quite accurately dubbed the "now" generation because in many ways they are in close touch with the latest and most important information. Whole new generations have grown up stimulated by television and other mass media. They constitute some of the best-informed generations this country has ever produced. Their children and their children's children will probably never return again to the authoritative "wisdom" of their elders. Professorial lectures are accepted in some situations, but the greater demand is for discussion between classmates and instructors. In all likelihood, this text will have value only to the extent to which younger generations will dissect it, rearrange it, and capture something of what it is trying to do. Younger generations do not regret that in making it their own, they may do harm to someone's brainchild.

On the other hand, youth alone merits only some plaudits. Mothers and fathers are not foolish persons who are totally unaware of what is going on in the modern world. Their generation has shouldered the responsibility of supporting and rearing the young. Henry A. Bowman, among others, has pointed out that one of the main functions of families is the fulfillment and development of parents.[17] This position is quite different from the usual stress placed upon familial concern for young children, adolescents, and young adults. This position asserts that parental generations must not be forgotten in the family picture because they, too, continue to grow and to derive satisfaction from life. Moreover, parents receive tremendous satisfaction from being responsive to both the young and the elderly.[18] In addition, parental generations are quite conscious of the needs of their own age categories and do not intend to neglect living as fully as possible in the present.

Finally, in keeping with a sensitivity for all generations, the elderly generations must not be overlooked. It is true that they are euphemistically called senior citizens or golden agers, but few older persons are misled by the harsh realities of their condition. Many of them have courageously and vigorously begun a social movement that assures their rightful place in society.

Many of the elderly are said to be overly sentimental and nostalgic about an archaic past, but they are also realistic enough to seek their own independence in the present. As many well know, dependency too early in life deprives persons of their sense of worth.[19] This alone should awaken young people who are well aware of their own generation's need to break the chains of dependency as soon as possible in order to develop their own potentialities in full.

As repositories of knowledge of the recent past, elders possess a wealth of information that could be lost to both the young and the middle-aged. In a number of ways, the experience of elders is not out of date. Their know-how in the arts of living remains as useful as ever. They have survived too long not to be credited with some knowledge of values, ideas, and actions that pay off in the long run. This text asserts that there does exist an empathy between the young and the old. In such programs as Foster Grandparents or Adopt-a-Grandparent, not only have the young and old benefited, but so have all those who have caught a part of the radiance that such generational contact provides.

MULTIGENERATIONAL ANALYSIS OF FAMILIES

In conclusion, two great social complexities, families and generations, are closely examined in this text. Families are viewed from a multigenerational perspective—a perspective that is rare as an organizing theme in the presentation of sex, marriage, and family systems.

Can we anticipate some of the doubts, questions, or resistance to a multigenerational analysis of families? The answer, of course, is yes. We do not deny that multigenerational analysis of families has its shortcomings, problems, and difficulties. Some of them follow.

The Possibility of Going Too Far Afield   Because families are of primary concern, it is desirable to see them in some context or perspective.[20] But, in tracing factors that play a part in shaping family life, the centrality of families may be temporarily forgotten. We can become so entangled with tangential issues as to lose sight of the main point. To avoid going too far afield with interesting, but not relevant, side issues, we must minimize our fascination with facets of family life and concentrate upon the family as a whole.

Disinterest in the Past or Future   Some young students argue that much of the past is inapplicable to the present. Times have changed, they declare, and past knowledge is obsolete and only of passing curiosity. The future, too, is dismissed as too vague, too far off, and too uncertain to motivate serious study. Families, they argue, are to be built in the present by understanding one's self, one's associates, and one's potential life partners. It would be a good argument if the premise of the primacy of the present were accepted. But it is not acceptable in multigenerational terms.

Past, present, and future *are* linked; we need to discover how, and what this linkage means in our lives.

Lack of Realism   Further, it is unrealistic to expect generations to live together with any semblance of harmony because so much of human history points in the other direction. Generations are far more familiar with violence, war, conflict, exploitation, and domination than they are with human dignity or understanding. This is sad, but true. We must agree with this rejection of efforts to reach some idealistic state of generational accord. But by analyzing an idealized position, we may discover real, valid goals.

Taking a positive position, we can anticipate the following advantages to be gained by looking at families multigenerationally.

Perspective   By guarding against going too far afield, multigenerational analysis of families can provide a fresh perspective. Families are not only approached from the context of the social order in which they exist, but they are placed in a time order that has often been overlooked.

An Antidote for Temporocentrism   There is no quarrel with the desire to live in the present as best one can. But much of the quality of life in the present depends heavily upon what has preceded it and where it can take a person or generation in the future. If innovations in family life are not really new, but have been tried before and failed, there is wisdom in learning how to avoid past errors. If valuable knowledge has, perhaps, been lost in the midst of rapid social change, there is good sense in retrieving what has temporarily been forgotten. *In family terms, multigenerational studies of families can reveal just how actions of past generations have led to current conditions.* Further, such study can suggest how the decisions made by present generations will affect the next generation and generations to come. In short, the present is placed in a time sequence in which our time biases are not allowed to exaggerate our own self-importance.

Relevancy   The cry for relevancy is especially strong among younger generations. Realistically, youth is critical of life all around it, a life in which it has no voice. Young generations are eager to get on with the business of living at the highest levels at which human beings are capable. The place to begin is with families. They did not just happen. They were woven out of the social fabric of the past and living generations and cannot escape that influence. If past generations had not been temporocentric, those of us now living would have a far different set of circumstances with which to deal. By adopting the multigenerational approach to family life, we need not continue to compound human errors; this is what is relevant. This is where we can begin and where we can profitably devote ourselves.

Families Are Emphasized   Some young people are quite justified in their outrage over family failures. Such persons have not received the love and care that is alleged to exist in most American homes. Divorce, desertion, demoralization, and physical or psychic separation of their parents have soured their lives. Unplanned, unwanted children have tried to enter the good graces of their parents but have received, instead, rebuffs and mistreatment. In recent years, the "battered child" syndrome, for example, has been discovered and discussed in professional and nonprofessional family-oriented literature. It is true that this dark picture may obscure the numerous instances of happy family life that others can report, but the fact that it persists for even a few, or could be spreading to many others, makes it less tolerable when the means and knowledge are at hand to prevent it. The approach we take in this text is no panacea for all family troubles, but it can be applied in a practical way to moderate family tensions and to prevent further spread of difficulties for future generations.

Emphasis upon Heritages and Traditions   Past traditions have both positive and negative effects upon present family life. It will not be difficult to find a number of entrenched attitudes or behavior patterns that quite literally squeeze the life out of families and family members. The subordination of women is one of these taken-for-granted patterns that has been challenged in the past but has mobilized many women in the present as never before. *Androcentrism* can be countered only by constant vigilance, and we will try to do this as we examine family life together.[21] Another negative impact has been the tendency to avoid sexual topics or to vulgarize them. This we will also guard against. Still another heritage is the subtle or not-so-subtle subordination or neglect of groups of people who may be black, American Indian, latin, or oriental. We can lay bare the realities of their conditions.

The positive features of heritages and traditions, however, can also be championed. Love, courtesy, appreciation, sensitivity, beauty, respect, and tolerance are not out of date and are part of the inheritance from past generations. In the effort to cope with social change, we need not make the error of tossing out babies with the bathwater. Value can be found in some traditions, and we will try to discover it as we move along.

Studying Families Scientifically It has taken many generations to arrive at the present state of our knowledge concerning families. Multigenerational study must rely heavily upon these accumulated family data. Family-life study has proliferated in the recent past, and we will draw upon a tremendous variety of investigations.[22]

One exercise of multigenerational analysis would be for each student to look carefully at his or her own family. Just how many generations of kinsmen and kinwomen have brought one's own family into being? What did paternal and maternal grandparents or great-grandparents have to do with current family circumstances? What personalities, what decisions, what judgments contributed to existing conditions in one's own family? What key events set the direction in which families are moving? What are the consequences of present generations' treatment of past legacies? What behavior has contributed to family solidarity or moved it closer to disintegration? What is taught or caught in the emotional atmosphere of one's family? What is being done to future generations? Where does the individual stand in family life? These would be valuable case studies that would bring multigenerational analysis of the family closer to each person's life and would make reaching for more abstract levels meaningful.

SUMMARY

In this introductory chapter, two major social systems are examined. The primary concern is with *families*, near-universal social agencies that render vital services or functions. The second concern is with *multigenerations*, those generations of the past and present that have developed ways of life consistent with specific sets of symbolic ideas, values, standards, norms, and behavior called traditions or heritages, and that will shape the generations to come.

Families are deliberately emphasized because variants of family life are taken into account. To do otherwise is to attempt to force all families into some common mold that does not really exist. There may well be common denominators that apply to every family, but we will realistically deal with *varieties* of families.

The term *generation* can mean a number of things. Generations can be viewed as developmental stages in a life cycle, cases of ranked descent, age cohorts, time spans, or internalizations of the spirit of the times. In this text, generations are defined as combinations of these interpretations, namely, as cohorts or thousands of persons who share similar, but not identical, experiences because they are born, live, and die within a common historical period.

Linkages *between* generations are not always smooth and harmonious. They may be broken, unhappy, or disrupted by conflicts over ways to think and act. Linkages *within* generations are also sources of conflict or confrontation. There are generational factions that effectively splinter generational solidarity over values and norms. Finally, there are linkages *between* generations within families, and these become subject matter for multigenerational analysis. Loyalties to families or to generations prevent attempts to find ways to satisfy both family needs and the needs of the peer group.

Families, themselves, become the locus within which various generations contend. Sometimes one generation is pitted against another. In other situations, two generations may join forces out of common sympathy. Illustrative of the first type are parents and children, sometimes working together and at other times locked in combat. Illustrative of the second type are parents and children joining together to prevent interference from grandparents, or grandparents and grandchildren joining in subtle conspiracy against the wishes of parents.

Power, or the ability to affect one's own life or that of another, is at the heart of much generational dispute. Some of the alternative ways to handle authority in families are mesoarchy, gerontocracy, or juvenocracy—dominance by middle-aged, old, or young generations, respectively. In an effort to achieve conciliation, much generational conflict over who shall rule can be minimized by recognizing the intrinsic worth of each generation and working for the common good of all. The promise of democracy calls for appreciation and understanding of each generation and not the superiority of one generation over any other.

Because this approach is not a well-traveled path, the unique feature of studying families multigenerationally raises some doubts or need for caution. Anticipating possible arguments against its use, we found that some could fault the approach on the basis of its going too far afield to provide a generational context for family living. Others have indicated a general disinterest in the past or future as not relevant to present generations making decisions concerning sex, marriage, and family life. Still others can point to the inability of generations to live together with any degree of harmony because, realistically, generations are far more familiar with confrontations and conflicts than they are with seeking compatibility.

Refuting these arguments, we shall seek out the advantages of taking a multigenerational approach to study families. This perspective places families in a time order that has been underestimated in more traditional or usual texts on family life. It serves as an effective antidote to temporocentrism, in which generations overestimate the importance of their times. It is relevant to the needs of younger generations who seek to achieve the highest levels of family living of which they are capable. While many families have achieved excellent rapport within their membership, there remain growing numbers of persons who find their families intolerable. Much of what they endure is due to antiquated heritages and traditions. These can be changed, but not without accompanying stress, anxiety, and pain for contending generations. If symbolic heritages contain some value, however, it should prove instructive to learn how generations have dealt with them in families.

Finally, generations of scholars have accumulated huge quantities of family-life data. These can be used to document where we now stand with respect to families and where we may be going in the future. Many students will find it rewarding to examine their own families to comprehend how many generations were involved in shaping the life they themselves lead.

One final point should be made. We will often hypothesize-theorize-posit about families and the impacts of multigenerations. Rigorous scientific inquiry may or may not support these allegations or relationships. Application to specific cases may or may not fit. But, let us see if there is merit in what we are about to do. The untrue will be exposed. The valid will make itself felt.

REFERENCES

1 William N. Stephens, *The Family in Cross-Cultural Perspective*, New York: Holt, Rinehart and Winston, Inc., 1963. The definition of family provided in this text originated with George Peter Murdock.

2 Melford E. Spiro, *Kibbutz: Venture in Utopia*, Cambridge, Mass.: Harvard University Press, 1956, and Melford E. Spiro, *Children of the Kibbutz*, Cambridge, Mass.: Harvard University Press, 1958.

3 E. Kathleen Gough, "The Nayars and the Definition of Marriage," *Journal of the Royal Anthropological Institute of Great Britain and Ireland*, vol. 89, part I, 1959, and David M. Schneider and Kathleen Gough, *Matrilineal Kinship*, Berkeley: University of California Press, 1961.

4 E. W. Burgess, "The Family as a Unity of Interacting Personalities," *The Family*, vol. 7, 1926, 3–9.

5 Harold T. Christensen, (ed.), *Handbook of Marriage and Family*, Chicago: Rand McNally & Company, 1964, p. 3. See also, Morris Zeldith, Jr., in Harold T. Christensen (ed.), *Handbook of Marriage and Family*, chap. 12, "Cross-Cultural Analyses of Family Structure," p. 466.

6 See Oscar W. Ritchie and Marvin R. Koller, *Sociology of Childhood*, New York: Appleton-Century-Crofts, Inc., 1964, and Dennis H. Wrong, "The Over-socialized Conception of Man in Modern Sociology," *American Sociological Review*, vol. 26, no. 2, 187–193, April 1961.

7   See John A. Clausen (ed.), *Socialization and Society*, Boston: Little, Brown and Company, 1968, and Orville G. Brim, Jr., and Stanton Wheeler, *Socialization After Childhood: Two Essays*, New York: John Wiley & Sons, Inc., 1966.
8   See Christensen, op. cit. See also William J. Goode, Elizabeth Hopkins, and Helen M. McClure, *Social Systems and Family Patterns: A Propositional Inventory*, Indianapolis: The Bobbs-Merrill Company, Inc., 1971.
9   See Margaret Mead, *Culture and Commitment: A Study of the Generation Gap*, Garden City, N. Y.: Doubleday & Company, Inc., 1970.
10   See Robert Bierstedt, *The Social Order*, 3d ed., New York: McGraw-Hill Book Company, 1970, pp. 177–179.
11   Lillian E. Troll, "The Generation Gap in Later Life: An Introductory Discussion and Some Preliminary Findings," *Sociological Focus*, vol. 5, no. 1, 21–23, Autumn 1971.
12   See William J. Goode, *World Revolution and Family Patterns*, New York: The Free Press, 1963.
13   See, for example, Floyd M. Martinson, *Marriage and the American Ideal*, New York: Dodd, Mead & Company, Inc., 1960.
14   Everett V. Stonequist, *The Marginal Man: A Study in Personality and Culture Conflict*, New York: Charles Scribner's Sons, 1937.
15   David Reisman, *The Lonely Crowd*, New Haven, Conn.: Yale University Press, 1950.
16   Lewis Feuer, *The Conflict of Generations*, New York: Basic Books, Inc., Publishers, 1969.
17   Henry A. Bowman, *Marriage for Moderns*, 6th ed., New York: McGraw-Hill Book Company, 1970, pp. 542–543.
18   See also Duane R. Carlson (ed.), *Generation in the Middle*, Chicago: Blue Cross Association, 1970.
19   See Richard A. Kalish (ed.), *The Dependencies of Old People*, Occasional Papers in Gerontology, no. 6, Institute of Gerontology, The University of Michigan–Wayne State University, August 1969.
20   See Gerald R. Leslie, *The Family in Social Context*, 2d ed., New York: Oxford University Press, 1973.
21   A term first brought to the attention of the author by Professor Suzanne Keller, Princeton University.
22   See, for example, Goode, Hopkins, and McClure, op. cit.

STUDY QUESTIONS AND ACTIVITIES

1   How do generations touch each other in the context of family life?
2   Could you state with some precision what generational heritages have done to your own family?
3   What heritages do you accept without question? Which traditions would you modify? What heritages would you reject for your own lifetime?
4   Being as honest as possible with yourself, what do you believe will be your own impact upon generations yet to be born?

5   Debate the advantages and disadvantages of studying families from a
    multigenerational perspective.
6   Offer one or more research designs that would empirically test the mul-
    tigenerational thesis in family life.
7   Select a number of texts in sex, marriage, and family systems and explain
    their organizing themes.
8   In what ways do you agree or disagree with your age peers?
9   Indicate in class discussions how close you feel to your parental generation
    and to your elders.
10 What are your expectations of finding value in examining families in terms of
    past, present, and future generations?

SUGGESTED ADDITIONAL READINGS

Cain, L. D., "Age Status and Generational Phenomena: The New Old People in Contemporary America," *Gerontologist*, vol. 7, no. 2, 83–92, 1967.

Davis, Kingsley, "The Sociology of Parent-Youth Conflict," *American Sociological Review*, vol. 5, no. 4, 523–534, 1940.

Feuer, L., *The Conflict of Generations: The Character and Significance of Student Movements*, New York: Basic Books, Inc., Publishers, 1969.

Hill, Reuben, and E. Konig (eds.), *Families East and West*, Paris: Mouton, 1970, chapter on the three-generation technique as a method for measuring social change.

——— et al., *Family Development in Three Generations*, Cambridge, Mass.: Schenkman Publishing Co., Inc., 1970.

Kalish, R., "The Young and Old as Generation Gap Allies," *Gerontologist*, vol. 9, no. 2, 83–90, 1969.

Mead, M., *Conflict and Commitment: A Study of the Generation Gap*, New York: Basic Books, Inc., Publishers, 1970.

Nye, F. Ivan, and Felix M. Berardo, *Emerging Conceptual Frameworks in Family Analysis*, New York: The Macmillan Company, 1968.

Part One

Past Generations

Chapter 1

Marriage and Family Structures

Human ingenuity has devised almost every structure possible for marriage and family life. Out of this array, consciously but more often unconsciously, American men and women have perpetuated those elements that seem to satisfy their needs. These specific structures, with supporting rationales, are part of the heritages from past generations to which we referred in the Introduction.

By examining them in this chapter, we can weigh to what extent they are acceptable to present generations. Three main options are open to present generations. They may accept heritages intact, modify them to meet contemporary conditions, or reject them entirely. If rejections or modifications have already occurred through past generations, present generations may restore or revive them. If, on the other hand, present generations invent what appear to them to be totally new ways to marry or to deal with family, they may discover that they have merely reactivated or relocated marital and family forms long used or adopted in other societies presently existing or societies of earlier times.

By attending to the myriad ways in which men and women live together, we will be made more aware of our own humanness, our own identity with the human family, our own wisdom or folly, and our own roles in seeking happiness on spaceship earth. Let us begin.

VARIATIONS IN MARRIAGE STRUCTURES

Marriage is the institution that regularizes relationships between men and women to permit them to live together to produce and maintain families. This regularizing has essentially taken four forms: monogamy, polygyny, polyandry, and group marriage.

Monogamy

Monogamy is the simplest, nearly universal, most frequently found form of marital combination. It consists of the union of one male and one female and endures for culturally prescribed periods, such as the lifetime of at least one partner. Some societies have gone as far as prescribing marriage as an indissoluable union for eternity. Two examples may be found among the Mormons of Utah and the Hindus of India. The Mormons recognize most marriages as lasting for a lifetime, but they also provide within their faith for "temple marriage" in which the priesthood of the Church of the Latter-Day Saints may unite a couple for all eternity. The now-discarded Hindu practice of suttee involved the ceremonial suicide of the widow, who joined her husband in death by sacrificing herself on his funeral pyre. This practice, too, suggests the inseparability of married couples even when death intervenes.

If there is social approval of plural mating, monogamy remains the most practical form of marriage. It is costly, after all, to acquire and maintain a number of spouses. Usually, only the prosperous and powerful can afford this luxury. Further, even if plural mates can be secured, their care and treatment call for diplomacy, infinite tact, and strong personalities to make a success of the venture. One wit once observed that Solomon of biblical fame *had to be wise* in order to live with his thousand wives.

Monogamy, however, is not a singular, monolithic form of marriage. It can be found in a variety of forms, as we have already noted differences in ascribed endurance—marriages lasting a lifetime and marriages spanning eternity.

Serial Monogamy   Americans usually take pride in a resolute defense of monogamy. But often they have in mind a particular form of monogamy: *one spouse at a time.* Marriage texts tend to stress preparation for one and only one marriage while recognizing that second and even third marriages are possible. In this, they may be remiss in failing to understand that one marriage may not be all that may occur in many American homes.

A monogamous marriage will normally last as long as the participants wish it to continue. If a couple, however, choose to have other, more compatible, marital partners, they legally dissolve their union and seek a new monogamous relationship with someone else. This type of monogamy is serial monogamy because a *series* of marital partners can be secured by one man or woman.

The late Tommy Manville was a celebrity who had eleven successive wives. Yet, Mr. Manville was said to have lived in monogamy. Similarly, but less dramatically, there are numerous cases of men and women having two or more spouses during their lifetimes. Divorce or death of a spouse do not merely indicate the termination of a monogamous marriage. These events may also signal the beginning of another monogamous marriage. Some 75 percent of divorced American men and some 66 percent of divorced American women have been estimated to eventually remarry.[1]

Some generations, such as those of the colonial United States, recognized the need for remarriage of widowers shortly after the death of wives. Men, they believed, could not carry on with children, homes, businesses, and farms without the aid of wives. On the other hand, the rigors of childbearing, child care, and household management under frontier conditions were often too much for wives, and it was not uncommon for men to have a series of wives because of their frequent deaths.

Present generations in the United States have engaged in serial monogamy for the same reason: the survival of many men and women despite the passing of their respective spouses. Older men and women have encountered considerable resistance to remarriages on the allegation that marriage is the prerogative of younger generations. Such disapproval has led to the secrecy of older couples' interest in each other or to the resignation that lonely widowhood or widowerhood is a normal condition of old age.

Nevertheless, the extension of life to a dozen or so years beyond age sixty in the United States has led to an increased interest in "retirement marriage" in which brides and grooms are in their sixties. One investigator, Walter McKain, has closely questioned these serial monogamists and reported on their common patterns.[2]

Criticism of Monogamy and Suggested Adjustments

Monogamy, as currently constituted, has been criticized for its failure to take extenuating circumstances into account. For example, monogamy seems well adapted to situations in which there is approximately an equal number of marriagable men and women. When this balance of eligibles is upset, however, some modifications of monogamy to meet the needs of the more abundant sex are in order.

Term Marriage Term marriage, in contrast to lifetime commitments, has been proposed as a remedy for disturbed sex ratios. The term of a monogamous marriage is specified as five or ten years.

This proposal was suggested in both England and Germany after World War II when there were serious shortages of single men. The intent behind the limitation of the marriage term to relatively few years was to enable single women to marry for at least some portion of their mature lives. Exclusive rights to a husband were not to last a lifetime, but rather were to terminate after a few years. The children from such a marriage would, of course, be legitimate and experience mainly the influence of their mothers. The once-married mother was not to marry again. The formerly married man, however, would be encouraged to marry other women, previously unmarried. These women would now have their turn at legitimate monogamy and legitimate children.

Term marriage was never taken seriously and made part of the legal and moral code. Its defects include the unwillingness of married couples to terminate their marriages within specified periods and the problems associated with the forced absence of husbands and fathers from their families. Further, there are those who prefer to remain single and to direct their efforts toward sustaining children and their families through such services as teaching, nursing, counseling, and social work.

Trial Marriage A second proposal to modify monogamy has been called trial marriage or companionate marriage. Early advocates of this form of marriage were Judge Benjamin Lindsey and Bertrand Russell.[3]

Lindsey and Russell specified four characteristics of trial marriage: (1) Young men and women would live together to determine their compatibility. (2) Appropriate techniques of contraception would be employed to prevent the arrival of children. (3) If contraception failed, children would be placed for adoption within the community. (4) Divorce laws would be liberalized to permit mutual agreement to terminate marriage, to provide for the return of all personal property owned prior to marriage, and to disallow alimony or any further financial obligation.

These proposals were quite revolutionary for the late 1920s, but some fifty years later, they have become, to some extent, the normal course of events for many American marriages. Current generations enter into monogamous marriages, but despite official vows to sustain marriage through a lifetime, they unofficially reserve the right to regard their marriages as being constantly on trial. Compatibility is tested, particularly in the early years of marriage. Contraception, in some acceptable form, is widely practiced by contemporary generations. Adoption, too, is widespread and has been extended to allow unwanted or neglected children to experience some form of acceptable family life. Divorce laws have been steadily liberalized to accept incompatibility as a legitimate reason to end an inadequate relationship. About the only item not included in Lindsey and Russell's proposals is outright admission that monogamous marriage in the United States is, in fact, trial marriage.

For those who want a monogamous marriage without legal trappings, the most recent example in the United States of trial marriage, as it is called on various campuses, is *the arrangement*.[4]

An arrangement consists of a man and a woman living together "without benefit of clergy" to determine their compatibility and to enjoy the advantages of heterosexual relationships without external legal pressures to maintain them. If the couple so determine, they are free at any time to end their common residency.

The advantage of such an arrangement seems to lie in its appeal to the free, unencumbered spirit of young generations who are not yet ready to accept the responsibilities of a lifetime commitment. The disadvantage lies in the ease with which one partner may exploit the other and so endanger future opportunities to enter into legitimate marriage.

Sexual Hospitality Sexual hospitality refers to extramarital affairs with the full knowledge and consent of a spouse. It represents a fundamental break with one of the most important bonds that unite a married heterosexual couple. Normally, marriage confers exclusive sexual rights. It is a partnership in which third parties are intruders.

One of the widely published characteristics of traditional Eskimo marriage was sexual hospitality to strangers or visitors. In a world in which possessions were few and portable, what more could a man share than one of his wives? It should be noted, however, that Eskimos did not necessarily practice monogamy, nor were they schooled in personal possessiveness.

Relatively few Americans actually practice sexual hospitality and fewer yet would universally recommend it. A certain amount of "wife swapping" or "wife sharing" apparently does exist among contemporary males in America. From the perspective of wives, "husband sharing" offers a welcome relief from the boredom of sexual exclusiveness with only one spouse. Swapping represents an emphasis upon sexual relationships and has its advocates among those who seek sexual variation with a variety of partners. It is, however, inadequate in its neglect of nonsexual relationships, for example, the status of different sets of children, and its transient nature, as in its stress on immediate gratification.

Quasi-marriage Marriagelike arrangements are called quasi-marriages. Examples may be found in man-mistress relationships or in common-law arrangements in which couples privately acknowledge their marriage to each other. Another example is concubinage, once found in the Far and Middle East. In this case, a man of wealth and power could acquire access to a woman without conferring upon her the status of being his wife or her children the status of being his rightful heirs.

Quasi-marriage, then, occupies the shadowy ground between monogamous marriage and nonmarriage. It merits attention because it suits the needs of some prominent persons to refrain from public acknowledgment of a legal marriage, as in the case of Eva Braun and Adolf Hitler.

Polygamy

Modern Western society is not unfamiliar with polygamy because past generations who shaped its heritage practiced polygamy in a variety of forms; present generations in other societies continue to retain remnants of polygamy; and present generations within modern Western society are both advocating and experimenting with contemporary versions of polygamous arrangements.

Polygamy consists of the mating of one person to two or more members of the opposite sex. If that person is a male, the polygamous form is identified as *polygyny*. If that person is a female, the polygamous form is known as *polyandry*. In order of frequency, with monogamy leading because of its practicality, polygyny is the second most common form of mating in societies around the world, with polyandry third.

Just as a rationale favoring monogamy has been handed down from past generations in Western society, so there are rationales for either polygyny or polyandry. Familiar refrains supporting polygyny include providing for sexual variety for men; companionship and the sharing of wifely duties by women; and increased wealth and influence through dowries, gifts, and multiple kinships. Cultural themes in favor of polyandry include a scarcity of women, prolonged absence of some men because of hunting or military obligations, and conformity to women-oriented practices such as matrilineage, matriarchy, and matrilocal residence.

Group Marriage   The rarest form of plural mating is group marriage. It differs from polygyny or polyandry because the emphasis is not upon a single man or woman having multiple mates but rather upon a group of men mating with a group of women. One of the best-documented instances of group marriage in the United States is the case of the Oneida community, a utopian venture in communal sharing including sexual access to consenting partners.[5]

Professional and popular attention remains focused upon group marriage as a viable alternative to monogamous marriage. Haughey reported a conservative estimate of more than 2,000 communes in 34 different states in 1971.[6] Rural and urban communes generally attract persons in the younger generations, typically between the ages of eighteen and thirty. Again, as with monogamy, polygyny, and polyandry, group marriage in all its forms is supported by some rationale, such as wider fellowship, removal from restrictions of "straight" marital structures, shared responsibility, and greater stress upon some fundamental purpose for life.[7]

VARIATIONS IN FAMILY STRUCTURES

There is far greater variability in family structures than there is in marriage structures. Families are subject to many more factors than marriages, and past generations have not hesitated to develop appropriate structures to take them into account.

Families in Terms of Participants

Nuclear Family   The nuclear family is widely held to be the basic building block in family structures. It consists of one male and one female and their children. These children may be biological offspring, or they may be adopted. Thus, two generations are normally found in the nuclear family unit, which lives independently of other family units. Three-

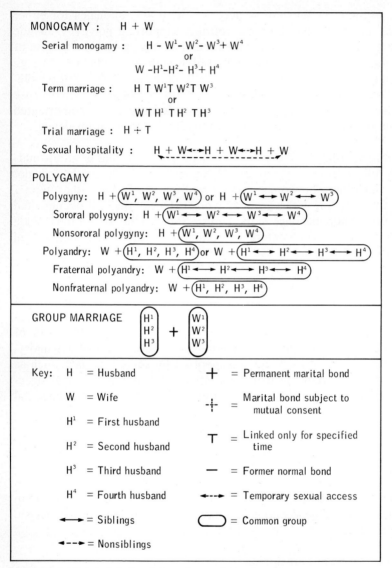

Figure 1-1 Summary of variations in marriage structures.

generation families may also be found, but they are usually only temporary arrangements to accommodate elderly parents in their final years.

The *independent nuclear family* has also been called the *conjugal family* because it stresses the union of husbands and wives of the same generation. All other generations rely heavily upon the strength of that union. If husbands and wives are devoted to each other enough to withstand external and internal divisive forces, all other generations, particularly children and elders, can be assured of their sustenance. This was the principal finding in a study of three-generation households in 1954 in Ohio.[8] This same pattern emerges as the family form best adapted to modern, industrial, urbanized societies throughout the world.[9]

When nuclear families are linked together, they are treated as *dependent nuclear families* and form *extended* or *stem* families. Such would be the case when married sons and daughters bring their wives and husbands and their dependent children to reside with their parents.

It should be noted that there is a distinction between households and families. A *household* is an enumerative term used by the United States census to include all those who have a common residence, despite the fact that they may not be members of the same nuclear family. Thus, servants, boarders, friends, distant relatives, and permanent guests can be counted as part of a household because they live under a common roof.

One of the most interesting variants of dependent nuclear families is the *joint family* of traditional India. Joint families come into existence when two or more brothers form a common household with their respective wives and children. Property is shared among them, including funds, facilities, and guardian deities.[10] They represent, however, a stage in Indian family life, because the death of one or more of the brothers signals the end of one joint family. A generation must mature before brothers become old enough to marry and to form another joint family of their own.

Robert Winch noted in the course of his Fourth Annual Ernest W. Burgess Award Lecture at the 1969 meetings of the National Council on Family Relations that there seems to be some inconsistency in finding the conjugal family system in modern, industrial technologies and also among primitive, hunting-gathering economies. He reconciled the findings by visualizing a curvilinear relationship between subsistence and the complexity of family structures. He noted: ". . . We have a nuclear family system at the primitive hunting and gathering level. The extended family system flourishes among agricultural peoples, and the nuclear system re-emerges as the economy becomes more complex."[11]

Families in Terms of Residence

A variety of terms have been developed to describe the residential patterns of nuclear families. If, for example, a wife or mother's kinship determines where a married couple shall live, the nuclear family unit is said to be *matrilocal* or *uxorilocal*. On the other hand, if the husband or father's kinship determines where a married couple shall reside, the pattern is said to be *patrilocal* or *virilocal*. Still another form is *avunculocal* family life in which residence is established for a nuclear family with or near a maternal uncle or with other male matrilineal kin of the husband.

Should the married couple alternate between paternal and maternal kins' residences, the arrangement is designated as *ambilocal*. When a married couple fail to establish a common household and continue to live apart, usually remaining in their parental homes, their relationship is described as *duolocal* or *natalocal*. Finally, if an option is provided for a married couple to live apart from all kin and independently choose some agreeable residence, then the nuclear family is said to be *neolocal*. This neolocal residential pattern has been ideally prescribed for American couples, but financial shortages may require an ambilocal pattern in the earliest years of marriage. Extenuating circumstances such as military or hazardous duty for a husband have led to natalocal residence for prolonged periods for a newly married wife.

Generational Views of Nuclear Families

Families go through recurring cycles of origination, development, and demise (see Figure 1-2).

Each generational member sees family life from a particular vantage point and identifies his family as presently occupying one phase of the family life cycle. When he is a dependent child, and sometimes a dependent adult, his nuclear family is seen as his *family of origin* or his *family of orientation*. This parental family has been called "the cradle of the personality" because it is within this unit that personalized habits, attitudes, values, and ideas are first shaped. In some ways, children, once processed or socialized by this family, probably are never the same again. The basic personality attributes are laid down within the family's framework, and all else builds upon them.[12]

When this same ego matures to the point of establishing another nuclear family, the new unit becomes an individual's *family of procreation*. It may also be called the *family of destination*.[13] A single nuclear family may, thus, be a family of orientation for a dependent child—a representative of the youngest generation—and simultaneously a family of procreation for the child's parents, the middle generation.

Families of procreation ultimately become *families of gerontation*, or aging families, in which survivors maintain a fairly vigorous family life

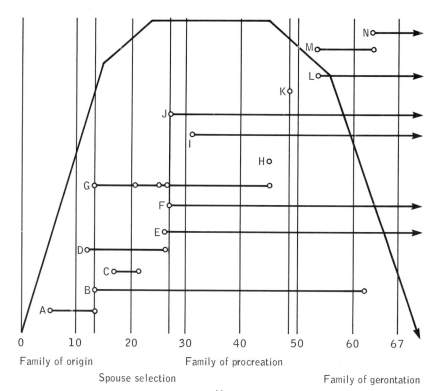

Figure 1-2 Schematic representation of individual course of life and family life cycle. (Source: Adapted from Matilda Riley and Anne Foner, *Aging and Society*, vol. 1, *An Inventory of Research Findings*, New York: Russell Sage Foundation, 1968, p. 410.)

as grandparents and great-grandparents. Inevitably, families of gerontation suffer dismemberment through the deaths of every participant. Postparental families enter eventually into "the stage of the empty nest," an apt phrase credited to Evelyn Duvall, in which everyone exits from the family through death.

Table 1-1 indicates the median ages of husband and wife at selected stages of the family life cycle from 1890 to 1980 in the United States. [14]

Table 1-1   Median Age of Husband and Wife at Selected Stages of the Life Cycle of the Family, for the United States: 1890–1980

Stage	1890	1940	1950	1960	1980
Median age of wife at					
First marriage	22.0	21.5	20.1	20.2	19.5–20.4
Birth of last child	31.9	27.1	26.1	25.8	27–28
Marriage of last child	55.3	50.0	47.6	47.1	48–49
Death of husband	55.3	60.9	61.4	63.6	65–66
Median age of husband at					
First marriage	26.1	24.3	22.8	22.3	22–23
Birth of last child	36.0	29.9	28.8	27.9	29–30
Marriage of last child	59.4	52.8	50.3	49.2	51–52
Death of wife	57.4	63.6	64.1	65.7	68–69

Source: Atlee L. Stroup, *Marriage and Family: A Developmental Approach*, New York: Appleton-Century-Crofts, Inc., 1966, p. 65. Used with permission of the National Council on Family Relations.

The approximate ages at which spouses would enter each phase of the family life cycle would be as follows:[15]

Stage of the family cycle	Husband's age	Wife's age
1. Childless couple	23.0	20.4
2. Expectant pair	24.7	22.01
3. Preschool family	25.4	22.8
4. School-age family	31.4	26.8
5. Teen-age family	38.4	33.8
6. Family in middle years	52.0	49.0
7. Family in later years	65.0	62.0

Families in Terms of Relative Numbers and Solidarity

A conjugal family, we should note, can consist of the minimal dyad of two members of the opposite sex. Further, this newly formed unit is a family in its own right and may remain a childless dyad in which the emphasis is upon the companionship of the married couple. This *companionate family*, however, is the nucleus upon which additional membership may be built. Conjugal relationships frequently, in fact, do result in the arrival of at least one child. At the first child's arrival, the family can be said to be *full.*

But just how "full" is a full family? A single fertile female may theoretically produce approximately thirty babies, if all are single births, during her child-bearing years. A number greater than thirty becomes possible only if there are multiple births of twins, triplets, quadruplets, quintuplets, and sextuplets. The world record is said to belong to Mrs. Fyodor Vassilet of Russia, reported to have given birth to sixty-nine children in twenty-seven confinements. There were sixteen sets of twins, seven sets of triplets, and four sets of quadruplets, all of whom survived to their majority.[16] Mrs. Vassilet herself lived only to the age of fifty-six.

Full families, in time, become depleted as generations come and go or refuse to live with each other. One or both members of a married couple may be absent from the family circle for a variety of reasons. Death, divorce, desertion, prolonged hospitalization, incarceration in a penitentiary, internment as a prisoner of war, separation, and even amnesia are sources of *broken families.*

Full families, however, need not experience the physical absence of parents to disintegrate. The moral fibers that hold married couples together may be severely strained. Children and other relatives may maintain a façade of solidarity before strangers, but the psychosocial distance between estranged couples introduces a whole new set of conditions. Poverty-striken families in East Topeka, Kansas, for example, have been studied as *failing families.*[17] Cuber and Harroff have studied *marriages of convenience* or *utilitarian marriages* among influential upper-class families who feel that they must "keep up appearances."[18] Ritchie and Koller have suggested *cracked*, not-fully-broken, families, employing the imagery of damaged, but still functional, chinaware.[19]

Families and Kinship

Past generations in cultures other than American have taught us that families must rely upon something stronger than whimsical ties of individual selection, of idyllic romanticism, or of undue haste. They maintained that the bonds that hold persons together in a family should be irrevocable, undeniable, and pervasive. The ties that they suggested would hold a family together were those of *kinship.*

Kinship has been popularized as *blood relationships*—those that are, in essence, genetic, biological, or physical in their linkages over generations. Blood, of course, does not carry genetic codes. Physical attributes are passed between generations via genes transmitted to the embryo at conception.[20] Nevertheless, the "blood" theory persists among laymen who speak knowingly about "blood brothers," "pure bloods," and "mixed bloods."

Kinship should be understood not only in terms of generational lineages that transmit genetic characteristics but also in terms of *affinity* —social and legal ties that include marriage, adoption, and common membership in clans, tribes, and totems. *Affines* are all those people said to be "related" because all agree that a relationship does, indeed, exist. Because they live and work closely together, affines can and do strongly affect generational life. Affines have much to do with the intangibles of life. They affect the quality of life by the ideas they convey and the models they hold up before oncoming generations. In short, affines have much to do with the preservation and transmission of *social heritages* within a family setting.

Kinship can be described as "near" or "remote" depending upon status as primary, secondary, or tertiary relatives.[21] Primary relatives are a person's parents and siblings in his family of orientation and his spouse and children in his family of procreation. Each of these primary relatives has primary relatives of his own and consequently is a secondary relative to the individual. Anthropologists can distinguish some thirty-three different classifications of secondary kin. Examples of secondary kin would be the subject's mother's mother, wife's father, sister's daughter, and son's wife.

Comparatively few Americans are interested in tracing their geneologies beyond one or two generations or in seeking personal association with tertiary kin, unless there is some glimmer of hope that such a search would yield prestige, wealth, or influence. One danger in geneological studies, as one student noted, was to run the risk of discovering a thief or a village idiot on one's family tree.

A recent study was made of some 300 students at Kent State University in which they were asked to trace their geneologies as far as their memories, aided or unaided by reference to written records, would take them.[22] Not only were the geneologies truncated or relatively sparse, there was a noticeable lack of information and concern for patrilineal kin. The strongest memories of these students were tied to matrilineal kin; this suggests the hypothesis that mothers are influential in holding middle-class American families together, whereas fathers are too preoccupied with their own affairs to sustain their ties with their patrilineal kin or promote these ties among their own children.

Efforts to Preserve Family Heritages

The closest Americans come to exploring mutual kinship are times when they meet as comparative strangers and try to find some common conversational ground in the name of cordiality. "Do you know So-and-So?" is an effort to break the social ice between unacquainted persons. Failing to find common ground, newly introduced parties drift apart.

Since strangers may be regarded as intruders and threats to the social order, preliterates find ways to incorporate them into their family systems. Nomadic Australoid family groups will sit together for hours when they meet in the open bush to determine, if possible, how they might be related. Failing to find a relationship, they move cautiously apart for their own preservation.

It has been a point of pride for a visitor to some exotic society to be adopted into a family and tribe and given a new name. Mistakenly, in unexcelled vanity, the visitor believed he was welcomed in this manner because of his personal virtues. Instead, preliterates were merely trying to find some means to place him within their kinship. Accordingly, he no longer threatened their heritage and would presumably enter into its preservation or defense. Because the stranger was now a "kinsmen," even though through adoption, he could be treated with the deference suited to his rank and status.

The ancient Chinese assimilated strangers into their families by painstaking adoption procedures. They would, for example, adopt a "daughter-in-law," a *t'ung-yang-hsi*, as an infant or toddler from some poor family and proceed to rear her as a future wife for one of their sons.[23] By this process, they helped preserve those special ways of living that characterized their particular families. The procedure amounted to raising a "daughter" so that the future wife did not come into their midst as an intruding, uninformed stranger. She was, instead, thoroughly familiar with her husband and his family heritage.

This is a far cry from American practice, in which spouses come from two diverse family backgrounds. As a result, they must first find each other and then work at adjusting their differences. Kephart's studies among over a thousand white college students in five colleges in the Philadelphia area indicate some of the American patterns in early dating. Median age at first date was thirteen for the sample. There were repeated experiences of infatuation. Median number of times infatuated was 5.6 for females and 4.5 for males. There was more than one serious love affair for these young men and women. Median number of love affairs for females in Kephart's study was 1.3. Males had a shade less number of love affairs than the females with a 1.2 median.[24] In brief, there is considerable screening of strangers as potential marital partners among American youth *prior to commitments*. This assures some common ground before marriage, but even then, a series of *adjustments* must occur before married couples can be said to be working out a mutually satisfying family life.[25] Chapter 11 discusses this screening process in greater detail. Chapter 12 suggests some essential adjustments newly married couples encounter despite the confidence with which men and women select each other.

There are two possible ways to keep loyalty to family heritages

intact. One is the *closed family system*, which focuses upon the fundamental privacy of families so that strangers are excluded from knowledge
of family affairs. We have already noted the Chinese pattern of early
assimilation of an adopted daughter to assure the uninterrupted preservation of unique family ways. We have also noted the American procedure
of early and continued screening of potential marriage partners by
individuals, followed thereafter by constant adjustment of differences to
achieve some mutually agreeable family life-style. Perhaps this system is
best adapted to the American style that creates a new family heritage with
every new family. In addition, the independent nuclear family effectively
keeps secondary and tertiary relatives at appropriate distances.

The second possibility is to develop an *open family system*. This
system is interested not so much in the *content* or *substance* of family
traditions as in the preservation of the *democratic way of living* in a
family. Each member, ideally, is free to express his own individuality
provided it does not interfere with the rights of other family members.
Strangers are also welcomed on this basis. The objective is "interpersonal
competence."[26] This quality is one of weighing personal behavior against
whatever impacts such behavior may have upon the welfare of other
family members. American families, ideally, seem to favor the open
family system and have been working toward that objective for several
generations.[27]

Termination of Conjugality

Kin-conscious preliterates have been less than successful in maintaining
conjugal ties. The imagery of the "noble savage" living close to nature
and free to express his needs and satisfy them easily does not square with
reality. Field anthropologists have discovered that husbands and wives
dissolved their union with far greater frequency among preliterate
societies than among sophisticated social structures. Not only are jealousy, pettiness, and cruelty grounds for divorce or separation, but also
disloyalty to family ancestors, infertility, laziness, disobedience, and
witchcraft.

Why is it that the termination of one or more dependent nuclear
families does not particularly disturb primitives, whereas the dissolution
of independent nuclear families seems to threaten the continuity of family
life in the United States? Among primitives, the kin networks that unite
living generations with their ancestors and with their future descendents
remain intact. The disintegration of conjugal ties does not destroy their
generational linkages; it merely permits men and women to find new
partners within a stable kinship system. Children and their parents are still
members of extended families and have established status.

The breakup of a marriage in the urban United States, however, is an event of far-reaching consequences. It means that living generations are cut loose in an open family system. Formerly married men and women must now return to the search-and-find procedures of unmarried, unattached persons or remain cut off from family life. Children are forced to find some way of continuing their life by alternating between parents, favoring one parent over the other, or seeking early independence. Elderly parents have to readapt themselves to the unanticipated return of their formerly married children as well as to renewed responsibilities to assist in the rearing of grandchildren. In short, the resources of family units are limited and are not easily redistributed in the urban United States.

Family Descent, Lineage, and Power

There are three remaining variables that help distinguish families wherever they may be found. These factors are descent, lineage, and power.

Descent The most common form of descent is *patrilineal descent*, social linkage through the male line. The second most frequent form is *bilateral descent*, a system that equally recognizes links with both male and female relatives—the system found in the United States. *Matrilineal descent*, ranked third, stresses the female line while ignoring the male line. Finally, and rarest of all, is *double descent.* In this pattern, the individual is assigned to his father's patrilineal group and to his mother's mother's matrilineal group. The double descent system ignores the father's matrilineal kin as well as the mother's patrilineal kin.[28]

Lineage The transfer of property between generations, tangible or intangible, whether the family's good name, crest, title, livestock, bank accounts, or lands, requires some orderly system. *Patrilineal inheritance* usually passes property to each generation of males, specifically from fathers to sons. *Matrilineal inheritance*, of course, reverses the procedure and permits mothers to confer properties on their daughters. In England in the twentieth century, the throne has passed from George V to Edward VIII, who abdicated in favor of George VI. The passing of George VI opened the way for Elizabeth II because there were no sons to inherit the throne. The present situation places Charles, the Prince of Wales, first in the line of succession. The inheritance, however, will not come from his father, Prince Philip, because he holds the rank of Prince Consort. The patrilineal line will, thus be ignored, and the symbolic leadership of Great Britain will be shifted through a matrilineal descent pattern.

Birth order plays a part in inheritance from past generations.

Primogeniture establishes the prior rights of the first born, the eldest in a series of children. This was the "birthright" that Esau lost from Isaac by the biblical deception of his parents, Rebekah and Jacob. *Ultimogeniture* is a rarer procedure in which the youngest child is favored.

Power   If the husband's, or male, lineage is held to be dominant, such families are *patriarchal*, literally, "father-ruled." It is a pattern entrenched in Judeo-Christian traditions that speak of the *fatherhood* of God and the *brotherhood* of men but exclude references to motherhood or sisterhood.

If the wife's, or female, lineage determines how families shall decisively act, the system is *matriarchal*. Lester Ward found he had given voice to the unspoken feelings of many American women of his times when he propounded his theory of *gynecocracy*, the natural leadership and superiority of females.[29] In the present, numbers of women are saying that women need no longer rely upon men to advocate women's rights. Rather, many have adopted the position that women, themselves, are best suited to champion women's rights. Men may try to empathize, but they can never quite understand the circumstances that gall women because their lives cannot fully comprehend the internal and external milieu in which women live. In this stance, growing proportions of women seem to be most eager to "liberate" all women from outmoded controls inherited from past generations.[30]

A third authoritative pattern within families is the dispersal of authority among several members. In this manner, families are *equalitarian*. Herein, frequent consultation, deference to all, and teamwork are needed to make the system effective. It is a most difficult pattern to follow because "pleasing everyone" becomes well-nigh impossible. To Americans, however, the joy resides in the struggle to achieve the ideal, not necessarily in its attainment.

SUMMARY

Past generations have developed a variety of marriage and family structures within which present generations currently operate. While acceptance of these forms has continued, they have not gone unquestioned or unchallenged. Contemporary generations of the seventies appear to be directly involved in modifying, rejecting, or reinstating marriage and family structures for themselves and for future generations.

Marriage structures take the form of monogamy, polgyny, polyandry, and group marriage. They are listed in order of their frequency in world societies, monogamy being near-universal and group marriage being the rarest and most experimental of all. While monogamy is the normal expectation in American marriages, a more realistic description is that of serial monogamy, that is, marriage to a number of spouses over a single lifetime.

Critics of monogamy have suggested term marriage, trial marriage, sex hospitality, and quasi marriage as alternatives to current procedures. Of these, trial marriage seems to have been established but lacks official acknowledgment. The other alternatives or modifications continue to be unacceptable to the vast majority of the American population.

Polygamous marriage has supporting rationales. The strongest is the comparative ease with which disturbed sex ratios are accommodated. Not only is there a normal attrition of males through successive generations, but an excess of one sex is a consequence of sex preferences, war, exposure to hazardous conditions, immigration, and job opportunities. Monogamy remains the only practical course for most persons even when polygamy is permissible.

Families display far greater variability than marriages. In terms of their participants, they are categorized as independent or dependent nuclear units. Studies of world trends indicate that independent nuclear families are well adapted to both primitive hunting and gathering economies and modern industrialized, urban economies. Dependent nuclear families, the style of past generations, are best suited to stabilized, agricultural economies.

In terms of residence, families may be matrilocal, patrilocal, avunculocal, ambilocal, duolocal, or neolocal. From the perspective of family life cycles, families move from families of orientation to families of procreation. Families of gerontation, or aging families, are just beginning to receive their share of attention in family studies. In terms of numbers and solidarity, families may be companionate or full. Full families may be broken or failing. They can remain somewhat intact, but they operate more at a level of convenience and appearances than at a level of vibrant, interpersonal competence.

Where family traditions are of great concern, primary, secondary, and tertiary relatives play important roles in their preservation. Strangers are carefully trained to respect established family ways. Under the American system, potential mates are screened and differences are adjusted. When conjugal ties are broken, there are few kin upon whom to rely.

Family descent, lineage, and authority either follow male and female lines or seek some equalitarian middle ground. The most recent example of attempts on the part of present generations to modify the influences of past generations has been the women's liberation movement. The ultimate goal in the United States is to make real the promise of equalitarianism. Dignity for all family members may be an impossible dream, but the joy of struggling to attain it provides the zest to keep trying.

REFERENCES

1   Jessie Bernard, *Remarriage*, New York: Harper & Row, Publishers, Incorporated, 1956, and Paul C. Glick, *American Families*, New York: John Wiley & Sons, Inc., 1957.
2   Walter C. McKain, *Retirement Marriage*, Monograph 3, Storrs Agricultural Experiment Station, Storrs, Conn.: University of Connecticut, January 1969.
3   Benjamin Lindsey and Wainright Evans, *The Companionate Marriage*, New York: Liveright, Publishing Corporation, 1927, and Bertrand Russell, *Marriage and Morals*, New York: Liveright, Publishing Corporation, 1929.
4   See, for example, "Morals on the Campus," *Newsweek*, Apr. 6, 1964, 52–59; Gael Green, *Sex and the College Girl*, New York: Dial Press, 1964; Ira L. Reiss, "How and Why America's Sex Standard's Are Changing," *Transaction*, vol. 5, no. 4, 26–32, March 1968; and "Sex in Academe," *Playboy*, vol. 16, no. 9, 193–195, September 1969.
5   See Constance Noyes Robertson (ed.), *Oneida Community: An Autobiography, 1851–1876*, Syracuse, N. Y.: Syracuse University Press, 1970.
6   John C. Haughey, "The Commune-Child of the 1970's," *America*, Mar. 13, 1971, New York: America Press, Inc.
7   Another useful source is Joann S. and Jack R. Delora (eds.), *Intimate Life Styles: Marriage and Its Alternatives*, Pacific Palisades, Calif.: Goodyear Publishing Company, Inc., 1972.
8   Marvin R. Koller, "Studies of Three-Generation Households," *Marriage and Family Living*, vol. 16, no. 3, 205–206, August 1954.
9   William J. Goode, *World Revolution and Family Patterns*, New York: The Free Press, 1963.
10 M. S. Gore, "The Traditional Indian Family," in M. F. Nimkoff (ed.), *Comparative Family Systems*, Boston: Houghton Mifflin Company, 1965, pp. 209–231.
11 Robert F. Winch, "Permanence and Change in the History of the American Family and Some Speculations as to Its Future," *Journal of Marriage and the Family*, vol. 32, no. 1, 9, February 1970.
12 Abram Kardiner et al., *The Psychological Frontiers of Society*, New York: Columbia University Press, 1945.
13 See, for example, Atlee L. Stroup, *Marriage and Family: A Developmental Approach*, New York: Appleton-Century-Crofts, Inc., 1966.
14 Stroup, ibid., p. 65.
15 Stroup, ibid., p. 65.
16 *Guiness Book of World Records*, rev. ed., New York: Sterling Publishing Co., Inc., p. 18.
17 "Hope for the Family That Is Failing," *Menninger Quarterly*, vol. 22, no. 4,

Topeka, Kans.: The Menninger Foundation, 15–21, Winter 1968.

18   John F. Cuber and Peggy B. Harroff, *The Significant Americans*, New York:
     D. Appleton-Century Company, Inc., 1965.
19   Oscar W. Ritchie and Marvin R. Koller, *Sociology of Childhood*, New York:
     Appleton-Century-Crofts, Inc., 1964, p. 161.
20   See, for example, H. Eldon Sutton, *Genes, Enzymes, and Inherited Diseases*,
     New York: Holt, Rinehart and Winston, Inc., 1961.
21   A. R. Radcliffe-Brown, "The Study of Kinship Systems," *Journal of the
     Royal Anthropological Institute*, vol. 71, no. 2, 1941. A secondary source is
     George Peter Murdock, *Social Structure*, New York: The Macmillan Com-
     pany, 1949, p. 14.
22   From an unpublished study by Marvin R. Koller and Jerry M. Lewis,
     Department of Sociology and Anthropology, Kent State University, Kent,
     Ohio, 1968 and 1969.
23   Arthur P. Wolf, "Adopt a Daughter-in-Law, Marry a Sister: A Chinese
     Solution to the Problem of the Incest Taboo," *American Anthropologist*, vol.
     70, no. 5, 864–874, October 1968.
24   William M. Kephart, "Some Correlates of Romantic Love," *Journal of
     Marriage and the Family*, vol. 29, no. 3, 471, August 1967.
25   See, for example, Jessie Bernard, "The Adjustments of Married Mates," in
     Harold T. Christensen, (ed.), *Handbook of Marriage and the Family*, Chi-
     cago: Rand McNally & Company, 1964, pp. 675–739.
26   Nelson Foote and Leonard Cottrell, *Identity and Interpersonal Competence*,
     Chicago: The University of Chicago Press, 1955.
27   For a method of research that tests the interpersonal competence theory, see
     R. D. Laing, H. Phillipson, and A. R. Lee, *Interpersonal Perception*, New
     York: Springer Publishing Co., Inc., 1966.
28   An excellent discussion of larger kin groups and kinship terminology occurs
     in Harold E. Driver, *Indians of North America*, Chicago: The University of
     Chicago Press, 1961, pp. 293–324.
29   Lester Ward, *Pure Sociology*, New York, 1903, pp. 296, 336–341, 345.
30   See, for example, "The Future of Women and Marriage," *The Futurist*, vol.
     15, no. 2, whole issue, April 1970.

STUDY QUESTIONS AND ACTIVITIES

1   What is the value of studying the variety of marriage and family forms
    throughout the world when most of us will be living in families or in marriages
    in the United States?
2   What rationales did you find in support of the overall marriage and family
    system in our society?
3   Can portions of some other styles of marriage and family be grafted success-
    fully upon American marriages and families? What would these be?
4   Would it take several generations to achieve drastic changes in American
    family life, or would you propose to make fundamental changes in social

structures within your own generation?
5 Examine a number of experimental marriage and family forms currently active within your own generation and determine if they are totally new in the experience of human history.
6 Select a combination of marriage and family structures different from that which you believe exists within the United States and suggest what its strengths and weaknesses might be.
7 Interview a nuclear family, guaranteeing anonymity, and indicate how this family does or does not fit the life-cycle model detailed in Figure 1-2.
8 In what ways is your family of origin different from all those known to you?

SUGGESTED ADDITIONAL READINGS

Barash, Meyer, and Alice Scourby, *Marriage and Family: A Comparative Analysis of Contemporary Problems*, New York: Random House, Inc., 1970.
Delora, Joann S., and Jack R. Delora (eds.), *Intimate Life Styles: Marriage and Its Alternatives*, Pacific Palisades, Calif.: Goodyear Publishing Company, Inc., 1972.
Geiger, H. Kent (ed.), *Comparative Perspectives on Marriage and Family*, Boston: Little, Brown and Company, 1968.
Goode, William J., *World Revolution and Family Patterns*, New York: The Free Press, 1963.
Lerner, Daniel, *The Passing of Traditional Society: Modernizing the Middle East*, New York: The Free Press, 1968, paperback.
Mace, David, and Vera Mace, *The Soviet Family*, Garden City, N. Y.: Dolphin Books, Doubleday & Company, Inc., 1964.
Makarenko, A. S., *The Collective Family: A Handbook for Russian Parents*, Garden City, N. Y.: Anchor Books, Doubleday & Company, Inc., 1967.
Nimkoff, M. F. (ed.), *Comparative Family Systems*, Boston: Houghton Mifflin Company, 1965.
Queen, Stuart A., Robert W. Habenstein, and John B. Adams, *The Family in Various Cultures*, Philadelphia: J. B. Lippincott Company, 1961.
Stephens, William N., *The Family in Cross-Cultural Perspective*, New York: Holt, Rinehart and Winston, Inc., 1963.

Chapter 2

History of Families

We have noted that generations characteristically are concerned wholly about their own times, their own affairs, their own problems, and their own satisfactions. In the day-to-day routines or in the midst of family problems that call for settlement in the "here and now," there seems little place for interest in past generations, particularly those of antiquity. Yet there are perceptive individuals within generations who see age-old ways of handling love, sex, marriage, and family that still affect their times. They note linkages with the past and develop "a sense of history," seeing present generations as merely the most recent living persons to be influenced by what has preceded them. All this is not to suggest that looking backward is somehow superior to considering the present or future. Rather, it is to suggest that past generations must be credited with originating and developing ways and means for men, women, and children to live together in some familial way.

Curiosity about how things began and how things changed has motivated scholars to speculate and to probe into almost every facet of human life. In this chapter, we examine in detail what they have found about the origins and transformations of family life. In chronological order, yet often overlapping or coexisting, the various modes of family life as found among the ancient Hebrews, Greeks, Romans, and early Western Christians are described.

ORIGINS OF THE FAMILY

William Graham Sumner once observed that "all origins are lost in mystery," but it is useful to consider, at least, what some family historians have authoritatively presented as the "facts" of familial life: transitions over time, etiology or causative factors, and ultimate linkage with present generations.

Representative Theories of Family Origins and Development

Theory of a Steady State and Its Social Erosion Plato and Aristotle theorized that, from the beginning, the basic condition of human family life was male domination, or patriarchy. This was, in their view, the natural and proper condition of humankind, a view somewhat colored by their own evaluation of the Hellenic ethos that made males the most favored creatures of the gods and females their loved, but subordinate, helpmates. Matriarchal or near-matriarchal families were known to Plato and Aristotle, but these represented, for them, an erosion of masculine privileges, the granting of favors or continued concessions by men, an unfortunate product of civilization and sophistication that came much later in the scheme of things. Their analyses have a familiar ring. Many men of contemporary generations allege that women are "going too far" in invading formerly exclusive masculine domains.

Sir Henry J. Sumner Maine supported this steady state theory in his *Ancient Law* by holding that patriarchy existed from the very beginning of human history. Maine contended that the unit of ancient societies was the family and that this unit was dominated by the most powerful male. It was, in his view, a natural unit in which status was determined by dominance-submission patterns based upon sheer exercise of brute authority. This unit was undermined, again in his judgment, by agreements or contractual arrangements in which the rights of participants were guaranteed. This meant that women and children eventually did succeed in wresting more and more power away from dominant males.

According to Maine, the *individual*, supported by the law of the land, became the unit of modern civilizations. While equality under the law would seem ideal to those interested in sharing authority, particularly if they were males, an inevitable part of this policy was the protection of the weak and the defenseless. Women and children would be protected against excessive masculine aggression. Community support, as expressed in the law, would guarantee this. Thus, Maine was convinced that patriarchal rule existed throughout antiquity until it was eventually modified by the codification of individual rights.

Edward A. Westermarck is also considered a steady state theorist. He insisted in his book *The History of Human Marriage* that throughout most of history, marriage was essentially monogamous. All other forms of marriage were mere fleeting aberrations that could not match the superiority and stability of the male-female pair and their common children.

Theory of Evolutionary Stages   Paralleling the mid-nineteenth century Darwinian promotion of organic evolution was the application of evolutionary theory to superorganic or sociocultural systems, including family systems. Johann Jakob Bachofen published his book *Das Mutterrecht*, "Mother Right," in 1861, a work that countered Plato, Aristotle, Maine, and Westermarck in their contention that the steady state of family life was predominantly patriarchal or monogamous. Bachofen believed that the earliest stages of family life were essentially promiscuous. Random matings and liaisons occurred in primeval hordes, as they do among herd animals. Thereafter, promiscuity gave way to a more durable stage of matriarchy, or gynecocracy. Two conditions brought about the change from promiscuity to matriarchy: (1) the scarcity of females due to female infanticide that led, in turn, to polyandry and (2) the close bond that naturally exists between a mother and her child. Finally, Bachofen held that patriarchy emerged from matriarchy as males made even greater inroads against the rights of mothers.

Lewis Henry Morgan advanced still another evolutionary theory, stating that families originated, as Bachofen believes they did, in outright promiscuity. Morgan, however, suggested that there were specific intervening stages leading eventually to monogamy. These stages were, in order, promiscuity, punalua (a Hawaiian term for "dear friend," which Morgan applied to inbreeding groups of men and women), polygamy (initially matrilinear because the identity of the father was often unclear, and later on, patrilinear, when men were willing to affirm their fatherhood), and finally, monogamy.

In 1927, Robert Briffault published *The Mothers*. In this work, he agreed with Bachofen's assessment of the primacy of mothers in families. This early stage, in Briffault's model, ultimately led to patriarchy as males established their rule over the entire family unit. Patriarchy, in turn, gave way to monogamy when women persisted in securing some basic rights for themselves.

Family theorists are strongly influenced by their own generational experiences, a temporocentrism to which we have already referred. Plato, Aristotle, Maine, and Westermarck developed steady state theories of male domination or monogamy that reflected the entrenched social orders of their times. Bachofen, Morgan, and Briffault, on the other hand, were sensitive to social changes that marked their generations and recognized social systems as dynamic, rather than static.

Historical speculation concerning family life among generations who left no written records is a legitimate exercise, but it does leave much room for doubt. On firmer ground, however, are historical accounts of ancient family life among the Hebrews, Greeks, Romans, and early Western Christians. These four societies overlapped each other chronologically and are credited with passing along generational heritages that continue to affect families of present generations in Western Europe and in the United States. By examining their specific contents, we can determine to what extent our heritages retain Hebraic, Greek, Roman, and Christian characteristics today.

ANCIENT HEBREW FAMILIES AND THEIR GENERATIONAL SIGNIFICANCE

Ancient Hebrew families developed one of the oldest family-oriented traditions in Western societies. Their life-styles serve as classic examples of family-centered life, in striking contrast to contemporary individual-centered life.

The Pentateuch, the first five books of the Old Testament, together with the Talmud, accumulated commentaries of Hebraic sages, constitutes the chief source of ancient Hebraic family life. It should be clear that these sources are not to be regarded as unassailable, sacrosanct documents that describe Hebraic family life with clarity, accuracy, and complete historical reliability. Rather, they should be viewed as the edited remains of centuries of revisions by countless and nameless scribes and authors. The data that come through to modern generations have been so sifted, recast, and reinterpreted that they must be treated as "hints of the past" rather than as the full, unexpurgated history of an ancient people.   .

Changing Locales of Ancient Hebrew Families

The earliest Hebraic families were desert nomads led by paternalistic, but autocratic, shieks. The very term "Hebrew" has been interpreted as "the people across the river"—in a sense, wandering strangers. Agricultural settlement in Canaan required modification of their former nomadic family life. With growing populations and the development of settled villages, towns, and cities, even greater modifications of their former desert existence had to be made. Ensuing generations experienced exile and global dispersion in the midst of suspicious, often hostile, neighbors and ushered in even more drastic changes in Hebraic family life.

Much of what is described as family life among the ancient Hebrews focuses primarily upon the settled agrarian life in Canaan, as these generations still retained the mores of their ancestral desert nomads and had not yet adopted enough of urban life to assimilate many non-Hebraic traits or patterns.[1]

A Family-centered Life

Marriage and family were at the heart of ancient Hebrew life. Every man and woman was to marry in order to become "a complete person." Celibacy was unacceptable even to those who chose to lead a thoroughly religious life as a priest or rabbi. To fail to use one's procreative and sexual drives in responsible adulthood was tantamount to nullifying or rejecting God-conferred gifts.

Ideally, marriage was to occur in midadolescence, when sons and daughters were still under the control of their parents. Most marriages were arranged by family go-betweens who took into account property advantages, economic capabilities, community reputations, and family alliances. Individualistic, self-centered, overly romantic liaisons were generally discouraged as too unreliable to achieve a lasting family unit. Now and then, however, the personal wishes or preferences of a couple would be taken into account.

A Realistic Approach to Sex

Both their earlier desert life and their later settlement in small agricultural towns required the full cooperation of both sexes. Veiling of women or cloistering them in secluded quarters would hamper their participation and movements. Accordingly, such practices were minimal in Hebraic life. Rather, sexual norms required men to protect neighbors' wives, menstruating women, prostitutes, female servants, slaves, captives, and non-Hebraic women. The incest taboo was a particularly important proscription in maintaining family harmony and solidarity.

These normative expectations were obviously transgressed or compromised. Samson's consorting with prostitutes to the dismay of his parents is a case in point. David's lustful usage of one of his general's wives, Bath-Sheba, is additional evidence that coveting one's neighbor's wife was not disavowed by persons even in positions of public trust. Seduction and rape are treated in some passages of Deuteronomy that prescribe death by stoning for both the fornicating man and the fiancee of another man if they were in a city in which help could have been summoned.[2] If the betrothed woman was seduced in the open country-side, only the man was to be put to death for his crime. The rationale behind this differential treatment was that in a city, the woman *could* have cried out for help, but did not. In the open country, on the other hand, she *may* have cried out for help, but there were none to hear her pleas.

Suspected adultery on the part of the wife was tested by an ordeal of swallowing "the water of bitterness" compounded of "holy" water and dust from the floor of the tabernacle, and swearing before a priest that she was innocent. If she was, indeed, innocent, no harm would come to her. If, however, she was guilty, it was believed that "her belly will swell and her thighs will fall away."[3] Those who could tolerate such unpalatable water and who were less conscience-striken could probably pass such a test even if they were guilty. Those, however, who had internalized Hebraic mores of complete fidelity to one's spouse undoubtedly condemned themselves prior to the ordeal, so that they were less likely candidates to survive the psychic stress of lying.

Selection of a Wife

Perhaps the earliest form of wife selection was outright capture. A second, formalized technique was contractual arrangements between families. The oft-cited case of Abraham sending his servant to secure Rebekah for his son Isaac illustrates this practice. Deep affection between men and women could also form the basis of a marriage. Jacob's enduring love for Rachel is a case in point. Esau chose two wives, Judith and Basemath, to the consternation of his parents, although he waited forty years before he openly defied his parents' authority.

Wife purchase was also possible. It took the form of a dowry, called *mohar.* Mohar served the dual function of compensating a family for the loss of a daughter's services and publicly confirming the socioeconomic status of the contracting families. While the mohar was given directly to the father, he often returned it to the bride so that she would not come to the groom without an estate. The bride who could reach her groom's household in the retinue of many servants and much livestock was a prize, indeed, and established herself favorably within her new domicile.

Bride service was still another form of securing a wife. Jacob willingly served Laban for fourteen years and even married Leah, the eldest daughter, before he could claim Rachel as his own. Most students of the ancient Hebraic family agree that the earliest form of marriage involved matrilocality. Patrilocal residence, patrilineal descent and inheritance, and patriarchy came later as men asserted their dominance in families.

Transition into Marriage

Moving from the unmarried to the married state among the ancient Hebrews required two steps. The first step was engagement or betrothal, speaking "in truth." The betrothal, called *erusin*, was a most serious step, as the ceremony pledged the woman to the man as his future wife. The pledge could be broken only by the man's death or his granting of a divorce. The usual form of erusin was to give a sum of money or its symbolic equivalent to the woman before witnesses. A document accompanied this gift, confirming the betrothal, provided the woman consented. An engaged man was consequently exempted from military service for as much as a year to permit him more time with his future bride, to protect her, to enjoy her company, and to assure his temporary freedom from the hazards of combat.

Erusin has significance for Christians, as it was this ceremony that bound the Virgin Mary to Joseph. Erusin corresponds to contemporary *engagement* to be married. Engagement obviously carries little of the serious pledging of loyalty that erusin did to the ancient Hebrews, as engagements are broken with considerable frequency by modern generations of men and women.[4]

Nissuin, or the final ceremony of marriage, followed erusin by a year or longer. Sexual consummation waited upon this second step. Later on, the usual practice became one of combining both erusin and nissuin rituals within a single ceremony. The rationale for this change was threefold: a shorter engagement reduced opportunities for sexual relations, jealous or rejected suitors would have little or no chance to abduct or harm the woman, and pledges of mutual devotion were speedily and publicly confirmed in marriage.

The Sacred Nature of Hebraic Marriage

Marriage was a serious step for Hebrews, as it was viewed as a religious act. The Hebrew term for marriage was *kiddushin*, meaning holiness or sanctification. Marriage was believed to be instituted by God. His Spirit, the *Shechinah*, was to be made evident in the daily acts of concern for the welfare of one's spouse. To treat each other with disdain was to be cursed, discredited, or out of touch with the Deity. Such a view was reinstated generations later in the Calvinistic doctrine of being "selected" by God for special blessings.

The Hebraic wedding ceremony was celebrated elaborately for seven days, symbolic of seven benedictions that were uttered during the nissuin ritual. These joyous celebrations, involving entire communities, well-wishers, and hangers-on, were feasts at which large quantities of food and drink were consumed.

It was at such a wedding in the village of Cana that Jesus is believed to have elevated marriage to the level of a sacrament, according to Roman Catholic teachings. A sacrament provides divine help for entering into various obligations or responsibilities. To save embarrassment for the newly wedded couple, whose wine supply was quickly depleted by the overenthusiastic guests, Jesus was said to have miraculously converted jars of plain water into wine. By this symbolic act, Jesus is said to have placed marriage on a par with other sacraments such as baptism, holy communion, or entrance into holy orders. Contemporary Roman Catholic couples receiving instruction in marriage attend what is known as "Cana Conferences," memorializing that ancient Hebrew wedding.

Monogamy and Polygyny

While monogamy was held as ideal, and the only practical course for persons of modest means, polygyny was not unknown among the wealthy or powerful Hebrews. Adam, Noah, Isaac, and Joseph are described as having only one wife, whereas Abraham, Jacob, David, and Solomon are equally well known for their many wives. In many instances, the presence of slaves, called servants, provided opportunities for either concubinage or for the hierarchal ordering of wives so that older wives could dominate younger ones.

Arguments in support of polygyny included the need for male children to inherit family property, the desire for many children (barrenness being a sign of God's disfavor), and the obvious affirmation of one's socioeconomic status, since wife purchase and maintenance were costly.

Intrigue, jealousy, and outright cruelty could occur among these many wives, as in the case of the banishment of the handmaiden Hagar and her son, Ishmael. Ishmael, the first son of the patriarch Abraham, is still acknowledged to be the founder of his people among faithful Islamic followers. The legendary abandonment by Abraham of Ishmael has been interpreted, interestingly enough, either as evidence of the fraternal relationship between Islam and Judaism or as a generational memory of the unbridgeable gap between the two great faiths.

A *levir*, a brother-in-law, had a moral obligation to marry his sister-in-law if his brother died. The sister-in-law, now a widow, had the right to call upon the levir to father children in his dead brother's name. Through *chalitza*, the ceremony in which the levir was publicly humiliated by being slapped in the face with a shoe, spit upon, and cursed, the widow could "save face" and the levir could evade a distasteful duty, since neither had chosen the other.

Of generational significance is the case of Onan and his hated sister-in-law, Tamar. The biblical story pictures Onan as "spilling his seed on the ground" or practicing coitus interruptus, withdrawal, rather than impregnating Tamar. God slew Onan on the spot for this "wasting of the seed." It is not self-evident why this biblical tale ends with Onan's death, but it has been interpreted by some religious scholars to mean that God's wrath falls upon those who disobey a divine directive to "be fruitful and multiply and replenish the earth." Present generations continue to search out ways and means to practice birth control within families or population control within societies. For those who follow Judeo-Christian doctrines, the case of Onan has frequently been cited as evidence of the immorality of "unnatural" birth-control methods.

Relative Status of Hebrew Men, Women, and Children

While ostensibly a husband was the head of a household and was addressed as *baal*, master of the house, wives exercised considerable authority. Within the home, her services were indispensable in following moral codes or in setting moral examples. A husband might play a priestly role, but without a helpful wife, he was severely handicapped. His wife supervised the children, servants, and kinsmen. She maintained supplies, prepared foods, watched over family property, and instructed the young in appropriate behavior. The virtues of such prominent wives as Sarah, Rebekah, Rachel, Ruth, Deborah, Abigail, Hannah, Huldah, and Esther brought them fame far beyond the confines of their own households. Their "good names" in a number of cases, have made shadowy figures of their husbands.

Nevertheless, the power of a husband was considerable. He could sell a child, usually a female, into slavery. He could sacrifice or threaten to sacrifice a child, even a male, as in the case of Isaac, or he could punish him unmercifully for unruly or outrageous behavior. The requirement to render homage, filial concern for parents, was a most serious admonition. As many interpreters of the Decalogue have noted, there is no biblical reference to a counter admonition of respect for children on the part of parents. On the other hand, there is little reason to doubt that a genuine feeling of mutual respect and admiration could develop between a son and father if time mellowed whatever antagonisms might have occurred between them.

Family unity was in jeopardy when properties or favors were transferred between generations. Jealousies could destroy brotherly relationships and splinter family solidarities. The rule of primogeniture, inheritance through the eldest son, kept family property intact but also meant that younger sons were subordinated to their eldest brother. Later on, primogeniture was abandoned in favor of equal division of family properties among the sons, but some effects of primogeniture survived through the allotment of double portions for the eldest.

Sibling rivalries could and did erupt, as in the cases of Jacob and Esau and, later on, of Joseph and his older brothers. The earliest tale of brothers appears in Genesis and concludes with fratricide, Cain killing Abel in a fit of jealous rage. Cain's searching question, "Am I my brother's keeper?" continues to taunt generations and has troubled contemporary, religiously oriented families.

Termination of Marriage

Divorce was a simple affair among the ancient Hebrews. A husband would hand his wife a bill of divorcement, a *get*, on such grounds as barrenness, laziness, sorcery, disobedience, incompatibility, or infidelity. Later on, wives received protection by the requirement of proof of claims against them and the return of their original property. Divorce of husbands by wives became possible if the husbands had defects of their own, such as "a loathsome disease," for example, leprosy, or "a vile occupation," such as being a tanner of hides or procurer of prostitutes.

Divorce was thus a secular affair. It would seem to be inconsistent with the prior view that marriage was *kiddushin*, holy or sanctified. One explanation for this paradox was that while the unity of husband and wife was held to be a divine blessing, the Hebrews realistically held that human beings were "a little lower than the angels" and therefore quite capable of failing to live up to their professed ideals.

Absolute divorce, the freedom to remarry another person after the dissolution of a marriage, was an option open to the ancient Hebrews. They believed that the real bonds that unite a couple are those that the couple themselves have forged. They did not believe that agencies such as community opinion or courts of law should require a couple to live together. In this regard for the internal solidarity of a home rather than reliance upon external agencies to keep couples together, the ancient Hebrews left ensuing generations a vital legacy. Hebrew families were not always happy and content, but they served their participants well because they took human shortcomings into account.

Unmistakenly, ancient Hebrew families affirmed a family-centered life, a realistic approach to sex, a recognition that spouse selection linked kinships, a need for cautious transitions from an unmarried to a married state, a view of family life as a sacred obligation, an allowance for the coexistence of both monogamy and polygyny, a flexible patriarchy that left room for the leadership and wisdom of able women, and a pragmatic approach to divorce and remarriage. These concepts continue to manifest themselves in contemporary family life. Present generations, however, accept them only with reservations, seeking to adapt them to dynamic social changes.

ANCIENT GREEK FAMILIES AND THEIR GENERATIONAL SIGNIFICANCE[5]

The Greeks of antiquity developed their own unique culture that has left its mark upon ensuing generations, particularly in the Western societies. Like the Hebrews, Greek families reflected the changing fortunes of Hellenic life. A common core of qualities emerged in the Homeric period. Family life, then, was essentially rural and patriarchal. Thereafter, self-governing city-states came into being and Greek family life became highly urbanized and sophisticated. Athens, center of scholarship, and Sparta, focal point of forthright chauvinism, were two of the most famous modes of Hellenic culture. To use both mind and body in noble service became the highest goals of Greek citizens.

Not all persons, however, were extended the full privileges of Greek citizenship. The institution of slavery still remained. Women were to be subordinate in their families. Elite males dominated Grecian ways, and they ruled their homes as surely as they believed their handsome gods ruled Mount Olympus.

The Status of Greek Women

During the early agrarian Homeric period, Greek women enjoyed a status similar to that of Hebraic women, valued comates of men. Later on, during the rise of the city-states, the position of Greek women became more like property than human beings. Women were given servile duties to perform or were placed in charge of slaves who performed family services.

Wife capture, the oldest form of securing a wife, gave way to wife purchase, gifts of cattle given to the father of the bride. These gifts were often handed over to the bride to become part of her dowry. Her husband had right of *usufruct*, or usage of the cattle, but knew that the cattle would have to be returned with the woman if the marriage should turn out to be a failure. Usufruct provided some assurance of stability to Greek marriages because the requirement to return such property made husbands think more seriously of the consequences if they ever dismissed their wives. Bride service and winning a bride through athletic prowess were two other forms of Greek marriage. In either case, wives were treated as valued commodities but not as equals.

Greek women were generally secluded in special quarters within urban homes and spent their days spinning, weaving, washing clothes, instructing slaves, and tending children under seven years of age. Shopping or gathering of household supplies was usually done by a husband or his slaves, but not his wife.[6] If they ventured outside, Athenian women were typically veiled and chaperoned. Extreme differences in age between spouses were possible. An unschooled childwife of fifteen would easily be under the tutelage of her worldly husband of thirty.

Spartan women, however, as wives and mothers of warriors, were a notable contrast to the harried housewife role of Athenian women. Spartan women were encouraged to engage in athletic contests, rhythmic dances, and outdoor exercises. Their clothing was brief, slashed, or minimized to allow free movement, a striking contrast with the sedate, flowing, and full garb of Athenian women. Spartan women were obviously not housebound slaves but were accorded some esteem as they gave their sons in service to the city-state.

The Status of Greek Men

Males were the valued sex, and considerable attention was paid to their proper rearing once they were taken from their mothers in childhood, whether in the more academic Athenian centers or in the rough barracks life of Spartans.

Greek citizenship was usually conferred around the age of twenty, and emancipation from their fathers left men free to select their own wives. Like their Hebrew counterparts, all Greek men were to marry, and legal codes were instituted to punish unmarried males, particularly those who delayed their entry into responsible matrimony.

The Status of Greek Children

Like women, Greek children were dominated by their fathers or guardians, known as *cyrios*. Infanticide was fairly common and was related to

Hellenic aversion for the physically unfit. Females ran the greatest risk of being killed, as they were viewed as inferiors to males, unsuited for military duties, and certainly costly because dowries had to be provided for their future marriages.

Children were given tasks of increasing difficulty as they moved through the age grades. Unquestioning obedience to authority was expected of children. Disobedience was a serious offense and could be punished by brutal measures, such as whippings until blood flowed or, in extreme cases, even amputation of the hands.

Superpatriotism of the Spartans

The Spartans developed a society that was the prototype of superpatriotism. The noblest service an adult male could offer was to be a warrior. Physical and mental conditioning for both men and women did produce some of the finest troops that ever took the field in combat. Not only the body but also the mind was toughened to endure whatever required raw courage and sheer fortitude. Their fighting spirit was sustained by a belief in the invincibility of their arms against all enemies.

The Spartan model of gallantry in battle has been repeated over many generations. Whipping men into physical condition is only one facet of military preparedness. Underlying the physical toughening must be an attitude of acceptance that no sacrifice is too great to achieve desired ends. In the Spartan system, families reinforced the fighting spirit by willingly sending their sons into military service. The legendary cry of mothers to their sons to return preferably as dead heroes on their shields rather than alive and disgraced was a powerful support for their fighting morale.

Emphasis upon Sensuality

Hellenic civilization glorified the human body. Unlike the Hebraic conceptualization of a supreme Deity as a gerimorphic, elder father figure, the ancient Greeks were polytheistic and portrayed their deities as eternally youthful. Physical culture emulated these joyful, playful, youthful gods and goddesses by encouraging gymnastics, calisthenics, and competitive sports. *Gymnos*, "nakedness," is derived from the Greek practice of engaging in exercises completely nude in a center now known as a gymnasium.

Sensual pleasures were to be enjoyed, but not necessarily between spouses. While traditionally devoted to monogamy, married Greek men often engaged in extramarital relations with concubines or prostitutes among slaves and war captives. The most famous prostitutes, *hetaerae—*

companions of wealthy men—were trained to cater to both the intellectual and aesthetic proclivities of men as well as to their erotic tastes.

Homosexuality was commonplace among the Spartans. Because sex
segregation was required in military barracks life, young boys would try
to sexually please their officers. Spartan girls, too, would seek out older
women to sexually comfort them during the prolonged absences of their
husbands in foreign campaigns.

Adultery, however, was regarded as a heinous offense. Athenian
men would execute, divorce, banish, beat, or imprison offending wives,
depending upon the degree of their sense of outrage. Sexual relations
between married couples were functional, prosaic affairs necessary to
produce children. Small wonder that wives sought out paramours who
might be more considerate than perfunctory husbands.

Three Facets of Love

Three elements of the love relationship were distinguishable to the
ancient Greeks: *eros, philias,* and *agape.*

Eros can be described as passion or sexual attraction that, in
essence, culminates in self-satisfaction. The sexual drive was, thus,
identified by the Greeks of antiquity as an innate force that requires
expression. But erotic love was never considered to be the totality of the
love relationship.

Philias love was defined as the considerate, other-centered love. It
could be demonstrated as brotherly or sisterly love or it could be applied
to the parent-child relationship in which each is considerate of the needs
of the other. It should be noted that philias love between "brothers and
sisters" of one's own social generation is probably easier to achieve than
philias love between parents and child because two generations are
involved. The assumption, which may or may not be correct, is that
relations within a single generation would generally be more cohesive
than those between two generations.

In the broadest sense, philias love could be extended to all generations and to all humanity. Thus, inadequate living conditions for any
person or collectivities of persons would be viewed as intolerable.
Acknowledgment of one another as "soul-brothers" is an example of
philias love among American blacks. World Campus Afloat, a project of
Chapman College, in Orange, California, takes hundreds of college
students throughout the world aboard an ocean liner converted into a
floating college campus. This venture is strongly motivated by philias
love, appropriately symbolized by its school song, "Brothers Around the
World."

Agape love was taken as the antithesis of eros love. It was sacrificial, even to the point of self-destruction. It was this type of love, Christians believe, that Christ practiced on the cross. To give one's life for the sake of others was the supreme sacrifice. It was agape love that is said to have motivated heroic deeds by soldiers, sailors, and airmen. In the day-to-day care and concern displayed by many mothers and fathers, agape love is manifested and goes unnoticed except for sentimental events such as birthdays, anniversaries, or special holidays. Such parental care is sacrificial insofar as the main thrust of parental efforts gives far greater priority to the needs of their children than to their own needs.

No one argues that one form of love as conceptualized by the ancient Greeks is superior to any other, but their analysis does help identify what some people mean when they ardently declare their love for a person. In this sense, the indebtedness to the Greeks of antiquity is great.

Marriage Stability

Divorce was relatively rare among the ancient Greeks although later codes formalized the possibility. Two major forms of divorce consisted of either the wife's leaving the husband, *apoleipsis*, or the husband's leaving the wife, *apopempsis*. If incompatibility or infertility were the cause, divorce was generally a private matter. If adultery was involved, however, a husband was required to publicly void the marriage. Refusal to do so led to *atimia*, loss of civil rights, a most serious matter in a society that had both slaves and freemen. Not only would the dowry be returned in the event of divorce, but the husband was duty bound to pay *sitos*, alimony. A final stipulation in statutory divorce was to have witnesses. These provisions had a stabilizing effect upon marriage because few would risk the possible economic losses and public disgrace that could result from divorce actions.

The Incest Tabu

Marriages between half brothers and half sisters, primary relatives who were related through one parent only, were permissible. However, marriages between parents and their children were regarded with horror by the ancient Greeks. The inadvertent marriage of the Theban monarch, Oedipus, to his mother, Jocasta, became the tragic theme of Sophocles' drama *Oedipus Rex*. Freudian psychology applied the Oedipus theme to sexual rivalries said to exist between a son and a father over access to a mother. Unresolved sexual rivalry between a daughter and her mother for the love of a father was identified as the Electra complex. This syndrome is based upon Aeschylus' dramatic trilogy, the *Aresteia*, in which her brother, Orestes, kills their mother, Clytemnestra, for her adulterous relationship with Aegisthus, an act disloyal to Electra's beloved father, Agamemnon.

In the end, what did past generations of ancient Greeks bequeath to posterity, particularly those ideas or systems that apply to family life?

The ancient Greeks affirmed the desirability of family stability, unity, and harmony, but they also understood the necessity to dissolve family ties if internal dissension, disloyalty, or infidelity jeopardized family life. They were deeply concerned over personal privileges, but their emphasis upon the elite led them to deny full legal protection for women, children, and slaves. They subordinated their family life to the state by encouraging both sons and daughters to devote themselves to public service. They glorified the beauties of both the human body and the human intellect. And they favored eternal youthfulness.

"Greek letter" fraternities and sororities found on many American college campuses have adopted some of these Hellenic values. Their fortunes have ebbed and flowed over the issue of elitism. Those who have persisted in exclusiveness are defended or attacked, depending upon the family background of their supporters or critics. In more recent years, elitist ideas have been modified or replaced by expressions of concern for the brotherhood or sisterhood of the human family.[7] Thus, it is evident that the life-style of the ancient Greeks, as with that of the ancient Hebrews, strikes a responsive chord among modern families and undoubtedly will be evident as generations evolve new modes of family life.

ANCIENT ROMAN FAMILIES AND THEIR GENERATIONAL SIGNIFICANCE[8]

While admiring and absorbing some aspects of Hellenic civilization, the Romans did develop their own distinctive ways, which becomes apparent when their families are studied.

Entrance into Marriage

Like the ancient Greeks and Hebrews, the Romans arranged their marriages through family representatives or go-betweens, provided a stabilizing dowry, or *dos*, whose principal was returnable to the bride's father in the event of death or divorce, and recognized a transitory period of engagement, betrothal, or *sponsalia*, a promise to marry. Monogamous marriage was idealized as sacred, a matter of deep concern to families, and a state responsibility. A bachelor's tax was levied against the unmarried, and those who were widowed or divorced were urged to remarry. Age at first marriage for girls was fifteen, and their husbands were typically five to ten years their senior.

Multiple Marriage Forms

The ancient Romans developed a most elaborate social-class system, and the many gradations of socioeconomic status created a complicated variety of marriage forms. If one married a member of one's own class, particularly intrapatrician or intraplebian, the marriage form was called *matrimonium justum*. It took many years to assign *matrimonium justum* status to intermarriages between patricians and plebians. *Matrimonium non justum* was actually legalized concubinage between a Roman citizen and a woman of a lower class. Their children could neither inherit property nor be recognized as a part of the citizen's family.

A distinction was made between those marriages in which the wife was either controlled by her father, despite the fact that she was married, or by her husband and his family. The former type was called *sine in manum conventione*, the latter *cum conventione uxoris in manum viri*.

Three subtypes of *cum conventione uxoris in manum viri* were recognized: (1) *confarreatio*, a patrician marriage involving elaborate sacrifices to Jupiter in the presence of priests and ten witnesses, (2) *coemptio*, a plebian marriage involving a bride purchase before five witnesses, and (3) *usus*, a plebian marriage involving bridal consent, a type of common-law union in which cohabitation had occurred for a period of one year and during which time the woman did not absent herself for more than three days.

Three other types of marriage were recognized: (1) *contubernium*, a marriage between two slaves or between a slave and a free person, (2) *concubinatus*, cohabitation between two unmarried free persons or a single freeman and a maidservant, and (3) *imparia matrimonia*, a mixed marriage between pagans and Christians that became common in the fourth century A.D.

The Powers of Roman Men

Authority was vested in the father, the head of a Roman household. His absolute powers were expressed in two ways: *patria potestas*, complete domination of his children, including the legal right to sell, beat, banish, or make arrangements for their marriages and to continue to own his son's property even when the son was mature, and *manus*, literally, the hand, symbol of his complete authority over his wife and their entire household.

The Status of Roman Wives

While still dominated by her husband, the Roman wife enjoyed far more freedom than her Greek equivalent. She was not confined to special female quarters, nor was she publicly ignored. Rather, she ruled over her own household with dignity and was frequently consulted by her spouse in familial matters. She was not veiled, as were Greek women who ventured outside. She was often publicly escorted by her husband. Two of her most important tasks were to supervise the domestic training of her daughters and to meet religious responsibilities to honor the household gods. The Romans believed that the spirits of deceased members of the household still hovered about their former homes and could become malevolent if not properly propitiated. Accordingly, Roman wives exercised considerable authority in supervising household worship of ancestral spirits.

Recurrent wars, with their concurrent absences or deaths of husbands, gained the Roman woman an unprecedented freedom to control her own destiny. Such circumstances also allowed opportunities for sexual infidelity in order to fulfill unsatisfied sexual drives.

Roman Children

Girls were somewhat under the tutelage of their mothers, but boys turned to their fathers for instruction in reading, writing, arithmetic, agricultural skills, and knowledge of laws. Freemen or slaves handled the early elementary education of boys, but by age fifteen, citizenship could be conferred upon a boy, who would be required to meet its first responsibility—protection of the state through military service.

Greek slaves were often tutors of Roman boys, as the Greeks were respected for their intellectual powers. Later on, young Romans were sent off to an academy in Greece to complete their education. Roman youths conducted themselves on these Greek campuses far from home in much the same manner as modern college students. While ostensibly oriented to intellectual pursuits, high spirits, fun, and young girls were three interests on which extracurricular activities centered.

Roman Divorce

The solidarity of Roman families was phenomenal in the ancient world. Divorce was practically unknown for hundreds of years. If it occurred, divorce was accomplished by mutual consent in the presence of witnesses. This form was called *divortium*. A special form of *divortium*, called *repudium*, was, however, necessary to dissolve a marriage on the basis of such grounds as adultery, poisoning, or "falsifying household keys" so that strangers might enter private household chambers. Under *repudium*, a husband retained his former wife's *dos*. If an innocent wife was divorced, however, her marriage portion or dowry was returned to her family.

In sharp contrast to the stability of these early Roman families, the later centuries of Roman history saw the rapid spread of divorce to all levels of society. In one notorious case, a woman had married and divorced twenty-three men; her last husband had previously married twenty other women. Easy divorce made a shambles of what were once proud and stable homes. Morality gave way to sheer licentiousness which, in the judgment of some historians, goes far in explaining the downfall of the Roman Empire. Self-seeking Romans could no longer hold the empire together. "Roman" and "debauchery" became synonymous.

Modern American society is frequently compared with that of ancient Rome. The "Zimmerman thesis" expounded in Carl Zimmerman's book *Family and Civilization* holds that the state of family life presages the state of a nation.[9] Joseph Folsom's contention in his book *The Family and Democratic Society* denies that changes in family life mean the inevitable decline of American society.[10] Rather, Folsom contends that family stresses and strains have come from practicing democracy in families. Greater freedom and responsibilities for men, women, and children may mean that difficulties and breakdowns in family life can increase, but they also may transform American society into one built upon justice and fair play for all participants. Such a society is not declining but is reaching out to affirm its ideals.

Roman preoccupation with legalisms that attempted to consolidate and formalize the status of men and women in a powerful society has not been lost despite the coming and going of intervening generations. Modern American families, like their ancient Roman counterparts, continue to provide the mentality needed to support a great world power. Roman rigidities that sapped the internal strengths of men and women originated or were reinforced in their families and are viewed by many, in younger generations, as unworthy of a society pledged to freedom. Changes along these lines seem to be underway among many families in the United States.

EARLY WESTERN CHRISTIAN FAMILIES AND THEIR GENERATIONAL SIGNIFICANCE

The inheritor of Hebraic, Greek, and Roman traditions was the early Western Christian family system. Hebraic influences run deep because Christianity did not emerge as a distinctive faith until more than a hundred years after the events surrounding the crucifixion of Jesus.

Christianity developed slowly from Jewish sects that awaited the Second Coming of the Mesiah. Its spirit and vigor might have diminished and disappeared altogether had it not been for the organizational skills of inspired leadership that formed cadres of believers. The New Testament was developed as the fulfillment of the Old Testament and reminded living generations of the birth, ministry, death, and resurrection of Christ.

The history of Christianity covering some two thousand years is documented and interpreted in countless publications. For the moment, however, we are concerned with the early Christian families as they departed from Hebraic traditions and brought into being their own distinctive ways. Their generations laid down the fundamental guidelines that set them apart from all others and have characterized or affected Christian generations to the present time.

An Ambivalence Concerning Marriage

The earliest Christians did not give primacy to marriage and family. Life in the present was secondary to life after death. The imminent return of the Messiah would usher in a spiritual life for which the faithful had to prepare. Christ, Paul, and many early Christian bishops were celibates, as spiritual life was their central concern. Virginity was believed to be the highest form of morality. Vows of chastity were admired because these meant full devotion to a spiritual life.

Yet marriage and family were treated with respect. Some scholars have held that growing laxity of marital ties and neglect of home life among the pagan Romans made the early Christians more eager to defend marital vows and to create a warm and affectionate family life among their followers.

This ambivalence toward marriage is evident today in the comparison between the Roman Catholic doctrine of marriage as one of the sacraments instituted by Christ and the Protestant modification of marriage legitimatized by secular authorities.

The Status of Early Christian Women

Women were generally distrusted as temptresses of men and directly responsible for the fall of mankind from God's grace. Women, not men, were held to be the original sinners because Eve was the first human being to consciously disobey God. When subservient to men in marriage and family, women were honored and beloved for their meekness and gentility. If virginal women sought to serve their Christian faith, they, too, were revered and encouraged. Unlike the ancient Hebrews, Greeks, and Romans, who vacillated in their assessment of women, the early Western

Christians were unequivocal about the proper place of women. Women were to be subordinate to the leadership of men.

Christian Concern for Children

The subordination of women was balanced, in part, by a softening of attitudes toward children. Infanticide and the selling of children were forbidden among Christians, although these practices continued for some thirty generations. Child abuse and child exploitation continued for many more generations, until laws forbidding them were promoted and enforced by outraged citizens in Western societies.

Ambivalence Toward Divorce

The earliest declarations concerning the termination of marital vows were ambivalent. On the one hand, men and women were encouraged to remain faithful to each other, regardless of circumstances. On the other hand, failure to practice Christianity or entrance into holy service were acceptable grounds for a termination of marriage vows.

The formalization of Western Christianity in the canon laws of the Roman Catholic Church has led to repeated affirmation of the indissolubility of a marriage as well as to exceptions to the general rule. On the one hand, the Roman Catholic Church refused to allow Henry VIII's marriage to Anne Boleyn and subsequently lost much power and influence in England. On the other hand, it has declared a marriage null and void from the beginning in its granting of *divortium a vinculo matrimonii*. Further, a separation, divorce from "bed and board," *divortium a mensa et thoro*, is allowed if a married couple cannot live amicably together. In this separation, a marriage is still considered to be in effect, and the couple is not free to remarry.

Early Christians did not return to the older Hebraic model of mutual divorce, with the privilege of remarriage if one wishes, for generations. Protestant denominations reluctantly accepted divorce as a merciful and Christian deed when human personalities were being destroyed in the name of family unity. Early Western Christians began the process of making more humane some of the past harsher treatment of participants in family life. They added a gentility and a generosity toward human imperfections that have endured to this day.

SUMMARY

The search for hard, conclusive data on the origins and development of family life in the Western societies of Europe and the United States has been only partially successful. Evolutionary, speculative theories have wavered from steady state to sequential stage models to explain family origins and development. Such efforts have not been as productive as examination and interpretation of historical records of distinctive family life-styles. In this chapter, the perspectives and families of the ancient Hebrews, Greeks, Romans, and early Western Christians were examined to determine to what extent their inputs have survived and affected present generations.

The Hebrews of antiquity stressed: (1) a family-centered life in which everyone should be married, (2) a realistic acceptance of sexual needs, often idealized, but more honored in the breach, (3) a serious appreciation of engagement as a transitory stage before marriage, (4) the undergirding of marriage and family with spiritual faith, (5) deep concern for the creation of the next generation, (6) recognition of essential contributions of women, (7) the freedom to terminate an intolerable marriage, and (8) insistence that the ultimate authority of families should be vested in males.

The ancient Greeks, by contrast, developed their own set of marriage and family expectations: (1) women were held to be inferior to men but essential as healthy mothers of oncoming generations, (2) men were to marry and maintain a proper home, although the state took precedence over individuals, (3) physical or sensual experiences were equated with spiritual purposes, (4) divorce and incest were strong tabus, and (5) while democracy was held as an ideal, elitism was actually practiced through slave ownership, citizenship for freemen, patriarchy, and special privileges for the favored few.

Admiration for the Greeks led the Romans to place their sons under their tutelage, but the Romans did produce a set of family values uniquely their own: (1) marriages were accorded legal status depending upon the social class of the participants, (2) male authority was reaffirmed, (3) women were publicly treated with some consideration, and (4) family life was undermined by prolonged absences of fathers and husbands, a changed morality that favored infidelity and personal gratification, and increasing dissolution of marital bonds.

Early Western Christianity developed out of Hebraic family life but consciously differed from and supplanted older Hebraic ways. Early Christians were ambivalent toward marriage, wavering between life in the hereafter and life in the here and now. On the one hand, virginity and vows of chastity represented primary devotion to a truly spiritual life. On the other hand, the excesses of pagan Romans revolted them, and they turned to the importance of marriage faithfulness and loyalty among men and women. Early Christians held women responsible for sinfulness and their appropriate status was one of subordination to men. Nevertheless, while holding women somewhat suspect, early Christians also elevated the status of children to innocents in need of support and kindness. In this latter stance, they were unique among ancient peoples of their times. Finally, early Christians also wavered in their attitude toward divorce. In general, they favored the outlawing of divorce, but they also provided legal loopholes to suit their spiritual needs. What appears to be ambivalence for some, however, may be nothing more than the ability of Christianity to move with the times, to accommodate the existence of new conditions, new ideas, and new needs.

These heritages are among the factors that continue to indicate the symbolic impacts of past generations upon present generational family life. Undoubtedly, modern generations do not accept them without reservations. As with generations who have gone before them, present generations will screen and sift these heritages to make them fit the times. Then, inevitably, contemporary modifications will be similarly treated by future generations.

REFERENCES

1 A useful source of the entire span of Jewish history is Abram Leon Sachar, *A History of the Jews,* 5th ed., New York: Alfred A. Knopf, Inc., 1967. Another source is Max I. Dimont, *Jews, God and History,* New York: Signet Books, The New American Library, Inc., 1962.
2 Deut. 22:23–29.
3 Num. 5:11–31.
4 See Ernest W. Burgess and Paul Wallin, *Engagement and Marriage,* Philadelphia: J. B. Lippincott Company, 1953, chap. nine, "Broken Engagements," and William M. Kephart, "Some Correlates of Romantic Love," *Journal of Marriage and Family,* vol. 29, no. 3, 470–474, August 1967.
5 Adapted from Panos D. Bardis, "The Ancient Greek Family," *Social Science,* vol. 39, no. 5, 156–175, June 1964.
6 Robert Flacelière, *Daily Life in Greece at the Time of Pericles,* New York: The Macmillan Company, 1965, p. 66.
7 Alfred McClung Lee, *Fraternities without Brotherhood,* Boston: Beacon Press, 1955.
8 Adapted from Panos D. Bardis, "Main Features of the Ancient Roman Family," *Social Science,* vol. 38, no. 4, 225–240, October 1963.
9 C. C. Zimmerman, *Family and Civilization,* New York: Harper & Row, Publishers, Incorporated, 1947.
10 Joseph Kirk Folsom, *The Family and Democratic Society,* New York: John Wiley & Sons, Inc., 1943.
11 A useful source on early Christian family life is Stuart A. Queen, Robert W. Habenstein, and John B. Adams, *The Family in Various Cultures,* Philadelphia: J. B. Lippincott Company, 1961, chap. 9, "The Legacy of the Early Christian Family," pp. 181–201.

STUDY QUESTIONS AND ACTIVITIES

1 It is commonplace to hear of the American family system described as a Judeo-Christian product. In what ways is this true and in what ways is it false?
2 Do you agree or disagree that the individual is the unit of modern civilization in contrast with family being the unit of ancient societies, as Sir Henry J. Sumner Maine contended?
3 Search available sources to determine what families are like in modern Israel, Greece, and Italy. In brief, what has happened to the generational heritages of these countries?
4 If fraternity and sorority representatives are available to the class, interview them to determine what they mean when they speak of "brotherhood" and "sisterhood."
5 Do families make history or does history make families?
6 In what ways is evolution at work in marriages and families of the United States?
7 Sketch in diagram form what you believe are the interrelationships between family and all other social institutions in the United States.
8 From all that you know, what do you consider to be the origins of contemporary families?
9 Debate the resolution: Modern marriage and family have nothing to do with ancient generations.

SUGGESTED ADDITIONAL READINGS

Bardis, Panos D., "Family Forms and Variations Historically Considered," in Harold T. Christensen (ed.), *Handbook of Marriage and Family*, Chicago: Rand McNally & Company, 1964, chap. 11, pp. 403–461.

Dimont, Max I., *Jews, God and History*, New York: Signet Books, New American Library, Inc., 1962.

Kenkel, William F., *The Family in Perspective*, New York: Appleton-Century-Crofts, Inc., 1960.

Leslie, Gerald R., *The Family in Social Context*, 2d ed., New York: Oxford University Press, 1973, chaps. 6 and 7, "The Development of Western Family Organization," I and II, pp. 155–218.

————, Richard F. Larson, and Benjamin L. Gorman, *Order and Change*, New York: Oxford University Press, 1973, chap. 7, "Family," pp. 485–516.

Reiss, Ira L., "The Universality of the Family: A Conceptual Analysis," in Ira L. Reiss (ed.), *Readings on the Family System*, New York: Holt, Rinehart and Winston, Inc., 1972, pp. 11–26.

Schultz, David A., *The Changing Family: Its Function and Future*, Englewood Cliffs, N. J.: Prentice-Hall, Inc., 1972, pp. 17–137.

Chapter 3

Cross-cultural
Study of Families

Cross-cultural study of families provides a perspective that fits well with our multigenerational approach.[1] That perspective allows us to appreciate the variety of ways that past generations met and resolved the universal problems of conducting personal, familial, and societal affairs.

Certainly one of the greatest events in human history has been the rapid dissemination of European-American ways among societies throughout the globe. The effects have been lethal for some societies, shocking for others, and troublesome for those societies that seek to defend their more firmly rooted traditions. In many instances, preliterate societies of past generations have been destroyed. Other preliterate societies that have made more recent contact with more sophisticated cultures have been sorely tested. And literate but preindustrialized societies have been forced to homogenize some of their traditions with those of Europe and the United States.

Fortunately, all records of known societies that succumbed to the introduction of European-American patterns have not been lost. Preliterate societies are particularly useful to study, and field anthropologists have labored diligently to reconstruct and preserve considerable portions of their cultures. But why select primitives or preliterates as particularly useful?

There are three reasons: (1) preliterates have developed systems that can be readily understood because they are relatively simplistic in comparison with literate societal structures and processes, (2) preliterate societies provide greater contrasts with literate societies because preliterates have chosen unique pathways unaffected by contacts and cultural diffusion from the rest of the world, and (3) preliterate societies manifest primitive fusion.

PRIMITIVE FUSION

Primitive fusion refers to the tendency of preliterate societies to merge or blend essential societal functions within families. Preliterate families carry on social control, protection, sustenance, shelter, and socialization. These functions have been transferred from families by literate, industrialized societies to such elaborate institutions as government, education, religion, and the economy. This process of transfer has never been completed, but the sharing of functions formerly allocated to families by other institutions has left families dependent upon many nonfamily systems.

THREE TECHNIQUES IN CROSS-CULTURAL STUDY

Case Study

One way to comprehend families as cultural products is to understand them as imbedded in an overall cultural system. A case study of family life involves seeing families in cultural context. Familiarity with the general cultural conditions enables one to recognize just how much the overriding culture has penetrated and shaped the family environment.

Paired Comparison

A second technique is to juxtapose at least two different family systems and to determine in what ways they are similar or dissimilar. Joseph Kirk Folsom used this item-by-item analysis of family patterns when he compared the details of Trobriand family life with those of the American family system of the mid-thirties.[2] Margaret Mead used the same technique when she contrasted the "storm and stress" period of adolescence found among American teen-agers with the smoother transitions between childhood and adulthood of Samoans.[3] For those interested in less serious, but pointed, use of paired comparisons, the satiric, tongue-in-cheek publications of Robert Nathan, *The Weans*,[4] Robert Linton, "One Hundred Per Cent American,"[5] and Horace Miner, "Body Ritual of the Nacirema,"[6] are well worth examining.

Systematic Processing: Human Relations Area Files

Descriptions of unique or paired cases of family patterns do not satisfy those interested in testing hypotheses concerning the families of the world. By developing organized topical categories based upon reliable field reports, a master file known as the Human Relations Area Files, better known by its acronym, HRAF, is available. This has been a major contribution of George Peter Murdock, who has spent well over two decades perfecting the HRAF.[7] Data from 862 societies, coded for statistical analyses on about fifty different indices, may be found in the *Ethnographic Atlas*.[8]

Qualitative field notes are reduced to quantifiable data in the *Ethnographic Atlas* and, hence, become amenable to statistical analyses that provide frequency distributions, correlations, and computation of chance probabilities for random samples of the world's cultures.

Three of Murdock's observations are particularly noteworthy. One is his recognition that "clusters" of societies exist with many features in common because they come from a common genetic source. This suggests the ability of generations to receive, retain, and transmit whole cultural systems—a thesis we have held in this text. Data from 862 societies of the world are organized into 412 clusters so that those using the HRAF may determine for themselves if they wish to develop their hypotheses as applicable to a single cluster, a number of clusters, or to a random sample of the world's cultural clusters.[9]

The remaining observations have further relevance for our study of the influence of multigenerations upon families. These involve the factors of geographic and generational separation. It is Murdock's contention that three degrees of latitude in any part of the world and three degrees of longitude in the tropics, distances of approximately 200 miles on the globe, are sufficient to minimize cultural diffusion between any two societies. Even more significant is his assumption that "at least 1,000 years of separation and divergent evolution are necessary before two societies derived from a common ancestor are likely to develop sufficient differences to be treated as independent cases for comparative purposes."[10]

In making these assumptions, Murdock may or may not be correct. However, there is considerable merit to his contention that cultures, though scattered, reflect their common origin and require the filters of geographic isolation and generational transmission before they can emerge as relatively independent and unique.

EXAMPLES OF CASE STUDY AND PAIRED COMPARISON AMONG FAMILIES

For our purposes, it will be useful to apply the above methods of studying cultural variations by concentrating upon family life itself. First, we can take a close look at the results of a case study of the Nyakyusa of East Africa. These people have been selected because they are notable examples of a generationally conscious society. They have worked out the problem of reducing generational conflicts by settling upon a system that passes authority on to younger generations without affecting the dignity of older generations.

The paired comparison procedure is illustrated by parallel versions of family life as interpreted by the Tungus of Northern Siberia and contemporary Americans. The Tungus are remote enough to be studied with considerable detachment. The brief summations of facets of American family life provide some examples of how detached, outside observers would report the life-styles of American families. Both the Tungus and Americans are people who have struggled with heritages from past generations to determine to what extent they are still applicable in present generations.

Case Study of the Nyakyusa—a Generationally Conscious Society[11]

Habitat and Economy   The Nyakyusa were residents of the marshy plains and foothills at the northwest corner of Lake Nyasa in Africa, territory now in the modern state of Tanzania. At least one generation, or possibly two, have passed since Godfrey and Monica Wilson lived among them to produce their field report.

Sedentary agriculturalists, the Nyakyusa subsisted on an economy of varied crops and husbandry of short-horned, humped cattle. Crops such as bananas, plantains, millet, maize, peas, potatoes, and cassava were grown in succession throughout the year. Adult men and women spent a good part of their days in crop maintenance. Sexual division of labor occurred in the form of men and boys being responsible for hoeing and women and girls for sowing, weeding, and reaping. Every man owned cattle, just as every woman owned some fowls. The food supply was, thus, stabilized, but hard work was still needed to meet daily needs.

Isolated from the outside world by high mountains on three sides of the Songwe river valley and on the fourth side by Lake Nyasa, off the main trade routes, the Nyakyusa were relatively free to develop their own ways untouched by fairly distant African neighbors, Arabic slavers, or European missionaries.

Political Organization Politically divided into one hundred independent chiefdoms, the Nyakyusa maintained some unity through recognition of common ancestry by kinsmen scattered over the many chiefdoms. Chiefs were required to follow the advice of commoners. Accordingly, no hereditary powers could be conferred upon a chieftain's kinsmen. Real political power lay in the hands of common village leaders who elected their replacements each generation.

Family Organization Kinship transcended village loyalties when movable and valued property such as cattle were involved. Cattle were prized possessions because with them a man could marry, live comfortably, gain prestige from friends by giving them feasts, and have something of value to bequeath to the next generation. It was the transfer of cattle from the groom's kinship to the bride's kinship that confirmed a legal marriage and so provided an economic basis for kinship networks.

Polygyny was the ideal, but plurality of wives was impossible for a man without good fortune over a considerable period of time. Few men under forty had more than one wife. Age at first marriage for men averaged twenty-five. Women married at puberty, about the age of fifteen.

Plural marriages increased wealth even further because a plurality of wives brought the services of more women and their sons and daughters to help acquire additional cattle through the bride price. Property passed not from father to son, across generational lines, but intragenerationally, between brothers. Not until a full set of brothers had died and bequeathed their stock could the son of the eldest brother, as an adult, acquire his father's or uncles' cattle.

Age, sex, and the control of wealth were the chief indices that determined social status. The status of chief was hereditary, but kinship to a chief did not automatically mean that an individual could become a chief. That determination remained with the village leaders, who were commoners. Women were publicly subordinated to men with the notable exception of the two "great wives" of a chief and the senior wife of a village headman, who cooperated with her husband in rites associated with ancestor worship. Seniority and wealth among men were respected, but esteem was gained by the manner in which wealth was shared or distributed. When a Nyakyusa male prepared numerous feasts for others, he acquired the greatest prestige among his fellows.

Age Grading   The outstanding characteristic of the Nyakyusa was their age-graded villages. Kinship constituted one linkage among the Nyakyusa, and chiefdoms another. But linkage with age peers occupied their daily lives and was considered to be the most important relationship the Nyakyusa experienced.

Boys slept in their fathers' houses and were made responsible for the proper care of their fathers' cattle. Close to dawn each day, the cattle were driven out of the village by the young boys, usually in a single herd with the cattle of their neighbors. The herd was returned to the village for milking in the early afternoon and then brought back to pasture until nightfall. This cadre of boy herders, usually between the ages of six and eleven, formed the nucleus of a future age village.

At about ten or eleven years of age, the boys made two major changes in their routine. First, they turned over the herding to their younger brothers and they, themselves, assumed the adult male's task of hoeing in the fields. Second, they no longer slept in their fathers' homes but joined an age village of boys. Encouragement for such behavior was given by their fathers who provided land adjacent to the village upon which the boys could build little reed huts for shelter. At first, these structures were playfully made miniatures and were wholly inadequate for sleeping or for shelter from torrential rains. When the huts were enlarged and made much more substantial, then each boy finally occupied his own hut.

Up to the time of his marriage, each Nyakyusa boy hoed his father's fields and ate food cooked by his mother. But he continued to sleep in his own hut amidst his age-segregated friends. It was commonplace to observe an unmarried man and his many friends taking turns at eating at the various homes of their respective mothers. Their comradeship was, thus, extended to activities other than common residency.

A single herd group of boys was not sufficient to form a single age village. Members of other herd groups would join them so that young boys found their circle of intimate friends decidedly enlarged by the time a true age-graded village was developed. About a dozen boys formed an age village and were quite willing to accept their younger brothers at first. However, by the time the eldest members of an age-segregated village were sixteen or eighteen, they began to reject younger boys as mere "children." Those refused entry into an established age village either formed their own age villages or joined age villages started nearby in another village.

"Closed" age villages concentrated upon the acquisition of wives, because only through husband-wife teams could the business of field cultivation and stock raising enable them to become independent. The men enlarged their shelters and brought nearby fields into cultivation. When a woman joined her husband to cook for him, to cultivate his fields, to enrich him with cattle and children, the man had arrived at full adult status.

Leadership in the age villages was "natural" in the sense that the strongest boy asserted his authority. When he finally remained unchallenged and unvanquished, he assumed full leadership of the age-graded community. This natural leadership began in the early herd groups when one boy would order others to bring back straying cattle, to fetch firewood, or to stop fighting. Headmen in the village would often designate one boy to control disputes in the developing age villages, but such leadership was nominal and temporary.

Formal Transfer of Generational Power   When eight or ten years had elapsed from the time of their first marriages, most men would then be about thirty-five years of age. A number of age villages in a chiefdom would then be officially recognized by their fathers' generation. The "coming-out" ceremony was called an *ubusoka*. After an *ubusoka*, the governing of the territory became the responsibility of the younger generation. More land and cattle were added to their domain as a further symbol of their full adulthood.

An *ubusoka* began when the eldest sons of a chief's contemporaries were about thirty-five years of age. The old chief was requested by his village headmen to let these sons "come out." The two eldest sons of the ruling chief and their respective village headmen were designated as the leaders of two new chiefdoms. Leadership at the local level already existed in the age villages, either through the assertion of natural leadership or through leadership appointed from fathers' villages. Such local leadership was confirmed or denied after an *ubusoka*.

A chiefdom was subdivided at the *ubusoka*. Four village headmen followed one chief's son and four village headmen followed the second son. "New fire" was symbolically kindled and distributed to those who elected to follow a particular chief. Boundary lines between the two new chiefdoms were clearly designated by the planting of two *ficus* trees. This variety of tree provided the bark cloth that was worn by the Nyakyusa.

A few months after an *ubusoka*, each of the young chiefs would marry two wives, even if they had already been married to other women. The new wives were designated "great wives" and the eldest sons of these great wives would become the inheritors of their father's chieftainship. Great wives were, themselves, daughters of neighboring chiefs and were married just prior to their anticipated menarches by symbolic wife-capture ceremonies. The wife captures were preceded by appropriate arrangements and affirmed by the transfer of cattle. Until the old chief died, there was a delicate balance of power between his two ruling sons and himself. Problems arose only in special cases when legal settlement could not be reached by the young chiefs and the cases were brought before him for final appeal.

Nyakyusa Generations

Three generations of males were distinguishable within the villages of the Nyakyusa: (1) those who were in the same generation as the former chief, basically elders, (2) those who were in the same generation as the ruling chief, the middle-aged, and (3) those who were boys and young adult males in the same generation as the sons of the ruling chiefs, the young. Each age grade or generation covered some thirty to thirty-five years. Each age village housed men who were within an age set of five to eight years. Just prior to an ubusoka, elders with ritual functions were sixty-five to seventy-five years of age; the mature men of the ruling generation were thirty-five to sixty-five years of age; and the males who had not yet "come out" were ten to thirty-five years of age.

Nyakyusa women changed villages much more often than the Nyakyusa men. First they left their fathers' villages to live in the villages of their husbands. Their husbands were usually ten years older than themselves. When a husband died, wives were assigned to their deceased husband's kin, usually a brother, and this necessitated still another residential change for the women.

The Chief Value of the Nyakyusa: Preservation of Generational Integrity

In essence, then, the underlying sentiment that bound the Nyakyusa to each other was their deep concern for generational integrity. Congeniality or "good company" was to be found in the companionship of age mates of the same sex. Each generation was consciously recognized as holding a legitimate status and was guaranteed political power in due time.

This is in sharp contrast with modern American family practices that tend to hold generations in tighter compartments to be dominated by older generations for an indefinite period. To be sure, those of the same age and same sex in the contemporary United States recognize each other and seek each other's companionship, but it is more of a defensive move to comfort each other from the pressures imposed by senior generations than, as in the Nyakyusa case, a consciousness of kind based upon early assurance that power will be theirs.

The Nyakyusa represent a singular case of a people who developed a consciousness about the generations in their midst and worked out an effective solution to the transfer of authority between generations. One did not hear about generational "gaps" or generational "conflicts" among the Nyakyusa as one does in modern American society. Instead, a potentially dangerous and conflict-ridden relationship had been converted into harmonious intergenerational and intragenerational expectations.

We would be in error if we assume that the Nyakyusa had stumbled upon an idyllic system to handle generational problems. Each generation in its own place and each generation guaranteed a central place in the total society are not perfect solutions to be emulated by all societies. The Nyakyusa were not free of conflict within their families, within generations, or between generations. In discussing their treatment of generations, we have extracted only a portion of their total culture. Full treatment would require more space than we can allot. What we have suggested, however, is that a people like the Nyakyusa have been aware of generational unrest and attempted to work out an amicable solution. Among American families, in a far more complicated system, generational aims continue to be thwarted or held in limbo for prolonged periods. What we are asking is an initial awareness of generational alienation, malaise, or dissatisfaction in order to move on to mutually agreeable generational patterns, particularly as they relate to modern family life.

An Example of Paired Comparison: The Northern Tungus and Americans of the United States[12]

The Northern Tungus occupied the headwaters of such great rivers as the Enissy, Lena, and Amur in Northwest Asia. Their territory ranged from Lake Baikal in Siberia, east to the Kamchatka Peninsula and the Sea of Japan. The northern limits were marked by taiga, forested highlands with frigid climates, and the southern limits by steppes, grassy plains with milder climates.

The Northern Tungus domesticated the reindeer and supplemented their diet and supplies by hunting elk, bear, wolf, musk-ox, wild boar, fox, squirrel, and sable. Such an economy required the wide dispersion of their population. This scattering of the Northern Tungus, or *Evenki* as they called themselves, led to a variety of distinctive subcultures, but these internal differences were not sufficient to destroy their common culture base. Shirokogoroff, the anthropologist who intensively studied the Northern Tungus, believed they possessed enough culture traits, complexes, and patterns in common to arrive at generalizations applicable to any subdivision of the Evenki.

The item-by-item comparison of the Northern Tungus' family system with that of Americans of the United States follows. Selected data represent what past generations of Evenki and Americans passed along to present generations and what present generations in both societies tend to preserve. Further, present generations contend with these practices and make their own refinements or modifications as they see fit.

PAIRED COMPARISON OF FAMILY PATTERNS

NORTHERN TUNGUS	AMERICANS OF THE UNITED STATES

I Control of Reproduction

A Ideology of birth

NORTHERN TUNGUS	AMERICANS OF THE UNITED STATES
The Northern Tungus know the physiological consequences of coitus. Women are understood to be the bearers of children. Spirits are everywhere and must be propitiated. Each child has three souls that could be taken from him by shamanism or by other spirits. Spirits of one's clan are friendly; spirits of other clans can be hostile. Spirits remain in or near human habitation. After death, spirits go to a good or bad place. They do not trouble the living.	Sexual intercourse is understood as a prior condition to pregnancy. Every neonate has a soul newly created by a personal and omnipotent Deity. The Deity is masculine and created man in his image. Thereafter, woman was created from a rib of the man and the woman's disobedience to the Deity necessitated punishment in the form of childbirth, pain, shame, hard work, and death for all future generations.

B Social and biological fatherhood

NORTHERN TUNGUS	AMERICANS OF THE UNITED STATES
Fatherhood is both social and biological, but fathers are not heads of families. Fathers act only with consent of all family members. Powers of fathers are further restricted by the clans to which their families belong.	The social and biological father of a child is one man. This man is responsible for the physical care and rearing of the child to independent adulthood, often delayed by prolonged education and military service (for men).

C Population control

NORTHERN TUNGUS	AMERICANS OF THE UNITED STATES
Contraception is unknown. Children are desired and excess children are adopted by other families in a clan. Spacing of children is four or five years apart. Childlessness is rare.	Contraception is widely practiced and publicly acknowledged in the mass media. Arguments concerning family planning center on proper procedures. Most mothers have three or four children.

Most married women have children starting at age twenty. Efforts to reduce births per family have been quite effective. Recent reports indicate that bare replacement has been achieved for many segments of the society, with 2.04 children born to each married couple. There is no known abortion. Infanticide is not practiced.

Abortion is viewed as morally wrong by segments of the population, but a counter-movement has resulted in a legalization of abortion by making it a woman-doctor decision, particularly in the first three months of pregnancy. Infanticide is both illegal and immoral and occurs rarely.

D Intercourse tabus in marriage

Intercourse is usually with one's husband or wife, but in the absence or unavailability of a spouse, other partners are acceptable and publicly approved.

Intercourse is confined legally and morally to a married couple. During menses or late pregnancy, coitus is avoided. Some wives and husbands seek either full sexual freedom or the right to extramarital sexual expression.

II Marital Status

A Marital pattern

Ninety-nine percent of marriages are monogamous. One percent is polygynous if a wife is barren or too old.

Marriage is serially monogamous, other spouses being possible with the legal dissolution of each marriage in turn.

B Age difference of mates

It is preferable to have near-age mates, but a husband may be as much as three years younger than his wife.

Husbands are usually two or three years senior to wives. Age differences of more than ten years exist, but are not encouraged.

Child brides from infancy to prepuberty are possible, but most girls do not consummate a marriage until fifteen to eighteen years of age.

Child brides are illegal. Typical age patterns at first marriage are twenty for girls and twenty-three for boys. Emancipation for marriage can come earlier by consent of parents or guardians.

C Ultimate control of marriage

Highest authority rests with the clan. The clan requires the fingerprints of all concerned in a marriage or divorce.

Marriage and divorce are defined, licensed, and regulated by government authority, usually divided among fifty-one major jurisdictions.

D Permissibility of divorce

Divorce is rare, but it can occur if husband or wife fails to fulfill their functions or are incompatible. Children remain in the husband's clan.

Divorce is permissible by grounds specified in legal codes. Stated grounds are often not the real grounds. Divorce is commonplace, although disliked and held to be emotionally frustrating. Children are generally awarded to wives.

E Status of the married and unmarried

All persons are encouraged to marry in order to provide economic cooperation between the sexes. Those who remain unmarried are asked to become attached to some economically functioning family unit.

Most, some ninety to ninety-five percent, marry and develop a family unit that provides economic services. Those who choose to be single can find food, shelter, clothing, and recreation by paying businesses designed to meet these needs.

F Status of the widowed

Widows and widowers must be re-married or attached to a family.

Widows and widowers may prefer their new independence, but often remarry. There is a surplus of widows and a shortage of widowers.

G Illegitimacy

Children born out of wedlock are not stigmatized. They are adopted by clans and nuclear families. The unwed mother would have enhanced her value because she has proven her fertility.

Illegitimate children are stigmatized but cared for by nuclear families or organizations. Unwed mothers are subject to criticism. Fathers, if known, can be charged with responsibility for children but are not required to marry the mothers.

III Marital Selection

A Endogamy

Northern Tungus usually intramarry, but foreigners may be acceptable as marriage partners.

There remains considerable social pressure to marry within one's race, religion, social class, nationality, or educational level, but there is also a widespread tendency to ignore these distinctions because they are held to be barriers to freedom of marital choice.

B   Exogamy

Marriage within a clan is incestuous and consequently avoided.

Consanguinity and affinity are barriers to marriage within nuclear families and close kin, but proscriptions begin to break down at the first cousin level of kinship.

C   Clan organization

There are four clans that are significant to an individual: two senior and two junior clans that exchange wives. A single clan exchanges wives with only two other clans, one of the same generation and one of the older or younger generation. The remaining clan is tabu as a source of wives.

Kinship has sentimental and, sometimes, practical meaning. Networks are often shattered by distance and social mobility, but emergencies and major events such as marriages, anniversaries, or funerals bring relatives together.

D   Territorial rights

Nuclear families have exclusive rights to their hunting and grazing lands.

Nuclear families live independently within their own domiciles, rented or owned, often indebted by mortgages.

E   Preferential mating

The levirate and sororate exist. Two brothers often marry two sisters. Crosscousins are preferable.

There is no levirate or sororate. Preferential choice of cousins is not formalized and generally avoided.

F   Personal choice

Individual choice is desirable but not mandatory. Families arrange marriages involving a bride price or *kalym*, gifts of horses or reindeer. Bride service is also possible for a poor man. A dowry often accompanies a bride to provide greater economic stability for a new marriage. Wife capture is possible but is made acceptable at later dates by kalyms and dowries.

Marriage is made freely by two consenting and qualified partners on their own initiative. Family approval is often sought after a personal choice has been made. Wedding gifts are more tokens of good wishes than they are substantial. Eligibles meet by chance or by subterfuge. Marriage may begin with little economic promise or just the price of the marriage license.

G   Virginity of bride

Virginity of the bride is not required. Most girls over twenty are nonvirgins.

Virginity of the bride has been idealized but is nonexistent in growing numbers and proportions.

IV Transmission of Status and Property

A Names

Families have no names. The personal names of former family chiefs are forgotten and forbidden to future generations.

Families are patrinymic, and there is much pride in many family names. Names are assigned to honor the living or to memorialize family members who have died.

B Property

Families are not stable units. They have no lands or property to bequeath. Clothing, utensils, and reindeer depreciate to extinction within a single generation.

Family estates are carefully bequeathed to heirs or allocated to kin according to legal formulas.

C Economic and protective obligations

A husband and wife team and their children form the fundamental unit of society. Failure to provide for each other's needs creates the neccessity for clans to reassign individuals to other nuclear families. The aged are tenderly attended up to the point of extreme senility.

A husband supports his wife and their dependent children. Responsibility for other relatives, particularly the aged, is increasingly shared with the larger community or total society.

D Marriage and economic exchange

Family representatives agree upon a kalym consisting of twenty-five to sixty reindeer or thirty horses in addition to cash, clothing, and other valued items. The kalym compensates the bride's family for loss of her services. The bride brings a dowry to her husband that returns a portion of the kalym. The kalym and the dowry must be returned if a marriage fails. Marital bonds are, thus, stabilized, and clans are economically aided.

There is no kalym or bride service. Gifts are given to the bride, often in the guise of "showers." Traditions call for the bride to bring her domestic talents to the new household while her groom provides the main financial support. Many women find this financial dominance-submission pattern objectionable because it reduces them to dependency upon men. Many argue that the development and identity of women as human beings or persons require them to be treated just as men are, unrelated to the opposite sex. One instance involves the use of "Ms.," which, like "Mr.," provides no identification of marital status. Further, while legal contracts still specify the rights and obligations of each spouse, there is growing interest in devising "couple contracts" mutually agreeable to both husbands and wives.

E   Marriage ritual

The man seeks the consent of a woman. Thereafter, go-betweens arrange the kalym, but not the dowry. An encampment is chosen and the negotiating clans and their friends gather during nonhunting interludes. The kalym is transmitted, after which the bride and her dowry travel to the encampment. A member of the bride's party is captured en route. A sacrifice of meat and wine is thrown on a fire for the groom's clan spirits. Feasting follows for three or more days, and the couple sets out for hunting territories granted to them by the husband's clan.

The man proposes marriage to a woman, although she has indicated her approval prior to any verbalization of feelings. The woman accepts, but she may or may not seek her family's approval. A formal engagement can be announced and wedding plans finalized. A ceremony is held before a religious or legal authority. The couple may consummate their marriage on their wedding night but may have "slept together" prior to the wedding ritual. A honeymoon of a few days or weeks may follow a wedding. Thereafter, the couple return to a home usually near the husband's place of employment.

V   Segregation Patterns

A   Location of home

A nuclear family lives in the hunting territory assigned by the husband's clan.

Ideally, neolocal, but often virilocal, the nuclear family lives near the husband's place of employment. Considerable distance between a man's home and his place of work often requires much time spent in commuting.

B   Composition of typical household

A husband and his wife and their dependent children form the nuclear family, but adopted children and old persons may be present as well as clansmen in need of support. Wigwams have a capacity of four to ten persons.

The nuclear family lives together. Kin may be present and are usually welcome for brief visits. Adopted children may also be present, but older persons and other kin are encouraged to seek other quarters for the sake of privacy.

C   Adolescent and unmarried housing

There is no segregation except for special locations assigned to family members within a common wigwam.

Brothers and sisters occupy separate rooms at adolescence if possible. If sent away to coeducational schools, the unmarried sexes are often separated in dormitories or private housing. However, parietal rules have been either greatly relaxed at many colleges and universities or effectively bypassed by students.

D   Sex segregation in public and private activities

Men are excluded from witnessing childbirth and also avoid menstruating women entirely.

Men and women may be together, within their specialized roles, at most occasions, including childbirth and menstruation.

VI   Role of the Sexes

A   Sexual division of labor

Men hunt, engage in war if necessary, load and saddle horses or reindeer, select campsites, and handle domesticated stock. Women bear children, dress skins, make clothing, maintain the wigwam cover, cook, educate young children, collect firewood, attend the campfire, and collect fruits and berries.

Heavy, dirty, or dangerous tasks tend to fall to the men, and lighter, cleaner, and safer tasks are assigned to women. In homes, women generally cook, shop, clean, decorate, entertain, and watch over children. Men usually work away from their homes in offices, factories, or laboratories and travel long distances in pursuit of business, professional, or commercial enterprises. There is growing effort to break down distinctions between "masculine" and "feminine" tasks. About two-thirds of all women work outside their homes at some period in their married life. Some make this a full-time, others a part-time activity as their family size changes.

B   Rank and power

Men and women generally consult each other. Women may become shamans or clan leaders. Juniors usually defer to seniors.

Men and women are generally regarded as political equals, but women are still discouraged from seeking the more powerful elected offices. Women ministers or spiritual leaders can be found, but they are still a rare species. Middle generations are in power, but both young and old question the wisdom of the middle-aged.

C Personal conflict

Rough language and wife beating do occur, but generally husbands and wives cooperate.

Wife beating is illegal, and husband beating is the subject of humor. Violence between men is viewed as "manliness" in circumstances of war, police action, or self-defense. Violence between women is regarded as "unladylike," but self-defense is acceptable.

VII Children's Roles

A Responsibility for child care

Women care for children. Half of the children die before maturity because of rigorous conditions.

Women are vested with child care. The vast majority of children survive their childhood.

B Discipline and power

Parents are very permissive. Children are loved and wanted. There is much fondling and kissing of children. Boys and girls are equally desired.

Parents and children usually show much affection for each other. The tendency is to be permissive at first, but to gradually develop discipline in children to accept group norms of larger significance. Mothers are expressive leaders, and fathers are instrumental leaders.

C Child labor

Children assume heavier workloads until, by age fourteen, a child is a full-fledged worker.

Child labor is sharply curtailed by law.

D Adoption and foster parents

Orphans are assigned nuclear families by clans of the fathers.

Orphans are wards of a court and are permanently or temporarily assigned to nuclear families or quasi families.

E   Education

Children are trained through observation of parents. Boys hunt birds by age seven, using bows and arrows or snares. By age ten, boys use rifles and by fourteen, bring in large game animals.

Girls help with children, carry water, and attend reindeer. By age eleven or twelve, a girl knows how to dress skins, sew clothes, and do light household tasks. Men have a worklife of about forty years, and women are at work up to age fifty-five.

From preschool through postgraduate training in college, formal training is provided boys and girls, men and women, by specialists who are not part of a child's nuclear family.

Informal training occurs in the home. Peer groups often gain increasing control of informal training. Worklife is being shortened, but thirty to forty years are possible lengths of service for men. Women do not retire from domestic chores until serious illness or senility occurs.

F   Pregnancy

A special wigwam is built for expectant mothers. Delivery of a child is from a stooped position, using crossbeam supports or with midwife assistance.

Most deliveries occur in hospitals under medical supervision. Some hospitals permit the presence of husbands during child delivery, and others do not.

VIII   Love Patterns

A   Prepuberty amorous behavior

Sexual life begins early. A common technique to quiet a baby is to tickle its genitals or to use masturbation. Erotic sex play is acceptable.

Sexual knowledge is generally available, but actual sex play is generally discouraged. Girls are typically overprotected, and boys are expected to be more sexually aggressive than girls.

B   Tender love and affection

Husbands and wives do care for each other. They share a deep interest in their children. Older persons are given the choicest portions of food, are tenderly considered, and often are adopted into a nuclear family.

Husbands and wives love each other and their children. There is a tendency for a special attachment to develop between a parent and a child of the opposite sex. Old persons are welcome as temporary guests but not as meddlesome members of a family.

C   Romance

Love relationships are expected to grow after a marriage.

Love relationships occur prior to marriage. At least one "right" marital partner is said to exist somewhere and that person is "found" in due time. The absence of love is often given as the reason to dissolve a marriage.

D   Premarital sex

Premarital sex is approved as normal behavior.

Premarital sex is often publicly disapproved but privately ignored as a tabu. The usual argument is that premarital sex is acceptable provided no one is "harmed."

E   Adultery

Adultery is not acceptable with foreigners.

Adultery can be used as a ground for divorce but is sometimes "forgiven."

F   Prostitution

Prostitution is unknown.

Prostitution is known and exists at all socioeconomic levels. The accessibility of nonprofessionals has reduced the number of professional prostitutes in some cities.

G   Special occasions for sexual license

Sexual license is acceptable when a husband or wife is not available.

Sexual license is generally disapproved but can occur away from the home.

H   Sexual differences

Womanliness and manliness are complementary polarities. There is no known homosexuality.

Homosexuality exists, and greater acceptance for it is being sought. Manhood and womanhood, formerly stressed, have given way to common tastes in styles, behavior, and clothes. The goal is freedom of expression, regardless of one's sex.

The Passing of Traditional Family Life

William J. Goode and Dorothy R. Blitsen are among the family scholars who have documented the gradual erosion of traditional family life throughout the world. Traditional families have experienced the pressures of urbanization and industrialization, but these twin pressures have not *caused* family systems to change.

As Goode notes:

> The usual definitions of urbanization or industrialization include so many factors that they are illogical candidates as factors of social change. If urbanism as a way of life includes anonymity, impersonality, heterogeneity of social contacts, separation of one set of social relations from another, and a developed technology, then we cannot easily use such a complex as a "cause" of social change in a primitive or peasant society. The whole complex itself *is* social change and we are reduced to analyzing the impact of this great complex on the *individuals* who come to the city or within its orbit. We cannot, however, use "the city" to explain broad societal processes; to the extent that the city exists already, those processes are already underway.
>
> The same illogicality is to be found in the use of industrialization as a "cause." In addition, various other factors are usually added—those found in the factory situation such as a free labor market, freedom to improve one's occupational position if one can do the job, a breakdown of feudal restrictions, increase of scientific and technological knowledge and attitudes and so on. Again, to the extent that such a complex has been established, it cannot be used to "explain" large scale societal processes; it *constitutes* those processes.[13]

Rather than using urbanization and industrialization as causal in explaining changes in family patterns, particularly in traditional cultures, Goode suggests that "the core element in industrialization is a *social* factor, the freedom to use one's talents and skills in improving one's job."[14] It is this factor that breaks kinship domination over individuals. Men, women, and children are no longer dependent upon family relationships. The "grip of generations" is thus effectively broken, and persons can become socially mobile, usually "away from" whatever heritage they may have acquired from their forebears.

Goode noted at least five different ways in which industrialization modifies traditional family systems wherever found.[15] These are: (1) residential moves to locales where frequent and intimate interaction with kin is reduced, although there are technical means to remain in contact such as phone calls, letters, wires, and occasional reunions (Murdock's study of cross-cultural comparisons of premarital sex norms for unmarried young women in 180 societies supports this contention), (2) different social-class mobilities among relatives, some being rapidly mobile while others lag far behind, creating barriers to contact because of contrasting life-styles, (3) individual achievement takes precedence in the value system over placement because of kin affiliation, (4) urban and industrial systems displace the services of large corporate kin groupings by providing such items as funds for education, personal loans, and protection from harm, and (5) through specialization, employment is more likely secured by an individual on his own merits rather than by intercession of relatives.

Dorothy Blitsten comes to many of the same conclusions in her study of worldwide changes in family patterns. She writes:

> The interconnections between organizations and institutions in societies make it inevitable that they influence each other. However, in modern technologically advanced societies, family life is more determined than determining. The effects of families on non-family activities—political, economic, religious, and educational—are not insignificant, but they are chiefly disseminated by individual members. The family exerts its influence on the abilities of its members to cooperate with their fellows; on their evaluations of the ethnic, religious, and racial traits of the people they meet; on their political preferences; and on their tastes and goals. However, family organizations as such do not directly determine the political or economic policies of modern societies in any marked degree. They do not initiate drastic social changes. On the contrary, in modern industrial societies family organizations are called upon to adjust their routines to educational and occupational programs and to fulfill their functions by means that are largely controlled by non-family organizations.[16]

The family, thus, *adapts* itself to the overriding conditions affecting societies. Blitsten sees three ideal-typical forms of family organization that are associated with particular social and cultural circumstances. These ideal-typical forms are *corporate* families, *autonomous, bilateral extended* families, and *autonomous nuclear* families.[17]

The Corporate Family The corporate family is found mainly in association with agrarian societies in which land is the chief source of wealth. Contact is difficult both intraculturally and interculturally because communication and transportation are underdeveloped. Challenges from external or internal agencies are practically nonexistent, and corporate families are free to dominate political life. Religious homogeneity undergirds "great family" domination and allows relatively few persons in upper-class populations to benefit materially at the expense of the bulk of the population at the lower-class levels.

A small middle class or intelligentsia may exist, but they are dependent upon the largesse of the few, but powerful, upper-class members. Younger generations are subordinate to their elders, and women are subservient to men. Such conditions existed in most societies up to modern times and persist in the Far and Middle East, in Latin America, and in Eastern Europe.

Autonomous, Bilateral Extended Families   Extended families constitute the chief organizational units of corporate families. As "modernization"[18] occurred in traditional societies, however, extended families gained increasing autonomy. The autonomous, bilateral extended family, thus, represents a breakdown of corporate family life, but not a complete break with the past. While land ownership continued to be the main source of wealth, ownership, control, and profit from other means of production, such as industrial plants or a financial empire, become possible means to escape the power of the land barons. Certain extended families were in a position to withdraw from the corporate network and to grant to their own membership considerable latitude to pursue their own interests. More than likely, such autonomous, bilateral extended families were to be found in the upper-middle- or upper-class levels of the society.

Autonomous Nuclear Family   Finally, the autonomous nuclear family emerged as a well-adapted form in highly industrialized-urbanized societies. Freed from dependence upon either corporate or extended families, autonomous nuclear families relied more upon nonfamily organizations for supporting services.

On the personal level, youthful generations no longer had to defer to their elders. Those who became sick or disabled could be given over to nonfamily organizations because the resources of the small nuclear families were limited.

These shifts in family types seem to be occurring throughout the world. What has happened is *generational domination within families has been displaced by generational domination within nonfamily organizations.* Generations continue to wield power, but their power is so dispersed within bureaucratic agencies that it is even more difficult to confront them and to seek further changes. Nevertheless, it is on this bureaucratic front that "the clash of generations" will continue for many years to come.

SUMMARY

Cross-cultural study of family life includes case study, paired comparisons, and the testing of hypotheses on a world scale. Samplings of world cultures have become possible by systematic organization of all known data from both preindustrial and industrial societies. The Human Relations Area Files (HRAF), for example, are cultural inventories that make feasible scientific investigation of family variables in comparison with American-European models.

The Nyakyusa are an example of a generationally conscious society. They have learned how to cope with generational conflict by granting increasing autonomy to their age-graded villages. The transfer of power between the young and the elderly is assured and never left in doubt.

An item-by-item comparison of the family system of the Northern Tungus of Siberia and Americans of the United States reveals families as both culture products and culture carriers. Through them, generations are adapted to their particular conditions.

Throughout the world, new generations are accelerating the passing of traditional family systems. Urbanization and industrialization are associated with the demise of traditional families but are not causative processes in themselves. Corporate and autonomous bilateral extended families no longer control as many generations as do nuclear families. Generational powers once vested in traditional families have been widely dispersed to bureaucratic organizations. Nuclear families find themselves rearing new generations to conform with the demands of complex, nonfamily organizations. Younger generations seeking changes from past generational patterns find new strategies are needed to cope with this wide dispersion of established generational power. If changes are to come, the very fabric of society will be challenged by impatient generations currently nurtured in nuclear families.

REFERENCES

1 Major comparative family sources are: Stuart A. Queen, Robert W. Habenstein, and John B. Adams, *The Family in Various Cultures*, 2d ed., Philadelphia: J. B. Lippincott Company, 1961; William N. Stephens, *The Family in Cross-cultural Perspective*, New York: Holt, Rinehart and Winston, Inc., 1963; Dorothy R. Blitsten, *The World of the Family*, New York: Random House, Inc., 1963; M. F. Nimkoff, *Comparative Family Systems*, Boston: Houghton Mifflin Company, 1965; H. Kent Geiger, *Comparative Perspectives on Marriage and the Family*, Boston: Little, Brown and Company, 1968; and Meyer Barash and Alice Scourby (eds.), *Marriage and the Family: A Comparative Analysis of Contemporary Problems*, New York: Random House, Inc., 1970. See also "International Issue on the Family," *Marriage and Family Living*, vol. 16, no. 4, November 1954; "Family Research Around the World, *Marriage and Family Living*, vol. 23, no. 2, May 1961; and "Cross-cultural Family Research," *Journal of Marriage and the Family*, vol. 31, no. 2, May 1969.

2 Joseph K. Folsom, *The Family: Its Sociology and Social Psychiatry*, New York: John Wiley & Sons, Inc., 1934, pp. 5–34.

3 Margaret Mead, *Coming of Age in Samoa*, New York: William Morrow & Company, Inc., 1961.

4 Robert Nathan, *The Weans*, New York: Alfred A. Knopf, Inc., 1961.

5 Robert Linton, *The Study of Man*, New York: Appleton-Century-Crofts, 1936, pp. 326–327.

6 Horace Miner, "Body Ritual Among the Nacerima," *American Anthropologist*, vol. 58, 503–507, 1956.

7 George Peter Murdock et al., *Outline of Cultural Materials*, 3d ed., New Haven, Conn.: Human Relations Area Files, Inc., 1950.

8 George Peter Murdock, *Ethnographic Atlas*, Pittsburgh: The University of Pittsburgh Press, 1967.

9 Ibid., pp. 3–4.

10 Ibid., p. 4.

11 Adopted from Monica Wilson, *Good Company: A Study of Nyakyusa Age-Villages*, Boston: Beacon Press, 1967.

12 Adopted and abridged from Joseph K. Folsom, op. cit., and S. M. Shirokogoroff, *Social Organization of the Northern Tungus*, Osterhout, N. B., The Netherlands: Anthropological Publications, 1966.

13 William J. Goode, *World Revolution and Family Patterns*, New York: The Free Press, 1963, p. 169. Used with permission of the publisher.

14 Ibid.

15 Ibid., pp. 369–370.

16 Dorothy R. Blitsten, op. cit., pp. 265–266. Used with permission of the publisher.

17 Ibid., pp. 252–254.

18 See William E. Moore, *Social Change*, Englewood Cliffs, N. J.: Prentice-Hall, Inc., 1963, chap. 5, "Modernization," pp. 89–112.

STUDY QUESTIONS AND ACTIVITIES

1 In what ways do you see societies around the world adopting American-European cultural patterns and so abandoning their own cultural ways?

2 To what extent can you determine the resistance to American-European systems in various cultures around the world?

3 Generalizations concerning the American family systems are not easy to make. What modifications would you make in the specific areas of sex, marriage, and family as described by the author in comparing the Tungus and contemporary Americans?

4 How does cross-cultural study of families provide perspective for Americans?

5 Note as many ways as you can how generations of the present have contended with the patterns of family life inherited from past generations.

6 What are the advantages and disadvantages of case study, paired comparison, and statistical analyses of family life?

7 Explain the statement, "Families are cultural products."

8 Can geographic distance truly separate cultural patterns, or has modern technology erased this physical separation?

SUGGESTED ADDITIONAL READINGS

Belshaw, Cyril S., *Under the Ivi Tree: Society and Economic Growth in Rural Fiji*, Berkeley: University of California Press, 1964.

Herskovits, Melville J., *The Human Factor in Changing Africa*, New York: Vintage Books, Inc., Random House, Inc., 1967.

Mahar, J. Michael (ed.), *The Untouchables in Contemporary India*, Tucson, Ariz.: University of Arizona Press, 1972.

Read, Kenneth E., *The High Valley*, New York: Charles Scribner's Sons, 1965.

Steward, Julian H., and Louis C. Faron, *Native Peoples of South America*, New York: McGraw-Hill Book Company, 1959.

Vayda, Andrew P., *Peoples and Cultures of the Pacific*, Garden City, N. Y.: The Natural History Press, 1968.

Woods, Sister Frances Jerome, C. D. P., *Marginality and Identity: A Colored Creole Family Through Ten Generations*, Baton Rouge: Lousiana State University Press, 1973.

Yalman, Nur, *Under the Bo Tree: Studies in Caste, Kinship, and Marriage in the Interior of Ceylon*, Berkeley: University of California Press, 1967.

(See also *Case Studies in Cultural Anthropology*, George Spindler and Louise Spindler (gen. eds.), New York: Holt, Rinehart and Winston, Inc. The studies deal with such cultures as those of the Tiwi of North Australia, the Cheyennes, the Bunyoro of Africa, the Washo of California and Nevada, the Palauan, the Magars, and Mexican villagers.)

Chapter 4

Status of the Sexes

In this and the next two chapters, three emotionally charged biases that have troubled the lives of individuals and their families for generations are examined. They consist of *differential* and *preferential* treatment accorded persons by reason of their sex, age, or race. Identified as sexism, ageism, and racism, these three prejudices and their accompanying discriminatory acts have a long generational history that is manifested most clearly within marriage and family systems. By considering this history, we can judge for ourselves the extent to which past generations have passed on their legacies and to what extent present generations are prepared to accept them.

There is a reciprocity to the concept of status whether it is based upon sex, age, or race. One cannot treat a conferred position in a social system without also treating related statuses or positions. If one discusses the position of women in a society, for example, such a position cannot be understood except in relation to the status of men. Similarly, the status of youth is inexorably linked with that of older persons. The status of blacks, Chicanos, or Puerto Ricans implies some relationship to the status of whites. Thus, if discussion seems to emphasize the subordination of one social category, it also should be understood that another category has been given a superordinate or superior status.

Further, much of the analysis of status has to do with its dynamics or roles. Roles are behaviors deemed appropriate for those who occupy particular statuses. In a sense, roles represent personal interpretations of conduct within the confining limitations imposed by statuses. They answer the needs of individuals who seek to determine just how far they may go in testing the restrictions imposed upon them by others.

In Chapter 2, we have already noted the statuses of men and women among the ancient Hebrews, Greeks, Romans, and early Western Christians. In this chapter, we can examine the implications and ramifications of these statuses as they were passed along to past generations of Western Europe and carried into the United States.

THE STATUS OF MEN AND WOMEN IN ANCIENT SOCIETIES

The Ancient Hebrews

The ancient Hebrews firmly established a patriarchal system. To be sure, women were respected *in their place*, particularly when they carried out their ascribed duties with zeal and loyalty in their families. Now and then, a notable woman would be recognized and would be raised to a superior status, but these were exceptions that proved the general rule. Essentially, the ancient Hebrews sought brides to perpetuate male lineages. As breeders of men and producers of obedient women, Hebrew women were honored because they accepted a male-centered system.

Hebrew women were passed along between male lineages by arrangements with patriarchs. They were expected to produce male children to perpetuate a husband's kinship. If Hebrew women were sterile, Hebrew men had the right to father children through additional wives or female servants. Female impurity was assumed in the conduct of public religious ceremonials. Women were separated from the men during public worship. Men, alone, carried out the religious rituals. Women did not count as persons in forming congregations of religious celebrants because only ten men with appropriate religious training could constitute a religious quorum. Hebrew men thanked their God with prayer, "Blessed Art Thou, O God, who did not make me a woman."

The Ancient Greeks

Ancient Greek women fared no better than ancient Hebrew women. They were honored only to the extent to which they could enhance the lives of men. Classes of women were ranked by men to the degree to which they could rise or fall despite their inherent sexuality. *Hetaerae* were accorded equal or high status with men because they were trained from childhood in social manners, art, and knowledge to be sexual and social companions for wealthy men. But *hetaerae* were often foreign women captured in battle or Greek females who had been abandoned by their families. Their training was calculated to please their male sponsors and not themselves or their families. Those women who filled the ranks of wives were far less educated than the *hetaerae*, far less knowledgeable about social amenities or the world outside their families, and certainly wielded minimal influence in ancient Greek society. Prostitutes constituted the lowest rank of ancient Greek women and were available for exploitation by men of minimal wealth or social position. Such prostitutes were either women from the lowest classes of ancient Greek society or were women captured in battle with foreign powers. City-states found these prostitutes to be lucrative sources of income and heavily taxed them to finance civic activities.

Greek wives were cloistered in special rooms, usually on upper floors, and generally remained out of the sight of men. Men preferred their own company and would rarely invite wives to attend banquets or public affairs in which wives could be viewed by other men. Spartan women were notable exceptions to the Athenian model of the guardianship imposed on women. Spartan women were granted far greater freedom than their Athenian sisters in terms of confinement to quarters or in restrictions on exposure of their bodies. They were encouraged to engage in active sports or athletic exercises wearing minimal or no clothing. Allegedly, these activities were conducted in special areas reserved for such female usage, but these spaces were not carefully guarded or screened to prevent men from observing or appreciating their physical prowess. Such a physical cult for women found its rationale in the Spartan concern for healthy male warriors. Here, again, we note that women were the means by which men achieved their own ends.

The Ancient Romans

A key characteristic of the Roman system was the effort to formalize the status of men and women through specific laws. Had the Roman legal machinery been a part of a complete totalitarian government, laws could have been passed and enforced with considerable impunity. As it was, the ancient Romans made an attempt to take into account the concerns of male citizens, varying the effect of laws depending upon the degree of influence held by classes of men.

Women, however, had little voice or influence in the passage and enforcement of laws affecting their lives. They were passed along, as we noted in Chapter 2, under the perpetual care of their fathers, their nearest male kin, or their husbands. They were denied the right to hold any public or civic office. Women could not appear as witnesses in legal cases, sign a will, or make contracts. Property could be received by women only from their husbands or brothers. Women were legally held to be imbeciles so that in a rare conciliatory move, Roman lawmakers acknowledged that women could plead ignorance of the law in certain instances and not be subjected to torture in other cases.[1]

Some women did acquire considerable wealth through the evasions of law by cooperative men. Limits imposed by law as to the amount of property women could acquire were ignored by some men who did not make public the fortunes they passed along to their wives.

Certainly one of the most portentous events was the passage and the impact of the *Lex Oppia,* a law passed in 215 B.C. that forbade women to own more than half an ounce of gold, to wear partly colored dresses, or to ride in carriages within a mile of Rome except on special public festivals.[2] Roman matrons reacted to the Oppian law as militant feminists. They canvassed all voters who could overturn the law and surrounded the homes of outspoken male opponents, threatening vengeance if these men persisted in their rigid stance. The lawmakers heard a series of debates on the issue and finally conceded that Roman women deserved better treatment than the offending law accorded them. The *Lex Oppia* was retracted and a new law passed, granting that women could wear many-colored dresses and whatever jewelry they pleased, and could ride in chariots without limitations as to distances from Rome.[3] It was a victory that had to be won over and over again under later European laws, but it did serve to warn men that women had political influences that could not be summarily dismissed.

Early Western Christians

The status of men and women was increasingly liberalized under Roman law, at least for the upper classes. Increasing freedom for both men and women, however, led to excesses in marital instability, sexual licentiousness, and family infidelity. Whether these conditions were impelling reasons to restore older rigidities between the sexes is not historically clear. What is known is that early Western Chrisitans sought a more moderate stance concerning the status and roles of men and women than did the earlier Romans.

One advocate of women's rights, Eliza Gamble, took a position that many have advocated in more recent years. It is that Jesus taught lofty principles of justice, self-restraint, and regard for the rights and feelings of all men and women that were later sharply altered by the aggressive church builder, Paul.[4] Thus, the promise of full participation in the sacred and secular life of a Christian society for both men and women was thwarted by the machinations of a domineering, energetic, masculine-oriented leader who won control of a movement that had started out in an opposite direction.

The divinity of man and the humanness of woman was revived by such Pauline writings as the following:[5]

> The head of every man is Christ; and the head of every woman is the man and the head of Christ is God.

> For the man is not of the woman, but the woman of the man. Neither was the man created for the woman but the woman for the man.

> Let your women keep silence in the churches, for it is not permitted unto them to speak.

> And if they would learn anything let them ask their husbands at home.

Northern European societies established long before the rise of organized Christianity had reached a level of considerable equality between men and women. However, the spread of organized Christianity over the centuries began to erode whatever gains had been made for a more balanced treatment of men and women. Women were subordinated to men in families, civic affairs, and religious worship. The grip of the Roman Catholic Church was slowly loosened in Europe, but the postulates that kept women in relative subjugation to men were never fully denied. Such a heritage was transplanted to the New World by European colonists and yielded slowly to generational factors brought on by social changes.

FACTORS INFLUENCING PAST GENERATIONS OF AMERICANS

Freedom-conferring social movements operated in the New World and acted as liberalizing influences on the relative status of men and women. Lantz and Snyder name these influences as secularism, humanism, democratization, frontierism, individualism, rationalism, urbanization, industrialization, access to education and economic independence, voting privileges, legal rights, and improved medical care.[6] Just how did these social forces operate to reduce barriers that denied the abilities of both men and women?

Secularism

Secularism places responsibility for social conditions upon persons and the social order they establish rather than upon divine commandments or interpretations of divine directives. It treats men and women as fallible persons who can and should be subjected to criticism and necessary changes.

Church and state were to be separated in the New World and no longer could some overriding religious dogma dominate the lives of American citizens. Men and women were to conduct their affairs as they thought best and not out of fear of eternal damnation. This does not mean that Americans deserted their religious heritages. Rather, it means that men and women chose for themselves which particular line of religious doctrine they wished to follow.

Humanism

Under humanism, the emphasis was to be upon the dignity and worth of all persons, both male and female. To be sure, humanism did not seek to enthrone men and women as perfect beings. Rather, humanism recognized their strengths and weaknesses, and seriously sought to deal with them. Where checks were needed to protect vulnerable people from those who would do them harm, such checks were instituted. Lawlessness was tried in the United States by the venturesome, but they soon learned that freedom did not include treating others callously. Where there was recognition of talent among men and women, past generations were not unaware that these talents should be encouraged to serve the interests of an expanding, progressive society.

Democratization

Concentration of power in the hands of a single person, a tyrant, a dictator, a Caesar, an absolute monarch, or some other autocrat meant disregard for the rights of others. The sharing of political power has been a long-drawn-out process that has taken generations to accomplish. In the United States, at least, the principle of democratization has been established while the process still continues. The lowering of the legal age and the extension of the franchise to women are generational achievements of considerable import. The proposed equal rights amendment to the United States Constitution is a key issue that suggests that the status of men and women in American society is still an unsettled area in the process of democratization. How far current generations wish to go in the direction of democratization remains to be seen.

Frontierism

Westward expansion was one of the great forces that built the United States. Living on a frontier demanded the cooperation, and therefore the equality, of men and women; the physical occupation of Western territories could never have been accomplished without their mutual support. Since they acted in concert as husband-wife teams, as the foci of families, forbidding territory was made to yield. The saga of the West has become a part of American folklore and has furnished many of the heroes and heroines for today's generations. Frontierism is part of the fabric of Americana, and whether it will ever be removed from American consciousness is a decision for present and future generations to make. New frontiers still exist. Undoubtedly they will be *social* frontiers that ask men and women to conquer their selfhood enough to live effectively with a multitude of human differences.

Individualism

Individualism is concerned with the uniqueness and inviolability of human personalities. Categorizing men and women as either ruggedly masculine or prettily feminine has been sharply challenged as part of the human liberation movement in the United States. Normative behavior is imposed by every group, but rigid stereotypes as to how men and women should act has been questioned by individualistic men and women. There is no magic formula to acknowledge individual differences among the sexes, but again in American society, accommodation of varied talents of men and women has been sought.

Rationalism

Rationalism, of course, is reasoning, a procedure that opposes blind submission to past traditions. In terms of the status of the sexes, rationalism exposes stereotypic thinking such as allegations that women are emotional while men are reasonable. Compulsory public education for both males and females should have long ago demonstrated the intellectual capacities of both sexes, but many remain unconvinced. Note, if you will, the passionate pleadings of defensive men who feel threatened by the thoughtfulness or intellectual brilliance of certain women. Or, reversing the picture, note the considered opinions of women who are aware of the protectiveness of men in behalf of women and who offer logical reasons for preservation of traditional feminine status and roles.

Urbanization and Industrialization

These twin processes are adequately treated in numerous sociological sources and thus do not need extensive discussion at this point. Suffice to observe that they are rooted in the past and continue to be felt. Pooling great numbers of men and women in cement and asphalt environments once served past generations of Americans. Questions are being raised by present generations as to how much further super-urbanization and industrialization should go. Would decentralization, planning, or other cooperative efforts make city and factory life more attractive, or should men and women be disposable, expendable cogs in urban-industrial machinery?

Spinoffs in Education, Economic Independence, Voting, Legal Rights, and Medical Services

The products of the processes just discussed include the expansion of educational opportunities, economic independence, voting privileges, equity under the law, and medical services for American men and women. These have, without a doubt, radically changed traditional views of the status of the sexes. We can look at some of these changes.

Political Potential of Men and Women   Political power would seem to be well within the grasp of women in the United States because they constitute the majority of the voters. But a real, durable feminist bloc has not emerged to date in the United States. In the presidential elections of both 1964 and 1968, it is true that more women voted than did men, but the end results were in each instance in favor of the continued domination of men. In both the United States Congress and state legislatures in recent decades, the already small numbers of women senators and representatives has further declined. In all branches of the government, vital political decisions are essentially those made by men. The political *potential* of women is evident, but it is rarely exercised.[7]

Economic Status of Women   Economically, women have prospered in the United States. Much property is either owned or bequeathed outright to them. As *consumers*, women are indisputably powerful, and few men would openly oppose their wishes in the marketplace. Products are designed to catch the eye of women as well as men. They are alleged to be efficient servants for both sexes, but an unattractive item will suffer in a fiercely competitive market. Comfort, safety, and beauty must be built into a product if it is to survive. Further, inflationary prices have come under attack because women, who are generally responsible for family shopping, seek a reasonable return for their outlay. Boycotts on foods have been recent examples of the type of campaigns aroused women can mount in awareness of their power as a group.

As *producers*, women continue to perform services of incalculable worth within their homes. Acting as chauffeurs, cooks, maids, caterers, nurses, hostesses, laundresses, gardeners, babysitters, corresponding secretaries, companions, and housekeepers, women serve in multiple roles that some men appreciate and others take for granted. As some men have discovered when their wives cannot act in some capacity, the payment of fees for professionals in these roles is excessive and burdensome.

Not only do American women labor *within* their homes at multiple tasks, but increasingly, they are finding paid employment *outside* their homes. Table 4-1 provides data showing the increased participation of American women in the labor force for well over three generations.

Employment for American women increased by four million between 1963 and 1968 with women and girls sixteen years of age and older making up two-thirds of the increase in the total civilian labor forces.[8] A gain of over a million women was made during this same five-year interval in the teaching or health professions or other professional and technical work that is essentially an *extension* of work formerly done in the home. In clerical positions in which women simply carry out policies of their employers, there was a gain of two million women as the 1970s approached.

By contrast, private-household work or work on farms declined for women during this five-year period. Unemployment rates for nonwhite women were particularly high, over 7 percent, when compared with women's general unemployment rate of about 4 percent. For nonwhite teen-agers sixteen to nineteen years of age, the unemployment rates skyrocketed to over 22 percent in 1968. By the end of 1969, the Interdepartmental Commission on the Status of Women reported that "almost half the women between 18 and 64 are either working or looking for work."[9]

Some barriers to the employment of women outside their homes are being removed. By the end of 1968, separate male and female employment advertisements were outlawed. Fifteen states and the District of Columbia specifically ban sex discrimination through fair-employment-practices laws and the federal government, since 1967, bans discrimination based on sex in federal employment, in employment by federal contractors and subcontractors, and in employment in federally assisted

Table 4-1 Participation in Labor Force of Women, by Marital Status and Age, United States, 1890, 1960, and 1969, by Percent

	1890				1960				1969			
	All	Single	Married	Other*	All	Single	Married	Other*	All	Single	Married	Other*
14 and over	18.2	36.9	4.5	28.6	34.8	44.1	30.5	40.0				
14–19					25.5	25.3	25.3	37.3				
16–19									37.2	37.1	35.4	51.8
20–24	27.0	33.6	6.4	54.7	44.3	73.4	30.0	54.6	56.6	69.4	47.9	62.9
25–34	16.8	53.4	4.7	53.6	34.5	79.9	27.7	55.5	43.4	80.9	36.9	63.5
35–44	12.7	46.1	4.4	48.4	42.4	79.7	36.2	67.4	49.3	72.3	45.4	66.4
45–54	12.5	39.6	3.8	35.9	48.4	80.6	40.5	68.2				
45–64									48.4	67.9	43.1	60.8
55–64	11.4	30.9	2.9	23.4	35.2	67.0	24.3	50.7				
65 and over	7.6	16.5	2.1	10.0	10.1	21.6	5.9	11.0	10.0	18.4	7.6	10.2

*Widowed and divorced. Sources: International Encyclopedia of the Social Sciences, New York: The Macmillan Company and The Free Press, 1968, vol. 8, p. 479, and U.S. Department of Commerce, Social and Economic Statistics Administration, Bureau of the Census, no. 332, 1970 p. 224. Used with permission.

construction projects. The largest single employer in the United States, the federal government, has thus given notice that it stands on the side of more equitable treatment of men and women in securing employment.

But employment opportunities do not mean concomitant payment for services rendered. A gap has long existed between what men and women with equal training and experiences are paid for the same job. Equal pay for equal work has become a battle cry for women who seek to remove still another barrier in the long struggle for parity with men. Whether this barrier, too, will be breached or removed depends in large measure upon some overall consensus that the heritages from past generations require modifications in the light of present circumstances.

ARGUMENTS FAVORING RETENTION OF UNEQUAL STATUS OF THE SEXES

Past generations have taught that the greater burdens of marriage and family are borne by women rather than by men. It is women who are supposed to be *homebound*. Whatever socialization women are to receive is justified on the basis of their domesticity, their family orientation, and not full participation in the affairs of human society.

Threats to Men

Men tend to view any encroachment on traditional male activities as a zero-sum game. At least, so runs the argument. Whatever gains women may make, a proportionate loss is alleged to occur for men.

What has really happened in the United States is that women have assumed a double burden of both family and nonfamily responsibilities, while men have continued to insist that their own work is essentially located outside their families. When masculine prerogatives could no longer be defended, men accepted women in routine, nonpolicy making, family-associated, dead-end jobs. Further, men took the opportunity to enter careers formerly the exclusive domain of females.

Weakness or Vulnerability of Women

The anatomy and physiology of the sexes have been cited as the fundamental differences between the sexes that necessitate differential and preferential treatment. For example, Evelyne Sullerot writes:

> It is necessary to bear in mind the different periodicities in the lives of men and women. The existence of every woman is made up of successive physiological stages which subdivide her life-span. Not only is the differ-

ence between these phases experienced subjectively, it is apparent in the body: puberty, defloration, maternity, menopause. The autopsy of an anonymous male body would merely indicate his approximate age and whether he reached puberty. . . . The autopsy of a similarly unknown female body would provide a more detailed profile of her sexual development: degree of sexual maturity, virginity, childlessness or number of births, menopause.[10]

Women are, thus, held to be body bound and not victims of male perspicacity. It is women who are said to need maternal protection during and after pregnancy. It is women who are said to be vulnerable to sexual assaults. It is women who go through menstrual cycles from puberty to menopause. It is women who nurse children through breast feeding. And, it is women who lack the musculature of men. These anatomical and biochemical differences have been offered as reasons why women are accorded the status ascribed to them.

Threats to Women

Not only are men threatened by changes from traditional statuses of the subordination of women, but so are women. Some women are aware of the particular advantages that have been theirs so long as they play acceptable feminine roles. For example, such women do not compete directly with men. Further, they are shown special amenities or courtesies. If they work, women are exempt from lifting heavy loads, night work, or operating under extremely hazardous conditions. If they remain at home, the financial responsibilities of supporting them fall to men. The training of women orients them to being daughters, sisters, wives, mothers, aunts, and grandmothers in the traditional sense; deviation from this socialization would be most uncomfortable to many.

ARGUMENTS FAVORING CHANGES TO EQUAL STATUS OF THE SEXES

Concerning the Advantages to Men

Rather than a threat to men, the liberation of women is alleged to mean the parallel liberation of men. It means freeing them from the need to prove their manhood in terms of aggressiveness, financial support, physical and emotional courage, and overattentiveness. They are no less men if they express their individualized tastes or interests in areas formerly defined as womanly or feminine. A wider range of alternatives is opened for them if equality between the sexes is ever achieved.

Concerning the Weakness or Vulnerability of Women

The anatomical and biochemical differences between men and women are indisputable, but they do not take into account a wide variety of physical and social phenomena. For example, women manifest what Ashley Montagu called "the natural superiority of women."[11] Both in morbidity and mortality rates, women display a tenacious grip on life. Rather than being weak, they outlive men and experience far less sickness or disability.

To compensate for her numerous tasks, there is an unending variety of laborsaving devices available to the American woman. Figuratively, modern American women have hundreds of "slaves" to clean, wash, store, and prepare foods, carry equipment, transport them distances, and educate and entertain them. All that is needed is to flick a switch, read an instrument, open a tap, tap a key, press a button, turn a dial, or insert a key. Indeed, most men do not use sheer physical brawn to perform their own daily tasks in the modern United States.

Menstrual or cyclical problems of American women have been reduced through effective hygienic measures, biochemical intake, sex education, and removal of predisposition to induce discomfort by greater psychosocial understanding.

Protective measures need to be extended to both men and women in any seriously hostile or threatening environment. They include security against sexual assaults or physical attacks, such as care in selecting friends and associates; police protection; training in self-protection; effective treatment of psychiatric cases; and experience in the maintenance of physical, psychological, and social health.

Concerning the Threats to Some Women

Advocates of equity between the sexes point to the normative socialization consciously or unconsciously foisted upon men and women. Women have a place on male terms and not as persons in their own right. The domesticity of women and the bravado of men are social products and, hence, are subject to changes. That some women would be threatened by changes in current social norms is to be expected and dealt with positively. Training of both boys and girls, men and women, is to be directed toward the sharing of family life, a life in which men and women work together to make their homes livable and their families satisfying. Women, as well as men, are to use their talents in service beyond that of family life. Both stand to gain their personhood and to shed statuses that shackle their ingenuity. Few advocates would claim that an idyllic state would be achieved between and among the sexes. What they do claim is that a more honest state of affairs can exist between men and women so that, together, they may build a worthy generational heritage.[12]

SUMMARY

We have attempted in this chapter to treat a highly complicated issue, the differential and preferential treatment of the sexes over the past generations and what these distinctions mean in terms of modern American men and women and their families. Obviously, we have skimmed the surface and only suggested what lies beneath.

Nevertheless, the status of men and women among the ancient Hebrews, Greeks, Romans, and early Western Christians has carried over into modern American family life. Moderated by the forces of secularism, humanism, democratization, frontierism, individualism, rationalism, urbanization, industrialization, access to education and economic independence, voting privileges, legal rights, and improved medical care, ancient and European judgments concerning the status of the sexes have required rethinking and new alignments. Politically and economically, women have been gaining by the changes, but the process is still incomplete. Political power still rests with men. Equal pay for equal work is more a rallying cry than it is a reality. Men and women work outside their homes, more by necessity than by choice. Within their homes, women in the contemporary United States continue to carry greater domestic burdens than do their men.

Finally, we have weighed a few of the arguments for and against radical changes in the status of the sexes in the modern United States. Threatened men and women, and arguments that status and roles are outgrowths of biological foundations, were contrasted with the potential liberation of men, the recognition of the personhood of women, and the counterarguments that American men and women are not as body bound as they have been led to believe. In the end, we can see the extent to which past generations continue to influence modern times and to what extent present generations seek to modify past heritages for themselves and for their children.

REFERENCES

1 John Langdon-Davies, *A Short History of Women*, New York: The Literary Guild of America, The Viking Press, Inc., 1927, p. 175.
2 Ibid., p. 178.
3 Ibid., p. 179.

4 Eliza Burt Gamble, *The Sexes in Science and History*, New York: G. P. Putnam's Sons, 1916, pp. 360–361.
5 Ibid., pp. 362–363.
6 Herman R. Lantz and Eloise C. Snyder, *Marriage: An Examination of the Man-Woman Relationship*, New York: John Wiley & Sons, Inc., 1962, pp. 21–30.
7 See, for example, Seymour Farber and Roger Wilson (eds.), *The Potential of Woman*, New York: McGraw-Hill Book Company, 1963.
8 See *American Women, 1963–1968*, Report of the Interdepartmental Committee on the Status of Women, Washington, D.C.: U.S. Government Printing Office, 1968, p. 11.
9 See ibid., p. 11.
10 Evelyne Sullerot, *Woman, Society and Change*, New York: McGraw-Hill Book Company, 1971, p. 51.
11 Ashley Montagu, *The Natural Superiority of Women*, New York: The Macmillan Company, 1953.
12 A tremendous literature has developed around the status of the sexes. For useful sources, see:
Edmund Dahlstrom (ed.), *The Changing Roles of Men and Women*, Boston: Beacon Press, 1971.
Betty Friedan, *The Feminine Mystique*, New York: Dell Publishing Co., Inc., 1963.
Ferdinand Lundberg and Marynia F. Farnham, *Modern Woman: The Lost Sex*, New York: Harper & Brothers, 1947.
Reische, Diana (ed.), *Women and Society*, New York: The H. W. Wilson Company, 1972.
William L. O'Neill (ed.), *The Woman Movement: Feminism in the United States and England*, Chicago: Quadrangle Books, Inc., 1971.

STUDY QUESTIONS AND ACTIVITIES

1 In what ways are families responsible for the differential and preferential treatment accorded men and women in the United States?
2 Invite panelists into class who consider themselves to be advocates of women's rights. Balance them with those who hold contrary views.
3 Prepare your own "position paper" on how you believe men and women should be treated in American society.
4 Debate the proposition that differential and preferential treatment of the sexes is based upon innate, nonremediable differences between the sexes.
5 What part do social definitions of femininity and masculinity play in the status and roles of men and women in the contemporary United States?
6 To what extent has the heritage of the ancient Hebrews, Greeks, Romans, and early Western Christians remained intact in the United States?
7 Read F. I. Nye and Louis W. Hoffman, *The Employed Mother in America*, Chicago: Rand McNally & Company, 1963, and determine how Nye and

Hoffman document the effects of outside employment of mothers upon their families and themselves.

SUGGESTED ADDITIONAL READINGS

Balswick, Jack O., and Charles W. Peek, "The Inexpressive Male: A Tragedy of American Society," *The Family Coordinator*, vol. 20, no. 4, pp. 363–368, October 1971.

De Beauvoir, Simone, *The Second Sex*, New York: Alfred A. Knopf, Inc., 1964.

Clavan, Sylvia, "Women's Liberation and the Family," *The Family Coordinator*, vol. 19, no. 4, pp. 317–323, October 1970.

Cowan, Wayne H. (ed.), *Witness to a Generation: Significant Writings from Christianity and Crisis, 1941–1966*, Indianapolis: The Bobbs-Merrill Company, Inc., 1966.

Davis, Elizabeth Gould, *The First Sex*, New York: G. P. Putnam's Sons, 1971.

Gordon, Michael, "The Ideal Husband as Depicted in the Nineteenth Century Marriage Manual," *The Family Coordinator*, vol. 18, no. 3, pp. 226–231, July 1969.

Grey, Alan L. (ed.), *Man, Woman, and Marriage: Small Group Processes in the Family*, New York: Atherton Press, Inc., 1970.

Hecker, Eugene A., *A Short History of Women's Rights*, New York: G. P. Putnam's Sons, 1910.

Mead, Margaret, *Male and Female: A Study of the Sexes in a Changing World*, New York: William Morrow & Company, Inc., 1970.

Roleder, George (ed.), *Marriage Means Encounter*, Dubuque, Iowa: W. C. Brown Company Publishers, 1973.

Yorburg, Betty, *The Changing Family*, New York: Columbia University Press, 1973.

Chapter 5

Age Grading

Just as past generations handed down a heritage that called for sharp distinctions between the sexes, a heritage that present generations seek to redefine in terms of equal treatment and opportunity, so too have past generations bequeathed their definitions of age grading. The passage of individuals along the life cycle from infancy, childhood, adolescence, youth, maturity, and old age was marked by a gerontocracy that mandated how younger age grades were to behave. Today, we observe considerable modification of this older pattern in and out of family life in terms of a mesoarchy with both youth and the elderly clamoring for recognition of their personal and social rights. In this chapter, we will describe age grading among a selected group of American colonists and contrast it to practices among contemporary Americans.

One distinction between the subject matter of Chapter 4 and this chapter is that, in the former, sex difference split the social experiences into two distinctive life-styles, whereas in the latter, age involves everyone in common experiences. Further, recognition of the age factor provides far more options over a lifetime than the duality of sex. In a sense, age grading becomes a common cause for generations, whereas sex differences tend to create a polarity among generations.

AGE GRADING IN COLONIAL NEW ENGLAND, PLYMOUTH COLONY

Treatment of Children

The Puritans sought to establish a religious community in the New World that took its moral code from the Hebraic laws as set down in the Old Testament. The head of a household was to be a stern patriarch who dominated his family. Children were to be obedient to his instructions, to suffer in silence, and to move toward adulthood as soon as possible. The most serious offenders in terms of stubbornness, willful rebellion, or cursing or striking a parent were liable to execution.[1] No record has been found that the letter of colonial law was ever actually carried out for children, but the spirit of the law was certainly felt by the very young.

The large open fireplace or kitchen provided the setting for the family gathering, each member entitled to a comforting place on the hearth. But this idyllic picture of a pleasantly engaged family is shattered by evidence of the sharp distinctions accorded children and adults. Many children were not allowed to sit at the same table with their parents but were required to stand through the whole meal. Each child had a standing place and a plate or trencher. Sometimes they stood behind the adults and took whatever food was handed to them. In other families, children stood at a side table; to supply their food, they were required to come to the parental table to fill their trenchers.[2]

Children were held to be inherently evil or inclined to be unruly and willful. Fathers and mothers were urged to create a religious atmosphere through family prayers, family reading of the Bible, and observance of the Sabbath. The Deity was a wrathful God who would strike children dead or make them suffer if they did not respect the moral codes of their elders. Because of the responsibility to build a New Zion in the wilderness, idleness was viewed as sinful. Children were to be useful to their families as soon as possible. Small boys were to weave garters and suspenders on small looms found in almost every family. They were to work in the fields with the crops or tend to cattle. Little girls joined their brothers in spring sowing and weeding of vegetable gardens. Starting at age six or seven, girls learned how to spin flax and wool. Tape and braid for shoelaces, belts, and hatbands were made by small children while they tended sheep or watched over their family's cattle. Domesticity for girls included training in cooking, sewing, spinning, weaving, and needlework on samplers. Memorization of a catechism or embroidering of some moral verse reminded children of their duties as subordinates to their parents. Work was the worst enemy of Satan, and Puritan parents were zealous that their children would be saved from his influence.[3]

Those children who were orphaned or who had poor parents were legally bound over to suitable adults who would carefully attend to their spiritual salvation by working them in homebound industry.

Children, then, were economic assets who contributed to the home by their labors. Most families averaged nine or more children, and it was not uncommon for wives to have as many as twenty. Infant and child mortality, however, was extremely high, and many did not survive the rigors of early childhood to reach maturity.[4]

It would be false to equate the stern and rigorous treatment of children with sheer cruelty. Undoubtedly, these parents displayed affection and concern for their children, but always with an eye to the common beliefs and practices of the day. Cruel and irresponsible parents were known to the community, and these eventually lost control of their children through laws that required their assignments to more conscientious adults.

The seventeenth, eighteenth, and nineteenth centuries saw more and more power taken from parents who worked their children excessively or who abused their parental powers in the United States. Indeed, the autonomy of families declined as state laws increased the restrictions as to what families could or could not do with their children. Some parents in the twentieth century who believe that they have absolute power over their own children soon discover that such is not the case. Modern children are protected by state and federal laws, and their mistreatment has brought shockwaves of outrage when child-abuse cases are brought to public attention.

Adolescence

Puritan children were considered little copies of their elders, who should enter the adult world as soon as possible. A child was not excused by reason of being young. Rather, a child was to take as direct a path to full adulthood as was possible. A transitional stage from childhood to adulthood—adolescence—was unknown, and the word itself had no currency until the twentieth century.[5] Thus, there could be no recognized phase in the life cycle that would be characterized as "storm and stress," and, accordingly, no juvenile delinquency in the sense that it is understood today. Children followed in the footsteps of their parents or guardians and took up their tasks early.

An "age of discretion," however, was recognized. This would occur around the age of fourteen when, for example, an orphaned child could choose his or her guardian.[6] The laws of Plymouth Colony were written to take effect at age sixteen when youngsters were said to be able to distinguish between truth and lying, between fair treatment of others and outright slander. At sixteen, boys were eligible for military duties.[7] Some wills specified that children "came of age" at fifteen and so could inherit property apart from widows.[8]

John Demos, a specialist on family life among the Puritans of Plymouth, wrote about the absence of adolescence: "Once the child had begun to assume an adult role and style, around the age of six or seven, the way ahead was fairly straightforward. . . . Here was no 'awkward age'—but rather the steady lengthening of a young person's shadow . . . the whole instinctive process through which one generation yielded imperceptibly to its successor."[9]

The Later Years

It was the elderly who dominated Plymouth Colony. To grow older was to increase the chances of gaining greater prestige and power. After age forty, a man could be called to take public office and so widen his influence. The major governing units were filled with men in their fifties and sixties. Nor did men retire or relinquish their powers. Typically, they would die in office.[10] Governor John Alden set a record by dying in office at age eighty-seven.[11]

Publicly, the elderly were said to be wise by reason of their many years of experience. Older persons were to counsel younger age grades, and the demeanor of the young was supposed to be one of "a bashful and modest reverence."[12]

Abject respect and reverence, however, were not automatically conferred upon the elderly. Beneath the surface, there was resentment that boiled to the surface in legal suits for damages against the elderly. There were children who abandoned their aging parents or refused to carry out the mandates of a will. Most of the aged and infirm received help from their children or relatives, but with an avenue of escape through open lands to the west or south, one of the greatest fears of the very old was the refusal of younger persons to sustain them.

CHANGES AFFECTING AGE GRADES IN THE UNITED STATES

The development and expansion of American society from small colonies, such as Plymouth Colony, along the Atlantic Seaboard to the Far West and the land in between does not come under our purview. What does concern us is how such processes as geographic and social mobility, work specialization and complexity, industrialization and urbanization, and transfer of functions from families to political and economic institutions affected age grades to produce contemporary conditions.

Geographic and Social Mobility

The open lands and the open opportunities for enterprising young men and women were two powerful invitations to break with past obedience to parents or established authorities. For those willing to take the chance to move into the vast wilderness to the west, there could no longer be traditional acceptance of subordination to older age grades. One did not have to wait upon one's family to reach some age of respectability or community acceptance. The New World beckoned the young and the strong to move to new ground and new territory that would test their mettle and personal character. Family names would not clear lands, build homes, establish businesses, or plant crops. Only individuals, sturdy men and women with sufficient drive and willpower, could perform these tasks. As they did so, the traditional age grades were realigned to accommodate the age grades that were truly contributing to the political and economic future of an emerging nation.

Work Specialization and Complexity

Common tasks for common age grades fitted the family-centered life of the early colonists. Such was no longer the case when the young, middle-aged, or elderly could learn the many specialties and trades in demand in an expansionist United States. A young man did not have to follow in his father's footsteps. Young women could break away from overprotective families that kept them in subtle social bondage. To offer some unique service, skill, or product was far more desirable in a community, regional, or wider market than that of the self-sufficient family.

Industrialization and Urbanization

Removing industry from homes and providing an independent workplace had profound effects upon age grades. Men and women joined a labor force rather than work for and with their families. With independent incomes and independent residence, their own needs took priority over those of their families. Large numbers of people could assemble in a thriving industrial complex and find employment and mutual support for their personal aspirations. The result was an upheaval in age grading that was better adapted to new technologies and a new family life.

Farber described this new status-providing function when he wrote:

> Among those social scientists who regard the family as deriving from universal functions, there is general agreement that changes in technology and the economy stimulate new routines and eliminate others within the family. These newly created routines may require family members to adapt to changes in circumstance by migrating, reorganizing their daily regimen, or developing new interpersonal life styles associated with professional or business advancement. The theory is that through these adaptations, the roles of parents and children are reorganized to fulfill family functions effectively in a new setting. This adaptive process establishes a "fit" between the requirements of an industrial system and the form of the family.[13]

Transfer of Functions from Families

Families, then, were not the political and economic centers of individual lives as industrialization and urbanization unfolded in the United States. Fathers and mothers were not the sole sources of food, shelter, clothing, recreation, protection, education, or employment. Indeed, mothers and fathers were, themselves, a part of the labor market and devoted themselves to servicing an impersonal economy or supporting a larger political force of increasing complexity.

Where children once were trained to begin as early as possible to contribute to their families, there came a new mode of families contributing to the welfare of children. At first, industry exploited child labor in a more extravagant fashion than families did in cottage-type industry. But, with improvements in technology making their work uneconomical and with growing awareness of excesses in exploitation of the very young, younger children and adolescents were removed through child-labor laws from industry and business. The task of these laws, supported through compulsory education and public taxes, was to delay the entry of children and adolescents into economic and political adulthood by prolonged study and preparation in schools. Children and adolescents, then, were held in high regard, but they were placed in the position of being economic liabilities rather than economic assets to their elders. As consumers rather than producers, young Americans hold awesome powers in the contemporary United States, a circumstance that rarely fails to amaze visitors from foreign lands who are more acclimated to traditional age grades of subservience to the elderly or middle-aged.

The American Elderly

Full power and respect came with advancing years for Plymouth colonists. With the passage of some three hundred years, the situation has drastically changed for the elderly in contemporary American society. As middle-aged persons, the elderly once tasted full adult status or age-grade independence. Currently, older persons find themselves in the "roleless roles" similar to those of their younger counterparts, the adolescents. Elders are confronted with vast amounts of time and energy, with minimal participation in middle-aged society. They are asked, if necessary, to invent behavior systems that will fill their years within their resources. It is no small order to fulfill in the face of decreased incomes, mounting physical disabilities, and polite forms of abandonment by those in a position to change their conditions.[14]

Like the adolescents, the age grade of the American elderly, and those who identify or sympathize with them, seeks a place of dignity within the total society. Their objectives were identified in The Senior Citizen's Charter, which emerged from the 1961 White House Conference on Aging. The charter called for each senior citizen to

> . . . be useful, obtain employment, based on merit, freedom from want in old age, a fair share of the community's recreational, educational, and medical resources, obtain decent housing suited to the needs of later years, moral and financial support from one's family so far as is consistent with the best interest of the family, live independently, as one chooses, live and die with dignity, and have access to all knowledge as available on how to improve the later years of life.[15]

In brief, American elders wish to be treated as *persons* rather than as *categories*. They find their families negating this objective and seek some redress of their grievances. In what lies ahead, we can explore what part families can play in meeting the needs of the elderly as well as all the generational age grades with which we are concerned.

INTERPLAY BETWEEN FAMILIES, GENERATIONS, AND AGE GRADING

Families initiate age grading in the contemporary United States, sustain it, and are, in turn, affected by it. Generational strife in and out of families varies from minor skirmishes to major warfare permeating every institutional framework of the larger society. We have suggested in the Introduction, "Multigenerational Families," that it is within families that generations touch each other's lives so intimately. What appears in miniature in the primary relationships of family life is magnified in the overall society that acts as family host.

Generation in the Middle

The present pattern consists of the generation in the middle, the middle-aged, parental generation, enjoying whatever powers come their way as well as suffering the criticisms of the younger and older generational age grades. Children are not brought into adulthood as quickly as in the colonial past, and childhood is further delayed by the new age grade of adolescence. Further, the elderly are shunted into early retirement both in their work and in their families. The result is a mesoarchy that is shaken now and then as both young and old demand their rights or greater privileges.

Parental generations have rights, too, and middle-age is the time normatively set aside for them to enjoy whatever they have achieved over many years of hard work. Nevertheless, middle-aged parents feel the pressures from age grades at their flanks. Younger age grades try the tactic of reminding parents that once they, the parents, were also young and filled with anxieties and problems foisted upon them by their parents. Older, grandparental generations grumble about the ingratitude and lack of respect from their own children or grandchildren. Altogether, it is a trying situation in which the middle-aged are torn by a sympathy for the very young, some understanding for the impatience of adolescents chafing under adult restrictions, an inkling of similar treatment when parents grow old, and yet adamant about their own achievements and needs. This conflict of generations appears to be the most acute within middle-class or upper-middle-class families. At these socioeconomic levels, material benefits have enabled whole generations of young people to experience the further luxury of criticizing their own social system. It is a performance that baffles parents, who view their children as ungrateful for their material comforts.

The dissatisfactions rooted in the family have been projected onto the larger screen of American society, particularly in the 1960s and early 1970s. A socially sensitized younger generation had come of age and voiced their criticisms of the rejection, insecurity, and discomforts suffered by ethnic, religious, racial, and lower socioeconomic families. Most members of the younger generations believed that changes can be made within the established system. For a minority, however, militancy, nihilism, and radical change were the only acceptable pathways. On the college campuses, and later in high schools, in the sixties and seventies, middle-class and upper-middle-class youth joined forces with militants from their own classes and with angry, frustrated lower-class youth to form explosive mixes that detonated numerous times throughout the land. The shootings of students at Kent State University and Jackson State University in the spring of 1970 were among the tragedies of this generational drama.[16]

Within families, parents, grandparents, and children can normally disagree as to what constitutes appropriate behavior for their respective age grades. Gathering thousands of hypercritical young adults on college campuses, granting them freedom from the restraints of earning a living, and encouraging them to examine social hypocrisies made the route of violent insurrection an appealing option. To their parental generation, schooled in hard work and familiar with a serious depression and wars, who made valiant efforts "to do the best for their children," such rebellions were either intolerable or almost unbelievable.

Lewis Feuer has brilliantly summarized the global history of the clash of generations as it unfolded in rebellious student movements.[17] Its roots, Feuer notes, lie within families. The clash of generations that begins with families operates in ever-widening circles until it reaches college campuses, the public streets, and major cities.

Whether in Russia, Germany, Italy, France, England, Turkey, Japan, China, Bosnia, South America, Africa, the Middle East, or the United States, perennial students, those who have found a way of life in their studies, have deliberately set about to challenge and, if necessary, tear down and rebuild the social order. The strategy has been typically to goad authorities, usually middle-aged, into bloody and often tragic countermoves. Political systems, historic conditions, or national ethos may considerably alter the precise patterns, but what essentially occurs, in Feuer's judgment, is a "de-authorization" of the elders by the younger generations.

In family terms, this is the familiar struggle of sons to free themselves from the shackles of their fathers. Privileged, uncommitted, intelligent, and sensitive students universally recognize alienating circumstances between age grades that are not of their own making. In the crucible of common experiences that mark a social generation (for American youth, these consist of postwar affluence, militant civil rights movements, advancing technologies, and rising expectations of the oppressed), young men and women join hands to oppose, sometimes quite violently, the continued degradation of the downtrodden, the forgotten, the exploited, and the suffering. The complacency and complicity of the middle-aged who are alleged to have mouthed devotion to ideals, but settled for systems far short of these ideals, are thus attacked.

A type of death wish has been suggested as a prominent feature of student dissent wherever it is found. Sacrificially and suicidally, idealistic young people seem willing to give up their lives, or affect their future lives, if it will somehow eventuate in the tearing down of an ongoing society they passionately oppose.

The reconstruction of "a better society," often, is not part of their policies. The price that has to be paid is "martyrdom for the right cause," and this is what some modern youths have already done in self-immolation. As the feudal samurai of ancient Japan followed the Bushido code, honor above life, so modern youths seek to be "campus Kamikaze" who will sweep evils away by their self-destruction. As 1970 came to an end, one Japanese superpatriot dramatized his opposition to any renunciation of war as a national policy by haranguing a military school, disemboweling himself by hara-kiri, and having his head cut off before the horrified eyes of his audience.

Generational Conflicts in Other Lands: Japan and Africa

Japan Filial devotion, respect for elders, ancestor worship, and obedience to authority have been a part of Japanese character for generations. But these qualities rooted in family life were badly shaken by the defeat of Japan in World War II. The humiliation suffered by their fathers and the institutionalization of political democracy did much to undermine the faith and trust formerly vested in older age grades by the young. Young students grew up in postwar Japan with a far different social climate than that of their parents schooled in obeisance, restraint, deification of the Emperor, and militant nationalism. Fathers or father figures such as teachers were revealed as incorrect in their vainglorious assumptions of infallibility, blind deference, invincibility, and perpetuation of myths. Accordingly, younger generations in Japan jettisoned whatever impediments may have been acquired by older generations and sought, instead, a newer and more promising system. Violent methods were condoned if they would bring about the needed changes.

The radical student movement in Japan, the *Zengakuren*, the National Federation of Student Self-Government Associations, consisted of young adults who wished to implement the promise of postwar personal freedom. Throughout their childhood, they had witnessed the hypocrisy of military apologists who either tried to reassert their authority or who attempted to pass themselves off as liberals when democracy was instituted. At times, Marxian communism seemed to hold the key to youthful salvation, but at other times, the home-born imperialists who were alleged to be stifling and exploiting workers, women, the poor, and

younger age grades were seen as "the real enemy." Factionalism continued to split the youthful revolutionaries, but major social issues such as
Japan's relationship with the United States could unite them as brothers-
in-arms. Political activism on a scale large enough to close down major
universities or urban centers such as Tokyo, itself, occurred in the decade
1960–1970.

The 1970s, however, promise change. A new generation is coming of
age. For them, post-defeat Japan is chiefly a historic event recorded in
textbooks to be studied by schoolchildren. The humiliation of surrender
on the battleship Missouri, the administration of General MacArthur, the
debris of Hiroshima and Nagasaki, the return of the defeated troops, and
the realignments of political loyalties were not part of their personal
experience. What they have seen is the growing prosperity and economic
recovery of Japan to a place of world prominence. Affluence is increasing
and spreading into more lives and families. Under such expanding
opportunities, generational unrest is quiescent. If the American experience is of any value, there remains the mistaken possibility of taking for
granted unlimited economic security. Japan will predictably witness a
renewal of ideological warfare against generational authorities. It appears
to be present among age grades in contemporary Japanese families.

Africa   The generations that can be realistically credited with the
emergence of sovereign African nations were those who were trapped
between the tribalism of their elders and the exploiters of their people.
Western education, first through missions and later through European and
American universities, tipped the scales toward generational freedom.
Young Africans exposed to political and economic freedoms of the West
longed to create such modes in their own lands. Men like Jomo Kenyatta,
Kwame Nkrumah, Julius Nyere, and Joseph Kasavubu were "mission
boys" educated in the West who were contemptuous of both colonial
powers and the primitive ways of their less-privileged brothers.

By refusing to be timid bureaucrats to a foreign power in their own
lands, such men revolutionized their followers into political prominence.
The political map of Africa was sharply altered during the mid-1950s and
early 1960s as a result. Some twenty-five new nations achieved political
autonomy during this period.

Independence, however, brought new bureaucracies, new paternal-
ism, and new tyrannies. The men who were thirty in 1945 and who
wielded power in their new countries now felt the wrath of new
generations who resented their domination. Critical of developments and
whetted by promises of economic improvements, generations born about

the same time as their new nations have again begun to show signs of unrest and further rebellion.

Families as Determined and Determiners

Unrest in the United States, Japan, or Africa is closely associated with families. The economic and political life of a nation fixes the conditions under which families must operate. If, for example, there is peace and prosperity, families can optimize the chances to remain intact and secure. If, however, there is open conflict and poverty, families are among the first to suffer the consequences. In this sense, families are "determined" or severely limited by conditions imposed by cooperating or conflicting generations.

On the other hand, families are also "determiners" in the sense that their active socialization of oncoming generations has much to do with societal outcomes. Infants, children, adolescents, and even young adults feel the impacts of accepted trainings for specific age grades. Their personalities are shaped and polished through family actions, family climates, and family models. Whatever personalities emerge from families, they tend to be "acted out" in the macrosystems of other social institutions. Once representatives of age grades with their unique personalities occupy important positions within the political and economic arenas of their own lands, their decisions become public policy and affect the destinies of millions.

C. S. Blumel, an English psychiatrist, made much the same point when he examined the personalities of prominent leaders who precipitated World War II. He wrote in his book, *War, Politics, and Insanity,* ". . . and now that the Second World War has come to a close we find that world-wide strife continues. This strife results not so much from a conflict of interests as from a conflict of personalities. In this conflict of personalities we find the stuff that wars are made of."[18]

SUMMARY

Stepping back to an example of age grading among Plymouth colonists, we briefly outlined the domination of children by their elders. Children among these early New Englanders were to enter adulthood as speedily as possible. An interim age grade between childhood and adulthood, a phase in the life cycle now known as adolescence, was then unknown. The low status of children was to be exchanged as they grew up for the moderate status of the middle-aged, and later, if approved by their peers or superiors, for the highest status possible in the gerontocracy.

Contemporary age grading in the United States has brought about drastic changes in the status of children and their elders. Children are said to have high status or consideration whereas their economic effects are to drain the resources of their respective families. Further, their childhood is prolonged or attenuated by requirements to remain under tutelage while they are prepared for entry into a complicated and diversified economic system. Defined as not quite grown up, adolescents have defensively created unique subcultural systems of their own to exclude all other age grades. Later on, more likely in college or beyond, gathered in reinforced strength in crowded campuses, they have demonstrated their capacity to rebel against oppressions which they contend are not of their own making.

Further, the power and status of the oldest age grade, the elderly, have been supplanted in favor of a new middle-aged domination. Parental generations find themselves shaping the lives of both their children and the children's grandparents. The elderly of the United States have been pushed into a "roleless role" similar to that of adolescents. The elderly are asked to remove themselves, to disengage from the societal mainstream, to make way for oncoming generations. Like their younger counterparts, they have defensively and militantly reacted. There is both sympathy and support for their cause, but the hard fact remains that they can no longer occupy center stage.

The parental generation finds itself trapped in the middle. On the one hand, it must be responsible for the socialization of the younger age grades and the care for the elderly. On the other hand, its own needs are unsatisfied. As parents, gratifications for the sake of their families and their responsibilities outside families are delayed. Most shocking from the parental perspective is the rejection of those material comforts given their young or adolescent children. Hard-won "advantages" are taken for granted by the young who develop an expertise at social criticism. The deauthorization of the parents has occurred with devastating regularity in such places as the United States, Japan, and Africa.

The entire drama begins in families, continues in families, and remains in families, as personalities developed therein are written large in their respective societies. Age grading, whether done by past generations or by present generations, has not been notably successful in achieving generational harmony, family happiness, and societal peace.

REFERENCES

1   Joseph M. Hawes, *Children in Urban Society*, New York: Oxford University Press, 1971, p. 13.

2   Willystine Goodsell, *A History of the Family as a Social and Educational Institution*, New York: The Macmillan Company, 1915, p. 399.
3   Ibid., p. 401.
4   Ibid., p. 396.
5   John Demos, *A Little Commonwealth: Family Life in Plymouth Colony*, New York: Oxford University Press, 1970, p. 145.
6   Ibid., p. 147.
7   Ibid., p. 148.
8   Ibid., p. 149.
9   Ibid., p. 150.
10 Ibid., p. 174.
11 Ibid., p. 174.
12 Ibid., p. 176.
13 Bernard Farber, *Family and Kinship in Modern Society*, Glenview: Ill.: Scott, Foresman and Company, 1973, p. 3.
14 See, for example, Irving Rosow, *Social Integration of the Aged*, New York: The Free Press, 1967.
15 *Aging*, U.S. Department of Health, Education and Welfare, March 1961, p. 14.
16 See, for examples, James A. Michener, *Kent State: What Happened and Why*, Greenwich, Conn.: Fawcett Publications, Inc., 1971, and Stuart Taylor and Associates, *Violence at Kent State, May 1 to 4: The Students' Perspective*, New York: College Notes and Texts, 1971.
17 Lewis S. Feuer, *The Conflict of Generations: The Character and Significance of Student Movements*, New York: Basic Books, 1969.
18 C. S. Bluemel, *War, Politics, and Insanity*, Denver, Colo.: The World Press, 1950, p. 7.

STUDY QUESTIONS AND ACTIVITIES

1   Does age grading represent a bias on the part of the particular age grade or generation in power in a particular society?
2   How has age grading been altered by present generations in the United States?
3   Can you explain how families originate, sustain, and develop age grading to the advantage or detriment of age grades in the contemporary United States?
4   What, in your judgment, is an appropriate way to deal with the needs of each age grade in the modern United States?
5   Can families, alone, set the status and roles of age grades in the modern United States?
6   What empiric evidence is there that clearly provides a picture of the needs of the young, the middle-aged, and the elderly in American society today?
7   What functions are performed by rites of passage as each age grade grows older?

8 Are the needs and desires of age grades in direct conflict and so unable to be satisfied?

9 What concessions are in order if each age grade is to develop a satisfactory posture within American society?

10 Do you see any possibility of restoring privileges once enjoyed by age grades in the systems of past generations?

SUGGESTED ADDITIONAL READINGS

Atchley, Robert C., *The Social Forces in Later Life: An Introduction to Social Gerontology*, Belmont, Calif.: Wadsworth Publishing Company, Inc., 1972.

Elder, Glen H., Jr., *Adolescent Socialization and Personality Development*, Chicago: Rand McNally & Company, 1968.

Handlin, Oscar, and Mary F. Handlin, *Facing Life, Youth and Family in American History*, Boston: Little, Brown and Company, 1971.

Koller, Marvin R., *Social Gerontology*, New York: Random House, Inc., 1968.

Miller, Daniel R., and Guy E. Swanson, *The Changing American Parent: A Study in the Detroit Area*, New York: John Wiley & Sons, Inc., 1958.

Neugarten, Bernice L. (ed.), *Middle Age and Aging: A Reader in Social Psychology*, Chicago: The University of Chicago Press, 1968.

————, and Karol K. Weinstein, *The Changing American Grandparent: Journal of Marriage and the Family*, vol. 26, no. 2, pp. 199–204, May 1964.

Silverstein, Harry, *The Sociology of Youth: Evolution and Revolution*, New York: The Macmillan Company, 1973.

Streib, Gordon F., "Intergenerational Relations: Perspectives of the Two Generations on the Older Parent," *Journal of Marriage and the Family*, vol. 27, no. 4, pp. 469–476, November 1965.

Chapter 6

Racism

Racism, a legacy of past generations with which present generations continue to struggle, is the most emotionally charged of the issues confronting families. Subordination of women by men, or of younger and older age grades by the middle-aged, pales into insignificance when contrasted with the tragedies visited upon whole societies or peoples in the name of race.

Interestingly, the term *race* is a relatively modern linguistic invention.[1] It came into usage in European languages in the sixteenth and seventeenth centuries coinciding with the rise of nationalism and its spread into lands occupied by people who were visibly or physically different from white Europeans. Lying at the heart of racism, despite claims to the contrary, has been both economic and political exploitation of the resources and the very lives of those people judged to be inferior or less-than-human beings.

The race-relations record of past generations of those who populated the United States is particularly notable because it stands in sharp contradiction of what many have called "The American Promise" or "The American Dream." Gunnar Myrdal identified it as "The American Dilemma."[2] The dilemma was how to proclaim the virtues of freedom, justice, and personal dignity, while simultaneously denying them to large numbers of people.

The performance of past generations, allowing for those few who protested and who tried to treat people compassionately, consisted of the removal and destruction of the first Americans, the misnamed American Indians, the enslavement of African blacks, the mistreatment of Orientals who were hired to labor in an expanding economy, and the lack of concern for Mexican Americans along the southern rim of the United States.

Such a historical record could be relegated to the past if its repercussions did not reach into the lives of present generations and their families. But, racism is a live issue and is witnessed daily in the lives of American Indians, American blacks, and Mexican Americans as well as in the lives of white Americans with whom they come in contact. There can be no going back to erase past generational behavior. There can only be a going forward into an understanding of what has happened and what can possible be done about it.

RACISM: WHAT IT IS AND WHAT IT IS NOT

Ambiguity of Racism

Unfortunately, racism has a great many referent meanings assigned to it and thus is filled with ambiguity. People of certain religious persuasions, such as Jews, have been called a race. Hypothetical ethnic types, such as Nordics, have been called races. Those who speak a common language, such as English, have also been identified as racial. Or those who have cultural origins in common, who are subjects of some nation, such as Italy, have been called races.

Further ambiguity is added when race is confused with acquired behaviors. Crime, ignorance, poverty, or sheer laziness have been attributed to innate racial sources. While there is only one species of mankind, visible differences among humanity are said to be the cause for whatever behavior is viewed as reprehensible. Confusing race with social classes, when so-called races are found in every social class, is an error of monumental proportions. The ambiguity continues to be supported because it frees persons from responsibilities for conditions under which racial minorities live. If it is believed that whatever conditions are found are due to genetic origins, to innate, biological differences, then it follows that races cannot be helped or changed to alter their environments. On the other hand, if the conditions under which racial types live are due to human ineptitude, neglect, and ignorance, then there is room for responsible change.

The contemporary view is that racial differences such as skin pigmentation; shapes of noses, lips, eyes, and cheekbones; or texture of hair are the results of genetic pooling or inbreeding of a given population.[3] These traits in no way imply inferiority or superiority of one race over another. *Racism*, the differential treatment of races, is, itself, an acquired or learned behavior that merely confirms or self-perpetuates the mythologies surrounding peoples who are said to be different from all other human beings.

Reverse Racism

While racism is deplored, particularly by those who are its victims, one defensive posture that has appealed to some is reverse racism. Claims of unique superiority or in-group strengths are developed together with claims of inferiority and cupidity for out-groups. Such a stance restores hope, pride, and dignity for people who have long suffered, and who continue to suffer, the indignities of rampant racism. The Pan-Indianism of American Indians, the black pride movement among American blacks, and the conceptualization of "La Raza" among Chicanos are examples of reverse racism in which the tables are turned upon whoever is held to be the oppressor.

Subtle Racism

Racism may also be deplored by those who consciously or unconsciously perpetuate it. The conscious racists explain that racism in the cruel sense should be rejected, but that racism is to be supported because it is "for the good" of both minorities and majorities. It allows each to live in their separate enclaves to develop whatever they believe is best for their own people. The unconscious racists are unaware of the torment visited upon individuals and their families by the use of words that defame or sully the reputations of whole peoples. Consider, for example, such terms as black eye, blacklist, black sheep, blackguard, black mood, blackball, or Black Tuesday. Contrast these with such terms as white lies, whitewash, white-collar, White House, White Knight, or the expression "the bride wore white." "Whiteness" connotes purity whereas "blackness" is said to be its reverse. Small wonder, then, that slogans such as, "Say it loud, I'm black and proud," are prevalent.

Subtle racism, of course, is not confined to language or rhetoric. It spills over into attitudes in schools, churches, businesses, organizations, and families. People marry and raise still another generation in racial fictions and subtleties.

RACISM AND FAMILIES

The links between racism and families are not easy to trace, but they are unmistakable in a number of ways. One way is to describe some of the characteristics of families affected by racism such as we shall do in Chapter Eight, where Japanese American families and black families are discussed. Another way would be to study the impacts of racism on family participants such as children, fathers, and mothers. Analysis of disputes that occur among families concerning such topics as inter-racial marriage or segregation versus integration is still another way. And, because of our multigenerational approach to family life, it would also be useful to consider the extent to which generational tensions and conflicts occur in families over the specific issues of racism.

Racism and the Chicanos

There is no question that black-white racism is the major model used in analyses of racism. But, even older racist patterns have been noted among contemporary generations because of the renewed vigor of the civil rights movement of the 1960s and the new militancy of the younger generations in the 1970s. There is growing awareness of the plight of Mexican Americans or *Chicanos*, a derivative of *Mexicano*, an in-group term that is gaining currency among the general population.

Their history antedates the history known to most schoolchildren, namely, that of the occupation of the East Coast of the New World by white Europeans and the gradual spread of settlement to the West Coast. Like the history of the American blacks that was forgotten for a time and has been revived in the form of black studies quite recently, Mexican American history was conveniently sidelined as a rather insignificant portion of the historical record, until rising demands have given it the prominence it deserves.

The earliest period, called the Indo-Hispanic, goes back to the development of Indian civilizations in Mexico, their subsequent defeat by Spanish conquistadores, the beginnings of the blending of both Indian and Spanish cultures, the colonization of the Southwest United States from central Mexico, and the independence from Spain in the early nineteenth century.

The second period is the Mexican period starting about 1810 and ending in 1848 that saw the development of Mexico as a political entity and its internal unrest that led to war with the United States and the loss of half of Mexico's original territory to the United States in the Treaty of Guadalupe Hidalgo.

The third period, 1848–1899, witnessed the entry of Anglo-Americans into the Southwest; the heavy investments in mines, cattle, railroads, and farming; and the assignment of Mexican Americans to minority status or second-class citizenship.

The fourth period, 1900–1941, saw the continued migration of Mexican refugees into the United States, not only into the Southwest but also into the Midwest and North; growing efforts to organize Mexican Americans into an effective political and social segment of the population; and a return of some migrants to Mexico during the Depression of the 1930s.

The contemporary period began with the entry of the United States into World War II and continued with more migration from Mexico, a revival of awareness in the cultural heritage of Mexican Americans, some improvements in living conditions, and now is characterized by a two-pronged effort to provide Mexican Americans a greater share of American life than they have heretofore enjoyed. One procedure is to employ militant incidents to dramatize the deprivations of the Chicanos. The other is to use nonviolent, legal means to secure educational advantages, civil rights, and equality of economic opportunity for Mexican Americans.[4]

Loosely translated, la raza means "the race," or "my people," to Chicanos. It carries with it a sense of the mixture of American Indian and white European peoples, not only in the genetic pooling but also in the cultural-historical interplay between them. Nominally Roman Catholic, usually capable of speaking Spanish, but not in all cases, a Mexican American tends to show some pride in his or her cultural background—historical experiences of a unique group of people—and a preference for native arts, crafts, and foods.

Inaccurate, stereotypic portrayal of Mexican Americans tends to romanticize them as descendents of great Spanish conquistadores or to denigrate them as lazy, dirty, drunk, criminal Indians who can only perform stoop labor in rural areas of the Southwest.[5] Far more accurate is the fact that the majority of Mexican Americans are urban residents and vary in social classes depending upon such occupations as farming, ranching, business, education, law, medicine, and politics. There are varying degrees of mixture between Caucasian and Indian ancestry and different degrees of assimilation and integration into the general society of the United States.

Further, there are subtypes of Mexican Americans, the *californio*, the *tejano*, and the *nuevo mexicano*, loosely those who settled in the states of California, Texas, or New Mexico, respectively. Within these subtypes, there are further subcategories depending upon the number of generations of settlement, the number of migrants from Mexico, the nature of acceptance by local Indian groups and by Anglo-Americans, and the desire to find identity within the mainstream of American society or within *La Raza*.

For our purposes, the set of values around which Chicanos rally is particularly important. These consist of a concern for kinship ties, strong loyalty to families, and individual worth assessed by such qualities as honor, respect, *machismo* (manliness), and being, rather than social achievements.[6] Psychologist Nathan Murillo identifies these values as a naturalness of style, a rejection of the Puritan work ethic in favor of physical and mental well-being, an expressive sharing of rewards and satisfactions with others, an interest in the here and now rather than in the future, and a sensitivity of individual feelings that requires tact, diplomacy, indirection, and courtesy.[7]

While recognizing the wide variety of families among Mexican Americans, there are certain familistic themes that repeatedly occur. It is these themes that allow a certain amount of generalizing about Mexican American family life.

The first of these is family centeredness. Life revolves around one's family, which takes priority above one's self. In terms of emotional and material support, family members are the first persons to consider. To be cut off from one's family is a serious threat to many Mexican Americans because the external world, including other families, can be hostile or negative in their treatment of strangers. One honors his or her family and never brings it shame or ill repute.

Not only is a person's nuclear family important, but so is a person's extended family. Grandparents, uncles, aunts, and cousins are visited, helped, advised, and kept abreast of family fortunes. Paternal relatives are given preference over maternal relatives, and there is also inclusion of *compadres*, godparents or sponsors of children, within the family circle.

Deference patterns require respect and obedience for the wishes of elders over the younger, and for men over women. Husbands and fathers are the absolute authority in the household. Few decisions are made without their approval or knowledge, and they may come and go without question from their wives or children. Masculinity or *machismo* is prized, but it cannot be abused without loss of respect within the local community.

Toward children, Mexican American fathers are permissive, gentle, warm, and close while the children are quite young. When children reach puberty, fathers withdraw to a posture of authoritarian distance and respect.

Wives and mothers are to be totally devoted to their husbands and children. While playing the roles of catering to the needs of husbands and children, women are respected. Personal needs of women, however, are secondary to their family needs. Differing from the husbands and fathers, Mexican American wives and mothers remain close to their children throughout their life. Growing up, marrying, and having children of their own does not break the mother-children relationship. Daughters and mothers are particularly close, affectionate confidantes because females are well schooled in familism. Both boys and girls are trained to assume family responsibilities when quite young. Caring for younger brothers and sisters, doing errands, taking small jobs to increase the family's income are highly approved training tasks for growing children. At adolescence, males begin to pattern themselves after their fathers. Peer groups of *palomillas*, friends of mine, become their testing grounds for an adulthood that is close at hand.

Such a familism is functional within the Mexican American traditions, but it becomes dysfunctional in contacts with what Mexican Americans call "the Anglo society." School attendance may be neglected if a son is needed to take his mother to a medical doctor because the mother does not have a command of English. His older sister will also keep away from school that day because her brother would not be there to protect her if any need arises. Pressed for decisions by an impatient Anglo, Chicano women or young men may hesitate because they are accustomed to seek a father's permission before they may accept or agree with some action.

The school attempts to teach democratic ideals, while at home, authoritarian parents are made uneasy by the exposure of their children to values that undermine family solidarity. Chicano children are taught English at school and speak Spanish at home. Such children are confused when their poor English is condemned at school and their poor Spanish is equally condemned at home. The teacher is usually a female and far more authoritarian than Chicano youth appreciate. Or, if marriageable young Chicano women show a preference for greater role flexibility than is traditional or if intermarriage is proposed between a Chicano and an Anglo, cultural values are at stake and Chicano youth does not know which way to turn.

Murillo suggests the alternatives confronting the bicultural Mexican Americans.[8] Some may want to cling to the past that may not be functional in the present. Some would try to blend the best of both cultural worlds and, in the process, dilute both into nonviable patterns. A third alternative would be to abandon Mexican American ways and join wholeheartedly into the Anglo world. This alternative would be feasible were it not for the racism, the prejudices and subtle acts of discrimination, among some Anglos. Murillo favors the fourth alternative of developing a unique identity of personhood within a Chicano framework that accepts differences and changes among all peoples. Generational differences between parents and Chicano youth are to be used as lessons in adaptation and flexibility in this alternative.

As with other minority groups, strategies for survival and self-actualization depend largely upon the understanding of majority groups. There are glimmers of a change in racist attitudes among majority groups, particularly among the younger generation, but that event has not fully unfolded to date.

Racism and American Indians

The "Vanishing Americans" have not disappeared from the United States.[9] Numbering well over 825,000 persons at present, American Indians are quite visible in the Navajo Tribal Chambers at Window Rock, Arizona, among the Pueblos of Taos, Cochiti, or Zuni, among the Apache fire fighters in the national forests, among the Seminoles of the Everglades, among the Mohawk structural steelworkers, or among militants who occupied Wounded Knee, South Dakota, for over two months in mid-1973. Heading the best-seller lists for many weeks, Dee Brown's book *Bury My Heart at Wounded Knee* provided an Indian's view of the winning of the American West, a view that had been swept aside by rationalizations that the need for expansion demanded the treatment that was meted out by whites, but now is documented as cloaked in broken treaties and cruelties almost beyond imagination.[10]

As with the Chicanos and other minorities, cultural diversity and unique circumstances make overall analyses difficult. Perhaps the full, detailed, historical record of each band, tribe, chiefdom, or state among American Indians will never be uncovered for the American public. Only a handful of professional scholars can begin to comprehend the immensity of the American Indian–White European contact in the New World. But, it is possible to appraise the circumstances under which contemporary American Indians live and to recognize, once again, the unmistakable imprints of past generations upon those living today. These socioeconomic conditions include the following:[11]

Forty percent of the Indian population lives below the poverty level.

Most Indians live in quarters built in 1939 or earlier.

Indian unemployment was three times the national average in 1970. Close to two-thirds of American Indian youth drop out of high school.

Life expectancy for reservation Indians is some twenty years short of the national life expectancy of about sixty-seven.

Official government policy toward American Indians has wavered from subjugation, guardianship, and denial of land ownership to return of lands; compensation for loss of resources; relocation; improvements in education, health, welfare, and employment; and efforts to terminate all responsibilities of wardship.[12] Recent policy includes gradual abandonment of federal responsibility coupled to an increasing acceptance of state responsibility for American Indians living within their jurisdictions. While some 57 percent, 477,458, are estimated to be eligible for federal services, the 1970 census indicated that approximately 310,000 Indians lived in such metropolitan centers as New York, Chicago, San Francisco, and Los Angeles.[13] Another 50,000 American Indians live in smaller urbanized areas of 2,500 or more population.

American Indians, again like other racial minorities such as the Chicanos, experience what Hyman Rodman has called "the lower-class value stretch."[14] Without abandoning general values held by the overall American society, their experiences dictate development of an alternative set of values as well. In this sense, they have "stretched" their values to enable them to cope with deprivations visited upon them by their lower social-class position. How can one be an American Indian in a non-Indian world? How can one be Mexican American in a non-Chicano world? How can one be black in a white world? These are the questions which racial-minority members seek to answer in their daily routines.

The blurring of differences among a people such as the American Indians is a problem for those who seek to evaluate American Indians positively or negatively. There is no "Indian language" or "Indian family," as those who come to study American Indians for the first time believe. There are Indian *languages* and Indian *families*. For those who wish to know the nature of cultural variations among American Indians at their zenith, the period before White European contacts, a useful source is Harold Driver's definitive work, *Indians of North America*.[15] Each cultural area, the Northwest Coast, Plateau, Plains, Prairies, Eastern Woodlands, Great Basin, California, and Oasis regions, produced distinctive types and subtypes. Every conceivable family structure or form is represented somewhere in the midst of these cultural variants. Past generations of American Indians adopted those forms and processes that seemed to fit their unique locales and needs.

Because of the past treatment of American Indians, however, there has been increasing recognition on the part of American Indians of more recent generations that they share a common lot, a common condition. By adopting the white man's perspective, faulty as it is, that American Indians are "all alike," American Indians have joined forces in *Pan-Indianism*. The Ghost Dance of 1890, founded by the Paiute, Wovoka, became a religious movement among American Indians that preached the restoration of the land, the return of dead Indians, and the return of the buffalo to the prairies. Similarly, the Peyote cult or the Native American Church is the principal faith of a majority of Indians living between the Mississippi and the Rocky Mountains and is also represented in parts of the Great Basin, southern Canada, and east-central California.[16] Its members consume the nonnarcotic dried buttons of the peyote cactus that induce varicolored visions and hallucinations. Combined with elements of Christianity such as baptism, the Trinity, the Cross, singing, praying, and testimonials, the Native American Church is viewed by some as a transitional institution that will lead American Indians into full acceptance of Christianity in future generations.[17]

The secular aspects of Pan-Indianism include widespread adoption of fashions from the Plains cultural area, the area most associated with "true Indians" in the white man's mind. Hence, regardless of origins in other cultural areas, American Indians have adopted the Plains war bonnet, the Plains war dances, and other Plains symbols. Through political and economic leadership, both from within and outside their ranks, American Indians have organized themselves with effective, collective efforts to have a place *as Indians* in modern society.[18] Neither the romanticized "savage" nor the bloodthirsty "savage" stereotype fits the modern Indians. Rather, they are a people to whom all Americans are indebted for their material and nonmaterial contributions to the American way of life. They deserve far better treatment and consideration than racism of past and present generations has accorded them.

Racism and Blacks

An analysis of black families will be found in Chapter 8, under the rubric of being "different" from white, urban, middle-class, Protestant families, the most general mode of contemporary American families. What can be accomplished briefly in this context of racism among past generations and its impacts upon present generations is to become aware of the diversity of black families depending upon what generational experiences has been theirs.

Black families, or as some prefer, families of Americans of African descent, are found at every socioeconomic level although it is true that there remain far greater numbers and proportions in the lower social classes than would normally be expected for a total people. They tend to live in urban centers, but there are still ample numbers living in essentially rural communities or enclaves. Large sections of inner-cities are dominated by black families surrounded by white satellite suburbs where *de facto* segregation is maintained—physical separation in fact, rather than *de jure* segregation or physical and social distance by reason of law. In authority, equalitarian, patriarchal, and matriarchal types are found among black families. It is the survival of matriarchal types among black Americans that has received the maximum attention in the mass media and that has sparked widespread debate as to its predominance and significance. Further, some black families are intact with husbands and wives and children, while others have husband-absent, wife-absent, or parent-absent conditions. Jessie Bernard has suggested that another dimension of black families is that they can have either a *respectable* or *nonrespectable* tradition.[19] By this, Bernard means family heritages of legitimate struggles to find a place in American society or a defeatism that insists that survival by illegal means, illegal in the sense of white society's laws, is the only road to follow in the black community.

Bernard has ably portrayed three different "social generations" among American blacks since the end of the Civil War.[20] The first generation went through the institutionalizing of freedom for blacks in the rural South. The second generation consisted of those families that fled the rural South to become residents in northern cities. The most recent generation is called the self-emancipating generation because they did not choose to wait for the white power structure to give them the equitable treatment they felt they deserved. These were the vocal, young, organized blacks who scorned the nonmilitant stance of their parents and elders who have been so patient and tolerant of mistreatment in the hands of whites. Action now, talk later, is the mood of this young generation who have been received with mixed emotions by their elders. Partly admired and partly deprecated, the admiration for the audacity of youthful blacks is based upon a long-restrained wish to shed minority status while the depreciation is based upon fear that excesses can be counterproductive and threaten whatever gains have been made patiently in the past.

The argument, if any, goes on both within families and within the larger black community. Which strategy is best? Should there be violent or nonviolent action to expose the housing, health, education, and employment conditions under which poor blacks actually live? Should there be encouragement or discouragement of interracial marriages or interracial efforts to reduce social distance between blacks and whites?

While legitimate interracial marriages are estimated to account for less than 1 percent of all marriages, there is ample evidence of illegitimate interracial, sexual exploitation resulting in a tremendously mixed population of black and white combinations. The result is considerable confusion as to who is black and who is white.

The argument goes even deeper than being visibly black or white or some combination in between. It extends into so-called black attitudes or sympathies. An "Oreo," for instance, is the derisive term applied to an American black who is black on the outside, but white on the inside. In short, such a person does not have black pride or self-pride, but takes his or her cues from the nonblack society. Caught between two worlds, black families and black individuals continue to struggle for self-actualization, a marginal status that compounds the normal efforts to be successful in a competitive society.

Racism and the Whites

When all is said and done, racism reaches into white families and white lives. It could not have endured for so many generations without the vocal or silent support of whites.

Richard Sennet, for example, does not equivocate when he points to what he calls the brutality of modern families.[21] Sennet explains that behind the facade of intimate family life of mothers, fathers, daughters, and sons in white suburbs is a closed circle based upon fear, guilt, and avoidance of strangers, particularly those of the nonwhite world. The former distance between fathers and sons and mothers and daughters is cut down as fathers try to treat sons as brothers and mothers and daughters treat each other as sisters. There is seemingly no generation gap that cannot be overcome through intimate communication and mutual experiences. But, as Sennet observes, underlying this drawing together is a pervasive "guilt-over-conflict" that includes black anger or hostility over a white-dominated society that moves very slowly to achieve its alleged ideals of justice and fair treatment for all its people.

Moves to achieve racial balance in public schools, such as the busing issue, have been received with mixed emotions in white suburban families who had thought they had escaped the need to contact a different racial, religious, or social-class group. Outraged, protective parents have demonstrated their rejection of moving children out of their neighborhoods, and many of their arguments such as inefficiency, cost, or lack of evidence that their children will receive a higher quality education are logically reasonable. But the root of the problem remains in the subtle racism that motivated separations between peoples of different racial categories.

Until the issue of racism is faced forthrightly, the lives of white families will continue to be affected by external turmoil and unrest founded upon racial exclusiveness.

White youth can and do escape the efforts of parental generations who have opted for racial segregation as their solution to racial tensions. Mass media such as films, television, newspapers, radio, or magazines carry incidents, events, or stories of racial significance. Growing visibility of blacks in advertising, entertainment, sports, business, and professions removes family-imposed blinders. And, leaving their families far behind to travel, to take a job, to enter college, or to volunteer their services, young people have increased their racial contacts to determine for themselves if their former protected family life had schooled them in the whole truth of, for example, black-white race relations.[22] What this young generation has found is that there has been hundreds of years of neglect of racial minorities and they, in growing numbers, choose to make some dent in perpetuation of such a system. It has been young people who have taken "freedom rides," engaged in sit-ins, teach-ins, be-ins, and "freedom marches." Without fanfare or public notice, young people have tried to treat people of other races with the respect they have long deserved. A "brave, new world" is not yet here, but to the credit of concerned younger generations, racism will no longer go unchallenged and unrecognized in the contemporary United States.

SUMMARY

Racism, the differential treatment of races, is an anomaly to contemporary American society because it stands in direct contradiction to proclaimed ideals of equity, freedom, and dignity for all its people. It is, nevertheless, a legacy from past generations that continues to confront American families in multiple ways. Racist labels are applied, for example, to people who belong to a religious faith, to people who speak a common language, or to people who have ethnic or cultural origins in common. Further, racism, itself, a factor in criminal behavior, in ignorance, in poverty, or in despair, is misinterpreted to justify its perpetuation. Outright racism, subtle racism, or reverse racism, the latter a reaction among peoples who have long been the targets of prejudice and discrimination from majority groups, continues unabated, and few know how it will run its course.

What is suggested in this chapter is the strong link between families and racism in the United States. This link is evident in the lives of Chicanos or Mexican Americans, for example. In their lives, one can witness the confusion of racist claims of innate inferiority with a mixed cultural history of contact between American Indians of Mexico, Spanish conquerors, and white European or Anglo-American along the southern border of the United States and Mexico. Strong familism and identification with *La Raza* has emerged among Chicanos as rallying points against racism.

Similarly, American Indians have suffered and reacted to racism over generations. Despite tremendous cultural differences among them, and despite different historical contacts with white Europeans from the Atlantic to the Pacific coasts, American Indians recognize a common treatment of their reduction to subordinant, minority status and all its accompanying degradation of a proud people. Their daily family life on or off reservations has been a struggle to preserve some of their heritage and identity in a world that threatens to dilute or deny their unique background on the American scene. Pan-Indianism in sacred and secular activities corresponds with the *La Raza* theme among Chicanos or black pride among American blacks.

Without question, the major model of racism at work applies to black-white relations in the United States. Recent generations have brought about a dramatic reversal of some of the racism of past generations that has remained in force. In Chapter 8, black families will be described and analyzed in greater detail, but in this chapter, the militancy of youth, both black and nonblack, is stressed. Complacency, patience, and retreat, the strategies of older generations, are being displaced by pride, militancy, and aggressive action on the part of young people.

In white families, racism also is being challenged. Whether subtle teaching or forthright teaching of racial inferiority-superiority goes on in families, white youth has begun to respond to the inequities visited upon racial and cultural minorities. Present studies may have missed the complicity of generations in the perpetuation of racism through families. Perhaps, future studies can be mounted to lay bare the links between families and racism as this chapter suggests exist.

REFERENCES

1 Brewton Berry, *Race and Ethnic Relations*, 2d ed., Boston: Houghton Mifflin Company, 1951, pp. 41–42.
2 Gunnar Myrdal, Richard Sterner, and Arnold Rose, *An American Dilemma: The Negro Problem and Modern Democracy*, New York: Harper & Brothers, 1944.
3 See, for example, Stanley M. Garn, *Human Races*, 2d ed., Springfield, Ill.: Charles C Thomas, Publisher, 1965.
4 Matt S. Meier and Fecliciano Rivera, *The Chicanos: A History of Mexican Americans*, New York: Hill and Wang, Inc., 1972, pp. xiv–xvi.

5   Ibid., p. xvi.
6   Ibid., p. xviii.
7   Nathan Murillo, "The Mexican American Family," in Nathaniel N. Wagner and Marsha J. Haug (eds.), *Chicanos, Social and Psychological Perspectives*, Saint Louis: The C. V. Mosby Company, 1971, pp. 99–102.
8   Ibid., pp. 107–108.
9   Robert F. Spencer et al., *The Native Americans*, New York: Harper & Row, Publishers, Incorporated, 1965, p. 490.
10 Dee Brown, *Bury My Heart at Wounded Knee: An Indian History of the American West*, New York: Holt, Rinehart and Winston, Inc., 1970.
11 Spencer and Jennings, op. cit., pp. 504–505; see also, William H. Kelly, "Socioeconomic Conditions of Contemporary American Indians," in Roger C. Owen, James J. F. Deetz, and Anthony D. Fisher (eds.), *The North American Indians: A Sourcebook*, New York: The Macmillan Company, 1967, pp. 611–620. See also, *We, The First Americans*, U.S. Dept. of Commerce, Bureau of the Census, 1970.
12 Theodore W. Taylor, *The States and their Indian Citizens*, Washington, D.C.: U.S. Bureau of Indian Affairs, 1972, pp. 76–78.
13 Ibid.
14 Hyman Rodman, *Lower-Class Families: The Culture of Poverty in Negro Trinidad*, New York: Oxford University Press, 1971, p. 195.
15 Harold E. Driver, *Indians of North America*, Chicago: The University of Chicago Press, 1961.
16 Spencer and Jennings, op. cit., p. 505.
17 Ibid.
18 Ibid., p. 506.
19 Jessie Bernard, *Marriage and Family Among Negroes*, Englewood Cliffs, N. J.: Prentice-Hall, Inc., Spectrum Books, 1966, chap. 2, "The Two Cultures," pp. 27–66.
20 *Ibid*, pp. 23–25.
21 Richard Sennet, "The Brutality of Modern Families," in Gwen B. Carr (ed.), *Marriage and Family in a Decade of Change*, Reading, Mass.: Addison-Wesley Publishing Company, Inc., 1972, pp. 142–158.
22 See, for example, Brewton Berry, "A Southerner Learns About Race," *Common Ground*, vol. 2, no. 3, Spring 1942.

STUDY QUESTIONS AND ACTIVITIES

1   What examples, if any, can you cite from your own experiences with outright, subtle, or reverse racism? Discuss your reactions to these experiences.
2   Suggest schematically the linkages between families and racism and then suggest research designs capable of testing your hypotheses.
3   Locate the referents used when people speak or write about races.
4   Is a person who is a product of miscegenation of black and white parents a black or a white?
5   Why does racism persist in the face of evidence that it harms both minorities and majorities in American society?

6   Is there a generation gap in attitudes toward racism in the modern United States?
7   In what ways has racism touched the lives of Chicano families and individuals?
8   Is racism taught or caught in families?
9   Examine the variant policies of the federal government toward American Indians from past to present generations.
10 Why is the black American–white American relationship the key mode to racism in the United States?
11 What can families do to combat racism in whatever forms it takes?
12 Can you project an American society of the future without racism?

SUGGESTED ADDITIONAL READINGS

Baughman, E. Earl, and W. Grant Dahlstrom, *Negro and White Children: A Psychological Study in the Rural South*, New York: Academic Press, Inc., 1968.

De Leon, Napthali, *Chicanos: Our Background and Our Pride*, Lubbock, Tex.: Trucha Publications, Inc., 1972.

Farb, Peter, *Man's Rise to Civilization, As Shown by the Indians of North America from Primeval Times to the Coming of the Industrial State*, New York: E. P. Dutton & Co., Inc., 1968.

Goldschmid, Marcel L. (ed.), *Black Americans and White Racism: Theory and Research*, New York: Holt, Rinehart and Winston, Inc., 1970.

Gossett, Thomas F., *Race: The History of an Idea in America*, Dallas: Southern Methodist University Press, 1963.

Grebler, Leo, Joan Moore, and Ralph C. Guzman, *The Mexican-American People: The Nation's Second Largest Minority*, New York: The Free Press, 1970.

Mack, Raymond W. (ed.), *Race, Class, and Power*, 2d ed., New York: American Book Company, 1968.

Moore, Joan W., *Mexican Americans*, Englewood Cliffs, N. J.: Prentice-Hall, Inc., 1970.

Moquin, Wayne (ed.), *A Documentary History of the Mexican Americans*, New York: Frederick A. Praeger, Inc., 1971.

Oswalt, Wendell H., *This Land Was Theirs: A Study of the North American Indian*, New York: John Wiley & Sons, Inc., 1966.

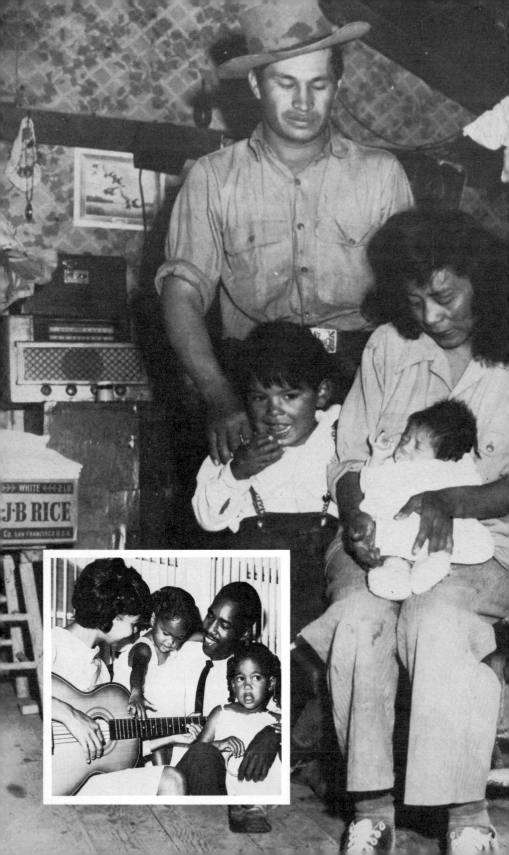

Part Two

Present Generations

Chapter 7

WUMP Families

The acronym WUMP refers to persons and groups who have the fourfold attributes of being *w*hite, *u*rban, *m*iddle-class, and *P*rotestant.[1] More familiar is WASP, an acronym derived from the words *w*hite, *A*nglo-*S*axon, and *P*rotestant. The use of WASP as a descriptive term stresses the national origins of persons or groups from England, whereas the less familiar WUMP is more appropriate for our purposes because it calls attention to the dimensions of urbanity and middle-class orientation. We will, thus, focus our attention in this chapter on WUMP families to provide some base line, some reference point, from which to examine those families that "differ" because they are nonwhite, rural, upper or lower class, and non-Protestant. Such families will be treated in greater detail in the next chapter.

In giving WUMP families a chapter-length description, there is no intention to idolize or idealize them. Rather, the objective is to assess their place in the family life of present generations of Americans. This particular group of families represents what we can call the "middle

Table 7–1   Number of Whites and Nonwhites, in Millions and Percent of U. S. Population 1960–1970

	1960	1965	1967	1968	1969	1970
Whites						
Numbers in millions	159.4	170.7	173.9	175.5	177.1	180.4
Percent of total population	89.5	89.1	88.9	88.8	87.1	88.0
Nonwhites						
Numbers in millions	20.6	23.1	24.0	24.4	24.8	24.9
Percent of total population	10.5	10.9	11.1	11.2	11.9	12.0

* Figures for 1970 are computed from U.S. Bureau of the Census reports, April 1970.

Source: U.S. Department of Commerce, Social and Economic Statistics Administration, Bureau of the Census, 1970, p. xiii.

ground," the somewhat typical group that sets the overall standards by which Americans may measure their relative status. In their own right, WUMP families are significant by reason of (1) their large proportions in the American population, (2) their influence upon the remainder of the population, and (3) their distinctive life-styles.

In racial terms, whites approximate 90 percent of the American population, although nonwhites have been increasing at a faster rate than the whites over the past decade and constituted approximately 12 percent of the total population in 1970.

It is no surprise that the American population is overwhelmingly urban rather than rural. Census definitions of urbanity have varied over the years, but there is little doubt that Americans have abandoned farms for the attractions of city, town, suburban, or nonfarm residency (see Table 7-2).

Table 7-2   Number in Millions of Farm Population and Percent of Nonfarm Population, United States, 1960–1969

	1960	1965	1967	1968	1969
Farm population					
Number in millions	15.6	12.4	10.9	10.5	10.3
Nonfarm population					
Percent of total population	91.3	93.6	94.5	94.8	94.8

Source: U.S. Department of Commerce, Social and Economic Statistics Administration, Bureau of the Census, 1970, p. xiii.

Precise enumeration of the composition and distribution of the American social-stratification system presents a more difficult problem. Not only is there considerable disagreement among social-stratification specialists on the nature and discrete parts of the social-class system of the United States, but there are contrasting findings on the proportions assigned to each social class. Most scholars recognize the contention of John Cuber and William Kenkel that social classes exist as a continuum; that is, they display minute differences on a gradual scale from one extreme to another.[2] Nevertheless, there is both popular and empirical usage of distinctive social classes, varying in number from three to six. Egon Bergel compares the percentages found in various classes by different social-class experts. The percentages vary according to their indices of social-class characteristics, the samples studied, and the times these samples were examined.[3]

I Classes according to income	
Upper-upper	1.0
Lower-upper	2.8
Upper-middle	18.1
Lower-middle	41.4
Upper-lower	13.2
Lower-lower	23.5

II Classes according to occupation	
Upper-upper	1.0
Lower-upper	2.8
Upper-middle	21.2
Lower-middle	19.0
Upper-lower	14.0
Lower-lower	42.0

III Classes according to education (males, 1954–1955)	
Upper	18.2
Middle	43.2
Lower	46.9

IV Classes according to education (U.S. census—Morris computation)	
Upper	13.2
Middle	37.2
Lower	46.9

V Classes according to Warner (Yankee City)	
Upper-upper	1.4
Lower-upper	1.6
Upper-middle	10.0
Lower-middle	28.0

Upper-lower   33.0
Lower-lower   25.0

    VI   Classes according to Warner (Jonesville)
Upper   2.7
Upper-middle   12.0
Lower-middle   32.2
Upper-lower   41.0
Lower-lower   12.1

    VII   Classes according to Centers (self-rating)
Upper   3.0
Middle   43.0
"Working"   51.0
Lower   1.0
(Refused rating)   2.0

    VIII   Classes according to Kahl
Upper   1.0
Upper-middle   9.0
Lower-middle   40.0
"Working"   40.0
Lower   10.0

Bergel reconciled these variations in social-class proportions by arriving at the following percentage distribution:[4]

Upper classes   3
Middle classes   37
Lower classes   60

Source: From *Social Stratification* by Egon Ernest Bergel. Copyright 1962 by McGraw-Hill Book Company. Used with permission of McGraw-Hill Book Company.

Recognizing social classes as merging almost imperceptibly, Bergel noted their usefulness as scientific constructs. He wrote, "To use a metaphor, we can count waves by their crests but cannot tell where they begin or end. The number of marginal people may be considerable, but the vagueness of the boundaries does not eliminate social classes from the reality of social life."[5]

The final WUMP-family attribute, Protestantism, applies to the approximately 55 percent of the American population that is religiously affiliated. The proportions have generally dwindled since 1950, but Protestants continue to constitute well over half the membership of organized religions in the United States.

The general composition of the U. S. population in 1970 was

Table 7-3   Number in Thousands and Percent of Protestant Affiliation,
All Religious Bodies and Protestant Membership, United States, 1950,
1960, 1965, and 1968

	1950	1960	1965	1968
All religious bodies Number of members in thousands	86,830	114,449	124,682	128,470
All Protestant Bodies Number of members in thousands	51,080	63,669	69,088	69,424
Percent of all religious affiliation	58.8	55.6	55.4	54.1

Source: U.S. Department of Commerce, Social and Economic Statistics Administration, Bureau of the Census, 1970, p. 42. Percentage computations added.

approximately 88 percent white, 95 percent essentially urban, 40 percent middle-class oriented, and 55 percent Protestant. The first two qualities of WUMP families were widely shared in the general population; the last two were more restricted. Taken together, WUMP families constituted a majority of all families in the United States as the 1970s began and will probably continue to dominate in the foreseeable future.

INFLUENCES OF WUMP FAMILIES

WUMP families affect American family life in a variety of ways. Their influences are intimately associated with (1) mobility patterns, (2) occupations, and (3) values or moral standards.

Mobility Patterns

In terms of social mobility, WUMP families are the generational source of upper-class families and the model for the upwardly mobile among the lower classes.

The relatively restricted ranks of upper-class families contrast sharply with the much larger proportions of WUMP families. Upward mobility into the upper classes requires a number of generations. Now and then one hears of some dramatic entrance into upper-class family life by some vigorous middle-class individual. The process, however, is usually much more prolonged. The genealogies of upper-class families frequently indicate the rather humble origins of their ancestors, although the search for historical records may be motivated by a more ambitious desire to be related to nobility or prestigious families.

While entrance into the upper classes may be delayed for generations, many WUMP families continue to aspire to the heights of the social-class system. "Getting ahead" is the popularization of these long-range ambitions, and while WUMP families may not identify upward mobility as an ultimate goal, the gradual improvement of their fortunes may, indeed, achieve this end. One factor that works against their accumulation of enough wealth to enter upper-class ranks is their practice of dividing the surplus amassed within a single generation into equal shares among family survivors. Thus, each middle-class generation maintains the same relative position in the social-stratification system, although movement into more comfortable life-styles is possible.

On the other hand, WUMP families may have some memories of lower-class affiliations. Often sentimentalized but more often rejected, these origins act as incentives that guard against slipping back into a downward mobility pattern. Increasing determination to "succeed" characterized such WUMP families.

Wealth, of course, is not the sole criterion of social status, but its attainment helps distinguish one socioeconomic level from another. In the upper classes, family fortunes are inherited from past generations. Interest or profit are high enough to allow them to leave much of the family estate intact. For the middle classes, however, wealth is earned or acquired within a generation or so. Upper-middle-class and lower-middle-class subdivisions indicate the greater or lesser amount of *surplus* or *discretionary* income beyond family needs of food, shelter, and clothing. With surplus income available, middle-class families may be able to begin to cultivate some taste for upper-class qualities. Because lower-class families are closer to the subsistence level, and many lower-lower-class families below the poverty level, the advantage of discretionary income may provide incentive for movement into the middle class for lower-class persons who seek a better life.

This desire for upward mobility has been challenged, particularly by younger generations of middle-class families who reject the crass "materialism" of middle-class strivings to "get ahead." Many middle-class parents are shocked to discover that the "advantages" they may have lacked in their youth, and for which they have long worked, are taken for granted, or even rejected, in the rhetoric of their children. The clothing, mannerisms, or life-style of the poor are often slavishly adopted by middle-class youth who believe the lower classes to be the most honest, the most uncompromised, or the least guilty of exploiting their fellowmen. Moreover, the idealization of the poor, the innocent, and the deprived in the midst of affluence has a certain appeal to sensitive middle-class youth. For WUMP youth, the idealization is reinforced by a Christian respect for humility and for a desire to relieve suffering. Nevertheless, both middle-class parents who have some vivid recollections of lower-class family life and lower-class families who currently experience serious difficulties in their daily lives are somewhat baffled by the glorification of deprivation.

Occupations

Occupationally, middle-class family heads serve many masters. As upper-middle-class proprietors of small businesses, as professionals, or as managers in business or industrial corporations, they carry out policies that not only serve their own needs but also support the life-styles of upper-class families. As members of the lower middle class, they act as sales personnel, clerks, skilled and semiskilled workers, and operators of small, independent, often handcraft-oriented businesses. In these occupations, lower-middle-class workers are likely to take their cues from middle management in order to protect their own interests as well as those of upper-middle-class families.

Because social class is a product of many factors, occupation is not sufficient to distinguish one social class from another. Nevertheless, occupation is itself a composite of multiple factors and has much to do with education, income, talent, prestige, and relative influence. Within present generations, broad occupational categories have been shifting as technical and mechanical advancements have taken physical labor out of what was once called "hard work." Untrained manual labor becomes less in demand; technical, professional, and persuasive skills more so (see Figure 7-1). By 1975, almost half of the occupations in the United States will be categorized as white-collar.

Middle-class occupations allow WUMP families to influence markedly the overall population. As teachers, social workers, judges, lawyers, ministers, and medical doctors, they unconsciously or consciously promote middle-class values. Persons in their care or sphere of responsibility, as well as personal associates, are directly influenced by this middle-class morality that overwhelms contemporary generations.

Values or Moral Standards

Representative middle-class values include industriousness, thrift, loyalty, stability, respect for property, self-restraint, harmony (often portrayed as getting along with others), and personal independence. Unlike the upper-class-family members who have inherited their status, middle-class-family members must achieve their positon on the basis of talent, judicious expenditure of thought and energy, and personal drive and ambition. In WUMP families, the Protestant ethics of self-reliance,

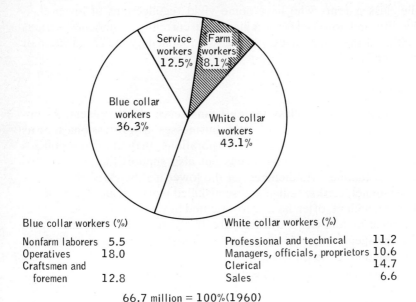

Blue collar workers (%)

Nonfarm laborers   5.5
Operatives   18.0
Craftsmen and
  foremen   12.8

White collar workers (%)

Professional and technical   11.2
Managers, officials, proprietors 10.6
Clerical   14.7
Sales   6.6

66.7 million = 100%(1960)

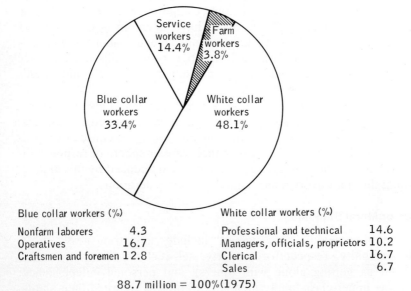

Blue collar workers (%)

Nonfarm laborers   4.3
Operatives   16.7
Craftsmen and foremen 12.8

White collar workers (%)

Professional and technical   14.6
Managers, officials, proprietors 10.2
Clerical   16.7
Sales   6.7

88.7 million = 100%(1975)

Figure 7-1 Changing occupational needs, United States, 1960 and 1975. *(Adapted from "Changing Occupational Needs," Road Maps of Industry, no. 1632, New York: National Conference Board, Dec. 15, 1969)*

sobriety, thrift, and integrity help reinforce these values. Hence, it is WUMP families that instruct their members to observe the laws of the land; to carry out the requirements of their professions, industries, and businesses; to apply themselves faithfully to their studies; and to serve their churches and their country. The rewards for this acceptance of duties are many. Chief among them are the outward signs of "inner grace," such as ownership of one's home. Ownership of a home, whether modest or elaborate, is a major accomplishment of WUMP families and one of their largest financial transactions. Comfort, protection, and the satisfaction of being one's own landlord are rewards of middle-class independence.

WUMP FAMILY LIFE

Linkage with Past, Present, and Future Generations

With Past Generations   WUMP families have relatively tenuous ties with past generations. Unless there are some benefits to be gained by retaining historical ties to distinguished relatives, there is little effort to preserve past records, to trace family origins, or to retain any tangible evidence of family roots. Family names are often Americanized to disassociate any negative ties with foreign or alien cultures. Thus, one objective of WUMP family members is "to make a mark" through their own efforts and not through unearned advantages conferred by former generations. This desire for a break with the past also has the advantage of not permitting the inadequacies of preceding generations to limit their ambitious strivings.

WUMP families, then, do not build either on the assets or the liabilities of past generations. They begin anew each generation to retain their middle-range statuses and to be, perhaps, a little bit "better off" than their parents.

With Present Generations   WUMP families typically maintain ties to collateral relatives from approximately three living generations.[6] These may vary from perfunctory contacts to almost daily and intimate associations. Further, WUMP families meet with children, parents, and grandparents of various kinsmen during joyous events such as weddings, graduations, and family anniversaries or in times of serious trouble, the latter being a surer test of their family loyalties.

In the normal course of events, however, WUMP families live as nuclear units of husband-wife teams and their dependent children. Unmarried, adult children may be tolerated for a time, but because personal independence is the major goal in middle-class life, they are encouraged to go their own way as soon as possible. Considering its responsibility fulfilled, the parental generation will subtly or openly push mature children out of the family.

Each family unit, then, establishes its own home, finances, routines, friends and associates, and range of interests. If solicited, aid in the form of loans, personal service, or advice is welcomed.

Each generation being essentially independent, WUMP parents seek to help their children attain adulthood. Children are expected to move steadily in the direction of increasing autonomy through education, training, and enriched experiences. On the other hand, parents take pride in being able to take care of their own needs, and to have a small surplus to bestow small or more lavish gifts upon their married children and their grandchildren. However, the return of gifts to the parental generation is minimal and often in the form of tokens of appreciation for past favors. Middle-class children—dependent or independent—grandchildren, and nieces and nephews are not held responsible for parents, grandparents, or uncles and aunts as these elder generations age. The courts sometimes require younger generations to accept some responsibility for the support of elders, but most legal effort is in the form of spreading costs to the larger community, whether it be local, state, or national. Through taxation, pension funds, social-security requirements, or encouragment to give to community or national charities, younger generations spread the costs of older generational dependency so that each WUMP family allegedly carries fewer financial burdens.

When the oldest generation passes away, family estates are likely to be relatively modest. Even if the family estate is large, it soon dissipates because equal divisions among family survivors reduce inheritances to minuscule proportions.

With Future Generations   WUMP families are not concerned with the eventual attainment of upper-class status in future generations. Individual family members may possibly attain "fame and fortune," but this is a personal rather than a family objective. Ambitious individuals may well carry their families farther up the socioeconomic ladder. If this occurs, credit is given to the person who has achieved success on his own.

In a sense, WUMP families encourage a type of *disassociation*, often called independence, from their primary and secondary relatives and so invite their own oblivion. Their children are expected to start their own families "a little bit better off" than those of the parental generation, but their class mobility is not anticipated to be very great. Ambition is focused on the status of their children, but this is quite different from making mobility into upper-class ranks the ultimate goal. Only in the larger sense, in the sense of future generations of *all* families, do WUMP families encourage the preservation of their particular set of values. As far as they are concerned, to be "successful" is to recognize the intrinsic worth of WUMP values and to promote them as guides of conduct for future generations.

This middle-range, white, urban, Protestant life-style, neither extremely selective in preferences nor scornful of excellence, neither overly aggressive nor particularly content with current conditions, neither extremely wealthy nor poor, has suggested to some observers that future generations in the United States will be caught up in "middle-class mediocrity," if this is not already the case. Envisioned is a society in which the ranks of the upper classes will be further reduced and the lower classes will merge with the middle classes through a redistribution of advantages by a vigorous program of guaranteed income levels, public housing, education, medical care, and mass leisure.

Family Roles

Husband-Father Roles   The WUMP husband and father is the nominal head of the family. There is often a conscious effort to achieve an equalitarian sharing of family authority with the wife and mother, but in many instances, she is the actual head of the family. Matriarchy is brought about through the demonstrated abilities of wives and mothers, through the adult female presence in the daily routines of the family, and through the absenteeism of the husband-father, who is preoccupied with his work, business, or profession.[7]

When he is the chief economic support of the family, a WUMP husband-father has considerable influence. He feels some loss of status when his spouse supplements the family income or if he, for whatever reason, falters or fails to provide sufficient family funds. He does welcome the added income of his wife in order to provide "luxuries" for the family, especially if this supplemental income can be added without open assaults upon his masculine image. Forced retirement by reason of age or health requires even greater diplomacy on the part of his spouse to sustain his self-image despite the reduction in his earning powers.

Unless services are provided through rental, apartment life, or condominium arrangements, the husband-father of WUMP families does the heavier or so-called masculine work in and around the home. He maintains the grounds by mowing, raking, weeding, fertilizing, and planting lawns; by building walls, patios, and grills; by fixing roofs and gutters; by painting or repairing exteriors and interiors; and by removing snow and ice. He keeps the family car or cars in running order. It is he who moves heavy furniture and appliances. He may also construct a recreation room, porch, or nursery addition or, if particularly versatile, may build an entire house from foundation to television aerial.

When children are all born, the WUMP husband-father "shares" the responsibility for their rearing with his wife. He anticipates, or comes to understand, his wife's preoccupation with their children, particularly when they are infants and toddlers. He provides a male model for both his sons and daughters, although he remains somewhat peripheral to his spouse's central role as manager-socializer. His disciplinary function is to support his wife in her more intimate association with the daily experiences of their children.

In whatever he does with his children, the WUMP father vividly remembers his own childhood and development. He is the children's link with an older generation. The WUMP father recalls his own socialization and selects those actions in word or deed that appealed to him and avoids those that did not. What is "good," what is "proper," what is "appropriate," however, must meet WUMP standards.

Wife-Mother Roles   The wife and mother may not be the nominal head of the family, but she is its neck; she turns the head and so "gets her way." Feminine strategies are eagerly cultivated and widely shared by WUMP wife-mothers. Her own talents as a person must be fulfilled and so she has been schooled to think of marriage and family as one of the normal experiences of life that prove her attractiveness and worth.

In the early years of marriage, personal and social life with congenial friends, usually peers of her own generation, constitute her chief sources of satisfaction. She may continue her education, her own work career, her own leisure interests, or she may encourage her husband to improve himself and, by extension, to improve their mutual chances for WUMP success.

When children arrive, however, her motherly role takes precedence over her own personal and social life. It continues during the dependent stages of the children's lives because there is little outside help, even with the sympathetic participation of her spouse; thus mutual plans for child rearing are implemented by the mother.

From her children, the WUMP mother receives satisfaction. Female children particularly receive her attention as she relives her childhood through them, with minor adaptations. Her WUMP background has taught her that male children should be aggressive, but not in an offensive, tactless way. As the male child approaches adolescence, she expects the father to guide him while she focuses more and more on bringing her daughter or daughters to womanhood.

Folklore passes along the aphorism that "a son is a son until he takes himself a wife, but a daughter is a daughter all her life." Empirical study, however, does support this theme that mother-daughter ties are, indeed, very close.[8] Moreover, it is daughters who are the guardians of their kin network. They keep in contact with parents, siblings, cousins, uncles, aunts, and grandparents. When some 300 students at Kent State University were asked to identify their kin network, they were able to recall chiefly those kin who were on the maternal side of their families.[9] On the paternal side, contacts were reduced over the years.

"The house" becomes the symbol of the WUMP wife-mother's domain. In its decor, her "touch" is in evidence. The rugs, drapes, furniture, closets, floors, walls, and windows, particularly their order and state of cleanliness, reflect her personality. Clothing, food storage and preparation, household budgeting, meal planning, entertainment, and "extras" come under her management. If there are family pets, she has supervisory or actual responsibility for their care and feeding, despite the children's allegations that they will be responsible. Family regulations are issued by the WUMP mother-wife on wiping one's feet, hanging clothes in their appointed places, playing in "safe" areas, putting away toys, or keeping bathrooms uncluttered.[10]

An efficient WUMP wife-mother does not permit her maternal role to dominate her life. Her children *are* important to her, but she does realize that much depends upon her husband to set the basic standards of their domestic life. By unobtrusively "fitting in," the WUMP wife-mother acts as her spouse's companion, his hostess, and living symbol of his good taste, stability, and responsiveness to others. She knows how to meet other wives and husbands and how to treat her husband's superiors and subordinates. She may make or break her spouse in his career development.[11] Often working at his side with customers, students, audiences, patients, or other clientele, the efficient WUMP wife-mother aids and abets his efforts. Her own schedules and desires are often altered to meet her husband's changing needs.

The upper-middle-class wife-mother often finds that she has excess time and energy to devote to civic services. These activities are motivated by such concerns as a sincere interest in those less fortunate, a desire to contribute to community life or away from household routines, to enjoy the company of other WUMP wife-mothers, and to enhance her husband's reputation, or her own standing, in the community. For special occasions, she may request the participation of her spouse as an escort or a source of needed support.

Roles of WUMP Children   The small nuclear family, with its intensive emotional investments, provides the earliest social structure and atmosphere of children. It is the responsibility of the children to absorb the ways of their families. Above all, they are expected to "behave," which in WUMP terms means to obey parents. For small children accustomed to consideration, the most serious sanction is the withholding or withdrawal of parental love. Because of the high emotional content of WUMP family life, such a threat produces results. The child's world crumbles when parental warmth is not there to reassure him in his highly dependent state. Later on, in adolescence, when peer approval is far more important than parental wishes, such a threat has far less impact.

WUMP children do not normally perform remunerative work, nor are they expected to do so. Whatever tasks they do take on are viewed as "instructive," teaching them moral lessons. With modern gadgetry, family work is more difficult to assign—a far cry from the farm chores performed by young children in the rural United States of past generations.

The real work of WUMP children is to learn. It begins informally in the home, through television, books, music, games, and imaginative play. Later on, the formal and increasing burdens of primary, elementary, secondary, and collegiate studies occur. Competition with other middle-class children is encouraged, but at no time is the *initiation* of overt fighting found acceptable. *Defensive* or *reactive* fighting, however, a posture that surfaces as national policy, is acceptable. Aggressive behavior is thus channeled into competitive sports, into excelling in education or extracurricular activities, or into earning honors for personal achievements. Particularly appealing are the "constructive" efforts of young persons from WUMP families. Efforts are deemed constructive when they emulate the work of the parental generation, such as the Junior Achievement program, which teaches business practices, or a junior volunteer program in which girls assist hospitals nursing and medical staffs.

WUMP children are also taught that persons in authority are to be treated with respect. These include teachers, school administrators, ministers, counselors, employers, police, and youth-group advisers. To the dismay of WUMP parents and grandparents, disenchantment with authority figures has occurred in the United States. Social strains between the generations became increasingly visible in the 1960s and have continued into the 1970s. A Gallup poll taken in 1971 reported that four out of ten students predicted that change in American society was likely to occur through a violent revolution within the next twenty-five years.[12] Such an assessment indicates the growing dissatisfaction with some of the guiding tenets of WUMP family life.

Sexual morality in WUMP terms means that appropriate expressions of sexual needs occur within marriage between married partners.

Sexual curiosity is to be met through an honest answering of children's questions at their level of understanding. Suspicion of strangers is inculcated, and any associations that could possibly expose children to sexual abuse are forbidden. A number of communities have organized mothers to display the symbol of a helping hand on their front doors. School children are instructed to come to homes that display this symbol if they need help. In this way, child molestations are less likely to occur.

Modesty in dress; careful use of language to avoid vulgarity; appropriate literature; rejection of sexually explicit films, magazines, or pictures; and sex-appropriate grooming are among the middle-class moralities. Pregnancy out of wedlock is a serious offense in WUMP homes and is concealed whenever possible. "Proper" hours, companions, and activities can hopefully prevent violations or sexual indiscretions. Such is the WUMP families' contention.

As with other fixed patterns of WUMP families, these values have been openly flaunted by emerging generations of WUMP youngsters. One source of this rebellious behavior is the discrepancy between the lip service paid to middle-class morality and the actual behavior of parents. This discrepancy (the younger generations have called it hypocrisy) has been glaringly exposed in the mass media. The gossip of rural villages of the past has become actuality in the printed words of a *Peyton Place* or the well-publicized studies of sexual conduct.[13] As a result, some WUMP youth have rejected the "standard package" of middle-class materialism and transparent respectability and have entered the ranks of the rebellious, the defiant, the militant, or the dropouts.

BEING WHITE

The major effect of being white is a strong tendency to underestimate the importance placed upon racial identifications such as skin pigmentation, texture of hair, or facial features. Most WUMP families associate with fellow whites and are rather shocked to discover racial sensitivities on the part of nonwhites. WUMP youth are unaware of racial differences when they are sheltered, guarded, or "suburbanized." Not until they are removed from their families do they begin to comprehend the indignities suffered by nonwhites.[14]

In many cases there is a deep sympathy among WUMP youth for those who differ racially. This sympathy is often translated into action through strong friendships, comradeships, and helping relationships that emerge from convictions that everyone is "a child of God." It comes as another shock when reverse racism is experienced. Friendly overtures may be rebuffed as tokenism—too little, too late, unsustained, and insincere. The youthfulness or common generational background of both white and black has helped overcome some of this lack of trust between the races, but there is far to go before racial differences can be defined with pride. Youthful generations as *agents of change* have been effective in the past. At this juncture in American history, it would appear to take many more youthful generations to come closer to the open society envisioned for the United States.

BEING PROTESTANT

Stability of the Family

One of the common mythologies is that Protestants promote or favor divorce. They are falsely accused of being willing to break up their homes almost at whim. The myth is given credence by their relatively high incidence of divorce in comparison with other faiths. Even when taking into account the large proportions of Protestants within the general population and the tendency to categorize most persons who are not clearly of some identifiable religious persuasion as Protestant, the data fail to indicate the *reluctance* of Protestants to secure a divorce. However, the real position of Protestants is that divorce is warranted only under certain conditions, which may be described as seriously threatening to the personalities of the husband, wife, or children. In the Protestant view, individuals must be free to develop their divinely granted talents and attributes. When individualism is stifled, when a family member is thwarted at every turn, then Protestants unhappily seek redress of grievances through the courts. This view is quite different from the popular notion that Protestants take their marriage vows lightly. Indeed, many years elapse before Protestants decide that their only recourse is to seek divorce.[15]

Primacy of the Individual over the Family

Individualism is enthroned in Protestant churches and is in accord with the belief that there is a direct line of communication between individual and the divine. Although other religious groups are also split among themselves on a variety of doctrines, perspectives, or interpretations, Protestants have broken into literally hundreds of denominations, churches, sects, and splinter groups. The Protestant view manifests itself in every institution it touches and is particularly visible in marriage and family. WUMP families encourage individual members to assert their uniqueness and so serve the general good, confident that this stress on personal freedom will strengthen family life rather than weaken it.

Love, Peace, and Brotherhood

Other Protestant virtues help to modify excesses that might emerge from the stress on individualism in WUMP families. Love, peace, and brotherhood are encouraged with the knowledge that human beings are quite capable of backsliding if they are not constantly reminded to control petty needs, immediate gratifications, or antisocial tendencies. That these virtues are quickly forgotten after Sunday services is evident in the secular world of competitiveness. To the extent that these proclaimed virtues are voided, circumvented, or ignored, generations of WUMP children and young adults find grounds to lose confidence and trust in their parents.

SUMMARY

WUMP families constitute one of the largest and most significant segments of family life in the United States today. These families have come to be regarded as the most typical Americans. Attention is directed to them, but not because they are to be idolized or idealized. Rather, WUMP families are given prominence because of their large proportions in the American population, their influence upon the remainder of the population, and their own distinctive life-styles. Each factor that helps delineate WUMP families is widely shared in the general population. In 1970, 88 percent of the total population was *white*. By 1970, some 95 percent of the population was classified as nonfarming or essentially *urbanized*. Social-class placement is more difficult to assess, but a rounded figure of some 40 percent indicates the *middle class* population in the United States. Finally, close to 50 percent of the population was *Protestant* in 1970.

By reason of racial affiliation or residence, WUMP families have much in common with the rest of the population. By reason of social-class position or religious preferences, WUMP families have less in common with the overall population. The latter two factors, however, are important enough to merit attention. Many upwardly mobile persons or families regard WUMP life as their ultimate objectives and so strive to emulate WUMP families.

Influences of WUMP families on American family life are closely associated with their mobility patterns, occupations, and values or moral standards. First, upper-class families have the benefit of their ancestral generations, whereas many generations must come and go before a small percentage of WUMP families may finally enter the upper echelons. Within their own ranks, however, upward mobility takes the form of being in a somewhat "better" position than that of one's parental generation. For WUMP families, upward mobility is frustrated by the practice of modest estates being equally divided among surviving family members so that there is little significant improvement in social status. Nevertheless, there is some satisfaction in the intrinsic worth of WUMP family life because it still rates "above" the life-styles of the lower classes or the less-advantaged. WUMP "success" may therefore consist of stabilizing a middle status, a goal many consider worthy in its own right.

The materialism of WUMP families, however, has been subject to considerable criticism by WUMP youth, who regard such values as a betrayal of Christian ideals that speak of love for all humanity. Youthful imitation of a less-privileged life comes somewhat as a shock to parents who do not remember their own lower-class experiences as being particularly attractive or desirable.

Occupationally, WUMP family heads hold a middle position between the seats of power and the marginally employable. They carry out policies and affect the lives of those they serve as users or consumers of their talents.

Because whatever they have or are, they have earned by sheer talent or perseverance, WUMP families uphold such values as industriousness, thrift, loyalty, stability, respect for property, self-restraint, cooperation, and personal intergrity.

Past generations are generally treated as relatively unimportant and best forgotten. Few WUMP families seek to learn the details of their generational ties by examining their kinship structures. Emphasis is placed on present generations, particularly one's peers. There is some interest in future generations, but essentially, children are to achieve their own independence in due time and will presumably not move too far up the social ladder from their parental generation. Independence characterizes the roles of husband-father, wife-mother, and children in WUMP families. Protestantism reinforces this individualistic theme, although it is modified by a deep concern for all human beings in every station in life. Nevertheless, the predominance of whites in American life tends to make WUMP families forget the depth of racial rejection found among nonwhites. Youthful generations, as change agents in WUMP families, have, however, begun to manifest their serious concern for respecting the rights and needs of racial minorities.

REFERENCES

1   Robert Blood, Jr., was among the first to use the acronym WUMP to replace the more familiar acronym WASP. The Anglo-Saxon influence is so diffuse that it was given less prominence in this chapter.

2 John F. Cuber and William F. Kenkel, *Social Stratification in the United States*, New York: Appleton-Century-Crofts, Inc., 1954.
3 Egon Ernest Bergel, *Social Stratification*, New York: McGraw-Hill Book Company, 1962, pp. 274–275.
4 Ibid., p. 277.
5 Ibid., p. 259.
6 See Bert N. Adams, *Kinship in an Urban Setting*, Chicago: Markham Publishing Co., 1968, pp. 50–52, for a discussion of relatively recent studies.
7 A useful source is E. E. LeMasters, *Parents in Modern America: A Sociological Analysis*, Homewood, Ill.: The Dorsey Press, 1970, Chap. 8, "The American Father," pp. 138–156.
8 See Theodore M. Newcomb and George Svehla, "Intra-Family Relationships in Attitudes," *Sociometry*, vol. 1, pp. 180–205, 1937, and Marvin Sussman, "The Help Pattern in the Middle Class Family," *American Sociological Review*, vol. 18, pp. 22–28, 1953.
9 From an unpublished study by Marvin R. Koller and Jerry Lewis, 1968 and 1969.
10 Ruth Shonle Cavan, *The American Family*, 3d ed., New York: Thomas Y. Crowell Company, 1963, p. 123.
11 William H. Whyte, Jr., has written extensively on the executive wife, for example, in "The Wives of Management," *Fortune*, vol. 44, pp. 86–88ff., October 1951; "The Corporation and the Wife," *Fortune*, vol. 44, pp. 109–111ff., November 1951; and in *Is Anybody Listening?*, New York: Simon & Schuster, Inc., 1952, chap. 8, *The Wives of Management*.
12 George Gallup, American Institute of Public Opinion, Princeton, N. J., published in *Akron Beacon Journal* (Ohio), 21 January 1971.
13 John F. Cuber and Peggy B. Harroff, *The Significant Americans*, New York: D. Appleton-Century Company, Inc., 1965, for example.
14 A useful source is Marcel L. Goldschmid, *Black Americans and White Racism: Theory and Research*, New York: Holt, Rinehart and Winston, Inc., 1970.
15 See Andrew R. Eickhoff, *A Christian View of Sex and Marriage*, New York: The Free Press, 1966, pp. 55–62.

STUDY QUESTIONS AND ACTIVITIES

1 In what ways do WUMP families set the standards for American society?
2 What part do generations play in placing families into the middle classes?
3 Develop a diagram or schema that indicates the status of WUMP families in the social structure of the United States.
4 Can you find evidence that suggests that future generations will alter the typically middle position of WUMP families in the United States?
5 Is identification or alleged sympathy for non-WUMP families by WUMP youth genuine or likely to be forgotten as WUMP youngsters grow up?

6 Are WUMP families unaware of or unconcerned about how non-WUMP families live?

7 What societal needs are served by those socialized in WUMP families?

8 What do you see as the strengths and weaknesses of WUMP family life?

9 How much of the tradition of past generations is preserved under WUMP family conditions, and how much is rejected?

10 Are you inclined to be positive or negative in your own appraisal of WUMP families in the United States?

SUGGESTED ADDITIONAL READINGS

Blood, Robert O., *The Family*, New York: The Free Press, 1972, Chap. 2, "The Stratification System and the Family."

Cavan, Ruth Shonle, *The American Family*, 4th ed., New York: Thomas Y. Crowell Company, 1969, Chap. 6, "Middle-Class Families.

Duncan, Otis Dudley, David L. Featherman, and Beverly Duncan, *Socioeconomic Background and Achievement*, New York: Seminar Press, 1972.

Faris, Robert E. L., "The Middle Class from a Sociological Viewpoint," *Social Forces*, vol. 39, pp. 1–5, October 1960.

Halebsky, Sandor, *The Sociology of the City*, New York: Charles Scribner's Sons, 1972.

Komarovsky, Mirra, *Blue-Collar Marriage*, New York: Vintage Books, Inc., Random House, Inc., 1967.

Koos, Earl L., "Middle Class Family Crises, *"Marriage and Family Living*, vol. 10, pp. 27–40, 1948.

Leslie, Gerald R., *The Family in Social Context*, 2d ed., New York: Oxford University Press, 1973, Chap. 9, "The Middle-Class Family Model."

Mills, C. Wright, *White Collar: The American Middle Classes*, New York: Oxford Book Company, Inc., 1951.

Tallman, Irving, and Ramona Marotz, "Life-Style Differences Among Urban and Suburban Blue-Collar Families," *Social Forces*, vol. 48, pp. 249–256, March 1970.

Chapter 8

Families That Differ
from WUMP Families

While WUMP families play a significant part in American family life, there are families that differ from them markedly in generational experiences. These "different" families are not deviant. This would imply that WUMP families are the ideal by which all other families should be judged. Rather, a more objective stance suggests that families that differ from WUMP families have emerged from *another* set of experiences and have responded with variant forms and processes in order to cope with their unique circumstances.

For illustrative purposes, black families, Japanese-American families, Jewish families, and non-middle-class families have been chosen as representatives. They have been selected from legions of "different" families because racially, socioeconomically, religiously, and historically they provide strong contrast with the white, urban, middle-class, Protestant families that have figured so prominently in family literature.

BLACK FAMILIES*

Black families do not constitute a monolithic, homogeneous type of family structure. Rather, there is a wide range of subtypes that manifests

*Jerry M. Lewis, associate professor, Kent State University, has provided insightful comments and aid in this section.

169

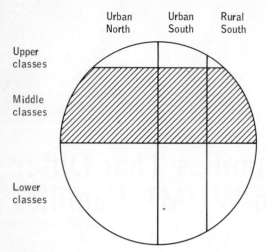

Figure 8-1 Black families in social spaces. (*Andrew Billingsley, Black Families in White America,* © *1968, p. 7. Reprinted by permission of Prentice-Hall, Inc., Englewood Cliffs, New Jersey.*)

tremendous diversity (see Figure 8-1). Andrew Billingsley estimates that roughly half of contemporary black families are to be found in the lower classes. About 40 percent are estimated to be in the middle classes. The remaining 10 percent are placed in the upper classes. Regionally, half of the black families in the United States live in the urban North and the urban West. The other half are about equally divided between the urban and the rural South.[1]

Subvariants of black families can be found within the upper, middle, and lower classes (see Figure 8-2). Upper-class black families are subdivided by Billingsley into "old" and "new" families. The "old" black families of the upper classes are there by virtue of "generational headstarts" which are the results of long histories of privilege, accomplishments, and the status of past generations. The "new" black families of the upper classes are there because of a supporting society and the combined efforts of individual family participants within a single generation. Representative of this latter group are black mayors elected to office in major American cities through the support of both black and white constituents.[2]

Middle-class black families are trichotomized by Billingsley into "upper middle class," "solid middle class," and "precarious middle class" families. Differentials in education, income, occupation, and life-style determine the degree to which these families retain their middle-class status.[3]

Finally, lower-class black families are subdivided by Billingsley into three categories that blend into each other: "the working nonpoor," "the working poor," and "the nonworking poor." The first category is headed by men who have the security and stability of unionized jobs in industry. These men are generally semiskilled and have acquired their abilities on the job. The second and probably the largest category, the working poor, is led by persons in unskilled and service occupations. Marginal incomes of the working poor range downward from approximately $3,000 a year. Billingsley's third and most highly publicized category of lower-class black families is that of the nonworking poor. This category constitutes approximately 25 percent of lower-class black families, whose heads are often unemployed and require the support of friends, relatives, and public welfare agencies.[4]

Data from the U.S. Bureau of the Census lend support for Billingsley's approximations. Money income alone for families of whites and blacks in 1968 differs sharply. Table 8-1 indicates that the lower income levels apply mainly to black families, higher income levels to white families. On the other hand, note that there are white families with minimal incomes as well as black families with high incomes.

Black Family Structure

Black family structure is most typically portrayed as headed by a female with a husband or father absent. The most recent census data do not

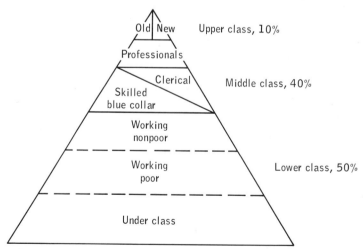

Figure 8-2   Black families by social class variants. (*Andrew Billingsley*, Black Families in White America, © *1968, p. 123. Reprinted by permission of Prentice-Hall, Inc., Englewood Cliffs, New Jersey.*)

Table 8-1   Distribution of Families by Income Level, Race, and Region,
1968

	Families					
	United States		North and West		South	
	White	Black	White	Black	White	Black
Number, in thousands	45,437	4,646	32,544	2,330	12,893	2,316
Percent	100.0	100.0	100.0	100.0	100.0	100.0
Under $1,000	1.5	3.9	1.3	1.8	2.2	6.0
$1,000–$1,999	2.9	9.1	2.2	5.8	4.4	12.5
$2,000–$2,999	4.5	11.0	4.0	9.0	5.7	12.9
$3,000–$3,999	5.4	12.3	4.9	9.5	6.8	15.1
$4,000–$4,999	5.6	10.6	5.3	8.6	6.4	12.6
$5,000–$5,999	6.7	8.8	6.2	8.2	7.9	9.4
$6,000–$6,999	7.6	7.6	7.3	8.6	8.3	6.5
$7,000–$9,999	24.0	17.6	24.1	21.6	23.7	13.5
$10,000 and over	41.9	19.1	44.8	26.8	34.7	11.5
Median Income	$8,937	$5,360	$9,318	$6,820	$7,963	$4,283
Percent with income less than $3,000	8.9	24.0	7.5	16.6	12.3	31.4

Source: U. S. Department of Commerce, Social and Economic Statistics Administration, Bureau of the Census, 1970, p. 324.

support this stereotypic view (see Table 8-2). Well over two-thirds of black families are nuclear families headed by a husband and wife, whereas less than one-third are headed by a female.

In terms of numbers of persons, black families are proportionally comparable with white families until larger numbers, such as six persons or more, are reached (see Table 8-3). In 1969, approximately 6 percent of all families had seven or more persons whereas approximately 15 percent of black and other nonwhite families had seven or more persons.

Those who have closely examined black family structures do report their heterogeneity an understandable response to past and present generational experiences.[5]

Generational Experiences of Black Families

A series of cumulative experiences over several generations explain contemporary black family life in the United States. First, there is the fact that black origins were *African* and not European. Secondly, there is the

Table 8-2   Households and Families by Type of Head and Race, 1969

Type of Head	Households		Families	
	Number	Percent	Number	Percent
Total in thousands	61,805	100.0	50,510	100.0
White				
Husband-wife	40,338	72.8	40,355	88.8
Other male head	4,318	7.8	1,028	2.3
Female head	10,738	19.4	4,053	8.9
Black and other				
Husband-wife	3,480	54.3	3,487	68.7
Other male head	793	12.4	200	3.9
Female head	2,139	33.4	1,387	27.3

Source: U.S. Department of Commerce, Social and Economic Statistics Administration, Bureau of the Census, 1970, p. 36.

group of experiences that center on slavery—the shattering of stable family life, the uprooting of millions from their native cultures, and the dehumanizing treatment of persons as property. Finally, there is the still extant and persistent myth of white superiority and black inferiority.

Table 8-3   Size of Families by Race, 1969

Size of family	All families (Number in thousands)		Black families and other nonwhites (number in thousands)	
	Number	Percent	Number	Percent
Two persons	17,392	34.4	1,393	27.5
Three persons	10,514	20.8	1,022	20.1
Four persons	9,642	19.1	856	16.9
Five persons	6,245	12.4	602	11.4
Six persons	3,510	6.9	459	9.0
Seven or more persons	3,206	6.3	741	14.6

Source: U.S. Department of Commerce, Social and Economic Statistics Administration, Bureau of the Census, 1970, p. 38.

African Origins   Past generations of contemporary black families in the United States were regionally West African. Centuries before European or foreign contacts, stable governments and thriving family systems were characteristic of West African life.

Marriage consisted of uniting kinship networks; while the wishes of couples were considered, the main objectives were to link lineages. West Africans were essentially patrilineal, although matrilineage was not unknown. Patriarchy was the outstanding authoritarian pattern, but this did not mean masculine tyranny over wives and children. Rather, men were made responsible for the welfare of their wives and children because of their kinship linkages. Fair treatment was ensured through heavy investments in bride prices, bride service, and bride payment. Bride payment involved the kinsmen of a groom placing a female relative—a daughter or a sister—with the kinsmen of the bride in order to compensate their loss of the bride's services as well as to ensure the fair treatment of a bride and her offspring among the groom's relatives.

Patrilocality was the most common form of residence for families, the wife or wives living in the home or compound of the husband and his kinsmen. Rarer forms were avunculocality, residence with the maternal uncle of the groom, or matrilocality, residence with the bride's relatives. Practically unknown was neolocality, independent dwellings for new families set apart from all other relatives.

Monogamy was the most common form of marriage, although polygyny was possible among the more wealthy or powerful. Polyandry was unknown in West Africa.

The socialization of children was the joint, major responsibility of both parents and their kinsmen. Mother-child ties were exceedingly close, but they did not exclude fathers, who were viewed as models of great moral integrity for the younger generations.

Slavery   The complicity of other black Africans in the slave trade is rarely stressed, but the total responsibility for the massive entrapment of millions of slaves and their subsequent shipment to the New World cannot be placed solely upon nonblacks. Norman Coombs, for example, notes how kings, chiefs, and tribal leaders enslaved prisoners of war, political enemies, and other tribesmen to secure guns, wealth, and power for themselves:[6] "European greed fed African greed, and vice versa."[7]

The vast majority of the enslaved, particularly those destined for North America, were males. The disproportionate numbers of females and small children effectively destroyed the chances of the slaves' maintaining some vestige of family life. Kinship that meant so much to Africans was, thus, forcibly sheared away, and the slaves were utterly helpless, abandoned, and without hope. Kept in holding pens such as those on the Isle of Gorree just outside the harbor of Dakar, Senegal, and packed into ships with minimal space, ventilation, sanitation, medical attention, food or exercise, thousands succumbed to illness and disease. The passage to the New World was marked by unprecedented cruelties. The seriously ill, diseased, injured, or dying captives were cast into the sea, still in chains, whenever it was deemed necessary. On arrival, black men and women, sold to the highest bidders for their labors and services, were effectively cut loose from their cultural heritage. Slaves were socially isolated from their masters, and from each other, by language barriers, differing tribal affiliations, and ignorance of other local West African customs.

The literature on the enslavement of millions of black men and women is one of the most damning records known. Now and then, one is tempted to see parallels between the enslavement of blacks and the enslavement of the Jewish people in biblical and modern times, for example, in the use of such terms as "ghetto," "genocide," and "slavery." Stanley M. Elkins, in explaining the character of blacks under the American slave system, sees some commonality with the characteristics of German concentration camp inmates. A slave-master relationship led to a childlike dependence upon Nazi Gauleiters among some Jewish prisoners, and a similar fawning, imitative, childish personality type emerged among some black slaves.[8]

Many would strongly object to such comparisons because there are vast differences between racial and religious discrimination, between planned genocide and the subtle, unplanned so-called genocide of today's American blacks, and between the familial-generational background of blacks and Jews.[9] The last factor, familial-generational backgrounds, goes far toward explaining the relative socioeconomic status of American blacks and Jews. Jews were sustained by their ancient heritages of religious and kinship solidarity, whereas blacks approached vertical mobility shorn of family or generational roots. Black men and women were at the lowest levels of emerging American society in the eighteenth and nineteenth centuries. Late in the twentieth century, the upward mobility of some black men and women has barely begun.

Latin and North American Treatment of Slaves Black slaves were transported to both Latin and North America because neither the indigenous Indians nor the immigrant white Europeans could satisfy the need for cheap, abundant labor. The treatment and conditions of black slaves, however, differed markedly in the two areas.

The Latin system provided some legal protection for slaves and was particularly influenced by the intercession of the Roman Catholic Church. Further, Spanish and Portuguese men lacked families of their own and were quite willing to legitimate marriages with black women. Manumission, the granting of freedom for slaves, was made possible by legal provisions that allowed slaves to secure their freedom by repayment of their purchase price. Many slaves won their freedom during the lifetime of their masters as a gesture of goodwill and appreciation. Others were set free upon the death of their masters. Marriage and family were possible for the free blacks. Illegitimate children of masters and slaves were freed upon baptism. Some slaves won their freedom by distinguished service in military campaigns. Women bearing ten children were set free. Emancipation societies banded together either to raise funds to win freedom for slaves by payment of purchase prices or to encourage the freeing of slaves as moral acts of honorable men.

Other factors in Latin American society softened the harsh burden of slavery and eventually brought slavery to an end. Tribal customs, languages, and social rank were kept fairly intact in the Latin slavery system because groups of men and women from the same tribes were moved en masse to South America. Further, freedom meant acceptance and assimilation into the general society. Donald Pierson's study of blacks in Brazil documents the "openness" of the Latin American system in sharp contrast with the "closed" system imposed on slaves and freed men in North America.[10]

There was no softening influence from a dominant church in North America. Few laws protected the rights of slaves. Slave owners in North America often had families of their own, and whatever intimacies developed amounted to sexual exploitation and not legitimate marriage. Black women were bred like animals to produce "field" or "house" slaves. If some form of marriage and family was recognized by slave owners, families of black slaves were still regarded as pieces of property that could be separated by sales of husbands, wives, or children at the will of their owners. Miscegenation was not legitimatized or given the social dignity accorded it in Latin America. Only in 1967 did the U.S. Supreme Court finally strike down the last antimiscegenation laws as unconstitutional.

Finally, emancipation did not bring freedom to blacks in American society. The "visible" chains of slavery were exchanged for the "invisible" chains of massive racial prejudice and outright discrimination. Reconstruction after the Civil War was an abysmal failure, and castelike conditions were imposed upon millions of blacks as "second-class citizens." Geographic and social mobility would seem to provide some escape routes to freedom, but as so many have observed, blacks were unable to escape their "skin prisons".

Geographic and Social Mobility of Blacks   The twentieth century has witnessed a mass exodus of blacks from the rural South to the urban North and urban West. The lure of better jobs, education, income, housing, and facilities brought millions to the industrialized cities. What then occurred was entrapment in cultural islands, or ghettos. How much of this segregation is credited to self-imposed separation as a defensive posture and how much to white rejection remains debatable. Studies of black families in "vertical ghettos" shed some light on the facts.[11] Paul Sites and Jerry M. Lewis, who have studied black families in "Hill Village" in industrial northeast Ohio, believe that the ghettos were formed primarily by blacks rather than whites.[12]

The whole story of black family life cannot be unfolded in a few short paragraphs in this text. But a few observations can help complete the picture of black family life given thus far.

First, we should recognize that upward social mobility began for many black Americans long before the present period. E. Franklin Frazier, for example, in his book *Black Bourgeoisie* gives evidence of a life-style for middle-class, and some upper-class, blacks that is unknown to many whites.[13] He also attacks the "make-believe" world in which they believe they escape the fate of their lower-class black brothers and sisters. His polemics are particularly strong in the final two chapters, entitled "'Society': Status without Substance" and "Behind the Masks."[14]

Second, a disproportionate number of black families in comparison with nonblack families continue to struggle for dignity, or what is even more important, for necessities. The precise conditions of black families and the significance of these conditions were reopened as moot questions by the controversial Moynihan Report.[15] The report depicted black families as a "tangle of pathology" and the root of the problems of black society. This interpretation has been widely and vigorously denied,[16] but the issue of black families as cause or effect remains. Was Moynihan correct in pinpointing black families as the source of black difficulties, or were his critics correct in stressing that the real issue lies in the sustained racism of white power structures? This latter view holds that whatever conditions exist in black families, they are the *effects* of rejection and not the causes of degradation.

The New Generational Mood   Two contrasting moods coexist within contemporary black families. The older generation are long familiar with the drive for civil rights and for integration within the larger society. Tactics generated by this mood are calculated "to overcome" segregation in housing, employment, recreation, transportation, education, religion, and government.

The newer mood, said to be represented by the younger generations, is one of increasing militancy, of an impatience with efforts to break the barriers of outright or subtle racism. The new mood seeks separatism, an inner pride based upon black justice, black interests, black experiences, black power, and black history. Younger generations of blacks seek to rediscover their West African roots, their cultural uniqueness, their manhood and womanhood.[17] It is an effort to determine their own strengths, their own beauty, their own contributions and not to demean themselves in a vain and impossible effort to be "white" on the "inside," "Oreos", who can never quite "make it" in White America.

Within black families, the two moods have the potential to split some conservative elders from their more radical children. On the other hand, there is a growing recognition that unites black families—that both moods can "set things straight." There is pride in the accomplishments of elders, and there is pride in the honesty of youth to openly accept themselves as human beings.

Contemporary Black Families   Most evidence indicates that the stereotype of black families as matriarchal, devoid of morality, dependent upon white society, disorganized, and incapable of building healthy personalities is a myth. Many black families are successfully coping with their conditions and are demonstrating a resilience to great odds that bodes well for their future. This is not to say that this optimistic appraisal will automatically dispel the stifling effects of racial prejudice that is present in American society. Racism is a heritage rooted, consciously or unconsciously, in the deepest recesses of human personalities and will not be eliminated by pious hopes, solemn pronouncements, elaborate studies, or dramatic or inflammatory rhetoric. Rather, the sufferings and gross errors of past generations will be slowly and painfully changed through monumental efforts by present and future generations. Some of these efforts will be initiated within American families.[18]

JAPANESE-AMERICAN FAMILIES[19]

Blacks constitute one of the largest minorities in the United States. When the U.S. Bureau of the Census reports data concerning "Negroes and other races," approximately 90 percent of the data concern blacks. There are, however, others to consider; by focusing on Japanese-American families, one of the smallest ethnic minorities in the United States, contrasting and informative data come to light (see Table 8-4).

The Japanese were encouraged to come to the United States because their labor and services were in demand in the late nineteenth century on railroads, in mining and smelting industries, in the fields, in fisheries, and in homes along the Pacific Coast and the Western states.

Table 8-4 Population by Race and Sex, 1930 to 1960, Numbers in Thousands*

Race and sex	1930	1940	1950	1960
Male				
White	55,923	59,499	67,129	78,348
Negro	5,856	6,269	7,299	9,098
Japanese	82	72	77	229
Female				
White	54,364	58,766	67,813	80,490
Negro	6,035	6,596	7,744	9,751
Japanese	57	55	65	244

*Prior to 1960, excludes Alaska and Hawaii.
Source: U.S. Department of Commerce, Social and Economic Statistics Administration, Bureau of the Census, 1970, p. 29.

Their numbers grew slowly, up to the 1930s, when anti-oriental prejudice began to reach fever pitch (see Table 8-5).

The Japanese were encouraged to come by emigration companies that guaranteed to employ them while they were in the United States. In contrast to the blacks, who came in chains and as property, the Japanese came as free workers who had the advantages of a strong government in their native land to protect their interests, a knowledge of and an identity with an ancient and unique culture, and the possibility of returning to their homes, families, and kinship systems when they had accumulated enough wealth.

Generations of Japanese-Americans

The first generation of Japanese-Americans are known as *Issei*, those who were born in Japan and who came to the United States to improve their economic conditions. The Issei were not motivated solely by ambition.

Table 8-5 Japanese Population in the United States, 1870–1940

Year	Population
1870	55
1880	148
1890	2,039
1900	24,327
1910	72,157
1920	110,010
1930	138,834
1940	126,947

Source: U.S. Department of Commerce, Social and Economic Statistics Administration, Bureau of the Census, 1970, p. 42.

They were also keenly interested in making a contribution to a growing, dynamic, bustling adopted land. Some Issei returned to Japan when they had accumulated the wealth they sought, but others remained in the United States and became citizens.

For the most part, the Issei were young, unmarried males. Some 23 percent were under twenty years of age when they arrived, and some 53 percent were under twenty-five years of age. Further, the sex ratio was highly disturbed. In 1910, for example, there were only 9,000 women out of the total 72,157 Japanese in the country, a proportion of some seven males for every female. About half of the Japanese were employed in some form of agricultural work, but others found work as domestics; in independent small businesses of their own; on railroads; and in canneries, lumber mills, mines, and smelters.

The well-developed agricultural methods learned at home, supported by their socialization as cooperative, hardworking, industrious people, enabled the Japanese-Americans to convert otherwise worthless ground into vegetable- and fruit-producing lands. Their capacity for organized productivity was both appreciated and envied by white competitors, an ambivalence that erupted at the outset of World War II.

Marriage between a Japanese-American male and a non-Japanese woman was well-nigh impossible. Some Issei returned to Japan for the express purpose of securing a bride. Most, however, used the "picture-bride" method. This consisted of an exchange of photographs between prospective brides and grooms with their mutual friends and relatives acting as go-betweens. When the match was acceptable, a proxy marriage could be performed in Japan and formalized by being entered in the husband's family records. If the parties to a proxy marriage knew each other in Japan, the marriage was entered with little attempt at subterfuge. In numerous other marriages, the picture brides and their grooms were total strangers. Prospective grooms resorted to deceptions such as posing in borrowed clothing; covering a bald head with a hat; or pretending that a building in the background was their own, when in reality, they may have owned no property as farmhands, laborers, or railroad section workers. Prospective brides, too, may have resorted to some chicanery in order to come to the United States, but, in the end, the marriages were generally stable and reasonably happy.

The second-generation Japanese-Americans are known as *Nisei*, those born in the United States. Neither the Issei nor the Nisei offered any population threat, despite Pacific Coast residents' fears of a Japanese population explosion. A number of factors worked against such a result. First, the numbers of Issei were relatively small. The peak years of Japanese immigration were between 1900 and 1908, when some 139,000

Issei entered the country. By comparison, approximately 10 million European immigrants entered during the same period. After 1908, Issei exceeded 10,000 in only two years, 1918 and 1919, and in every year, females exceeded males by a ratio of two to one. The preponderance of females was due to the normal desire of earlier male immigrants to marry, but the entry of women was never sufficient to allow some 40 percent of the men to marry.

Second, the Gentlemen's Agreement between Japan and the United States which took effect in 1908, stated that the Japanese authorities would voluntarily restrict passports for skilled or unskilled laborers. Laborers who had already been in the United States or who had blood relatives there were immune from the restrictions. By 1924, immigration was sharply cutdown by a quota system which was particularly effective with Orientals. Between 1909 and 1924, some 118,000 Issei arrived, an average of 7,375 per year. Either because of achievement of wealth or a combination of harassment and disillusionment, some 40,000 Japanese left the country during the same period, about one-third of the original immigrants. As a result of this attrition and through normal death, the Issei and the Nisei never exceeded the peak population of 139,000 in the years 1900 to 1908. In fact, Japanese-Americans experienced the *loss* of an entire *generation* between 1930 and 1940 because the Issei had entered their non-childbearing years and the Nisei had not yet reached these years. When war broke out between Japan and the United States in 1941, the average age of the Issei men was about sixty and that of their wives about fifty. Most of the Nisei were only in their early twenties.

The history of Japanese-Americans, particularly in California, is one of economic gains despite organized and unorganized discrimination. Efforts were made to make Japanese-Americans ineligible to purchase land and to deny them citizenship. The only recourse left to the Issei and the Nisei was to invest their energies in their families and friends, and this they did with vigor. The third generation, the *Sansei*, were to prove the merit of their ways.

One unique group within the Nisei generation should be noted. These were the *Kibei*, American-born children of Issei, citizens of the United States by birth but educated in Japan. The Kibei experienced marginality because the traditional ways in Japan were never quite acceptable to them, and they were never quite "at home" in the United States because of unfamiliarity with education, and racial-cultural and language barriers. The result was isolation and alienation, even from other Nisei who had remained in the United States and who were educated and acclimated to Western ways.

The elaboration of generational distance from Japan is perpetuated in these linguistic terms of Issei, Nisei, Sansei, and Kibei. The great-grandchildren of Issei are addressed as *Yonsei*, literally, the fourth generation. The fifth generation, children of the Yonsei, are known as *Gosei*. As Lyman has noted, "Japanese-Americans are the only immigrant group in the United States who specify by a linguistic term and character-ize with a unique personality each generation of descendents from the original immigrants."[20]

Generational Contacts within Japanese-American Families

Oriental and Occidental traditions coexisted in Japanese-American homes with some degree of toleration and resignation on the part of the Issei and the Nisei. Japanese-American children could not help but acquire a command of the English language, a knowledge of Western ways, an attraction to the land in which they were born through their formal schooling and through their greater contacts with Caucasians than was possible for their parents. The Issei retained stronger memories of Japanese ways and frowned upon the freer ways of Westerners, such as dancing in each other's arms or informal relationships between the sexes.

Efforts to keep the Nisei "within the fold," through arranged marriages, for example, were sources of friction between the generations. *Baishakunin*, family friends who acted as go-betweens, were sometimes called into the generational strife by the Issei. Interestingly enough, the persistence of long-established prejudices among the Japanese-Americans themselves included checking to determine if prospective brides or grooms were related to the *Eta*. The Eta is a caste of Japanese who are excluded from polite society in Japan because of such "defiling" occupations as the tanning of hides or the disposal of the dead. George Devos and Hiroshi Wagatsuma have detailed the exclusion of the Eta in Japan in their study, *Japan's Invisible Race*.[21] In this instance, prejudice and discrimination are clearly as much a part of the mores of Japanese as they are of Americans. When victimized by those who subscribe to prejudice and discrimination, Japanese-Americans are quick to complain —and rightfully so in the United States. In the case of the Eta, however, the "long memories" of the Issei included their own brand of social exclusiveness.

Early Japanese-American family life was a fascinating mixture of traditional Japanese ways and newer American perspectives. One classic case may be found in Louis Adamic's book *From Many Lands* and is detailed under the significant title, "Young American with a Japanese Face."[22] To both the Issei and the Nisei, their families were comforting refuges from the pressures of a sometimes hostile external world. In their homes, holidays, particularly New Year's, were elaborately celebrated in Japanese style. Japanese foods were served. Training in the Japanese language was encouraged. Associations of *kenjin-kai*, Issei from the same prefecture in old Japan, could be maintained. And, most important of all, Japanese morality could be carefully taught and practiced. Nisei could learn the meaning of *on*, obligation; *shushin*, morals; *ai*, love of parents for children; and *giri*, repayment of *on*.

Finally, the Issei could pass along to the Nisei what Professor Harry H. L. Kitano has called the *"Enryo* syndrome."[23] *Enryo* is a Japanese term that covers the combined qualities of reserve, restraint, deference, and diffidence. It involves self-control, obedience to authority, and willingness to sacrifice oneself for the sake of others. Enryo traditions have served the Japanese-Americans well, particularly during the dark days of World War II, when Japan and the United States were locked in battle on the Pacific.

One would assume that Japanese-American family life would be characterized by austerity, formality, control of personal feelings, and submission to the wishes of the Issei. As many Japanese-Americans can testify, this stereotypic view is far from the truth. Japanese-American families can be characterized by informality, warm or cordial intergenerational relationships, and a bicultural way of life in which the Issei encouraged and sustained the entry of the Nisei into American society.

Evacuation, Relocation, and Return to Honor

The Issei, Nisei, and Sansei generations stood together in one of the most amazing records of family solidarity in the midst of adversity that ever befell a segment of the American population. The attack on Pearl Harbor in December 1941 raised anti-Japanese feelings to fever pitch. Longstanding animosity reached a climax of war hysteria in which every Japanese-American was held to be a secret agent of the Japanese militarists who had schemed to bring about the downfall of the United States as a world power. All past deeds of proven loyalty and constructive investments in the American society were swept aside as clever screens for the real disloyalty of Japanese-Americans. Sabotage and disloyalty were thus suspected but never proven.

Wholesale removal of Japanese-Americans to so-called relocation centers far from the Pacific Coast war zones was a cruel blow to these families who had labored so long and hard to establish homes, businesses, and property investments. The hasty sales of these products of years of sacrifice involved serious economic losses to Japanese-American families, who had every reason to be embittered and resentful of such ill treatment. Full restitution was never made for these losses, nor could Americans ever make amends for the ignorance and thoughtlessness that caused the uprooting of families and sending them to live in camps comparable to the concentration camps of European Jews under the Nazis.

When the magnitude of the hysteria was finally realized, efforts began to restore Japanese-Americans to their rightful status as American citizens, which included allowing the men to serve in the armed forces. The valor and fine service records of Japanese-American soldiers in both the European and the Pacific theaters during World War II are well documented, and won for these soldiers an enduring respect and admiration. The postwar years, covering the formative years of the Sansei, have witnessed a growing and continued admiration for the contributions of Japanese-Americans to the United States. The admission of Hawaii as the fiftieth state of the Union brought more Japanese-Americans into the mainstream of American society, and this time, the economic, political, artistic, educational, and cultural achievements of Japanese-Americans were clearly recognized. *Giri*, repayment, a concept learned in Japanese-American homes, could have been bitter. Instead, to the credit of Japanese-Americans, their attitude was one of tolerance and forgiveness —living monuments to the Issei who came to help build the United States.

JEWISH-AMERICAN FAMILIES

American society has been called a society dominated by the Protestant ethic. It is at least a Christian nation. Who then, are these Jewish-Americans, small in number, "the perennial minority," who have made such an impact that they represent one of the three major faiths in the United States? To understand Jewish-Americans it is advisable to become familiar with the ancient, medieval, and modern European Jewish generations that preceded them.[24] It is, however, with the more recent generations of Jewish-Americans and their families that the present discussion is concerned.

The most recent data available in the 1970s indicate that there are some 70 million Protestants, 48 million Roman Catholics, and 6 million Jews in the United States.[25] It should be clear that there are degrees of religiosity, or degrees of identification with one's family faith, and so, many are Jews in name, but not by actual practice in homes, temples, or community life.

R. A. Schermerhorn has listed some ten different qualities that set Jewish-Americans apart from all other Americans, even their close

Christian neighbors and friends.[26] These are (1) survival for some two thousand years as a minority faith in Christendom, a reminder of an indebtedness to those "people of the Book," (2) religious scholarship that has been transformed into devotion to secular education, professionalism, and economic success, (3) dispersion to every corner of the earth and yet a strong sympathy for the State of Israel and their coreligionists, (4) religious endogamy that has attempted to thwart interest in interfaith marriages, an exclusiveness that has brought the charge of religious snobbery, (5) bicultural family life that perpetuates a faith that has resisted assimilation for generations, (6) ghetto experiences now transformed into self-segregation in suburban communities, (7) political emancipation that has enabled them to enter and fully participate in civic life, (8) strong identification with city life, (9) a view of the United States as "the Promised Land" of religious freedom, and (10) a variety of strategems to maintain an ancient faith in the contemporary United States.

American Jews have been a part of American history as far back as Revolutionary War days. However, the first, second, and third generations of American Jews of contemporary society trace their origins to two waves of Jewish immigrants in the late nineteenth and early twentieth centuries. The first Jewish migrants were German or Ashkenazic Jews from Western Europe, arriving between 1820 and 1870. The second wave, from 1870 to 1920, came from Southern and Eastern Europe. As Harry Golden expressed it, "only in America" have so many Jews found their dreams realized.[27]

Closer study, however, reveals that Jewish-American families still have many problems to face. In such major cities as Boston, Cleveland, Los Angeles, Muncie, Nashville, New York, Philadelphia, St. Paul, and Minneapolis, prejudice continues to exist.[28] The issues may differ, but many Jewish-Americans are conscious of their identity and consequent subtle rejection. They are torn between assimilation in American Society and their—unique religious—cultural identities and heritage.

Jewish-American Family Life Reputation

The reputation of Jewish-American families is quite flattering. They are said to be paragons of stability, economic strength, generational concern, close kinship ties, interpersonal warmth, solidarity, and religious fervor. One hears that juvenile delinquency is rare and that young adults are eager to emulate their parents and grandparents in achieving *sholom*, family peace and harmony. It is a positive stereotype, but one that misses the mark by a fairly wide margin.

Stuart Rosenberg's study of Jewish identity in the United States[29]

and Bernard Rosen's study of Jewish adolescents[30] lend support to the
thesis that Jewish-American families face considerable internal tensions
that threaten their future. The most detailed generational study of
Jewish-American families was made by Sidney Goldstein and Calvin
Goldscheider in 1968 in Providence, Rhode Island.[31] About 19,700 Jews
were living there in some 6,000 family units. Sampling 25 percent,
Goldstein and Goldscheider found 1,500 families to be a well-educated,
fairly prosperous group. Successive generations had experienced upward
social mobility but at the same time had the problem of maintaining a
religiously oriented family life. The home, sometimes described as the
"fortress of the faith" by Jews, is apparently more in danger from internal
dismemberment than from external criticism or assaults.

As Table 8-6 indicates, for the Jewish population of Providence,
Rhode Island over twenty-five years of age, 85 percent were married and
less than 1.5 percent were divorced or separated. However, slight
increases (of family breakdown) are noted over the generations, from the

**Table 8-6   Marital Status of 1,500 Jewish-American Families, Providence,
Rhode Island, 1963–1964, by Generation and Age**

Generation and age	Marital status				
	Single	Married	Widowed	Separated and divorced	Total percent
All ages					
First generation	1.2	79.6	18.2	0.8	100.0*
Second generation	7.0	86.5	5.3	1.2	100.0*
Mixed parentage	6.7	89.1	1.0	3.2	100.0
Third generation	7.7	89.3	1.7	1.4	100.0
Total	5.5	85.3	7.7	1.4	100.0
25–44 age group					
First generation	2.4	95.2	1.2	1.2	100.0
Second generation	6.4	91.3	0.8	1.4	100.0
Mixed parentage	7.7	89.1	0.0	3.2	100.0
Third generation	7.8	89.9	1.0	1.3	100.0
45–64 age group					
First generation	0.6	88.6	9.1	1.2	100.0*
Second generation	7.4	86.5	5.0	1.0	100.0*
Mixed parentage	4.7	88.2	3.5	3.5	100.0
Third generation	8.2	87.8	2.0	2.0	100.0
65 and over age group					
First generation	1.5	66.5	31.7	0.3	100.0
Second generation	6.3	65.2	27.7	0.9	100.0

*Includes less than 1 percent unknown marital status.
Source: Sidney Goldstein and Calvin Goldscheider, *Jewish Americans: Three Generations in a Jewish Community*, Englewood Cliffs, N. J.: Prentice-Hall, Inc., 1968, p. 107. Reprinted by permission of the authors.

Table 8-7   Religious Identification of 1,500 Jewish-American Families, Providence, Rhode Island, 1963–1964, by Generation and Age

Generation and age	Religious identification				Total percent
	Orthodox	Conservative	Reform	Other	
All ages					
First generation	41.1	42.4	11.6	5.0	100.0
Second generation	14.9	61.0	20.1	4.0	100.0
Mixed parentage	7.1	56.7	34.0	2.2	100.0
Third generation	6.3	49.0	35.3	9.4	100.0
Total	19.8	54.1	21.2	4.9	100.0
25–44 age group					
First generation	22.6	50.0	19.0	8.3	100.0
Second generation	12.5	63.8	20.7	3.0	100.0
Mixed parentage	7.7	62.4	27.6	2.3	100.0
Third generation	4.5	51.9	36.7	6.8	100.0
45–64 age group					
First generation	35.1	49.1	11.1	4.7	100.0
Second generation	16.0	61.3	18.6	4.0	100.0
Mixed parentage	5.9	42.4	49.4	2.4	100.0
Third generation	18.4	32.7	28.6	20.4	100.0
65 and over age group					
First generation	51.8	33.5	10.2	4.5	100.0
Second generation	17.9	45.5	28.6	8.0	100.0

Source: Sidney Goldstein and Calvin Goldscheider, *Jewish Americans: Three Generations in a Jewish Community*, Englewood Cliffs, N. J.: Prentice-Hall, Inc., 1968, p. 177. Reprinted by permission of the authors.

earliest to the latest. Those born in the United States of mixed parentage (one parent born in the United States and the other in a foreign land) had the highest proportions of separations and divorces, further evidence of a departure from the usual Jewish norms of family stability.

The data on religious self-identification in Table 8-7 are most revealing because they indicate the extent of the departure from traditional orthodox Judaism. The Orthodox wing of Judaism tends to follow as closely as possible the ancient ritualistic requirements of the faith. The Reform wing is concerned with changes to be made in the light of knowledge and circumstances in the modern world. The Conservative wing represents those who seek to conserve what they consider to be the most valuable aspects while adapting to the conditions of contemporary American society. As Table 8-7 indicates, there is a pronounced tendency to move from Orthodoxy to Conservative and Reform practices as generations become more Americanized. Those of mixed parentage are particularly prone to this shift.

Table 8-8   Family-centered Rituals in 1,500 Jewish-American Families, Providence, Rhode Island, 1963–1964, by Generation and Religious Identification (Percentages)

Generation and rituals	Orthodox		Conservative		Reform	
	Always	Never	Always	Never	Always	Never
Sabbath candles						
First generation	84.9	5.8	51.8	19.6	24.0	32.0
Second generation	62.2	19.3	38.6	21.0	26.5	32.8
Third generation	60.0	30.0	32.1	28.6	11.3	35.8
Total	75.2	12.1	40.3	22.3	22.8	34.6
Passover seder						
First generation	90.8	1.7	85.1	3.6	64.7	3.9
Second generation	80.7	7.6	83.5	4.4	74.3	6.8
Third generation	80.0	10.0	77.3	2.3	71.4	8.2
Total	86.5	4.2	83.8	3.9	71.4	7.5
Kosher meat						
First generation	82.8	10.2	55.1	13.3	20.8	27.1
Second generation	72.3	10.1	34.4	27.0	14.4	47.9
Third generation	60.0	20.0	25.0	31.0	3.8	63.5
Total	77.7	10.7	36.9	25.1	13.3	48.4
Separate dishes						
First generation	82.9	13.1	41.2	53.9	6.5	89.1
Second generation	64.4	33.1	24.8	69.7	7.0	90.4
Third generation	60.0	30.0	20.2	78.6	2.0	98.0
Total	74.7	21.4	27.4	67.9	5.6	92.1
Chanukah candles						
First generation	88.3	7.0	72.3	21.1	56.0	26.0
Second generation	81.4	14.4	79.8	9.3	68.9	17.9
Third generation	100.0	0.0	84.5	9.5	66.0	18.9
Total	86.2	9.5	78.6	12.1	65.5	20.1

Source: Sidney Goldstein and Calvin Goldscheider, *Jewish Americans: Three Generations in a Jewish Community,* Englewood Cliffs, N. J.: Prentice-Hall, Inc., 1968, p. 203. Reprinted by permission of the authors.

With each successive generation attendance at synagogues dropped, but even more telling in this family-centered faith is the movement away from religious rituals in the home. As the Sabbath begins at sundown on Friday night, candles are lit by the mother. As Table 8-8 indicates, regardless of religious identification, this practice is becoming increasingly abandoned by successive generations of Jewish-Americans.

At the Passover festival, Jewish families have a ritualistic family dinner in which they recall the Exodus of Jewish slaves from Egypt. This dinner is called a *seder*, which means "order," or a prescribed form of observing the holiday. In Goldstein and Goldscheider's sampling, the Jewish-Americans of Providence, Rhode Island, moved away from holding seders with successive generations, except for Reform Jews.

The word "kosher" means "ritually clean," and the restriction of family diets to kosher meats is a strong indication of retention of the ancient dietary directives. In the sampling each generation found it more difficult to observe these restrictions and rapidly abandoned the practice.

In Table 8-8 the separate dishes category refers to the effort to separate meat and dairy products at family meals. This practice stems from the ancient statement that "a kid is not to be cooked in its mother's milk." This means that each ritually observant Jewish family must have two separate sets of dishes and utensils, one for meat and one for dairy foods. For the Passover festival, lasting approximately one week, the usual sets of dishes and utensils are put away and two new ones are used. Thus, a truly devout Jewish-American family would have at least four sets of dishes. As Table 8-8 indicates, this practice, too, has been notably abandoned by younger generations.

The lighting of Chanukah candles in Jewish homes usually coincides with Christmas in Christian homes. In Jewish-American homes, a new candle is added each day in celebration of the restoration of the Temple by the Maccabees. At the end of eight days, the candelabrum is fully lit. Chanukah is a particularly joyous festival because each day the children in the family receive a new gift, in contrast to the Christian practice of gift giving on a single day. Table 8-8 indicates that Jewish-American families in the Providence sample tended to retain the ritual of Chanukah candles and to increase its use with successive generations.

NON-MIDDLE-CLASS FAMILIES

Middle-class biases of American family sociologists have increasingly come under attack. Veronica Heiskanen, for example, has examined some 534 articles based on marriage and family research reported in the *Journal of Marriage and the Family* between 1959 and 1968.[32] She found a blurring of socioeconomic characteristics that overwhelmingly contributed to the emphasis upon middle-class family life. College students, essentially middle-class, were sampled in 72 of 289 empiric studies; 53 studies were basically middle-class oriented with some admixture of upper-class persons; 19 studies dealt with lower-class strata; 90 studies combined middle-class and lower-class families; and 55 studies involved "no strata" because they made vague references to high school students, couples, housewives, or agency clients.[33] The result has been "a wholehearted endorsement of the 'cultural homogenization' theme and . . . the rejection of diversity as a conceptual alternative."[34] Heiskanen concludes that the wide range of family-life strata merits concern. "The whole human social experience contained in the realm of the family" should continually be examined.[35] It is for precisely this reason that this chapter was written.

Upper-Class Families

One family sociologist, who deserves recognition as one of the few who did not and does not follow the middle-class bias attributed to the profession, is Ruth Cavan. Through the years, she has brought together a wealth of data concerning variants of upper-, middle-, and lower-class families. An indebtedness to her is acknowledged in the descriptions that follow.[36]

Using Lloyd Warner's subdivision of classes into "uppers" and "lowers," Cavan describes the "upper-uppers" as well as the "lower-uppers."

The Upper-Uppers   At the pinnacle of the social class system are the upper-upper-class families, the products of many generations. Some eight or nine generations have helped establish Eastern upper-upper-class families, some four or five generations stand behind Middle-Western upper-upper-class families, and in the Far West, two or three generations have been sufficient to place families in the upper-uppers.

Indebtedness to past generations is acknowledged in these families in the form of great pride in family names, crests, heirlooms, and jointly owned family estates. Surviving elders are particularly respected, not only because they have personal knowledge of grandparents and great grandparents but also because they often control the families' inherited wealth. Upper-upper-class families manifest a strong tendency for cultural homogeneity, not only in their origins but also in the amassing of fortunes, educational training, emphasis upon family continuity, philanthropies, and the cultivation of manners and good taste. Trust funds, from which they may eventually draw interest on investments, are established for the children.

Social isolation from other class levels is assured by providing the youngest generation with nurses, governesses, tutors, companions, and escorts who may not be members of the upper-uppers but who are well versed in their employers' family traditions and expectations. Private schools at home and abroad complete the formal education of the youngest generation and set them apart from others in personality organization, aspirations, and interests.

Typically, marriage is rather late or deferred. The later twenties or early thirties seem to be the most typical ages for marriage. "Approved" persons are selected from a circle of friends and acquaintances. In some instances, marriage between distant cousins is very acceptable because it tends to preserve or consolidate family heritages. The debut is one form of introducing young women of upper-upper-class families to young men of the same class.

Marriages generally produce few children. Also, there is a relatively high proportion of elderly members found in upper-upper-class families. Life expectation is high, since these families command life-supporting, life-sustaining facilities not normally available to other families.

Such a broadly sketched picture of upper-upper-class families goes far to explain why so many family sociologists have tended to neglect them. The upper-uppers have achieved a stable pattern that needs only maintenance. Essentially, there are only two alternatives confronting upper-upper-class families. They may either maintain their present status, or they may go down; the latter option is rarely taken. One, then, does not study upper-upper-class families in the same manner as other families. With other families, one can consider alternative methods for upward mobility, ways and means to improve upon current patterns, and the possibility of their failing to maintain the status quo and sinking into lower socioeconomic conditions. With upper-upper-class families, upward mobility is out of the question, improvements are superfluous, and the chances of downward mobility are minimal.

The Lower-Uppers   There is a stratum just below the upper-uppers that does seek change. It is the level of the lower-upper-class families, or the *nouveau riche*, the newly rich, whose acquisition of considerable wealth within one or two generations places them in a strategic position of possibly entering upper-upper-class families. Their tremendous wealth enables them to buy status symbols, such as expensive homes, elegant cars, and the advantages of travel and education that might otherwise be far out of reach.

Such families are close to and yet removed from upper-upper-class families. Whatever ambitions for upward mobility exist, the most likely candidates for acceptance will be the youngest generation, the children of the *nouveau riche.*

Marriage occurs a little earlier in the lower-upper-class than in the upper-upper-class. Children are few and are carefully groomed to associate with upper-upper-class age peers in private finishing schools, resorts, and exclusive country clubs. In some ways, the lower-upper-class families are more ostentatious than the upper-upper-class families they hope to emulate. The lower-upper-class families need more generational time to become accustomed to upper-class life-styles. The grace and poise of upper-upper-class families have not yet become part of their personalities. Every effort is made to train lower-upper-class males to enter a respected business or profession and lower-upper-class females to make a "good" marriage.

One aspect of lower-upper-class families that merits further study is their relationships with upper-middle- or lower-middle-class collateral kin. Such persons have been left behind in the family's history of upward mobility. Sentimentally, there may be value in maintaining some contacts, but practically, the advantages lie in breaking these ties in favor of opening up new associations with upper-upper-class individuals.

Lower-Class Families

Lower-class families are also subdivided into upper-lowers and lower-lowers. The difference between the two subdivisions is in the degree of economic stability, which is influenced by such factors as wages, jobs, and home ownership. Upper-lower-class individuals could suffer from layoffs, but unions have protected their rights through collective bargaining in business and industry. Some upper-lower-class families have accumulated enough wealth to move away from lower-lower-class neighborhoods. For these families, a modest home with more living space is a proud achievement. Cavan chooses to call upper-lower-class families the "nouveau bourgeoisie."

The lower-lower-class families merge downward toward the so-called declassed—vagrants, delinquents, and criminals—who are attuned to their own contracultural values, which are quite alien to middle-class mores. Economic stability is practically nonexistent or extremely precarious for lower-lowers, who may be on or off relief rolls. Whatever family history exists may be found on the records of social agencies that have aided these multiproblemed families.

Lower-class families, in general, have minimal generational roots in American society. They are often described as "new arrivals" and as having great cultural diversity in terms of ethnic origins, languages, standards, faiths, and social ambitions. Some notable exceptions to the general rule can be found among those who are racially different from WUMPs. A strong case can be made for the large percentages of lower-class black, American-Indian, and Spanish-American families, whose generational roots go far deeper than those of many middle-class or upper-class families. In explanation of this phenomenon, an examination of family histories reveals the disruption of generational continuity that places these groups in, near, or below the poverty levels of the country.

Whereas upper-class families are graceful patriarchies in which patrilineage places men in leadership positions and women in "enhancement roles" and middle-class families are equalitarian in cooperative husband-wife roles, lower-class families are often characterized by a dominating patriarchy or a strong matrifocal subtype in which a mother or grandmother dominates family life. Unlike middle-class families, which at times debate the issue of working wives and mothers, lower-class families call upon all family members—men, women, and children—to work.

Hyman Rodman is one family scholar with a sustained interest in lower-class families. In a recent work, *Lower-Class Families: The Culture of Poverty in Negro Trinidad*, he offers a theory of lower-class families.[37] One feature of this theory is that much of what is called characteristic of lower-class families in the United States may not be universally valid. In an environment of different attitudes and social structures, the lower-class-male role of worker-earner may not be a serious loss. Earning capacity may not be regarded as the measure of a man. When this is the stance of lower-class families, the lower-class-male role is not diminished. Neither do lower-class families suffer by a man's inability to support his family when ways and means to distribute functions among other kinfolk, friends, or community organizations can be found. Rodman's interpretations suggest one caution: lower-class families should be observed in their own milieu rather than in that of the middle class.

Of all classes, lower-class-family members are reputed to marry the earliest, and to have rather brief, sexually exciting courtships. Lower-class families are typically large, and often unplanned.[38] They move frequently to improve conditions or to escape meeting long overdue rents. Lacking verbal finesse, they resolve hostilities by physical abuse and obscenities. Wife beating, child abuse, and fights between men are not uncommon, particularly when frustrations increase. Escapism takes a variety of forms, including separation, desertion, absenteeism, delinquency, crime, alcoholism, gambling, and sexual escapades. A note of caution is needed regarding these escape forms: they are contingent upon the particular community and the tenor of the times. Indeed, studies indicate that a number of lower-class families are able to counter their external environment to an extent that permits some of their children to "escape" through upward social mobility.[39]

Cavan acknowledges that lower-class families are the basic population pool from which middle-class families draw their strength.[40] There is nothing in their condition that is innate or inevitable. The very presence of the impoverished in the otherwise affluent United States is the result of a socioeconomic system that places large numbers at the bottom and fewer and fewer at the top. In some ways, the system perpetuates itself through the personalities shaped in the early socialization of all classes. The system is amenable to changes, however, as educational, political, and economic agencies and interest groups explore other alternatives.

SUMMARY

Far too often, students of family in the United States have neglected families that differ from WUMP families. In this chapter, we have examined a few such families—blacks, Japanese-Americans, Jewish-Americans, and non-middle-class families. In these contemporary families, the experience of past generations are reflected. How these families fare speaks remarkably to the point; namely, how close is the United States to its ideals of freedom and respect for human differences?

Black families are not found to be monolithic; rather, they show tremendous variations. Socioeconomic differences produce a number of subtypes, and social-class differences among blacks reveal the extent to which publicity has been concentrated upon the nonworking poor black family. Most black families can be found in nonstereotypic situations at every class level. Moreover, the most common family structure includes both husband and wife. However, much remains to be done before black families achieve economic equality with white families. The generations that were uprooted from established West African family life and sold into slavery have left their mark unmistakenly upon contemporary black families. Present generations stress their distinctive contributions to American society.

Japanese-American families have long struggled with their racial and cultural differences. Although a very small minority on the American scene, they have quietly made invaluable contributions by their diligence, family solidarity, and ability to retain their cultural heritage, despite the rejection of uninformed Americans. The height of their suffering came in the early years of World War II, when they were suspected of disloyalty to the land they had supported. The bravery, courage, and solid evidence of loyalty of Japanese-Americans were amazing rewards for ill-treatment, and Americans were shamed into acceptance—a lesson well taught by generations of Issei, Nisei, and Sansei.

A religious minority, Jewish-American families, were examined as entities flourishing in a Christian United States. Their reputation is generally a flattering stereotype of family stability and close identification with a heritage from ancient generations. However, evidence on both national and community levels indicates that the reputation must be modified. An ambivalence between a desire to maintain a religiocultural heritage and a desire to be accepted by fellow Americans colors Jewish-American family life.

Finally, upper and lower-class families in the United States play distinctive roles with middle-class families. Families become part of the upper-class only after many generations of accumulated experience. The oldest upper-class families can be subdivided into the upper-upper-class and the newest into the lower-upper-class. Both upper classes, however, draw upon the middle class for their fundamental sources. The lower classes, in turn, are the pools of population from which middle-class families draw their strength and resources. For lower-class families, with the notable exception of racial barriers, an untold number of generations are needed to achieve upward social mobility.

In conclusion, each of the subtypes of upper- and lower-class families have distinctive life-styles. They are to be regarded not as superior or inferior to middle-class families, but as families responding to a heritage bequeathed by past generations.

REFERENCES

1 For the basic data and framework concerning black families, we are indebted to Andrew Billingsley, *Black Families in White America*, Englewood Cliffs, N. J.: Prentice-Hall, Inc., 1968.
2 Ibid., pp. 8–9.
3 Ibid., pp. 131–137.
4 Ibid., pp. 137–142.
5 See Jessie Bernard, *Marriage and Family Among Negroes*, Englewood Cliffs, N. J: Prentice-Hall, Inc., 1966.
6 Norman Coombs, *The Black Experience in America*, New York: Twayne Publishers, Inc., 1972, p. 29.
7 Ibid., p. 29.
8 Stanley M. Elkins, *Slavery: A Problem in American Institutional and Intellectual Life*, Chicago: The University of Chicago Press, 1963, pp. 82–87.
9 See, for example, Raul Hilberg, ed., *Documents of Destruction, Germany and Jewry, 1933–1945*, Chicago: Quadrangle Books, Inc., 1971.
10 Donald Pierson, *Negroes in Brazil*, Chicago: The University of Chicago Press, 1944.
11 William Moore, Jr., *The Vertical Ghetto: Everyday Life in an Urban Project*, New York: Random House, Inc., 1969. See also Louis Kriesberg, *Mothers in Poverty: A Study of Fatherless Families*, Chicago: Aldine Publishing Company, 1970.
12 Paul Sites and Jerry Lewis, "Evidence for a Black Family Culture," unpublished paper on research supported by the Center for Urban Regionalism, Kent State University, Kent, Ohio, presented at the joint meeting of the Ohio Valley Sociological Society and the Midwest Sociological Society, May 1969.
13 E. Franklin Frazier, *Black Bourgeoisie*, New York: The Free Press of Glencoe, Inc., 1957, pp. 195–238.
14 Ibid, pp. 195–212; 213–232.
15 Daniel Patrick Moynihan, *The Negro Family: The Case for National Action*, Washington, D. C.: Office of Policy Planning and Research, U. S. Department of Labor, March 1965.
16 See, for example, Lee Rainwater and William L. Yancey, *The Moynihan Report and the Politics of Controversy*, Cambridge, Mass.: The M.I.T. Press, 1967, and Robert Staples, *The Black Family: Essays and Studies*, Belmont, Calif.: Wadsworth Publishing Company, Inc., 1971.
17 Alex Haley, *Before This Anger*, a black American finds his ancestry in the Mandinka tribe of West Africa, forthcoming.

18 Jerry Lewis and Paul Sites, "Decision Making in Black Working Class Families," unpublished paper, Kent, Ohio: Kent State University, 1969.
19 Partially adopted from Bill Hosokawa, Nisei: *The Quiet Americans*, New York: William Morrow & Company, Inc., 1969.
20 Stanford M. Lyman, "Japanese-American Generation Gap," *Society*, vol. 10, no. 2, pp. 55–63, January/February 1973.
21 George DeVos and Hiroshi Wagatsuma, *Japan's Invisible Race: Caste in Culture and Personality*, Berkeley: University of California Press, 1966.
22 Louis Adamic, *From Many Lands*, New York: Harper & Brothers, 1940, pp. 185–234.
23 Hosokawa, op. cit., pp. 211–212.
24 See Abram Leon Sachar, *A History of the Jews*, 5th ed., New York: Alfred A. Knopf, Inc., 1967, and Max I. Dimont, *Jews, God and History*, Simon and Schuster, Inc., 1962.
25 *Statistical Abstract of the United States, 1970*, 1970, pp. 41–42.
26 R. A. Schermerhorn, *These Our People: Minorities in American Culture*, Boston: D. C. Heath and Company, 1949, pp. 381–387.
27 Harry Golden, *Only in America*, Cleveland: The World Publishing Company, 1958.
28 See Eugene J. Lipman and Albert Vorspan, *A Tale of Ten Cities: The Triple Ghetto in American Religious Life*, New York: Union of American Hebrew Congregations, 1962.
29 Stuart E. Rosenberg, *The Search for Jewish Identity in America*, Garden City, N. Y.: Doubleday & Company, Inc., Anchor Books, 1965.
30 Bernard Carl Rosen, *Adolescence and Religion: The Jewish Teenager in American Society*, Cambridge, Mass.: Schenkman Publishing Co., Inc., 1965.
31 Sidney Goldstein and Calvin Goldscheider, *Jewish Americans: Three Generations in a Jewish Community*, Englewood Cliffs, N. J.: Prentice-Hall, Inc., 1968.
32 Veronica Stolte Heiskanen, "The Myth of the Middle-Class Family in American Family Sociology," *The American Sociologist*, vol. 6, no. 1, pp. 14–18, February 1971.
33 Ibid., p. 17.
34 Ibid., p. 17.
35 Ibid., p. 18.
36 Ruth Shonle Cavan, *The American Family*, 4th ed., New York: Thomas Y. Crowell Company, 1969, pp. 85–111, 134–153.
37 Hyman Rodman, *Lower-Class Families: The Culture of Poverty in Negro Trinidad*, New York: Oxford University Press, 1971, pp. 176–189.
38 See Lee Rainwater, *And the Poor Get Children: Sex, Contraception, and Family Planning in the Working Class*, Chicago: Quadrangle Books, Inc., 1960.
39 See Walter C. Reckless, Simon Dintiz, and Ellen Murray, "Self-Concept as an Insulator Against Delinquency," *American Sociological Review*, vol. 21, pp. 744–746, December 1956; Frank Scarpitti, Ellen Murray, Simon Dintiz, and Walter C. Reckless, "The 'Good Boy' in a High Delinquency Area: Four

Years Later," *American Sociological Review*, vol. 25, pp. 555–558, August 1960.
40 Cavan, op. cit., p. 152.

STUDY QUESTIONS AND ACTIVITIES

1 What are the particular assets of black families, Japanese-American families, Jewish families, and non-middle-class families in the United States?
2 In what ways have past generations affected these non-WUMP families?
3 Have present generations in these families met their unique situations in appropriate ways? How would you suggest they handle their special problems?
4 Select some other racial, socioeconomic, religious, or ethnic family type and determine to what extent they share characteristics of the families discussed in this chapter.
5 Would you predict that families trying to maintain some type of unique generational heritage will fail to do so in the United States?
6 What factors suggest that assimilation of cultural differences is inevitable in the United States?
7 What factors promote pluralism in family life in the United States?
8 Of the four family types described in this chapter, with which do you especially empathize? Why?
9 Invite representatives of "different" families to come to your class and interview them in order to better understand their needs, values, and efforts.
10 Propose a research design that would test stereotypes of non-WUMP families.

SUGGESTED ADDITIONAL READINGS

Adamic, Louis, *From Many Lands*, New York: Harper & Brothers, 1940.
Coombs, Norman, *The Black Experience in America*, New York: Twayne Publishers, Inc., 1972.
Edelman, Lily (ed.), *Face to Face: A Primer in Dialogue*, A Jewish Heritage Book, B'nai B'rith Adult Jewish Education, Anti-Defamation League of B'nai B'rith, Washington, D.C.: Crown Publishers, Inc., 1967.
Gordon, Albert I., *Intermarriage: Interfaith, Interracial, Interethnic*, Boston: Beacon Press, 1964.
Harrington, Michael, *The Other America: Poverty in the United States*, Baltimore,: Penguin Books, Inc., 1963.
Kramer, Judith R., and Seymour Leventman, *Children of the Gilded Ghetto: Conflict Resolutions of Three Generations of American Jews*, New Haven, Conn.: Yale University Press, 1961.
Kriesberg, Louis, *Mothers in Poverty: A Study of Fatherless Families*, Chicago: Aldine Publishing Company, 1970.

Mack, Raymond W., *Race, Class, and Power*, 2d ed., New York: American Book
   Company, 1968.
Rodman, Hyman, *Lower-Class Families: The Culture of Poverty in Negro
   Trinidad*, New York: Oxford University Press, 1971.
Sklare, Marshall, *America's Jews*, New York: Random House, Inc., 1971.
Van Den Haag, Ernest, *The Jewish Mystique*, New York: Stein and Day
   Incorporated, 1969.

Chapter 9

Generational Dissension

Generational relationships run the gamut from harmony to disharmony, from continuity to discontinuity, from consensus to dissension. In this chapter, we will examine generational dissension, particularly as it occurs in contemporary American families.

Generational dissension, of course, is not new. It has caught the attention of social historians, philosophers, and theorists for centuries. Julián Marías has brought together some of the more recent thinking about generational discontent, unrest, and malaise in *Generations: A Historical Method*,[1] in which a sample of the theories of Justin Dromel and José Ortega y Gasset provides a useful comparison of late-nineteenth- and early twentieth-century thought with our own multigenerational approach.

DROMEL'S FOUR GENERATIONAL PRINCIPLES

Justin Dromel, a Marseilles lawyer and political writer, in 1861 published *The Law of Generations*, which propounded four principles:[2]

> **1** The predominance of a generation lasts some sixteen years, after which a new generation succeeds it in power.

2 During a generation's dominance, the one to follow completes its political education and criticizes its predecessor.

3 A generation's social ideal is superior to, and in a sense in conflict with, that of its predecessor.

4 The work of each generation is special, unique, uniform, and exclusive.

Dromel's idea that a generation predominates for about sixteen years seemingly differs from our own approximations of twenty to thirty years (see page 7). The twenty- to thirty-year interval was used because it covers the period of the maturation and socialization of a new generation before it truly "takes over" from its elders. The fifteen- or sixteen-year interval used by Dromel constitutes the *median* number of years between children and parents. This allows an equal number of years on either side of that figure during which generational dissension can, and often does, occur. In this sense, Dromel's assignment of sixteen years to each generation is not so different from our own twenty- or thirty-year interval.

Dromel's second principle is more pertinent to generational dissension. It stresses the *inevitability* of generational dissent, because, as Dromel noted in his remaining principles, each generation believes its own social ideals are superior to those of its predecessor and, consequently, seeks to reify its ideals as it emerges as the dominant generation. Some twelve years after Dromel's publication, Antoine Cournot explained the same inevitability by noting that there was always "the gradual renovation of ideas . . . from the imperceptible replacement of older generations by the younger."[3] Cournot pointed to the "replacement of generations" while Dromel pointed to the alleged superiority of a generations' "social ideals" or social values. Bernard Farber, in his book *Family: Organization and Interaction,* has made "orderly replacement" a central feature of his own analyses of contemporary American family life—much in the fashion of Cournot.[4]

ORTEGA'S VIGENCIAS

Marias was particularly impressed with the thinking of José Ortega y Gasset in his book *The Modern Theme.* Ortega repeatedly stressed the importance of *vigencia,* binding custom that consists of laws, usages, traditions, and beliefs that prevail in a given society or collectivity.[5] *Vigencias* are not too different in the general sense from Sumner's folkways and mores or, in the more specific sense, from what Farber has called "symbolic family estates." These *vigencias*, or, simply, traditions are sources of contention between and among generations. We shall deal with a few of them among American families.

Ortega assigned *vigencias* to five distinctive generational periods. These generational intervals of fifteen years, approximately the time of dominance of a single generation according to Dromel, covered seventy-five years, the average life expectancy for contemporary men and women. The generational periods with their respective *vigencias* are as follows:[6]

1 The first fifteen years: *childhood.* There is no historical participation; what the child receives from the world hardly has historical character. Hence, the child's world changes much less from one period to another than does the adult's during the same dates.

2 From fifteen to thirty: *youth.* A person is receptive to his surrounding; he sees, hears, reads, learns, and in general permits himself to be permeated by the preexisting world that he had no part in making. This is a period of learning and passivity.

3 From thirty to forty-five: *initiation.* Man now begins to act, to try to modify the inherited world, trying to impose his own innovation on it. This is the period of preparation, during which man struggles with the preceding generation and attempts to remove it from power.

4 From forty-five to sixty: *dominance.* The world man tried to begin at an earlier age now prevails. The men of this age "are in power" in every walk of life; it is the period of control. Yet at the same time these men prepare to defend this world against innovations proposed by the younger generations.

5 From sixty to seventy-five, or more in cases of great longevity: *old age.* These are men who are survivors from past periods. . . . there are fewer men of this age than in previous groups. Old men are . . . "outside of life" and this is the role they must play; that is, they are witnesses to a previous world who carry their experience in that world while remaining aloof from contemporary struggles. Such is the function of senates and councils of elders.

Ortega's schema are certainly interesting and provocative. We should note, however, that social changes today are occurring at more frequent intervals than Ortega allows for, and that his constant referral to "men" does not take into account the increasing pressures from women who seek their own personhood.

GENERATIONAL DISSENSION IN THE PRESENT

Generational theorists are caught up in the *vicengias* of their own times. In the case of Dromel and Ortega, evolutionary patterns were of primary concern, and their views on the inevitability of generational strife fitted their times. In more recent years, however, revolution, sharp breaks with the past, and strong protests have taken center stage.[7] Family-life literature repeatedly emphasizes generational strife, discontent, disunity, alienation, schisms, or "gaps." Such a predominance of generational difficulties may be due to the belief that current problems are far more important than those of the past, but more likely, they concern students of the family because life in the present *is* under strong attack from many quarters.

Generational dissension is most visible in contemporary American families where the generations meet at the most intimate levels. Whether generational interactions are hostile or amicable, they are projected upon family screens, magnified out of proportion because observers are socially close, made personal through consanguine and affinal kin, and dramatized by members of various generations.

Families themselves, however, are dependent upon the state of affairs *outside* family life. Larger social issues pervade family life and conspire to test its internal consistency, its ability to cope. What often appears to be a small, internal affair is a larger issue "writ small" within a family circle. That such quarrels are duplicated in families everywhere validates this view. By examining *social change, social control,* and *social values,* we can pinpoint at least a few of the more prominent generational conflicts that surface in American homes.

Social Change

The dynamic nature of contemporary American society has been documented by so many observers and studied by so many analysts that it needs no duplication here. What is noteworthy, however, is the *acceleration* of social change in an unprecedented manner. Alvin Toffler has popularized this idea in his compelling book *Future Shock.*[8] His thesis is that the swift flow of events, the rapid tempo of human affairs, the impermanency of relationships, and the quick obsolescence of the past have left many people bewildered, lost, or traumatized, unable or unwilling to deal effectively with the present because it will soon pass away and be transformed into something else.

Writing about "the 800th lifetime," Toffler notes that

if the last 50,000 years of man's existence were divided into lifetimes of approximately sixty-two years each, there have been about 800 such lifetimes. Of these, fully 650 were spent in caves. Only during the last seventy lifetimes has it been possible to communicate effectively from one lifetime to another—as writing made it possible to do. Only during the last six lifetimes did masses of men ever see a printed word. Only during the last four has it been possible to measure time with any precision. Only in the last two has anyone anywhere used an electric motor. And the overwhelming majority of all the material goods we use in daily life today have been developed within the present, the 800th, lifetime.[9]

Toffler goes on to note that American society has moved from an agrarian to an industrial economy and is now on the threshold of a superindustrial economy in which manual and skilled labor are becoming superfluous and service management is becoming paramount. Being tightly bound in a network of social ties, events occurring anywhere have immediate reverberations throughout the world.[10] Transience, impermanency, rootlessness, diversity, alternatives, and the explosion of knowledge challenge whatever generational *vigencias* survive. Every social institution stands in the floodtide of social change and can be swept away. This applies particularly to contemporary American family life and is manifested in what we have called- "generational dissension."

In Toffler's view, families have been effective "shock absorbers" in the past. In more traditional terms, families have been called "fortresses" against adversity, man's "castle," or "safe harbor" from the storms of change. Toffler suggests, however, that the family may well be in for shocks of its own. Antagonists of contemporary family life see the family as obsolete because, to them, families serve no useful purpose under changed circumstances. Protagonists, however, see family as a refuge of tranquility in times of great social upheaval.

Toffler, however, takes neither a pessimistic nor an optimistic view of American families confronted with accelerating social changes. Rather, he predicts that family life will, more likely, "break up, shatter, only to come together in weird and novel ways."[11] In short, Toffler, a keen observer of rapid social change, sees families as surviving, but in imaginative, diverse forms compatible with a world of impermanency.

Impact of Impermanence upon Marriage That husband-wife relationships are today being redefined is evidenced by the fact that young couples have stated that they wish to treat marriage quite differently from their parental generations. Marriages bound by religious and legal ties are far too rigid for youthful tastes.

Many younger couples are both advocating and practicing what have been called "arrangements." In these arrangements, they live together as long as they are mutually satisfied. Licensing by states or religious ceremonials by established churches are believed to be unnecessary. Older generations point to the advantages of making public records: setting limits on ages for marriage, checking for venereal diseases, assuring that there are no impediments, such as an earlier, still-in-force marriage, and making each party responsible for the other and for any children born of the union. Further, older generations stress the values of appearing before like-minded coreligionists to affirm age-old moralities. To elders, "arrangements" are both shocking and foolhardy. To some young couples, however, arrangements make good sense.

What matters to such couples is that they can make or break their arrangements on their volition. If they stay together, it is because they choose to do so out of mutual trust and confidence and not out of fear that society will punish them if they do not behave in some approved way. As one participant observer expressed it, "Love has married us. We need nothing else." Thus, impermanence based on love freely given or withdrawn is held to be of far greater value than permanence based on laws or moral threats.

Younger generations clearly favor marriages that endure only as long as partners *choose* to remain together. Older generations may sympathize with this youthful confidence in love, but they also believe that youngsters would be well advised to be able to have legal recourse should unforseen circumstances occur. Such matters as access to and use of jointly owned property, support for children and mothers, and custody or visiting rights should be anticipated.

One would think that with liberalized grounds or interpretations of grounds for divorce, as well as the increasing adoption of "no-fault" divorce actions, the argument that legal marriages are too difficult to shed would be weakened. Or one would think that with growing confidence in birth-control measures, the arguments of elders that innocent children could become involved would lack force. Neither generation, however, can accede to the wishes of the other because, in the end, impermanence and unfettered commitment are arrayed against permanence and religio-legal responsibility, and these are not negotiable issues. For each generation, they are "givens" that squarely meet contemporary conditions.

Impact of Impermanence upon Family   Increasing mobility, whether geographic in terms of changing locales or vertical in terms of socioeconomic levels, has left its mark upon families and effectively separates younger from older generations. Older generations have already established themselves within communities or found their place within social-class levels. Younger generations are still searching for their destinies, for their careers, and believe they cannot or should not be tied down. "Homes" are starter homes to newly married couples, and they much prefer a quickly discarded apartment to the permanent housing of long-married couples. Whether they be students, technicians, or executives, young couples must be prepared to move as opportunities develop. A certain proportion of young families are also willing to move for the sake of variety rather than living in boredom with too familiar territory.

In the meantime, older generations are either satisfied with their lot or have come to realize that their present location and status are about as far as they are ever going to go. In aging, their concerns are rooted in a single community, in their friends, and in conserving whatever resources they may have acquired.

Generational dissension manifested in localized issues is often a result of mobility or nonmobility. Local disputes over school taxes, welfare programs, or highways are cases in point. Zoning, income taxes, and planning for recreational facilities also reflect generational preferences.

One of the significant developments in the United States has been the movement of the population out of central cities into surrounding suburbs. The high-speed highways that circle major cities in America are symbols of the growth of suburbia. The move to the suburbs has become so widespread that the real life of a city is increasingly conducted in a ring of satellite cities. The central city is abandoned to the poor, the aged, and racial and ethnic minorities who still consider it their home. Through urban renewal programs, these residents are soon shunted aside to make way for high-rise office buildings; fountained plazas; expressways; and mass entertainment, commercial, educational, medical, or governmental centers to serve the needs of suburbanites.[12]

The process of urban exodus eventually makes everyone a suburbanite. In the seventies, the process has only begun. This expansion and dominance of suburbia obscure the human conditions imposed upon families headed by middle-aged and elderly couples. As we have noted many times before, it is the young who have their eyes on the future. The middle-aged and the elderly stress the past. In the present, however, their coexistence does not always smoothly mesh. Instead, with their needs and interests at odds, discontinuity ensues. The young are geared to change. The elders are geared to stability.

Social Control

Along with change, social control constitutes a whole new arena for generational dissonance. Social controls are the ways and means that bind individuals to their respective groups. As a field, social control is appealing to authoritarian elders but is repugnant to freedom-minded youth.[13] We will now examine generational dissent over such issues as the expression or repression of sexuality, identification with parents, and the achievement of autonomy within the broader field of social control.

Expression or Repression of Sexuality Few would deny the existence of erotic feelings. How and under what circumstances these feelings should be expressed is an issue that has split generations of contemporary Americans. Our society has emerged from a repressive history of Puritanism, asceticism (a certain amount of self-denial or self-mortification), and an excessive prudery concerning sexuality. But just how far the trend toward sexual permissiveness has gone is not yet clear.

Laws, for example, have typically lagged far behind the real sexual mores of the times, and the present is no exception. It is still illegal for an unmarried adult man and an unmarried adult woman to have sexual intercourse voluntarily in any state, an act called fornication. It is also illegal for a married person to have coitus with someone other than his or her spouse, an act identified as adultery. Further, it is illegal for a man to engage in coitus with an underage girl, even when she consents—an act known as statutory rape. Yet, numerous studies and reports reveal these sexual acts are commonplace, discussed openly, and form part of the plot films, "family" newspapers, and magazines.[14]

Few legal cases are based upon outright violations of statutes that deal with sexual codes. Sexual escapades may well be associated with a legal case before the court, but sexual violations are incidental to a case and have little to do with the major charges placed against an individual or a couple.

One may well ask why these outdated laws remain in force. Does honoring them "in the breach" serve any purpose? Evidently, laws of this nature serve as expressions of civil morality. They may serve no other purpose than to note norms that are easily evaded. But they are far more significant as evidence of the durability of generational traditions.

The old double standard of sexual expression—freedom for men and repression for women—long espoused by past generations and currently defended by many in the over-thirty generations has been sorely weakened. Its demise, however, is still premature in the 1970s. Those under thirty tend to support a single standard for sexual expression, an acceptability of sexual experimentation, whether premarital or nonmarital, for both men and women. But even youthful generations accept the norm of sexual exclusiveness with their spouse as they both grow older. Interestingly enough, this is precisely the pattern of primitives—a comparatively free period of sexual experimentation while fairly young and a commitment to marriage when fully adult.

Identification with Parents   Kenneth Keniston noted in his analytical text *The Uncommitted, Alienated Youth in American Society*:

> In more static and less complex societies, parents rightly bring up their children to be like themselves in central ways. Young men do what their fathers did; young women copy their mothers; even in societies sufficiently complex to offer several options (e.g. to be a tiller of the soil, a warrior, or a priest) these options are clearly epitomized by the members of the older generation. To be sure, parents and children can often disagree, and the transition to adulthood is not always smooth. But relatively static societies usually permit something approaching a total identification of the younger generation with the one before it. From his father or others of his generation a man learns not only the personal qualities expected of an adult, but the religious outlooks and practices, the ways of working, the ways of dealing with relatives and non-relatives in the community. Relatively total identification means that a young man or woman can choose an exemplar present in the community and emulate him or her in full confidence that what proved adequate for one generation will prove adequate for the next.
>
> The problem of identification is inevitably more complicated for young Americans. Partly because of the pace of social change, identification must be cautious, selective, partial, and incomplete. Work changes; the skills essential to our parents no longer suffice for us; it is a rare (and usually unsuccessful) farmer or carpenter who does exactly what his father did. Women, too, know in their bones that the way they were raised as children may not suffice for their children, and anticipate that the fashions of child-rearing will continue to swing as they have in the past. To choose to be exactly like one's father or mother is to choose obsolescence; indeed it is literally impossible, if only because a pattern of life considered normal forty years ago would evoke such a different (and incredulous) response from one's contemporaries today.[15]

Empiric evidence that supports Keniston's analysis is abundant, but we will content ourselves with our own unpublished study of some 300 college students at a large midwestern state university. The data indicate that age peers were far more significant as models than parents.[16] The cues for conduct came from youthful colleagues and not from elders.

It is quite ego-deflating for parents to learn that they are not considered important models in work, morals, or family life itself. Generational dissonance, again, occurs when parents silently or openly plead with their children to emulate them and discover that it cannot, and will not, be so.

The Struggle for Autonomy   Generational dissent is also part of the struggle for autonomy on the part of younger generations. On the one hand, parents have held power over their children; on the other, children are gaining increasing power over their own lives. If all is to go smoothly, a delicate point must be reached when parents must learn to let go and children to be self-directing. Older generations tend to hold on longer than necessary for the well-being of the young, when, in fact, it is their own interests that are being served.

One can sympathize with older generations in their desire to cling to their parental powers, but we must realize that generations must inevitably part and go their separate ways. Like the booster rocket stages used for lunar explorations, each generation provides enough impetus for the next generation to explore the elusive future. Also like the boosters and the upper stages of lunar rockets, each generation must separate— one half dissipating in lower space and the other entering higher voids to determine what lies ahead. Fathering and mothering have some terminal point at which time the generations move apart—sometimes easily and sometimes marked by cries of outrage and disbelief.

Undoubtedly, the achievement of autonomy is a lifelong process, initiated in childhood and sustained in young adulthood. Erik Erikson, among others, has made much of the psychosocial stages through which American children pass in their early socialization.[17] He contends that the resolution of each stage can be either helpful or harmful and will affect later stages of life. For example, little children learn either trust or mistrust from their parents depending upon their handling. Trust comes from parental concern and distrust from parental neglect. In gaining control over their bodies in such matters as toilet training, dressing, or feeding, children experience either acceptance or rejection. In the United States, at least, children learn to compete actively with others or fail to compete. If they succeed, they acquire a sense of adequacy that builds self-confidence. If they fail, they acquire a sense of inadequacy that shadows their lives. As preadolescents, they either have a sense of self-worth or are troubled by a sense of inferiority that is not easily shed. As adolescents, individuals affirm their identities or experience *identity confusion* that colors much of their future.

Erikson's analysis has much to commend it. He sees younger generations as being acted upon by older generations; he is also aware of the subjective responses of younger generations in terms of independence or dependence. What Erikson neglects, however, are experiences beyond childhood. Orville G. Brim, Jr., among others, makes up for this shortcoming by stressing "socialization through the life cycle."[18] Socialization continues to prepare younger generations for adult roles "yet dimly seen."[19] This process continues in college, in graduate school, in job training, in military service, in love affairs, and in widening circles of friends and neighbors.

In the course of achieving autonomy, younger generations seriously quarrel with their elders over being forced to choose between their childish idealism and their more adult realism. As dependent children, younger generations are filled with idealistic visions. As increasingly independent individuals, they soon discover the harsher realities of life from which, it would seem, their parental generations sheltered them. Unless it is understood as a strategy of socialization and not one of deliberate falsehood, this shattering of ideals can be considered betrayal and hypocrisy on the part of elders. Older generations have felt, in the more recent past, that children can absorb only limited information and so have engaged in what amounts to progressive revealment of truths rather than full details, including the many shortcomings of human society. A new breed of adults, however, has appeared that refuses to shed ideals gained in childhood. They ask that ideals be realized and accordingly have called their elders to account.

Values in Jeopardy

Change and control are areas of generational dissent, but far more basic are social values. The extent to which one generation can convince the next that the values that guide them are appropriate will determine whether they can live together harmoniously or not. When values can no longer be shared, each generation will seek its own independence.

The Case of the Vietnam War While many events have been prominent in the 1960s and early 1970s, none approaches the national magnitude of the Vietnam war. This war has been one of the most controversial in American history. Some have said that it began and was supported by a determination to aid a free nation fighting for its life. Others have insisted that a frightful toll in lives and property has been exacted to pay for the selfish ambitions of the powerful and wealthy. The publication of the *Pentagon Papers* in the midst of the war was a startling event.[20] The papers revealed what many had long suspected: clandestine decisions in which the American public was manipulated to believe that its sacrifices could achieve honorable ends.

However, the story of the Vietnam war, with its public confessions of human errors, does not concern us here. What does is the extent to which the war has affected generational dissent—particularly as expressed within families.

Since some perspective is lost because the event is still close at hand, there is very little empirical data to ascertain what the war has done to generational relationships. Some information, however, suggests that many of the younger generation, particularly those who were or are subject to military service, have turned sharply away from their elders, viewing them as complicit, unfeeling or dedicated to values that traffic in human suffering. The bonds of mutual love and respect are often severed between parents and children under such circumstances. The children of prominent "war hawks" have received attention in the media—those who drop out of college, turn to drugs, roam the world aimlessly, or involve themselves in political activism and social service. But some of the less publicized, less prominent children of middle- and lower-class parents have also lost faith in their elders. When such parents continue to speak of love, kindness, gentility, and piety, their words cannot mask their deeds. Their children no longer find comfort in their counsel.

Escapism   The realities of adulthood shatter the idealism of youth, and escapism or retreat from reality is a familiar tactic to meet the situation. Younger generations have increasingly turned to drugs or "drug abuse," to the dismay of their elders. They, in turn, point to the long-established alcoholic tradition of their elders. Just as many young people regard the smoking of marijuana as harmless, so have older persons defended their own drinking habits as being sociable and harmless when enjoyed in moderation. In either case, once an enjoyable experience has been established, there is the strong possibility of repetition and a widening search for even greater euphoria. Such have been the case histories of both drug addicts and alcoholics.[21]

The fight for legalization of the sale and use of alcoholic beverages is past history. The fight for the legalization of "harmless" drugs is more contemporary and still heated. Some of the long prison terms for drug offenders are strongly reminiscent of the sentences for rumrunners and bootleggers during Prohibition.

One fact that emerges from the debate over drug abuse is the increasing dependence of both old and young on a variety of medications. There seems to be a pill for everything—for insomnia or keeping awake, for hyperactivity or depression, for anxiety or listlessness. "Happiness through pills" has been identified as a national drug problem and not one of generational disagreement. Furthermore, many businessmen have marketed harmful or useless pills for profit. These members of the older generations add fuel to the youngsters' claim of hypocrisy. This further widens the generation gap between generations.

Values in Work and Leisure   The old-fashioned virtues of satisfying work and rewarding leisure are questioned by younger Americans. They are profoundly aware of the "rat race," the "treadmills to oblivion," or the tedium of whatever their parents' generation have done with their lives. One frequently hears young adults say that they want "something more" than work interspersed with leisure. Money, savings, or frugality strike some of the young as absurd values upon which to stake one's life.

It has been said that the values of the "new breed" revolve around a determination to improve the quality of life for every level of American society. It is an attempt to fulfill "the American dream." This is "the good life" many of the younger generation seek, and it is a far cry from the self-centeredness of their elders.

Values in Science and Reason   In academic circles, at least, science and reason are enshrined values. They seem to be shared by many of the younger generation who come to college campuses to learn. However, a more socially conscious generation that distrusts mechanistic science and cold-hearted reason has developed. Science and reason are replaced with humanitarianism and with emotionality, values long submerged in the contemporary United States, as far as the young are concerned. What is needed, they say repeatedly, is an enlargement of their family circles, their feelings of primariness, their desire for brotherhood and sisterhood. These values excite young people far more than prosaic data and colorless logic.

Concerned service to drug addicts, the suicide-prone, or the poor are examples of a growing humanitarianism among the young. Expressiveness in dancing, singing, clothing, or frank discussion have become the hallmarks of those among the younger generations who rate feeling above reasoning.

Neither science nor reason has saved society, and modern youth has turned to spirituality, to unabashed mysticism, to find their way. Fundamentalistic conversions have attracted many youngsters far more than conservative, circumspect, church congregations. Oriental philosophies have flourished more than Western thought.

Whether by unconventional dress, beliefs, or practices, the younger generation seeks to both shock and shame elder generations into closer conformity with their own values. Their vision is one of a youth-led society, a reversal that sorely troubles elders who see the present time as "out of joint" and the source of youthful dissent.

SUMMARY

Generational dissent is not new to human history, but formal study of it is still fairly new. Theorists such as Justin Dromel and José Ortega y Gasset have stressed the inevitability of dissent from the perspective of evolution. Because we are concerned with present generations in the United States, the contemporary view is one of drastic revolution, a fundamental change in direction that brings about generational outcry. In this chapter, social change, social control, and social values are examined as sources of generational discontinuity, particularly as manifested in contemporary family life.

The rate of social change has become so rapid that impermanence or transcience are viewed as a better adaptation than permanence. Such a fast tempo of life has developed that families, once regarded as refuges from the frantic pace of life, have themselves often become arrangements or liaisons in which men and women prefer to come and go as they please.

Older generations testify to the virtues of permanent, legitimate, responsible relationships with spouses and children. Younger generations dissent enough to experiment, for a time at least, with relationships that are more fragile. In addition, rapid change means greater mobility for families. Many families feel no need to be committed to one community. Everything is seen as portable, exchangeable, duplicated elsewhere. The preference for stability on the part of the elderly means that they are the ones who remain behind. The political and social issues in communities are treated very differently by the stable elderly and the mobile young. In this instance, generational dissent takes the form of arguments hammered out in local elections and local politics.

Generational dissent also occurs when social controls are at stake. Youth seeks to be free, while older generations cling to their powers. Dissent also centers on the expression or repression of sexuality. Dissent develops as alienation in which parental generations are not regarded as appropriate models for contemporary youth.

The extent to which generations can share values will determine if they can live together harmoniously or in dissent. With increasing frequency there is an aversion to former values because these have become identified with a demoralizing conflict in Vietnam, with the tedium of work and leisure, and with the failure of science and reason to achieve a livable environment for all Americans. Humanitarianism, emotionality, and spiritual rededication motivate the "new breed" and turn them away from their elders. What is most striking is that generational dissent has reached such an impasse that young and old generations cannot agree on escapist techniques upon which they depend.

REFERENCES

1 Julián Marías, *Generations: A Historical Method*, trans. Harold C. Raley, University,: The University of Alabama Press, 1970.
2 Ibid., pp. 32–33.
3 Ibid., p. 39.
4 Bernard Farber, *Family: Organization and Interaction*, San Francisco: Chandler Publishing Company, 1964, pp. 29–30.
5 Marías, op. cit., p. 81.
6 Marías, op. cit., pp. 96–97.
7 For example, see Walt Anderson, (ed.), *The Age of Protest*, Pacific Palisades, Calif.: Goodyear Publishing Company, Inc., 1969, and *The Annals of the American Academy of Political and Social Science*, vol. 382, March 1969.
8 Alvin Toffler, *Future Shock*, A Bantam Book Published by arrangement with Random House, Inc., New York: Bantam Books Inc., 1971.
9 Ibid., p. 14.
10 Ibid., p. 15.
11 Ibid., p. 239.
12 See, for example, Robert F. Winch, *The Modern Family*, New York: Holt, Rinehart and Winston, Inc., 1971, pp. 135–137.
13 One of the early texts was Joseph S. Roucek and Associates, *Social Control*, 2d ed., New York: D. Van Nostrand Company, Inc., 1956. It stands in contrast with Arlene S. Skolnick and Jerome H. Skolnick, *Family in Transition: Rethinking Marriage, Sexuality, Child Rearing, and Family Organization*, Boston, Mass.: Little Brown and Company, 1971.
14 One classic study is Lester A. Kirkendall, *Premarital Intercourse and Interpersonal Relationships*, New York: The Julian Press, Inc., 1961. A research study of interpersonal relationships based on case histories of 668 premarital intercourse experiences reported by 200 college-level males.
15 Adapted from "Social Change and Youth in America," by Kenneth Keniston, in *Youth: Change and Challenge*, edited by Erik H. Erikson, © 1961 by the American Academy of Arts and Sciences, © 1963 by Basic Books, Inc., Publishers, New York.
16 Jerry Lewis and Marvin R. Koller, an unpublished study of 300 college students, their kinship patterns, and their "significant others."
17 Erik H. Erikson, *Childhood and Society*, 2d ed., New York: W. W. Norton & Company, Inc., 1963.
18 Orville G. Brim, Jr., and Stanton Wheeler, *Socialization After Childhood: Two Essays*, New York: John Wiley & Sons, Inc., 1966.
19 Ibid., pp. 18–24.
20 Neil Sheehan, Hedrick Smith, E. W. Kenworthy, and Fox Butterfield, *The Pentagon Papers*, New York: Bantam Books, Inc., 1971.
21 A useful study is Andrew T. Weil, Norman E. Zinberg, and Judith M. Nelsen,

"Clinical and Psychological Effects of Marijuana in Man," *Science*, vol. 162, pp. 1234–1242, Dec. 13, 1968.

STUDY QUESTIONS AND ACTIVITIES

1 What issues separate generations, and how are they manifested in families?
2 What "symbolic family estates" have you inherited? Has your acceptance, modification, or rejection of these *vicengias* led to family dissent or quarrels?
3 If you could leave your children a worthy heritage, what would it be?
4 Restate Dromel's generational stages in more contemporary terms.
5 Do you believe the author correct in his assessment of social control, social change, and social values as the key areas at issue between and among generations? What other areas would you include?
6 Suggest examples of how major events in the world or in the United States have become family-centered dilemmas.
7 Over what values do you and your parents disagree?
8 Suggest a list of key social changes that you have witnessed within your own lifetime. How have these separated you from other generations?
9 Argue for and against the licensing of marriage by the state.
10 Discuss the following: In the United States, at least, children learn to actively compete with others or fail to compete. If they succeed, they acquire a sense of adequacy. If they fail to compete, they acquire a sense of inferiority that is not easily shed.

SUGGESTED ADDITIONAL READINGS

Anderson, Walt (ed.), *The Age of Protest,* Pacific Palisades, Calif.: Goodyear Publishing Company, Inc., 1969.
Edmiston, Susan, "How to Write Your Own Marriage Contract," *Ms.*, Spring 1972.
Farberow, Norman L. (ed.), *Taboo Topics,* New York: Atherton Press, Inc., 1963.
Floyd, H. Hugh, Jr., "Dilemma of Youth: The Choice of Parents or Peers as a Frame of Reference for Behavior," *Journal of Marriage and the Family,* vol. 34, no. 4, pp. 627–634, November 1972.
McCaghy, Charles H., James K. Skipper, Jr., and Mark Lefton (eds.), *In Their Own Behalf: Voices from the Margin,* New York: Appleton-Century-Crofts, Inc., 1968.
Streib, Gordon F. (ed.), *The Changing Family: Adaptation and Diversity,* Reading, Mass.: Addison-Wesley Publishing Company, Inc., 1973.
Weinberg, Arthur, and Lila Weinberg, *Some Dissenting Voices: The Story of Six American Dissenters,* Cleveland: The World Publishing Company, 1970.
Wylie, Philip, *Generation of Vipers,* New York: Rinehart & Company, Inc., 1942.

Chapter 10

Generational Consensus

Whether on a microscale, as between two individuals, or on a macroscale, as between generations or, most commonly, between politicoeconomic blocs, it is much easier to deal with dissension than it is to deal with consensus. One explanation is the frequency with which discord, discontent, and differences culminate in violence, conflict, and rejection. The long history of the human species seems to be one of perennial aggressiveness, hostility, or destructiveness to achieve objectives. The price of survival has been the crushing of human lives, whether by physical death or by social death, that is, powerlessness, the inability to control one's destiny.

Perhaps this explains the portrayal of history as a never-ending series of "cold" and "hot" wars. It has been war or the threat of war that has dominated history, and not the relatively peaceful "interludes." Peace is often viewed as an apparently calm period in which the "seeds of destruction" are sown and brought to maturity. In other words, what are satisfying arrangements for some are unsatisfying for many others.

Apparent consensus is not good enough. Real consensus is necessary before generations can learn to fulfill their lives without fear.

Having discussed generational dissension in terms of change, control, and values in the preceding chapter, it would seem useful to balance the discussion with an exploration of the possibilities for consensus—a congruence of ideas and values that promotes generational accord, particularly in regard to family life.

GENERATIONAL COMMON GROUND

The young, middle-aged, and elderly generations share more common ground than they may realize. The model or schema appears somewhat as in Figure 10-1.

This configuration portrays all generations as acquiring, over time, some degree of power. The younger generations are typically beginning their bid for more control over their times. The middle-aged are more likely to be found at, or near, the pinnacle of their careers. And the elderly are somewhat removed from their former power status.

Such a schema suggests that the spread of both time and circumstance keeps each generation from understanding the position of the others. Further, it suggests that the middle-aged seem to be in the most favorable position to understand the difficulties of youth and the complaints of the elderly. In addition, the middle-aged know where they have been and where they will soon be. The schema also illustrates the widest gap—between the young and the elderly, with the middle-aged acting as mediator. But, most important of all, the schema recognizes the common life trajectories, the common experiences, the common direction, and the common ground upon which each generation stands.

If there is any truth in such a conceptualization, there is, then, some room for generational consensus—some way for generations to stand together to enhance each other's lives. With this prospect, future generations have a better chance of achieving consensus.

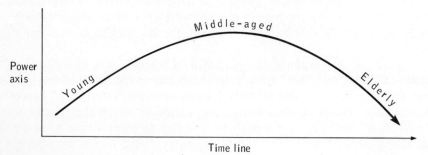

Figure 10-1   Generational common ground.

Searching for "A Happy Family"

One specific bit of common ground is the search for "a happy family." All generations complain that they have been seriously deprived by "missing out" on what they believe to be effective family life. Their frustrations are heightened when they learn through personal contacts or through the mass media that there are, or have been, many "successful," "adjusted," "happy," "flexible," "open," or "vital" families.[1] Such terms are used advisedly because there are many ways to be content, encouraged, or pleased with family life. Nevertheless, what emerges is the disbelief, the feeling of being cheated out of life chances, and the feeling of loss that accompanies the discovery that a good family life is possible.

The common search for happy family life does not mean that one single form of marriage, such as monogamy, must be relied upon to solve all generational problems. Rather, there is ongoing experimentation with workable formulas that bring men, women, and children together in some mutually satisfying way. This is precisely what is going on among the young, middle-aged, and elderly. However, many people refuse to believe that alternate life-styles can and should exist. This issue is only one of many that will have to be resolved.

Common Generational Needs

Generational consensus is possible, because all generations share the same basic needs. At least, generations seem to be moving in the same direction, although sometimes on separate courses. They might yet come together to achieve their goals.

Students of sociology become somewhat familiar with the various generalized "wishes" or "needs" hypothesized by Florian Znaniecki, W. I. Thomas, Vilfredo Pareto, Max Weber, Talcott Parsons, Karl Mannheim, and Arthur Maslow. The list compiled by Amitai Etzioni represents one of the more recent attempts to summarize the barest outlines of human needs.

In Etzioni's terms, the fundamental needs are (1) *affection* (solidarity, cohesion, or love), (2) *recognition* (self-esteem, achievement, or approval), (3) *context* (orientation, consistency, synthesis, meaning, or "wholeness"), (4) *repeated gratification* (an anti-neutrality inclination), (5) a degree of *stability* in the pattern of distribution of rewards, and (6) *variance in social structure* (variety of roles and norms to provide outlets for different personalities).[2] The first four are seen as "basic"; the remaining two are of a "second order" because they emerge from the first four. It is the frustration of these six needs that alienates generations, while the removal of frustrating barriers would go a long way toward achieving generational consensus.

These needs may not be satisfied simultaneously, as, for example, in the case of the desire for both variety *and* stability. But many families have proven themselves successful in bringing variant personalities together without seriously damaging the family structure. The same is true for universities that bring the broadest spectrum of disciplines together on a common campus. Stability is threatened when certain personality types seek to dominate or disallow others. In terms of family, the inability to tolerate other generations, the view that others are superfluous, obsolete, and anachronistic, stands in the way of consensus.

Specific Generational Needs

The reduction of alienation and the achievement of consensus depend on two other conditions: *participation* and *authenticity.* Etzioni has discussed them thoroughly in *The Active Society*, stating, "Ultimately, there is no way for a societal structure to discover the members' needs and adopt to them without the participation of the members in shaping and reshaping the structure."[3] Defined by Etzioni, authenticity is a "relationship or structure whose appearance and underlying reality are responsive to human needs."[4] In other words, pretense, hypocrisy, or outright dishonesty must be replaced by openness, integrity, and demonstrated sincerity.

One need not be a genius to see through the transparent admonitions of mothers and fathers who urge their children to behave for their own good. The parents who demand good grades or the mother who pleads that her daughter "act like a young lady" are expressing their own needs, not those of their children. The young resent being pawns in the "games" of their parents. To be used or manipulated is inauthenticity in action.

One ploy that needs to be recognized is the withdrawal stratagem, in which persons disavow association with or responsibility toward others. In families, it may take the form of withdrawal of love in order to secure conformity. This, too, is inauthentic because parents and children, young or old, educated or uneducated, rich or poor, black or white are *irrevocably* related to each other. There is no hiding place in our rather limited biosphere. Fleeing from each other only delays the time when persons and groups must come together.

In correlating consensus and control, Etzioni has suggested a typology of societies that goes far in explaining where American society now stands and where it might go in the future. A *passive society*, in his view, is one in which consensus and control are comparatively low. Those primitive societies in which political power is tribally segmented, with little or no apparatus for societal consensus, are of this passive type. Those societies in which there is high control but low consensus are *overmanaged* societies. Tyrannies, dictatorships, or ruthless oligarchies fit this category.

Drifting societies are represented by capitalistic democracies, such as that of the United States. Such societies are high on consensus but relatively low on controls.

And, finally, there is the ideal: *active* societies that are relatively high on both control and consensus.[5] Etzioni readily admits that active societies are utopian and do not now exist. Rather, they are projections for the future.[6] To achieve high degrees of control and consensus, "participatory democracy" may allow each generation to take part in shaping postindustrial and posturban society. Thus, young generations will be encouraged to build upon rather than destroy the bonds that unite the generations.

BRIDGE BUILDING

Thus far, we have stressed common ground that exists among and between generations. The common path or life cycle, the keen interest in a satisfying family life, the common generalized needs, and the more specific needs of participation and authenticity that could lead to a truly "active" society have been noted.

But, there are still gaps in need of bridging if consensus is to be achieved. Empirical data are being gathered that document the physical contact patterns of kindred in urban settings.[7] Physical contact, however, does not in itself constitute interactional patterns. Interactional patterns, by their very nature, can bring generations closer together in a family setting or can result in dissension or discord. For our purposes, bridge building includes (1) clear communication, (2) confrontation, (3) constructive argumentation, and (4) appropriate exchange or negotiation.

Communication

Clear communication depends upon saying what you mean and meaning what you say. It is part of the authenticity that Etzioni regards as paramount to an active society. The field of expertise known as conflict resolution might be applied to generational communication. This field usually concentrates upon diplomatic negotiations between political-economic power blocs. Some might consider this form of communication deceitful, indirect, and inauthentic. Others can accept the need for tact, finesse, and consummate skill in the search for consensus with complicated matters. Through conflict resolution, most persons can find clues to the settlement of differences, whether in the area of international diplomacy or of generational discord.

Ten precepts of conflict resolution that have achieved results are:[8]

1 Keep alert for symptoms of rising frustrations as proposals are set forth and deal with these before they become unmanageable.

2 Even if conflict arises out of communication of differences, continue to keep communication channels open.

3 It is essential to keep calm enough to draw upon intellectual reserves rather than upon emotional abilities.

4 All communication should be confidential enough to permit communicants some room for retreat, denial, or reorganization.

5 Examine closely the temperament of the chief spokesmen because this knowledge suggests what communicative procedures will be most effective.

6 Alternative "victories" are needed so that all communicants emerge with some prize of their own.

7 Candidly recognize when an impasse is reached, that is, when communication has revealed what appear to be insurmountable differences.

8 Identify as much common ground as possible.

9 Break larger issues into smaller components so that these may be discussed or explored.

10 If communication seems to be leading to a "victory" for one side and a "defeat" for another, further communication can provide for the sharing of "victory."

Those who have worked with the practical problems of tension reduction in families have translated these guidelines into ground rules for constructive quarreling, particularly as they apply to developing consensus between husbands and wives. For example, Henry Bowman, a pragmatic family-life educator, has offered the following:[9]

1 Unless cumulative experience suggests the contrary, each may assume that what the other says and does during the quarrel is the product of the tension involved and is not a true reflection of that individual's personality.

2 Each may assume that whatever judgments he makes during the quarrel are invalid. The judgments upon which action are based are better formed at a time when the individual is relatively calm and has regained his perspective.

3 Both may try to keep the quarrel within bounds. It need not be allowed to spread to other aspects of their relationship, their situation, or their personalities that had nothing to do with its origin. The couple need not shift from attacking the problem to attacking each other.

4 A quarrel may be kept private. It need not be allowed to occur in the presence of others, especially children.

5   A quarrel may further a couple's adjustment, if, instead of letting it generate ill will and insecurity, the couple forget it when it is over, let bygones be bygones, carry no grudges, and take a step forward in the clarified atmosphere following the storm.

6   Since the marriage is more important than the feelings of either party and in most cases much more important than the difference which precipitated the quarrel, it is important that each be willing to go more than halfway to effect a reconciliation. Sometimes the first step in this direction is easier for the person less at fault because his pride is not so great an obstacle to an apology.

7   The sooner after the quarrel the couple return to the pattern of affection and conversation which characterizes their marriage, the easier it will be; the longer they delay such a return, the more difficult it is likely to be.

Confrontation

It is important to get down to the real issues that divide generations if consensus is ever to occur. Much time and energy are lost in emotional rhetoric or in the dredging up of peripheral issues. It is precisely in this paring away of extraneous matters to reveal the real problems that *confrontation* has an important part to play. Confrontation is the climactic point at which problems must be resolved.

In the tragic confrontation documented in *Bury My Heart at Wounded Knee*, the destruction of Amerind preliterates by land-hungry European literates took place.[10] For many years, the expansion of the westward frontiers was defended, or rationalized, as "manifest destiny." In the 1970s, this confrontation can be seen as the contact between preindustrial societies and industrial societies that called for resolution. Historical hindsight reveals what happened. Sentimental appreciation of American Indian life in the past has been growing. Living generations of American Indians, however, have confronted non-Indians with their own longings for dignity, physical space, and growth. This time around, Amerinds are hopeful that consensus can be reached, that cultural pluralism can be encouraged rather than crushed.

Constructive Argumentation

In the discussion of communication, we have examined the differences between destructive and constructive quarreling. It is worth reiterating, however, that destructive quarreling goes off the target and further alienates participants. Constructive quarreling, by contrast, sticks to the central issue and reaches consensus. Destructive quarreling amounts to character assassination from which retreat is most difficult. Constructive quarreling seeks to solve problems. Destructive quarreling examines faults. Constructive argumentation examines strengths or assets.

Exchange or Negotiation

Finally, the ability to negotiate differences is vital to consensus. With tongue in cheek, one anonymous wit has suggested the following:

Suggestions to Teenagers on How to Get Along with their Parents
Don't be afraid to speak their language. Try using strange-sounding phrases like "I'll help you wash the dishes" and "Yes."

Try to understand their music. Play Glenn Miller's "Moonlight Serenade" on the stereo until you become accustomed to the sound.

Be patient with the underachiever. When you catch your dieting Mom sneaking salted nuts, don't show your disapproval. Tell her you like fat mothers.

Encourage them to talk about their problems. Try to keep in mind that to them, things like earning a living and paying off the mortgage seem important.

Be tolerant of their appearance. When your Dad gets a haircut, don't feel personally humiliated. Remember, it's important to him to look like his peers.

And most vital of all: If they do something you consider wrong, let them know *it's their behavior you dislike*, not themselves.

Remember, *parents need to feel they're loved*!

Returning to a more serious vein, the achievement of generational consensus requires careful bargaining practices. Demands on either side may be negotiable or nonnegotiable. Certainly, the right to exist is a nonnegotiable issue between and among generations. The negotiable demands, by comparison, allow room for a trade-off in which all sides can win some advantages. The manner or life-style of existence is negotiable. Many have remarked on the absence of humor, the dead seriousness of young Americans when they press their demands. To them, playing "games" with persons' lives leaves little room for humor. It is a perspective that merits respect and admiration from other generations that have tried to erect a screen of blissful ignorance about the life conditions of others.

There are, apparently, all sorts of games to be played with other peoples' lives. Game theory has attracted considerable attention in a wide variety of contexts—for purposes of economic gain, for the passage of legislation, or for social-psychological advantages, as in the popularized version of gamesmanship portrayed by Eric Berne in *Games People Play: The Psychology of Human Relationships*.[11] Such games as the "zero-sum game," in which there can be only one winner of scarce resources, "constant-sum games," in which there may be one big winner and at least one small winner, or a three-sided game, such as "lion, tiger, and fox," in which two powerful players and one thoughtful player can develop satisfying combinations are fascinating laboratory experimentations. But this is far removed from life itself.

Anatol Rapoport appropriately cautions:

> Presently the large gap between laboratory and life is viewed as a formidable obstacle in the task of developing a scientific approach to conflict resolution. It is indeed an insuperable gap, if one assumes it must be crossed by an inductive leap from a microcosm to macrocosm. Such a leap is possible only if the same "laws" govern both the events in the laboratory and those of the cosmos—as, for example, physical laws. No such universal laws are discernible in human affairs. Therefore, there can be no question of an inductive leap but only of patient bridge building from the study of miniature conflicts under controlled conditions and with clearly defined issues to large conflicts among ambivalently identified actors for poorly defined "stakes" obscured by myriads of interlocking issues.[12]

The "patient bridge building" that Rapoport mentions is worth stressing. Patience is a difficult quality to cultivate when generations find themselves engaged in mortal combat. It is so much easier for the "haves" to plead for patience than the "have nots." In generational terms, it is understandable why the elders recommend patience and the upcoming generations act out their impatience. Yet, patience is not simply a waiting game. It is an asset to those unheralded heroes and heroines who, step by step, have used available time to advantage. The so-called revolution or overnight reversals of the status quo did not just happen. They were the product of prolonged efforts to reach consensus. In the moves and countermoves of life situations, the "winners," in the end, are the patient ones who continued to think about what needed to be done.

Finally, it is the understanding who are flexible and the ignorant who are inflexible. Those who comprehend the nature of generational differences are in a far better position to continue to negotiate, build bridges, or seek consensus than those who must have their own way and so isolate or cut themselves off from further help. At the family level, this means that generations must continue to counsel with each other or suffer the consequences of dissension.

The Developmental Stake and Generational Consensus

Another theory, derived from the studies of Vern L. Bengtson and Joseph A. Kuypers, suggests how generational understanding can be achieved. This theory centers on the concept of the "developmental stake."[13] Bengtson and Kuypers call attention to "perceptions" of intergenerational differences. They consider these perceptions just as important in relationships between generations as differences in philosophy, attitude, or action within generations. These perceptions emerge from two myths: the *fear-of-loss* myth, in which each generation fears it will somehow lose something of value if it is not careful and the *developmental stake* myth, in which one generation's rejection of another generation's values is believed to negate that generation's reasons for living.

In the studies of Bengtson and Kuypers, both parents and children believe that there is disagreement in interpersonal relationships such as family procedures, tolerance, and lack of respect. But there is a different type of divergence from that point. Children perceive values dealing with morality, politics, and life goals as generational points of friction, whereas parents perceive their children's personal habits and traits as points of stress. Older generations are saying that, in time, youth will grow up and change its perspectives. Younger generations are saying that they already have changed, and that these changes deal with fundamental values and life goals.

Just what developmental stake or need for another generation is there? Youth sees parents as expendables who are to be cast off because they have completed their nurturing and socializing functions. Parents view younger generations as heirs, as carriers of values, as essential in sustaining generational continuity. Youth wishes to *establish* itself. Parents wish to *validate* themselves.

Bengston and Kuypers' point of view is conciliatory and generous. They believe that awareness of differences between generations will help. Parents should also understand that the urgings of youth do not forecast the imminent collapse of social structures, but rather suggest constructive changes. Youthful desire for autonomy does not necessarily mean wholesale rejection of all that older generations hold dear. Most important, Bengtson and Kuypers warn against the "moral error" of one generation's trying to validate itself through the control of another. In the end, each generation must let the other go free.

SUMMARY

Generational dissension is far easier to contemplate than consensus. History is portrayed as a neverending series of "cold" and "hot" wars. Indeed, peace may be viewed as an apparently calm period in which "the seeds of destruction" are planted and brought to maturity. Real rather than apparent concensus is necessary for generations to enhance each other's lives.

"Common ground" does exist between contending generations. Each generation walks the same paths at different times and under different circumstances. Often the generations seem to lose sight of each other, but their common experiences eventually bring them closer together. This common ground includes the search for a "happy" family life; the fundamental needs for affection, contentment, repeated gratification, recognition, some degree of stability, and variance within social structures; and more specifically, participation and authenticity. A utopian society, or an "active" (filled-with-life) society, is possible if both consensus and control are at a high level.

Where common ground is lacking, bridge building among and between generations can bring about consensus. This process calls for clear communication, confrontation, constructive argument, and appropriate exchange or negotiation. Consensus, a congruence of values, a like-mindedness, requires patience and education.

REFERENCES

1 A number of studies can be so interpreted if one takes the positive rather than the negative approach that so many prefer. See, for example, Wesley R. Burr, "Satisfaction with Various Aspects of Marriage over the Life Cycle: A Random Middle Class Sample," *Journal of Marriage and the Family*, vol. 32, no. 1, pp. 29–37, February 1970.
2 Amitai Etzioni, *The Active Society: A Theory of Societal and Political Processes*, New York: The Free Press, 1968, pp. 624–625.
3 Ibid.
4 Ibid, p. 626.
5 Sarajane Heidt and Amitai Etzioni (ed.), *Societal Guidance: A New Approach to Social Problems*, New York: Thomas Y. Crowell, 1969, pp. 24–28.
6 Ibid., p. 26.
7 Bert N. Adams, *Kinship in an Urban Setting*, Chicago: Markham Publishing Company, 1968.
8 Editorial Research Reports, *Challenges for the 1970's*, William B. Dickinson, Jr., chief ed., Washington, D. C.: Congressional Quarterly, Inc., 1970, p. 154.
9 Henry A. Bowman, *Marriage for Moderns*, 6th ed., New York: McGraw-Hill Book Company, 1970, p. 404. Used with permission of McGraw-Hill Book Company.
10 Dee Brown, *Bury My Heart at Wounded Knee: An Indian History of the American West*, New York: Holt, Rinehart and Winston, Inc., 1970.
11 Eric Berne, *Games People Play: The Psychology of Human Relations*, New York: Grove Press, Inc., 1964.
12 Paul Swingle (ed.), *The Structure of Conflict*, New York: Academic Press, Inc., 1970, p. 40.

13 Vern L. Bengtson and Joseph A. Kuypers, "Generational Difference and the Developmental Stake," *Aging and Human Development*, vol. 2, pp. 249–260, 1971.

STUDY QUESTIONS AND ACTIVITIES

1 Suggest and criticize ways to bridge generational gaps.
2 Do your own family experiences agree with Bengtson and Kuypers' thesis that generational *perceptions* of differences are as important as the differences themselves?
3 What common ground exists between generations?
4 Do you agree or disagree that failure to achieve or experience a happy family constitutes serious deprivation?
5 In what specific instances have you uncovered what you consider to be inauthentic behavior in your family or in your own generation?
6 Categorize societies around the world as "passive," "overmanaged," "drifting," or "active." Compare your decisions with those of your classmates.
7 Translate the ten precepts for conflict resolution into personal, familial, and generational terms.
8 Contrast constructive and destructive quarreling.
9 What is achieved by confrontations over family or generational issues?
10 Do you share Bengtson and Kuypers' view that, in the final analysis, one generation cannot find validation by dominating the lives of another?

SUGGESTED ADDITIONAL READINGS

Alexander, C. Norman, "Status Perceptions," *American Sociological Review*, vol. 37, no. 6, pp. 767–773, December 1972.
Bengtson, Vern L., and Joseph A. Kuypers, "Generational Difference and the Developmental Stake," *Aging and Human Development*, vol. 2, pp. 249–260, 1971.
Benson, Leonard, *The Family Bond: Love and Sex in America*, New York: Random House, Inc., 1971.
Cavan, Ruth S., "Family Tensions between the Old and the Middle-Aged," in R. F. Winch, R. McGinnis, and H. R. Barringer (eds.), *Selected Studies in Marriage and the Family*, New York: Holt, Rinehart and Winston, Inc., 1962.
Edwards, John N., and Mary Ball Brauburger, "Exchange and Parent-Youth Conflict, "*Journal of Marriage and the Family*, vol. 35, no. 1, pp. 101–107, February 1973.
Elkin, Meyer, "Conciliation Courts: The Reintegration of Disintegrating Families," *The Family Coordinator*, vol. 22, no. 1, pp. 63–71, January 1973.
Silverstein, Harry, *The Sociology of Youth: Evolution and Revolution*, New York: The Macmillan Company, 1973.
Swingle, Paul (ed.), *The Structure of Conflict*, New York: Academic Press, Inc., 1970.

Chapter 11

Preparation for Family Life

In the previous chapters, our focus has been on the multigenerational study of families. This chapter concerns the processes by which men and women meet and marry in the United States. Men and women are alleged to choose each other freely, but the selection processes have been studied for generations and are neither as free nor as mysterious as young people caught up in marital preparations may believe.

The entryways to marriage and family are rather ritualized in more traditional societies. In the modern United States, however, a number of personal options are involved. Because they set a life pattern that can be enriching or debasing, decisions in marital choices are critical. Young men and women can settle their destinies on the basis of how well, or how poorly, they prepare for marriage.

MATE SELECTION OR SPOUSE SELECTION?

In marriage and family literature, the term applied most often to preparatory stages is *mate selection.* Mating, of course, occurs throughout the

227

animal kingdom. It has little to do with the sociocultural factors that distinguish Homo sapiens from other creatures. The term *mate selection*, however, implies that it is the mating of heterosexual couples that passes on life to the next generation.

To incorporate both mating and the transmission of generational values, the term *spouse selection* is preferable for multigenerational analysis. Spouse selection takes into account the various ways that generations have prepared men and women to be *husbands* and *wives*, and not simply mates. Preparation for marriage and family life depends heavily upon how generations define the status and roles of husbands and wives. Once generations determine what is expected of them, the preparations for marriage become bounded by sociocultural limits. As these objectives change, new generations must reshape the forms imposed by older generations.

A TYPOLOGY OF MARITAL PREPARATIONS

Figure 11-1 suggests a number of configurations that are either current or possible, depending upon husband-wife goals.

Type A, the "open-ended megaphone," approximates the process of spouse selection in the United States up to now. There are minimal requirements for eligibility. Almost all men and women are assumed to be ready for marriage if they are of age, free to marry, and mutually agreeable. Termination of marriage, however, is viewed as much more serious, and is made more difficult by the imposition of selected "grounds" to validate divorce.

Type B, the "closed cone," represents the pattern that many would like to impose on marriage because they find divorce abhorrent. Proponents of the closed cone would retain the freedom to enter into marriage, but they would make it impossible to break up a marriage after it has been consummated. Because it would allegedly make persons think more seriously about their marital preparations and choices than at present, advocates of the closed cone believe it to be superior to the open-ended megaphone.

Type C, the "reversed megaphone," recognizes that the problems of marriage are not so much matters of exit as they are of entrance. Accordingly, much greater preparation for marriage would be needed than exists at present. The few who meet the entrance requirements would be given much more leeway to terminate the marriage if problems proved to be insurmountable. Marriage educators could approve of the reversed-megaphone pattern because persons entering marriage would be far better prepared to deal with marital problems and therefore less likely

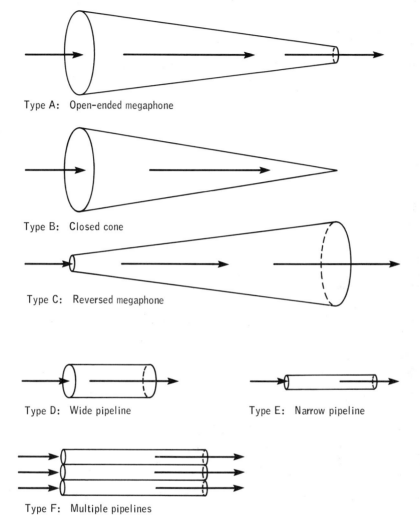

Type A: Open-ended megaphone

Type B: Closed cone

Type C: Reversed megaphone

Type D: Wide pipeline

Type E: Narrow pipeline

Type F: Multiple pipelines

Figure 11-1 Patterned configurations in spouse selection.

to divorce. Marriage would be treated as a profession, a commitment to a way of life requiring deliberate, hard-won training. Once qualified for marriage, as in any profession, persons could choose to leave it as circumstances dictated.

Types D and E, the "wide pipeline" or the "narrow pipeline," make the entrance into marriage either easy or difficult and match the exits from marriage with identical procedures. The wide-open entryway to marriage seems to have powerful support. The wide-open exit, a departure from the older open-ended megaphone configuration, is a pattern that present generations seem to want established. "No-fault" divorce laws are gaining in popularity as a far more honest definition of marital incompatibilities than the older pattern of finding one party to a divorce "guilty" and the other "innocent." The narrower matrimonial channel would restrict marriage to the "qualified" and permit all others to engage in nonmarital activities. While allowing some margin for error, the narrow pipeline would keep divorce actions under far greater control than currently exists. Such a pattern might be acceptable to a highly regimented society or subsociety but, more likely, would be rejected in the United States.

Finally, Type F, "multiple pipelines" of various dimensions, allows a variety of marital preparations or entryways. The advocates of this form would legitimate whatever marital forms or procedures were found acceptable by various groups of persons. Consenting adults would determine for themselves which pathways they would travel and prepare themselves accordingly. Type F marital configurations are not as far off in the future as many might think. Multiple pipelines can be given legal substance when lawmakers are convinced that de facto conditions of multiple ways to be married already exist.

THE MULTISTAGE FILTER THEORY OF SPOUSE SELECTION[1]

By fixing the open-ended megaphone configuration in a vertical position, a funnel-like pattern emerges. At the top, or entryway, the opening is very large to accommodate maximum numbers. At the bottom, increasing restrictions have brought about highly selected marital partnerships. Those who enter the funnel encounter a series of "filters" that screen or sort persons as potential spouses. Such is the barest outline of marital preparation as it is currently conceived by marriage and family theorists (see Figure 11-2). It is a pattern that effectively pulls together a wealth of accumulating data on what seems to be the process of spouse selection within the United States.

Theoretically, as in Bernard Farber's model of spouse selection, every heterosexual adult within one's society, or even beyond one's society, is permanently available as a potential spouse.[2] But this huge reservoir of potential spouses is effectively reduced by the available supply of possible partners with whom an individual might associate. In the United States, at least, dating is the process whereby persons become better acquainted. Proximity limits potential partners to those persons fairly close to one's own locale.

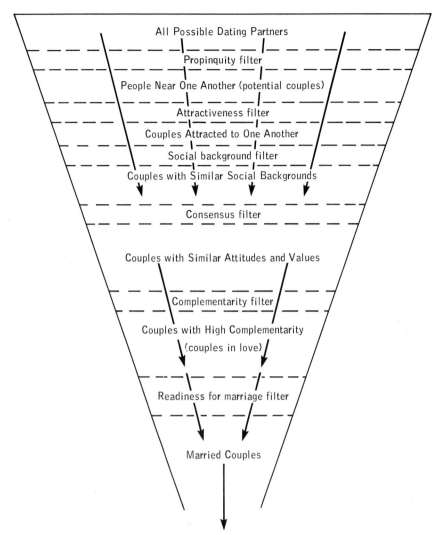

Figure 11-2 The multistage filter theory of spouse selection. (*Adapted* from J. Richard Udry, The Social Context of Marriage, *2d ed., Philadelphia: J. B. Lippincott Company, 1971, p. 13*)

As persons come to know each other, they accept or reject relationships according to the multistage filter theory of spouse selection. Consciously or unconsciously, the couples who accept one another are drawn together by the similarity of their social backgrounds, origins, or traditions. Closer contact, experience, and consideration enable each participant to see those personality factors that reflect key attitudes and values. If these attitudes and values are similar or compatible, the couple draws closer together. Ultimately, couples determine if their attitudes, values, wishes, or needs complement or reinforce each other enough to screen out all other potential spouses. Finally, as the multistage filter theory explains, couples in love reach a stage of readiness and commitment to each other, and so emerge as married couples.

A CRITIQUE OF THE MULTISTAGE FILTER THEORY OF SPOUSE SELECTION

There is much to commend the multistage filter theory. It suggests that informally, often unconsciously, men and women are prepared for marriage. Education courses in marriage and family have also attracted thousands in public schools and universities, although far greater numbers have not experienced such training or even found it desirable. Nevertheless, many studies have confirmed the sifting, screening, filtering conception of spouse selection. Whether the filtering processes operate in every case in precise, logical order is questionable. Little is said or explained concerning those persons who are turned back by the filters to prior stages to try again to find other partners. And, finally, far greater numbers pass through the filters than do not.

Age-specific marriage proportions in early 1970 were approximately 67 percent for males fourteen years old or older, and 62 percent for females fourteen years of age or older.[3] Starting at the mid-twenties for both men and women and continuing into the fifties and sixties, the age-specific marriage proportions ran well into the 80 percentiles.[4] The filters apparently work, but such high proportions of self-selected and mutually agreeable married couples suggest that persons encounter little difficulty getting past them.

In many ways, preparation for marriage and family, in the United States, at least, is left to chance. The chance factors are essentially those that generations, both past and present, have bequeathed to those about to enter marriage and family life.

Despite the consensus on attitudes and values, despite the high complementarity, and despite the readiness for marriage, incompatibles do seem to get together and proceed to make life miserable for each other and for those whose lives they touch. Relatively high rates of divorce, desertion, and separation testify that selective partnership still leaves a wide margin for error. Even more damaging testimony comes from studies that show the gradual disenchantment, the gradual erosion of unity, for many married couples.[5] Today most of us appear to recognize that preparations for marriage and family life are quite lax and that when intolerable conditions exist as a result of careless choices or decisions, the appropriate action is to dissolve the relationship without recriminations for either party.

Dating as Preparation for Marriage

Just how does dating help prepare couples for marriage? It is a fairly common practice in the United States, although other societies are known to encourage the free association of unmarried couples as an initial stage of marital preparation. In most of the known cultures of the world, dating serves no useful purposes, because other conditions make it either unnecessary or unwanted. These conditions include the relative homogeneity of the population, the greater acceptance of premarital sexual permissiveness or its reverse, and the greater control of the elders over the young through early and arranged marriages.

To Americans, however, dating is alleged to be instructive in terms of getting to know members of the opposite sex, in testing one's own sexuality, in gaining social graces, or in discovering attributes that lend themselves to forming compatible partnerships. In brief, Americans have great faith in dating as marital preparation.

The differences between dating and spouse selection, however, are profound. For example, dating has a fun orientation. It involves enjoying oneself in the company of one or more persons of the opposite sex. Conversational skills, popularity, participation in various events, sexual dalliance, relaxing, posing, laughing, teasing, dancing, or social drinking are all prominent aspects of dating. Spouse selection, by contrast, is a serious enterprise. Its concern is with determining which person will become a lifetime helpmate, sharing the joys and sorrows that make up marriage and family life, and shows the greatest promise for flexibility, adaptability, growth, or strength in the unknown vicissitudes that lie ahead.

Dating is commonly confused with spouse selection because the two processes often coincide. What is dating for some is spouse selection for others. After all, when one person grows serious about the other, dating still continues and can be said to be fused with the selection process.

Dating in its purest form is the American gateway to spouse selection. Formal selection occurs as dating becomes "steady," prolonged, exclusive, and a fairly conscious exploration of personalities and social backgrounds in order to determine marital potentials. The qualities that make for a good date, however, are not necessarily the same qualities that make for a good spouse. Fun orientation has its place and certainly relieves tensions built up from routines, drabness, or sheer survival. But conversational finesse, exercise of social amenities, joking, or popularity do not meet the long-range demands of marriage and family life such as dedication and loyalty to one's spouse, mutual support and comfort, ability to meet emergencies, or the socialization of children.

Because dating does have a fun orientation, its short-run nature allows participants to present themselves as good-natured companions. But as many discover to their chagrin, the masks or imagery are torn away when a marital partner is required to sustain his or her performance through many years. There apparently are many more actors and actresses in real life than there are on the stage.

American norms tend to treat dating as adolescent behavior in which the immature can mimic their elders in heterosexual-couple activities. Dating, however, does not apply exclusively to relatively young generations. One revealing finding is that divorced persons often remarry quickly, in contrast to the delayed response of younger persons contemplating a first marriage.[6] Prolonged dating serves no purpose for older generations because the persons involved have (or think they have) a much clearer picture of what they are seeking. In addition, we should consider the remarriages of widows and widowers of advanced ages who find a second or third marriage a source of great satisfaction. In these marriages of the older generations, we find even greater recognition that dating is enjoyable but does not truly prepare persons for daily life together. Time is far more precious to the elderly, and they choose not to waste it in dating. In defense of the young, of course, dating generally begins in adolescence and is an important part of their lives for years. Their readiness for marriage is delayed because of rising educational, economic, or political standards.

The Propinquity Filter

Propinquity, or nearness, has remained one of the least conscious factors in spouse selection. To be sure, as persons gain more freedom to go beyond their home communities, they widen the choices available to them. But during much of their childhood and adolescence, their circle is limited to those persons living near their homes. It is in this sense that parents have much to do with the early choices of persons with whom their children associate and among whom they may select spouses.[7]

Propinquity, of course, operates in a number of settings. Attendance at a college or university requires residence on or near a campus, and while the stated function is education, the latent function is to bring great numbers of potentially attractive persons together in a spouse-selection pool. By taking a job or a position in a highly populated locale, persons are thrown together, thus the chances that they will meet potential spouses increase. People frequent certain haunts—resorts, parks, sport centers, beaches, hotels, bars—because propinquity is essential to "chance" meetings. In the comparative isolation of a cruise ship, many persons claim to have selected each other when, in reality, propinquity, whether contrived or not, brought them together. Untold numbers of spouses can trace their earliest contacts to the relative isolation of living and working within some highly limiting setting, such as military service or a temporary job assignment. As James H. S. Bossard expressed the impact of propinquity, "Cupid has wings, but he does not fly very far."[8]

Attractiveness

Sheer propinquity is, of course, necessary but not sufficient to bring couples together. One person is to be selected out of the many who are near. Perhaps no student of marriage and family has analyzed the process of how attractiveness works in couple selection as well as Willard Waller in *The Family: A Dynamic Interpretation*.[9] He described the process as "unwilling involvement," because he was aware of the reluctance of some couples to become "too close" on the basis that persons can hurt or exploit each other in couplehood. Some degree of caution is normal. For those who throw caution to the winds, "affairs" become highly risky liaisons that lead to much personal grief.

Waller analyzed the involvement process as consisting of six steps or stages:[10]

1 Coquetry
2 The line
3 Light love
4 Lovers' quarrels
5 Separations
6 Pair unity

The initial steps come close to what the multistage filter theory of spouse selection calls "attractiveness." Coquetry or flirtatiousness can be a cultivated art, and it has most often been portrayed as deliberate scheming. But, in Waller's terms, *everyone* is unconsciously engaged in "being himself," and this constitutes coquetry or is attractive to *preconditioned*, potential partners. By manner, dress, facial expression, or expressed views, individual men and women are noticed. They stand out of the crowd and secure the attention and interests of observers.

"The line" is a bit cynical, but it follows coquetry quite closely. In brief, not only must a person be attractive to another but the attractiveness must be sustained. This is the function of the line. As in coquetry, a line may well be rehearsed and consciously improved upon, or, more likely, it forms part of the personality so that one can speak to a comparative stranger with some ease.

The stage of "light love" goes beyond coquetry and the use of lines, to some mutual recognition of an interest in couplehood. The bonds of the couple are not strong, and they are rather free to break away from each other whenever they choose. Typically, one of the partners feels more emotionally attracted than the other, but this feeling is kept under control and is not revealed.

Quarreling and separations are common hazards that threaten to break couples apart once they have moved into the light love stage. They do not occur in *all* cases, but Waller sees them as being incorporated into the involvement process because they do, indeed, unite couples as never before. Original attractiveness has brought couples close enough to reveal differences. If the couples can resolve these differences through quarreling, they have become problem-solving "teams." Their attractiveness for each other is more confirmed than ever in such a turn of events.

Whether brought about by a quarrel or without a dispute, leaving each other for extended periods of time may be necessary for couples attracted to each other. An "out-of-sight, out-of-mind" pattern becomes possible. But, if the separation has heightened the sense of loss, attractiveness is confirmed and the couples seek ways and means to come together again.

And, finally, in Waller's view, the twosome enters into a state of "pair unity"; two have become one. Couples have an unique history of their own. They have private jokes that only they can understand. They celebrate their montheversaries or anniversaries and speak of "their song," "their place," and "their plans." It is a relationship in which a third party is an intruder by reason of his or her unfamiliarity with what has transpired in the history of the couple.

In this analysis, Waller explains *how* attractiveness seems to work for most couples in the United States. But, the reasons *why* they find each other attractive is another matter. Some can explain attractiveness on the bases of individual tastes. Sociologists, however, are among the first to stress that individual preferences are social products. Tastes are not matters of whimsy but are shaped by the conditioning of one's society. These prior inputs are the social backgrounds that the multistage filter theory presents as narrowing down choices, once attraction is felt.

Similarity of Social Backgrounds

Reminiscent of Franklin Henry Giddings' "consciousness of kind," similarity of social backgrounds provides a common foundation.[11] In modern terms, this is *homogamy* in action—the choice of persons who are similar to each other rather than dissimilar. A number of studies affirm the high similarities of couples who choose each other on the bases of religion,[12] race,[13] social class,[14] intelligence,[15] nationality,[16] occupation,[17] or generation.[18]

Yet, there are elements of *heterogamy* to a smaller or larger degree in most relationships. Heterogamy is *preferential* mating in which individuals prefer that which they lack. In these areas of dissimilarity, couples find that opposites do not attract each other, but rather tend to strongly oppose each other. As the couples find complementarity, the differences become strengths rather than weaknesses (see Figure 11-3). If, however, they grate upon each other, social differences or oppositions lead to conflict, pain, and disunity. The only exceptions are those rare instances in which highly dissimilar couples reach consensus through their common delight in constant fighting or their abilities to maintain an appearance of solidarity.

In sum, homogamous selections demand little "social engineering" to bridge whatever gaps still remain between a man and a woman. Heterogamous choices, by contrast, demand considerable efforts to devise ways and means to achieve pair unity (see Figure 11-4).

Consensus

Similarity of social backgrounds, then, does operate to bring couples together, but the selective process continues among those who share similar attitudes and values. Herein lies acknowledgment that individuals are "ready to act" toward similar or common goals.

Most individuals tend to forget the origins and development of their own attitudes and values. These "inner," "psychic," or highly personal

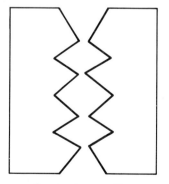 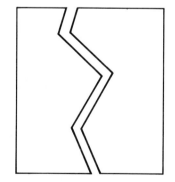

Couples in opposition   Couples complementing each other

Figure 11-3 Symbolic representation of opposition between couples in comparison with complementary needs among couples. *(From an idea suggested by George Masterton)*

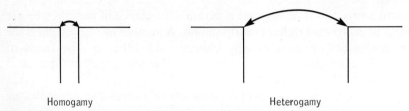

Homogamy   Heterogamy

Figure 11-4   Bridging the gaps between homogamous and heterogamous selections. *(From an idea suggested by Evelyn Duvall)*

features are *also* "inputs" based upon what past or present generations
have promoted. Few have created new attitudes or values. Most have
selected from their societies those alternatives that seem appropriate for
them. In this context, as with most systems that perpetuate themselves,
couples are free to match attitudes and values that offer minimal threat to
the status quo.

Complementarity

The chief proponent of complementarity in spouse selection is Robert F.
Winch. His theory of complementary needs has been tested for more than
twenty years with varying results and refinements. The basic propositions
are as follows:[19]

> **1**   In mate-selection each individual seeks within his or her field of
> eligibles for that person who gives the greatest promise of providing him or
> her with maximum need-gratification.
> **2**   There is a set of needs such that if person A behaves in a manner
> determined by a high degree of need X, A's behavior will prove gratifying to
> the need Y in a second person, B.
> **3**   These two needs, X and Y, in the two persons, A and B, are said to
> be complementary if:
> **a**   Type I complementariness: X and Y are the same need, and the
> need is present to a low degree in B.
> **b**   Type II complementariness: X and Y are different needs. In
> this case specific predictions are made about selected pairs of needs. That
> is, taking account of the particular X, with respect to some Y's it is
> predicted that B will have a high degree and with respect to others that B
> will have a low degree.

For example, in Type I complementariness, if one spouse has a high
need to receive recognition, it would be predicted that the need for
recognition would be held to a low degree by the other spouse. In Type II

complementariness, if one spouse had a high need to be dominant, the other spouse would have a high need to give deference.[20]

Winch has recognized that the theory of complementary needs is not universally applicable. The complementarity is an important part of the spouse-selection process under the following societal-cultural conditions:[21]

1 The marital relationship must be culturally defined as a rich potential source of gratification.

2 The choice of mates must be voluntary (i.e., not arranged) and bilateral (i.e., both man and woman must possess at least the power of veto).

3 There must be provision for, and preferably encouragement of, premarital interaction between men and women in order to provide the opportunity for testing out personalities of a variety of potential mates.

The theory of complementary needs was designed to predict the type of person an individual will select for a wife or husband once the needs of that individual are understood. As we have indicated, empirical study over the years has produced a better than chance result in some studies and unsupported results in other studies. Therefore, we should keep in mind that theories which help us comprehend and deal effectively with such complexities as spouse selection should not be mistaken for the complexities themselves.

It should be clear that the theory of complementary needs was not designed to predict marital happiness. Winch clearly states that complementary couples are not necessarily happy couples. For example, a masochistic woman might select a sadist for a husband, but such a marriage would be loaded with controversy and could be broken under the burden of conflict.[22]

By finding reinforcements, aid, and comfort in the other person, individuals reach a state of mutuality identified in American society as "love." In one sense, love is *unselfish* because it motivates persons to give as much as they can for the sake of others. On the other hand, there is a strongly *selfish* side to love because of an impelling desire to receive love once it has been given. Reciprocity, mutuality, exchange, interchange, and complementarity are among the nuances in the English language that convey the two-sided nature of love, which is *the* reason to move ahead into marriage as far as many Americans are concerned. The loving relationship may not be vocalized or openly acknowledged among couples, but its presence is felt or believed to be affirmed through the conduct of each participant.

Love as a *prior* condition to marriage seems quite logical to

Americans. But its intensity has been criticized as occurring too early to be sustained for many couples. Observers of the American culture have often commented that love should be treated as an *ensuing* condition, one that develops as persons truly support each other over the years. Ardent declarations of love are well and good prior to marriages, but many wives and husbands have noted the erosion of love as the years pass. Those who have been successful in their marriages labor long and hard to make giving and receiving a fundamental part of their relationships. As some have expressed it, *"Creeds* are wonderful, but *deeds* based on creeds are even better."

Readiness

Lastly, readiness for marriage brings loving couples together in a confirmed relationship. Normally marital readiness in the United States occurs in the late teens and early twenties. The pressure imposed by generational peers is to be like others, to join others as they move from singleness to marriage. As many admit, their readiness for marriage was brought to a critical point when they observed their age peers getting married while they had hardly begun to contemplate seriously such a move. Others, of course, are not stampeded into marriage. Such persons seek nonmarital, non-family-oriented values and are willing to delay spouse selection or, perhaps, permanently reject marriage for themselves. The goals unmarried persons seek are frequently of great social consequence because they serve so many others. In this context, persons who choose to remain single should not be criticized. *Marriage by choice* remains a more important norm in the United States than *marriage by coercion.*

Because marriage is a big step, certain transitional stages have been developed over many generations. These are, in sequence, engagement, wedding, and the honeymoon.

Figure 11-5 represents proportionately the time and energy spent on successive, transitional steps to marriage. The engagement is far more important than the wedding, and the wedding, in turn, is far more important than the honeymoon. Note the difference between the honeymoon and marriage itself. The honeymoon is obviously part of the marital state, but it does not rate as marriage over the long run because it is a euphoric, idyllic stage in which, for the moment, the couple can be blissfully out of touch with the woes and cares of real life. When the honeymoon is over, marriage has actually begun.

The wedding deserves far more study and comment than appears in these pages. It is a rite of passage that is dominated by the prominence of

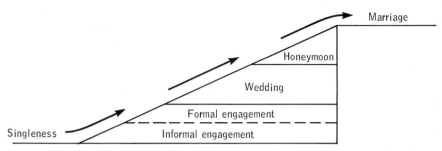

Figure 11-5 Transition into marriage.

the bride in the United States and the joining of two kinships. In this analysis, however, it is an interlude that partially tests the ability of the couple to work together on a common enterprise in full view of the public. Simple or elaborate, it expresses an affirmation filled with meaning to the participants and observers.

It is the engagement, however, to which particular attention is given here. Strangely enough, engagement is a transitional step that many people seem to underestimate. Its informal aspect concerns only the couple themselves. This is the extended period in which a private understanding is reached. Without it, the couple cannot go forward. Informality is followed by formality. In this phase, again rather lightly regarded by participants in the United States, persons closely related and distantly concerned are notified of the couple's intention and readiness for marriage. A prevalent attitude is that engagement, formal or informal, serves no major purposes. But this not true.

The functions of engagement are threefold: (1) to make explicit an implicit relationship between the couple, (2) to bring the couple closer to marriage without actually being married, and (3) to explore seriously those matters that can threaten or dissolve a proposed marriage.

The first function removes all speculation between the couple. Their intentions are declared, and they are free to treat each other accordingly. Gamesmanship is traded off for honesty. Further, outside persons need no longer guess or speculate on the couple's involvement with each other. They are about to be married and, as such, no longer circulate among other potential marriage partners. Their eligibility for marriage has become exclusive rather than inclusive.

The second function is a sobering one. It permits the couple to examine marriage closely before moving ahead. If the couple finds strong evidence that their contemplated marriage stands little chance to survive, they are well advised to end the engagement. Moving ahead to a "social suicide" is avoided by moving back to singleness.

The third function of engagement is to examine seriously those matters vital to the couple. Whereas, in the past, trivial matters, such as what to do on a date or what friends are doing, occupied their attention, engagement provides the final opportunity to consider those key items that can make their lives together a success or failure according to their own sense of values. What values are important to each? What guides their actions, and toward what ends? How do they feel about children, housing locations, friends, occupations, morality, and relatives? To leave matters undetermined and unresolved, in the fond hope that "things will work out" when they are faced in marriage, is to add additional burdens and strains to a relationship upon which so much already depends.

SUMMARY

Spouse selection in the United States has been characterized as an easy-to-enter but not-as-easy-to-exit situation. Solutions that have been suggested include making it impossible to exit (a no-divorce or closed-cone pattern), far greater preparation or qualifications than currently exist (a reversed-megaphone pattern), easy entrance and easy exit (a wide-pipeline pattern), difficult entrance and exit (a narrow-pipeline concept that acknowledges that only a few will be involved in marriage), and the acceptance of alternate marital styles (a multiple-pipeline configuration). In brief, current patterns of spouse selection are being questioned in the United States and have become subject to a variety of suggestions or experimentations.

The prevailing pattern is that of the open-ended funnel which gathers the largest assortment of persons possible, passes them through a series of filters or screens, and eventuates in married couples. This multistage filter theory, moving through dating, propinquity, attractiveness, similarity of social backgrounds, consensus, complementarity, and readiness for marriage, pulls together much of the state of current knowledge of how Americans choose each other as husbands and wives.

While the multistage filters seem to work in the approximate order described, they are by no means insurmountable barriers to marriage for most people. Most couples can arrive at what they believe will be a successful marriage. But chance probabilities are also at work. What appears to be a selection process is, in actuality, the results of generations of effort to which men and women are subject. Some persons operate within the system, taking as much advantage as possible of alternatives. Others seem to drift into marriage or are unaware of what is happening to them.

Marriage is a serious relationship, and this analysis has suggested that much depends upon how well participants prepare for it. The current spouse-selection pattern in the United States has much to commend it. Nevertheless, there is room for improvement, and present generations have consciously promoted either a better use of patterns that now exist or a new set of alternatives that will allow men and women to move in the directions they wish to go.

REFERENCES

1 Suggested by Alan Kerckhoff and Keith E. Davis, "Value Consensus and Need Complementarity in Mate Selection," *American Sociological Review*, vol. 27, no. 3, pp. 295–303, June 1962.
2 Bernard Farber, *Family: Organization and Interaction*, San Francisco: Chandler Publishing Company, 1964, pp. 106ff.
3 *Statistical Abstract of the United States, 1970*, 1970, p. xiii.
4 *Marriages, Trends and Characteristics: United States*, ser. 21, no. 21, DHEW Publication No. (HSM) 72–1007, U.S. Department of Health, Education, and Welfare, Public Health Service, September 1971, p. 7.
5 See, for example, Boyd C. Rollins and Harold Feldman, "Marital Satisfaction over the Family Life Cycle," *Journal of Marriage and the Family*, vol. 32, no. 1, pp. 20–28, February 1970.
6 Hugh Carter, Paul C. Glick, and Sarah Lewit, "Some Demographic Characteristics of Recently Married Persons: Comparisons of Registration Data and Sample Survey Data," *American Sociological Review*, vol. 20, no. 2, pp. 165–172, April 1955.
7 Marvin R. Koller, "Residential Propinquity of White Mates at Marriage in Relation to Age and Occupation of Males, Columbus, Ohio, 1938 and 1946," *American Sociological Review*, vol. 13, no. 5, pp. 613–616, October 1948.
8 James H. S. Bossard, *Marriage and the Family*, Philadelphia: University of Pennsylvania Press, 1940, p. 82.
9 Willard Waller and Reuben Hill, *The Family: A Dynamic Interpretation*, rev. ed., New York: The Dryden Press, Inc., 1951, pp. 174–192.
10 Ibid, pp. 181–190.
11 Harry Elmer Barnes (ed.), *An Introduction to the History of Sociology*, Chicago: The University of Chicago Press, 1948, pp. 744–765.
12 Robert H. Coombs, "Reinforcement of Values in the Parental Home as a Factor in Mate Selection," *Marriage and Family Living*, vol. 24, no. 2, pp. 155–157, May 1962.
13 Leonard Broom, "Intermarriage and Mobility in Hawaii," in *Transactions of the Third World Congress of Sociology*, vol. 3, *Changes in Class Structure*, London: International Sociological Association, 1956, pp. 277–282.
14 August B. Hollingshead, "Cultural Factors in the Selection of Marriage Mates," *American Sociological Review*, vol. 15, no. 5, pp. 619–627, October 1950, and William J. Goode, "Marital Satisfaction and Instability: A Cross-

Cultural Class Analysis of Divorce Rates," *International Social Science Journal*, vol. 14, no. 3, pp. 507–526, 1962.
15 Robert F. Winch, *Mate Selection: A Study of Complementary Needs*, New York: Harper & Brothers, 1958.
16 Coombs, op. cit.
17 Richard Centers, "Marital Selection and Occupational Strata," *American Journal of Sociology*, vol. 54, pp. 530–535, 1949, and A. Philip Sundal and Thomas C. McCormick, "Age at Marriage and Mate Selection: Madison, Wisconsin, 1937–1943," *American Sociological Review*, vol. 16, no. 1, pp. 37–48, February 1951.
18 Raymond Firth, "Marriage and the Classificatory System of Relationship," *Journal of the Royal Anthropological Institute*, vol. 60, pp. 235–268, 1930.
19 Robert F. Winch, *The Modern Family*, 3d ed., New York: Holt, Rinehart and Winston, Inc., 1971, p. 488. Used with permission.
20 Ibid., p. 488.
21 Ibid., p. 489.
22 Ibid., p. 504.

STUDY QUESTIONS AND ACTIVITIES

1 Contrast dating with mating in the United States today.
2 Why the term *spouse selection* preferred to *mate selection*?
3 Have each member of the class make a numeric count of persons of the opposite sex that have been in his or her "field of eligibles" and indicate various reasons why they were rejected as potential spouses.
4 How much formal preparation for marriage have you experienced?
5 What informal preparation for marriage seems to you to be useful in choosing a husband or wife?
6 In what ways have generational influences been at work in the spouse-selection processes?
7 Argue for or against the various patterned configurations in spouse selection found in Figure 11-1.
8 Does getting married prove that couples have made wise use of the entryways to marriage?
9 Discuss in small groups what couples mean when they say they are in love. Report back to the assembled class to determine to what extent each small group dealt with the same or different aspects love between men and women.
10 How many drift into marriage, and how many thoughtfully prepare? Why do these differences occur?

SUGGESTED ADDITIONAL READINGS

Adams, Bert N., *The American Family: A Sociological Interpretation*, Chicago: Markham Publishing Company, 1971, chap. 10, "Love and Mate Selection in the United States," pp. 203–233.

Adams, Bert N., and Thomas Weirath (eds.), *Readings on the Sociology of the Family,* Chicago: Markham Publishing Company, 1971, Part IV, "Dating and Mate Selection," pp. 167–256.

Bell, Robert R., *Marriage and Family Interaction,* Homewood, Ill.: The Dorsey Press, 3d ed., 1971, part II, "Dating-Courtship," pp. 73–230.

Bowman, Henry A., *Marriage for Moderns,* 6th ed. New York: McGraw-Hill Book Company, 1970, Part 2, "Marriage Preparation and Partner Selection," pp. 101–311.

Coser, Rose L., *The Family: Its Structure and Functions,* New York: St. Martin's Press, 1964, Part two, "Limitations on Marital Selection," pp. 91–247.

Cox, Frank D., *Youth, Marriage, and the Seductive Society,* rev. ed., Dubuque, Iowa: Wm. C. Brown Company Publishers, 1967.

Ktsanes, Thomas and Virginia Ktsanes, "The Theory of Complementary Needs in Mate-Selection," in Robert F. Winch and Louis Wolf Goodman (eds.), *Selected Studies in Marriage and the Family,* 3d ed., New York: Holt, Rinehart and Winston, Inc., 1968, pp. 517–529.

Sullivan, Joyce A., *Selection of Dates and Mates: An Intergenerational Study,* Columbus, Ohio: Office of Educational Services, The Ohio State University Libraries, 1972.

Chapter 12

Husbands and Wives

Generational continuity, we have repeatedly noted, requires men and women to come together to set the foundations for yet another generation. The life cycle is, thus, renewed and sustained from generation to generation. For those using this text, marriage and family patterns were being established from the time they started moving out of childhood and into adulthood. When an individual contemplates how much time is spent in preparing for marriage, it appears to be most of one's life. This chapter deals with couples who are not preparing for, but have arrived at marriage.

Figure 12-1 is a keystone pattern suggesting the steps that help prepare men and women for the roles of husbands and wives. The keystone indicates that boys and girls move from childhood through somewhat different paths into adolescence and young adulthood, approach each other through certain marital preparation experiences, and culminate their lives in a husband-wife relationship. Husbands and wives are thus visualized as being in a keystone relationship toward which they have been building their entire lives.

A number of criticisms can be leveled against this concept. First, the

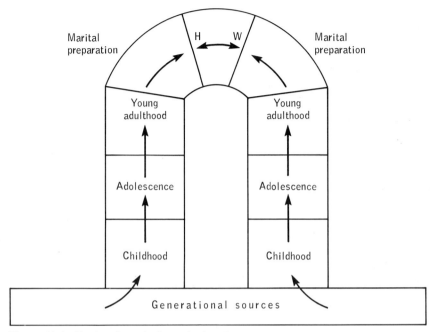

Figure 12-1 Husbands and wives: the keystone.

generational backgrounds of two individuals may be far from common ground, but rather quite separated and divergent. Second, their childhood, adolescence, and young adulthood may not be so neatly parallel, but twisted, shattered, delayed, or disrupted. Third, the preparation phases may not progressively approach each other. And, fourth, the husband-wife relationship is not necessarily the culmination of a man's or woman's existence. Many persons believe that fulfillment is not necessarily found in marriage and family life.

There is no major quarrel with these criticisms. The keystone concept is only a heuristic device to portray normative expectations from which one may anticipate an untold number of variations. What the concept does suggest is that becoming a husband or wife is a key step in one's life. It is a relationship that is new and strange for first marriages and one that requires the rest of one's life to strengthen. Upon this key relationship will be built other lives in the next generation. Depending upon how the relationship is handled, men and women can go on to other relationships and commitments. As many discover, the husband-wife relationship requires constant attention because, in the end, when others lives have shed their dependency upon the couple, husbands and wives remain together until death separates them.

BEFORE AND AFTER MARRIAGE

What is so new about the status of husbands and wives? A before-and-after picture of the husband-wife relationship may help explain this newness:

Before marriage	After marriage
Dreaming	Reality
Could walk away from problems	Must face problems
Making promises	Fulfilling promises
Choice of partners	Partner chosen
One kinship network	Two kinship networks
Need consult only oneself	Must consult with another
Contemplate different roles	Play a definite role

Before becoming a husband or wife, a man or woman can imagine, dream, or conjure up an idea of how the future will be with one's spouse. It is wonderful when cherished dreams come true, but, unfortunately, reality shatters many a dream. To project a vision of blissful happiness or tremendous consideration for one's spouse is delightful, but when spouses fail to consider one another over the many years of living together, when communication breaks down, and when one causes the other pain and sorrow, the vision fades, blurs, or is abandoned.

Before marriage, young couples with problems could separate and leave them unresolved. After marriage, mutual problems demand mutual decision making. Separations or denying the existence of problems only delays ultimate solutions.

Prior to marriage, young people, often in good faith, make a number of promises to each other. Good intentions motivate such promises, and they are most appealing or attractive to young men and women considering marriage. But fulfilling promises is quite another matter. Actions are not as easily carried out, as ebullient youth begins to discover.

In marriageable ages there is a certain exhilaration that a number of eligible persons are possible or available. Popularity with men or women is most flattering to the ego. But once the option is exercised in marriage, one must work with that choice. That many cannot live with their choices and believe they can continue to choose partners, despite their status as husbands or wives, is not a new phenomenon among young, middle-aged, or elderly generations.

There are those persons who marry to escape their parents or kinship networks. By marrying, however, they have merely compounded their kinship networks; each spouse now has to contend with a whole new set of relatives while retaining his or her own.

Further, having reached some recognizable stage of personal and social maturity, a young man or woman has cultivated the art of consulting his own mind, feeling, self. Yet, in marriage, there are two minds, two selves to satisfy, and consultations must take the form of what *we* should do and not what *I* want to do.

Finally, young men and women have seen any number of role models of husbands and wives. Close-up views have been available in their homes and in the homes of friends and relatives. Mass media have suggested an even greater array of models. The "moment of truth," however, has arrived as men and women become husbands and wives themselves. Now they must carry out the behaviors they deem appropriate for marriage. It is a real-life drama that is occurring, and one's being is at stake.

For these reasons, it is important that new husbands and wives devote as much time and energy as possible to their untested relationships.

GIVING TIME AND ATTENTION TO BEING HUSBANDS AND WIVES

Because the relationship is so vital, there is considerable margin for error if husbands and wives treat their status and role too lightly.* Wives who are pregnant prior to their marriage or who have children shortly after their marriage are more familiar with the wife-mother status and role than they are with the wife status and role. Those men who become husband-fathers soon after their marriage also miss out on what it is like to be exclusively a husband. Learning to be a husband or a wife is difficult enough without the further complications of one or more children who demand, and need, tremendous attention in their own right. Turning away from this task too early because of added responsibilities, complications, or distractions has affected many families, if the testimonies of thousands of college students over the past two decades are true. Children born and reared by husbands and wives who have minimal solidarity or pair unity have suffered the consequences of this inattention. Divorce, desertion, or chronic bitterness have often resulted in the lives of parental or child generations.

ADJUSTMENTS FOR HUSBANDS AND WIVES

Two personalities, two different life experiences, two individuals from different sexual worlds come together to become a husband-wife team. Since marriage constitutes minimal social distance, their spoken and

*Status is the position one holds in a social system, husband and wife status being examples. Role is the dynamic aspect of holding a particular status; it consists of specific behavior patterns within a given status. Thus, married men and women take on the statuses of husbands and wives but their interpretations of how to behave differ widely.

unspoken hopes and fears, their unconscious value systems, their special sensitivities are brought to the surface. One finds it difficult to hide from one's spouse whatever eccentricities or combination of intimate details constitute oneself. These qualities and attributes need *adjustment* if they are to be made to work well in marriage. Despite all prior efforts to select the spouse of one's choice, adjustment becomes the work of husbands and wives for the rest of their lives. A lawyer who has witnessed many divorce actions once remarked, "If only these men and women would work as hard on their relationships *after* their marriages as they did *before* they were married, my domestic relations cases would be negligible."

The traditional pattern for many generations has been to encourage the *wife* to adjust. Such a pattern made sense in a day when marriage constituted the chief investment, the way of life, for women. Men, by contrast, were admonished to be good husbands, which meant to provide economic security but not necessarily to try to enhance the psychosocial needs of their wives. A neat division of labor kept "men's work" and "women's work" apart. Woman's "place" was in the home, a man's in the "outside" world.

But times have changed. Men's work and women's work are no longer so separate and distinctive. The "place" of men and women can be in or out of the home. Women need not rely upon their husbands for economic support or for much of their psychosocial needs. Men and women determine together what they consider to be appropriate husband-wife behaviors. Lacking a formula, they are free to make whatever arrangements seem to fit their unique dyad. Certainly, husbands, as well as wives, must now learn to adjust to their new status. Today we live in a new generational world quite capable of making human errors but also quite filled with chances for success.

Robert Blood identifies this new relationship as "syncratic power" when he writes:

Under modern economic and social conditions, patriarchalism tends to give way to a new norm of equality between husbands and wives. In contrast to patriarchy where the husband theoretically has absolute power and may issue orders which the wife dare not question (much less, resist), in equalitarian marriages ordering and obeying give way to mutual consultation and negotiation. No one may give orders, one may make only requests which may or may not be accepted. Either sex may initiate such requests and either is equally free to refuse. Indeed, the old sex distinctions supposedly become irrelevant to this new power structure, since the roles of husband and wife in decision-making are presumably identical and therefore interchangeable.

In addition to equality of status, a second feature of the modern ideal is shared power. Theoretically, equality might be achieved by separately exercising autonomous jurisdiction over two equal halves of the marriage: I will make half the decisions and you make half. But the 50/50 concept which is often applied to contemporary decision-making does not refer to unilateral decision-making by separate-but-equal partners, but to joint decision-making. Ideally all decisions are made together; 50/50 describes the amount of influence exercised by the two partners in every decision, not the number of decisions each makes separately.

There seems little doubt that this picture of shared-equal (or "syncratic") exercise of power represents the normative power structure for the advanced countries of the world.[1]

SPECIFIC ADJUSTMENTS OF HUSBANDS AND WIVES

The overall adjustment in marriage is that of two personalities operating with a minimum of conflict. Ernest Burgess and Leonard Cottrell expressed the same idea in more positive terms by writing that a well-adjusted marriage was one "in which the attitudes and acts of each of the partners produce an environment which is favorable to the functioning of the personality of each, particularly in the realm of primary relationships."[2]

But what are the specific areas of adjustment over which husbands and wives can contend? A comprehensive listing and full analysis of each would burden the reader and cannot be given in the space limitations of a single chapter. Nevertheless, a few outstanding areas can be considered. These are in-laws, finances, sexual expression, sociability, family goals, and awareness of alienation. We will treat each of these in turn, some in greater depth than others.

In-laws

Two decades ago, Evelyn Duvall made a pioneering and thoughtfully penetrating study of 5,020 men and women throughout the United States in terms of their in-laws.[3] This study dealt with the problems confronted by new husbands and wives as they struggled to establish themselves independently from their parental families. Often well-intentioned efforts to assist young couples by parents, siblings, grandparents, or other relatives were seen as "interference" and "meddling" by young husbands and wives. Unsolicited advice, for example, particularly from relatives, was not received with gratitude, but, rather, was interpreted to mean that a young husband or wife was not yet ready to behave in a mature way or could not stand on his own.

Of all the in-laws, females were held to be the most troublesome. An abundance of mother-in-law jokes reflects the resentment of mothers-in-law. Barbed humor serves a useful purpose because under the guise of laughter, serious problems may be attacked. On the other hand, Duvall uncovered hundreds of cases in which mothers-in-law were revealed as constructively helpful to newlyweds. The mother-in-law stereotype was thus exposed for what it is: a partial truth. When married couples produce children, mothers-in-law become grandmothers. Stereotypic thinking portrays *them* as gentle, sweet old ladies who spoil their grandchildren. Thus, the same women are popularly portrayed as both troublemaking mothers-in-law and as overindulgent grandmothers.

Avoidance of in-laws is a popular ploy in American folklore. Husbands and wives may, indeed, find that this strategy works, but it may also work in reverse. Husbands and wives have not so much excluded relatives from their lives as found that relatives have excluded them from whatever benefits might have accrued had contacts been retained. Even more to the point, avoidance does not work as effectively as many husbands and wives believe. Rapid transportation and communication bring relatives close, sometimes at great expense or inconvenience. Social amputation is a drastic measure and should be applied only when it is necessary to maintain the integrity of the marriage. Short of this, husbands and wives should cultivate the ability to work with as many variant personality types as possible, particularly those primary and secondary relatives who shaped the lives of their spouse.

Many students of family life in the United States had apparently missed this effort to work *with* relatives rather than *against* them. For a number of years, it was taken for granted that urban, nuclear families were characteristically isolated from their kin. Yet, as early as 1951, Marvin Sussman's doctoral thesis established evidence that parental aid to young married couples was substantial.[4] Sussman, and those who followed his lead, continued to examine the evidence of efforts to maintain intergenerational continuity and found that direct and indirect aid flowed to husbands and wives from parental generations in far greater proportions than previously surmised.[5] By 1968, Bert Adams and others were synthesizing empirical and theoretical efforts in the study of kinships in urban settings.[6]

The research of Judson T. Landis and others has revealed that in-law adjustments are growth tasks for husbands and wives chiefly during the earliest years of marriage.[7] The middle and later years of marriage bring other problems, while in-law problems fade or settle into some workable or tolerable pattern.

Financial Adjustments

Given the affluent economy of the United States, the inescapable reality of family finances comes home to new spouses. In generational priorities, young, often unmarried couples frequently place money management far down on their list of concerns. But as one person observed, "Money isn't everything. It is the *lack* of money that is everything." For those accustomed to affluence or easy access to money, of course, financial stability poses no problems. It is only when husbands and wives find that their needs cannot be supported by their earned incomes that finances loom higher on their list of concerns.

Citing lack of funds as the cause of husband-wife problems, however, is missing a vital point: Couples may live successfully at various socioeconomic levels. What *is* essential is that husbands and wives determine for themselves just how they intend to use money—money being a means to an end and not an end in itself. Decisions concerning family finances reflect the personality organization of husbands and wives, particularly their acquired attitudes toward money and what ends it serves. Further, the manner of dealing with money is rooted in generational training. Many husbands and wives try to retain old habits and patterns or adopt a life-style far above their means.

Many areas in family finances need the attention of husbands and wives. Financial decision making and record keeping or budgeting are two of the most vital. Other areas are the use of cash or credit, installment purchasing, housing, insurance, and consumer education. Not everyone is an expert in such areas, but competence can be acquired by those who care to take the time and effort. The suggested readings at the end of this chapter should help in this search, and there are numerous other sources upon which to draw. Consumer education, for example, has received considerable attention by both private and governmental agencies, and these resources are available in most communities. For the sake of brevity, a few comments on financial decision making and budgeting will have to suffice.

Husbands and wives must determine for themselves just how their income is to be distributed to meet their needs. Options include a husband dominant–wife submissive pattern, a wife dominant–husband submissive pattern, a joint decision-making process, a separation of husband and wife income-outgo pattern, and a combination of sharing and independent decision making. The husband dominant–wife submissive pattern is a manifestation of the old patriarchal system in which the wage-earning husband makes all financial decisions. The subordinant wife is doled out funds to maintain the household. The wife-dominant pattern with the husband submissive is not uncommon. It occurs in those relationships in which a husband acknowledges his inability or lack of interest in managing money and so turns over all decision making to his spouse. Joint decision making in handling money is more attuned to an equalitarian marriage and has much support from those husbands and wives who favor democratic policies in most other areas of their lives. The complete separation of the incomes and outgoes of husbands and wives fits the individualistic orientation of men and women who are concerned with personal rights and freedoms within the framework of marriage. And, finally, the pattern of combined sharing and independent decision making is used when couples find that in certain areas, one spouse is the better judge of what to do, while in other areas, there is still need to mutually determine where and how money should be spent.

Budgeting was approached in past generations as *a plan for savings.* Given financial uncertainties in a basically cash economy, thrift seemed the wisest course to pursue. Present generations see budgets as *plans for spending,* and this attitude reflects the greater confidence or affluence of the times and the widespread use of credit. Money, as we have stated earlier, is chiefly a means to an end and not an end in itself. Some, of course, hold a contrary view: that money can and should be a goal for families, because its accumulation and access allow them to rise in the social-class system through the generations. Pragmatically, couples learn in their budgeting that *flexible* planning for spending has much to commend it. On the one hand, needs change over the years. On the other hand, emergencies can and do develop, and so some type of savings can be built into budgets to anticipate them. The needs may be pleasant ones, such as the preparations for a trip, a new car, a home, or a special gift. However, the needs may have a painful aspect, as in the case of accidents, sudden ill health, or disasters.

The *flexibility* of budgets cannot be overemphasized because husbands and wives need as much control of their financial affairs as possible. To carelessly overspend, to recklessly promise to pay out income not yet earned, means that others command their financial resources. Easy credit or attractive installment plans invite husbands and wives to "spend now, pay later." Only they can determine to what extent they will use these methods, and if they are naive, they may pay dearly for their choice. The flexible budget typically allows for intelligent spending *and* savings within the limits of one's income. Control, in any case, remains where it belongs—in the hands of husbands and wives to determine their own destinies.

Sexual Expression

Volumes have been written on human sexuality, whether premarital, marital, extramarital, or postmarital.[8] Elderly and middle-aged generations have witnessed the progressively easier access to sexual information during their lifetimes. Younger generations, by contrast, seem to have given human sexuality a more "open" treatment from the beginning, in the sense of franker discussion and acceptance of divergent views and practices. Yet, there remains considerable reticence and ignorance among what many assume are well-informed individuals. Sexual sophistication in the United States in the 1970s is often more apparent than real.

Here we can deal only briefly with marital sexual expression. We do stress that this area of husband-wife adjustment is a long-range one that occupies the remainder of their lives together. In-laws and financial adjustment are serious areas to consider, but where adjusting sexual expressiveness is concerned, the flood of information and the acceptance of divergent views have not washed away what Masters and Johnson have called "human sexual inadequacy."[9] Perhaps the concept of sexual expressiveness between husbands and wives has been delayed by the judgmental errors of older generations. Perhaps the difficulties, when they occur, should not focus on faulting any generation, since the state of our knowledge either is not that thoroughly developed or has not been effectively diffused throughout American society.

One problem for many couples is the overromanticized, unrealistic view of marital fulfillment common in the United States. This myth holds that one man or one woman will provide every conceivable satisfaction to his or her partner under any and all conditions. Fantasizing one's spouse as being everything from an adoring, tender lover to an exemplary friend is an attractive fiction but one that lends itself to serious disappointment in the hard light of reality and human limitations. No man or woman can be realistically expected to cater to every whim of a spouse. Indeed, it is because too much has been expected of spouses that some schools of thought suggest alternatives such as three- and four-party arrangements.

The usual approach to marital sex has been to recognize differences genitally, physiologically, psychologically, and socially and then to recommend some procedures that will bring about sexual satisfactions for husbands and wives. The most common is the *sex-manual approach* that urges the achievement of mutual orgasm as the ultimate objective for husbands and wives. Techniques to slow the husband's erotic responses and to speed the wife's responses are elaborated in these manuals.

But sexual expressiveness between husbands and wives is too important an issue to be made so restrictive. Rather, the objective needs broadening, as we have suggested, in the term *sexual expressiveness.* Certainly, orgasm or release of sexual tension is desirable, but the thousandfold ways to express oneself sexually in marriage with one's spouse indicate that present generations have far to go to achieve adjustment in this sensitive aspect of their lives.

Sexuality cannot be divorced from the total personality of husbands and wives, nor can it be separated from nonsexual facets of marital life. For example, failures in sexual adjustments are blamed upon individual husbands or wives or specific husband-wife combinations. More likely, sexual maladjustments are reflective of failures in such prosaic matters as financial arrangements, treatment of relatives, sharing of household tasks, or use of leisure time. Inability to communicate one's inner longings, even with one's life partner, is much closer to the target of adjustment in sexual expressiveness than some direct attack on sexuality as *the* target.

One premise in the concern for sexual adjustments of husbands and wives has been that husbands and wives have an *exclusive* relationship to each other. It is not new to suggest that this very exclusiveness, this *closed* association, is a root cause of failures in sexual expressiveness. What is new is increasing popularity of "open marriage."[10] Nena and George O'Neill have summarized the contrasts between "open" and "closed" marriage in somewhat idealistic terms:[11]

Open marriage	Closed marriage
Dynamic framework	Static framework
Open to the world	Shuts out the world
Open to each other	Locked together, closed in on one another
Spontaneous	Calculating
Additive	Subtractive
Creative, expanding	Inhibiting, degenerative
Infinite potential	Limited potential
Honesty and truth	Deception and game-playing
Living in the now	Living in the future, or with hang-ups from the past
Privacy for self-growth	Smothering togetherness
Flexibility in roles	Rigid role prescriptions
Adaptable to change	Threatened by change
Individual autonomy	Possession of the other
Personal identity	Selfhood subjugated to couplehood
Incorporates others—	Shuts others out—

grows through companionship with others	exclusivity limits growth
Equality of stature	Unequal status
Open trust	Conditional and static trust
Open love	Limited love
An open, expanding energy system	A closed, self-limiting energy system
Freedom	Bondage

The enthusiasm of the O'Neills for "open marriage" is apparently unbounded and their advocacy of it has apparently won the attention and support of many, particularly those who are youthful or young in heart. Some caution, however, would seem to be in order for those who would embrace it too quickly. The qualities of open marriage are presented as "good," those of closed marriage as "bad." Such may or may not be the case. Open marriage carries with it, as described by the O'Neills, numerous idealistic conditions. If "spontaneity," "honesty and truth," "open trust," and "open love" are lacking in husbands and wives, open marriage does not speedily bring them about. Further, such qualities might well be found in monogamous couples and, accordingly, these closed marriages do not constitute "bondage."

Sociability

The open marriage concept seems to imply or lead to the sexual participation of others in a dyadic marriage. Sociability, however, does not necessarily invoke a sexual emphasis as much as it seeks to challenge couples to include others in their marital life. If the sensuous nature of open marriage were separated from the concept, would open marriage be as popular as it seems to be among some young men and women? Imagine, if you will, a best seller that suggests that husbands and wives practice "sociability."

By *sociability*, we are referring to a reaching out to others in terms of friendships, service to those in need, exploration of other cultures or subcultures, travel, sports, entertaining guests, and visits. Reading or discussion with others are further extensions of sociability. In brief, sociability calls for the couple to reach out to others and to enable others to reach out to them.

Yet, as simple a concept as sociability seems to be, numerous couples find it difficult to practice. Exhausted husbands home from a day's work and bored wives, also having completed a day's work, whether inside or outside the home, find they are not compatible in terms of enlarging their contacts with others. The compulsive "workaholic" husband or the "self-occupied" wife are recognizable types who have made inadequate adjustments in marriage as far as sociability is concerned.

The solution in most cases is, first, to recognize that sociability has been neglected. Thereafter, mutual discussion and open communication can suggest how husbands and wives, together or separately, may incorporate selected people into their lives.

Family Goals

Prior to marriage, it is assumed that couples determined for themselves what purposes would be served by marrying each other. But, because much preparation for marriage is exceedingly lax in the United States, such an assumption is unwarranted. Many couples seem to drift into marriage, rather than consciously and conscientiously exploring what they intend to accomplish through their union.

It is never too late, however, to begin the process of searching for family goals together. Expectations, hopes, ambitions, fears, or hazards need an airing almost periodically in marriage because conditions are constantly changing. Failure to discuss these underlying concerns invites the maladaptations that couples need to avoid.

Alienation

Alienation is the reversal of falling in love. Just as couples came together before their marriage, they may always move apart. Few couples are forever blissful, close, and content with each other. Most have moments of great social distance or alienation and at other times think, feel, and act as close-knit team. Willard Waller and Reuben Hill offer an example of the alienation process as it moves to and through divorce:[12]

1   A disturbance in the affectional-sexual life of the pair (loss of rapport, withholding of affectional response)

2   Mention of the possibility of divorce (equivalent to the declaration of love in early spouse selection)

3   Appearance of husband-wife solidarity is broken (Others witness a break in the husband-wife partnership.)

4   Decision to divorce (not necessarily hasty; more often the result of long deliberation and suffering)

5   Crisis of separation (The dismemberment of whatever the couple have built together may be enough of a threat to enable the couple to reconsider.)

6   Divorce (as severance of husband-wife relationship)

7   Period of mental conflict and reconstruction (To return to a state of singleness calls for readjustments that are quite painful for both individuals and a couple-oriented society.)

Because the husband-wife relationship is central to the development of future generations, great care is worthwhile and necessary to make marriages work. Conscious and continuing thought and effort will result in an enriched relationship whose influence will be felt in generations to come.

SUMMARY

Husbands and wives constitute the keystone in an archway pattern. The archway involves a relationship toward which they have been moving for much of their lives. Depending upon their generational roots, childhood, adolescence, young adulthood, and particularly their preparations for marriage, husbands and wives form a union that may be solid or weak. Other generations, notably their children, will build upon the husband-wife relationship, but, for themselves, the husband-wife dyad requires constant attention for the remainder of their lives together. The husband-wife stage is entirely different from being single and stands in stark contrast to being simply an individual or adult man or woman. It is not a stage in life to be lightly treated or to be hurried past. Rather, it requires continued building and attention.

Patriarchal patterns of the past generations are giving way to a syncratic power among contemporary husbands and wives. Their relationship is on a sharing, equal basis and demands that each personality be enhanced. Husband-dominant and wife-subordinant patterns, in American marriages, at least, are giving way to an adjustment pattern that accommodates personality needs and meets adjustment problems.

Specific areas in need of adjustment include in-laws, finances, sexual expression, sociability, family goals, and awareness of the process of alienation.

Expertise and advice in these areas are available to husbands and wives. But in the end, they must become engaged in a conscious and conscientious effort to set their own destinies together.

REFERENCES

1 Robert O. Blood, *The Family*, New York: The Free Press, 1972, pp. 427–428. Used with permission.
2 Burgess, Ernest W., and Leonard S. Cottrell, *Predicting Success or Failure in Marriage*, New York: Prentice-Hall, Inc., 1939, p. 10.
3 Evelyn Millis Duvall, *In-Laws: Pro and Con*, New York: Association Press, 1954.
4 Marvin B. Sussman, *Family Continuity: A Study of Factors which Affect Relationships between Families at Generational Levels*, Ph. D. dissertation, Yale University, 1951.

5 Harry Sharp and Morris Axlerod, "Mutual Aid among Relatives in an Urban Population," in Ronald Freedom et al., *Principles of Sociology: A Text with Readings*, New York: Holt, Rinehart and Winston, Inc., 1956, pp. 434–435. See also Marvin B. Sussman and Lee Burchinal, "Parental Aid to Married Children: Implications for Family Functioning," *Marriage and Family Living*, vol. 24, pp. 320–332, November 1962.

6 Bert N. Adams, *Kinship in an Urban Setting*, Chicago: Markham Publishing Company, 1968.

7 See Judson T. Landis and Mary G. Landis, *Building a Successful Marriage*, 5th ed., Englewood Cliffs, N. J.: Prentice-Hall, Inc., 1968, p. 329.

8 See *The Encyclopedia of Sexual Behavior*, Albert Ellis and Albert Abarbanel (eds.), two volumes, New York: Hawthorn Books, Inc., 1961.

9 William H. Masters and Virginia E. Johnson, *Human Sexual Inadequacy*, Boston: Little, Brown and Company, 1970.

10 Nena O'Neill and George O'Neill, *Open Marriage: A New Life Style for Couples*, New York: Avon Books Division, The Hearst Corporation, 1973.

11 Ibid., p. 264.

12 Willard Waller and Reuben Hill, *The Family: A Dynamic Interpretation*, rev. ed., New York: The Dryden Press, Inc., p. 514. Used with permission.

STUDY QUESTIONS AND ACTIVITIES

1 Do all marriages require adjustments? Why or why not?

2 Suggest what qualities are brought to a marriage according to the archway conception.

3 What makes the status of husbands and wives so different? After all, are they not the same individuals after marriage as they were before?

4 In what ways do husbands and wives have to change as they move from being newlyweds to middle and old age?

5 Does marital adjustment constitute a static condition, or does it suggest a dynamic process to you?

6 Give examples of syncratic power for husbands and wives.

7 By sampling available husbands and wives, test the hypothesis that some areas of adjustment take a longer period of time than others.

8 Debate the validity of Burgess and Cottrell's definition of successful marriage.

9 Make your own critique of the ideal-typical construct of open marriage.

10 If you believe one specific area of adjustment is far more significant than any other, explain why.

11 Assume a hypothetical income that you and your spouse may have and suggest what you believe would be an appropriate budget. Give evidence that your allocations are based upon your knowledge of actual costs for goods and services.

12 What part do generations play in influencing the husband-wife relationship?

SUGGESTED ADDITIONAL READINGS

Bernard, Jessie, *The Future of Marriage*, Cleveland: The World Publishing Company, 1972.

Bigelow, Howard F., *Family Finance*, Philadelphia: J. B. Lippincott Company, 1958.

Carr, Gwen B. (ed.), *Marriage and Family in a Decade of Change*, Reading, Mass.: Addison-Wesley Publishing Company, 1972.

Cohen, Jerome B., *Personal Finance: Principles and Case Problems*, Homewood, Ill.: Richard D. Irwin, Inc., 1964.

Fullerton, Gail Putney, *Survival in Marriage: Introduction to Family Interaction, Conflicts, and Alternatives*, New York: Holt, Rinehart and Winston, Inc., 1972.

Jones, Kenneth L., Louis W. Shainberg, and Curtis O. Byer, *Sex*, New York: Harper & Row, Publishers, Incorporated, 1969.

Landis, Judson T., and Mary G. Landis, *Building a Successful Marriage*, 5th ed., Englewood Cliffs, N. J.: Prentice-Hall, Inc., 1968. See the following chapters: "Achieving Adjustment in Marriage," "Sex Adjustment in Marriage," "In-Laws and Marriage Adjustment," "Finances and Adjustment in Marriage," "Getting Your Money's Worth," and "Buying Life Insurance."

Lopata, Helena Z., *Occupation: Housewife*, New York: Oxford University Press, 1971.

Murstein, Bernard, and Vincent Glaudin, "The Relationship of Marital Adjustment to Personality: A Factor Analysis of the Interpersonal Checklist," *Journal of Marriage and the Family*, vol. 28, no. 1, pp. 37–43, February 1966.

Peterson, James A., *Married Love in the Middle Years*, New York: Association Press, 1968.

Stinnett, Nick, Linda M. Carter, and James E. Montgomery, "Older Persons' Perceptions of Their Marriages," *Journal of Marriage and the Family*, vol. 34, no. 4, pp. 665–670, November 1972.

Troelstrup, Arch W., *The Consumer in American Society: Personal and Family Finance*, 4th ed., New York: McGraw-Hill Book Company, 1970.

Chapter 13

Socialization of Children

Entry into marriage signals the climax of one generation's life and the beginnings of the foundations upon which the next generation will build its life. Husbands and wives will continue to grow as individuals and, as the passage of time and circumstances dictate, to make adjustments to marriage. But husbands and wives cannot focus their attention solely on their own needs. They must look to the next generation—to reproduce, nurture, and socialize them, at least in their childhood and, if possible, well into adolescence and young adulthood.

Alice Rossi has astutely analyzed this transitional point between the generations by writing:

> The timing of a first pregnancy is critical in the manner in which parental responsibilities are joined to the marital relationship. The single most important change over the past few decades is extensive and efficient

contraceptive usage, since this has meant for a growing proportion of new marriages, the possibility of and increasing preference for some postponement of childbearing after marriage. When pregnancy was likely to follow shortly after marriage, the major transition point in a woman's life was marriage itself. *This transition point is increasingly the first pregnancy rather than marriage.* It is accepted and increasingly expected that women will work after marriage, while household furnishings are acquired and spouses complete their advanced training or gain a foothold in their work. This provides an early marriage period in which the fact of a wife's employment presses for a greater egalitarian relationship between husband and wife in decision-making, commonality of experience, and sharing of household responsibilities.

The balance between individual autonomy and couple mutuality that develops during the honeymoon stage of such a marriage may be important in establishing a pattern that will later affect the quality of the parent-child relationship and the extent of sex-role segregation of duties between the parents.[1]

The conception and delivery of children can be terminated by abortion. Parental responsibilities can be transferred to others by adoption, by hiring or using surrogates, or, most drastically, by abandonment. Or, parents can choose to withdraw their concern for a child by neglect, minimal attention to physical or psychic needs, or by driving a child away by unremitting cruelties. Nevertheless, as Rossi noted, "We can have ex-spouses and ex-jobs but not ex-children."[2]

TRAINING FOR PARENTHOOD

What is astounding to some, but true, is the minimal training or relative neglect of preparations for parenthood in the United States, in sharp contrast to the elaborate preparations, strategies, and efforts that go into entering marriage. Again, Rossi notes four circumstances that work against the ability of American parents to perform adequately. These are (1) inadequate preparation to deal with sex, home maintenance, child care, interpersonal competence, and empathy, (2) limited realistic training for parenthood during pregnancy, (3) abrupt entry into parenthood upon the arrival of a child, and (4) lack of guidelines to successful parenthood.[3] Hans Sebald agrees with Rossi's appraisal of American parenthood by identifying it as "the last stand of the amateur."[4]

In short, while parents have a vital task to perform in their own name and in the name of their society—to rear children from a state of complete dependency to as complete an independency as their society permits—they begin with many handicaps. They have minimal preparation for the arts and skills of parenthood. Instead, their attention is focused upon their new roles as husbands and wives, their work careers, and their assessment of the extent to which they will allow agencies outside their family (friends, neighbors, playmates, associates, employers, special interest groups, schools, mass media, and the church, for examples) to share in the process of training their children.

SOCIALIZATION: WHAT IT IS

Socialization is the overall process of taking neonates and making them into persons capable of living in society. In one sense, the process amounts to transforming infants from helpless newborns into adults helpful to themselves and others. In another sense, socialization is an educational process in the broadest meaning of the term. It allows each generation to imprint successive generations with whatever values, ideas, knowledge, skills, arts, or beliefs are deemed worth perpetuating. Socialization *begins* in families, is *sustained* in families, but ultimately moves *outside* families as the life cycle takes individuals beyond familial care.

A point worth stressing is that each generation is not simply a passive agent that is being acted upon. It is also active in the socialization process. Each generation determines, to some extent, how far it will allow itself to be influenced by other generations and what it, in turn, proposes to give to other generations.[5]

SOCIALIZATION: WHAT IT IS SUPPOSED TO DO

Socialization, as conceived by social scientists, is a broad, all-encompassing process in which an individual encounters, moves through, and is affected by human groups throughout his or her lifetime. There are no formulas or correct ways to draw "appropriate" end products from human associations.

Parents constitute the first of a series of groups that neonates will eventually meet. Whatever parents do, consciously or unconsciously, begins the whole process of socialization. As we have noted, not only is their preparation for parental roles inadequate, but they represent every conceivable social level. "After all," as Ritchie and Koller expressed it, "realistically, convicts, racketeers, alcoholics, confidence men, ambitious politicians, conniving businessmen, sadistic tyrants, and thoughtless braggarts are, or have been, parents."[6] There are few or no impediments to becoming a parent, and all kinds of values have been promoted by whatever parents say or do. Their values make up much of the social content to which new generations are exposed.

Under such circumstances, socialization cannot be called a success or a failure. Rather, socialization works, mindlessly, unguided, to produce a variety of social types capable of living within human societies. It is only when specific parents, families, or special-interest groups achieve *unanticipated* results in oncoming generations that *they* regard socialization as a failure. "Why can't they be like us?" is the familiar lament of parental generations. But the socialization process has worked *in every instance.* It has either made new generations into close approximations or duplications of prior or existing generations, or it has generated opposition, resistance, or hostility between generations.

SOCIALIZATION IN THE UNITED STATES: PARENTAL FUNCTIONS

American society as a whole remains uncommitted to any specific model of an adult man or woman. Within subgroups, however, such models do exist. The results are the widest possible array of personalities and family life-styles. This may be the saving grace of American society, or its downfall, depending upon how much social tolerance each subgroup is willing to grant others.

To pinpoint parental functions that apply to the broadest variety of subgroups, then, is a most difficult task. But we can suggest some universals, providing it is understood that the precise ways of carrying them out are left to the discretion of parents.

Denaturalization

It is difficult for some to accept the concept of a newborn child as an animal, a *Homo sapien* to be sure, but nevertheless a creature that is not automatically full-blown "human." The human quality is *acquired* through the socialization process in which the ways of mankind are added to the biological attributes of a neonate. As the child grows up, his or her physical maturation runs somewhat parallel with socialization. The two processes, however, cannot be separated; they intertwine, interact, and mutually affect each other. Scientists have labored for generations to separate out the effects of maturation and socialization, but the two processes have so blended that the task seems impossible. What has been judged originally to be the result of maturation has turned out to be an end product of socialization. Conversely, a supposed product of socialization has ultimately been linked to biological processes.

The appeal of animals—the uncritical acceptance of animals as they happen to be, creatures responding to their biological drives, capable of learning or training only in some limited sense—applies to newborn children. Infants are natural in whatever they do—eliminating, sleeping, eating, exploring. They are unroutinized, undisciplined, and without modesty, language, religion, prejudice, or desire to harm others. Their appealing innocence or guiltlessness, in terms of the ways that man has been inhumane to man, captures many a heart and makes sacrifices or adult inconveniences worth the effort. Whether babies, infants, or young children, their spontaneity, unbridled enthusiasm, and playful creativity are much admired.

But, as concerned citizens asked in a White House Conference on Children and Youth, "What happens to the enormous and universal national resource of creativity that is evident in the infant and preschool child?"[7] What happens is that children are made to conform to the social molds that are set for them by parental generations. The traditions of the past, the silent influence of prior generations, are passed along to children through the socialization process. Children learn to become "human" and to socially restrict their biological natures.

No child or even young adolescent, unless very precocious, would take the time, energy, or interest to read through these pages. In essence, to read this text would be unnatural for a child. This is what happens to each generation as it is called upon to take its place human society. Each generation must inhibit itself, restrict itself, or denaturalize itself, and parents, operating within their respective family substructures, begin and sustain this process.

Disciplining

Untrammeled, unfettered living—freedom to do as one pleases—has long been the dream of individuals. But this goal eludes human beings because they must take each other into account in order to survive. Of all creatures humans are the most ill equipped for survival as isolated individuals. Man is a *social* animal, dependent upon others to satisfy his needs. What men and women have created *together* dominates and epitomizes human life.

Accordingly, disciplining begins with infants and is applied with mounting pressures and in greater variety as children grow up to adolescence and young adulthood. The comparative helplessness of the infant makes disciplining no great challenge. However, as maturation continues, children gain increasing mobility and sophistication in resisting discipline. At some point, typically at adolescence, some balance is reached between external disciplining and internalization of social controls. If all goes as anticipated, the internal or self-controls grow ever greater while the external disciplining diminishes. For those adults who have somehow never mastered the art of self-discipline, there are societal measures that can be brought into play. These may range from ostracism to lowered ratings on the job to imprisonment. In the last case, the protective crib and the restrictive playpen of infancy are exchanged for the barred reformatories and concrete cells of penitentiaries.

Americans have not been consistent over the generations on the matter of discipline. On the one hand, they recognize that some discipline is needed. On the other, they appreciate the freedoms that can develop from political, religious, or economic systems that encourage individuality. These are usually identified as democracy, Judeo-Christianity, and free enterprise. Wavering somewhere between discipline and permissiveness, American parents have tried to steer a middle course, but have, more often, moved closer to one side or the other as they socialized their children. The overly disciplined generations have sometimes been called the "silent" generations, rebelling only mentally, with rare individuals now and then acting out their hostilities or dissatisfactions. The "permissive" generations are most conspicuous because they include those impatient youths who are uncomfortable, unhappy, or disturbed by even the mildest forms of discipline.

Protection

The young do not automatically recognize dangers. Unless their environs are "childproofed," serious damage or bodily harm can occur within seconds. Common dangerous objects are sharp knives, open flames, household cleaners, glassware, drugs, staircases, or discarded tin cans. Some children have lost their lives through suffocation when they played with plastic bags over their heads. Dangerous toys are typically spotlighted during the Christmas buying season. Abandoned refrigerators are favorite hiding places for playful youngsters.

Less easily recognized are the more subtle forms of childhood dangers, such as playmates who cruelly ridicule, shame, or frighten companions. Thoughtless neighbors; ill-prepared teachers; or books, magazines, films, or television programs that cater to the bizarre or sensational can harm children.

The dilemmas of protection come to parents when they are called upon to determine at what point they have either overprotected or underprotected their children. Overprotection, for example, occurs when parents refuse to allow the ideas they have placed in their children's minds to be tested against contradictory ideas or perspectives. This may apply to religious instructions or to avoiding contacts with those who are "different." Underprotection, by contrast, consists of placing children in stressful or threatening situations in which there is a "sink-or-swim," toughening, nonsupportive condition. Under such circumstances, children adopt whatever stance allows them to survive.

In the United States, overprotection produces so-called feminine characteristics, such as sharpened skills with shades of meaning, indirection, submissiveness, or the seeking of interpersonal harmony. Underprotection, American style, leads to "masculinity." These qualities include bravado, directness, aggressiveness, or self-assertion. Either sex, of course, can receive overprotection or underprotection, and this goes far in explaining the blending of "feminine" and "masculine" qualities found in many personalities.

Interpretation

The family acts not only as carrier of culture, but also as an interpreter of that culture. It selects certain aspects of its society and so provides a screening effect, stressing some factors, treating others matter-of-factly, and underestimating or undervaluing still others.

The interpretative function of parents is no simple task. If there is a clear-cut, standard way of looking at some phenomenon, as might be the case in religious dogma or in some educational philosophy, then there is little to do except present the accepted line. But such is often not the case. Parents determine for themselves what they wish their children to experience and what meaning they will apply to the experiences. Misinterpretations and distortions are also possible, and children will generally accept these as uncritically as they do any other interpretation or construction put upon an event or series of events. It is only after many years of separation from their parents that children acquire contradictory evidence and the process of unlearning or discarding erroneous meanings can even begin. Deep-seated biases against people who are "different," authority figures, or complex organizations have their roots in parental interpretations or treatment of cultural "reality."

Personality Development

Personality is the subjective reflection or internalization of sociocultural experience. It is the result of the unique ways in which individuals of different physical and psychic makeup have received socialization and made it their own. Personality, then, is the chief end product that children take with them from family life.

To be sure, personality is fluid, ever changing, and altered by experiences well beyond family life, but, in the main, there is a durable residue or core personality pattern that carries the brand of family living wherever an individual wanders.

Concerned parents, recognizing the lifetime effect of personality development, are generally eager to build into their children's personalities such "virtues" as initiative, expressiveness, appreciation, kindness, honesty, integrity, and leadership. But, here again, there is no tried-and-true formula to guarantee such outcomes. What parents *can* do is to try by direct example, by becoming models to demonstrate and exercise these qualities in themselves. Beyond this, parents cannot go.

Freedom Giving

Highly committed to the concept of freedom in the United States, parents have been torn between their disciplinary functions and their freedom-giving functions. The two functions seem totally incompatible, but they are not.

American parents have accepted in large measure the concept of freedom *in the negative sense.* This means that freedom is viewed as being unrestricted, unconfined. In short, freedom consists of *not* being chained, denied, hindered, or stopped from satisfying one's inalienable rights. The Bill of Rights, for example, codifies this concept of freedom by such rights as the freedom to assemble, to publish information, to petition, to redress of grievances, or to defend oneself. In brief, these rights are *not* to be denied or proscribed. They are rights about which early Americans had firm convictions in view of their treatment by European authorities.

In American family life, this "we-will-not-stand-in-your-way" approach of parents is often held to be sufficient evidence of freedom giving. Instead, it has amounted to an abdication and easy out, a way for parents to tell children that they are free to do as they please without the parents being accused of stifling them.

What has been neglected or understressed by American parents is freedom *in the positive sense.* Another step must be taken if negative freedom is to achieve effective results. It is the step of *helping* children develop their capacities or potentials to join with others in improving the world in which they live. This positive freedom calls into play the disciplinary function discussed earlier. It amounts to actions that enable, rather than actions that allow, a person to do as he pleases. It means that not any way will do, but rather that certain ways must be acquired. Hard work is involved, and no amount of sugar coating can disguise the painstaking efforts that persons must make in order to achieve specific goals.

Enrichment of Family Life

The prolonged period in families of origin need not be a boring, dulling, routinized interlude. For both parents and children, family life can be enriched or vitalized if they care to work at it. James Bossard and Eleanor Boll make much of "table talk" in their concern for family enrichment.[8] For example, family members have to eat, but nutrition need not be the sole purpose of meals. They may well provide a socializing experience in which symbolic interaction, in the form of conversation or discussion, can invigorate a household. News, issues, plans, interpretations, ideas, hopes, fears, and general good fellowship can become a part of a family at dinner. A systematic taping of family table talk over an extended period of time appears to be an excellent indicator of the degree to which families are alive and exciting or dead and lacking in companionship.

Problem Solving

Finally, in the array of parental functions, parents have a problem solving job to do. The number and variety of problems brought to parents by their children almost defy imagination. Parents are called upon daily to judge situations and to take prompt and judicious action to resolve them. In all their decisions, appraisals, and reactions, they attest to their generational know-how. The newest generation, the children, long remember "the little things" their parents did when dilemmas or difficulties arose. How does a parent handle sibling rivalry, provide sex education, deal with a child's playmates, cope with neighbors? What should be done about, or for, family pets? What should be the appropriate attitude toward money? What tasks are appropriate for the child? Under what circumstances are children to be given free rein or denied their requests? These and thousands of other questions must be answered by parents, and they *are*, somehow, sometime during the course of parenthood. Parents cannot wait upon clear, complete, and definitive knowledge because such knowledge is lacking. It is with unclear, incomplete, and indefinite knowledge that parents have to work, and they do so daily as their children grow up.

IS FAMILY THE MAJOR INTERVENING VARIABLE IN SOCIALIZATION?

Investigators are alleged to find no difficulty in documenting the place of families as intervening variables in the socialization of their children. Yet, there is seemingly contradictory evidence from scientific studies. The works of Lee Robins[9] and Walter Toman[10] support the importance of family life as the key variable in the socialization of children. The studies of Glen Elder[11] and Orville Brim,[12] in contrast, suggest that families can be regarded as only one of many socializing agencies that shape the lives of successive generations.

The Robins Study: Deviant Children Grow Up

The Robins study was a longitudinal study of 524 child-guidance-clinic patients who were compared with 100 nonpatient children of the same age, sex, race, intelligence, and neighborhood as the former patients. A complete set of patient records covering some twenty-two years of a formerly active psychiatric clinic in St. Louis was made available to a team of research workers under the direction of a psychiatrist and a research professor of sociology. Eight additional years had elapsed since the psychiatric clinic closed its doors, and this provided an interval of approximately thirty years between the childhood of the patients and their adulthood. By finding the former child patients now grown to adulthood, the study was well under way.

The Robins study affirmed the hypothesis that "antisocial behavior in childhood not only predicts the full-blown picture of antisocial behavior that is diagnosed sociopathic personality, it also predicts the level of antisocial behavior in adults whose psychiatric picture is pre-empted by psychosis or who have less antisocial behavior than that required for a diagnosis of a sociopathic personality."[13]

The family setting of the young sociopaths was found, in the Robins study, to be highly predictive of adult antisocial behaviors. Two-thirds of the child patients had mothers and fathers with behavior difficulties or outright psychiatric problems. Sociopathic behavior or alcoholism on the part of the fathers predicted sociopathy in the children. Psychosis in the mothers predicted psychosis in the children. And freedom from psychiatric illness in either of the parents predicted mental health in the children.[14]

Love-oriented or adequate discipline and punitive or too-strict discipline in childhood were *both* effective in reducing the presence of convictions and imprisonment in adulthood. On the other hand, excessive leniency, inconsistent discipline, and disinterest of parents in their children were associated with records of conviction when these children became adults.[15] Broken homes, in themselves, were not found to be predictive of subsequent adult problems, such as criminal behavior. Much more significant was the presence or absence of family harmony or disharmony.[16] And lastly, the *fathers' behaviors*, such as desertion, excessive drinking, chronic unemployment, and failure to support, were found to be far better predictors of behavioral problems in their children than the behaviors of the mothers.[17]

The Toman Study: Family Constellation

Drawing upon some 3,000 case histories, Walter Toman also supports the thesis that families play prime roles in the generational outcomes of individual lives. His thesis is that "whatever people a person chooses for spouses, friends, partners, assistants, superiors, and the like will be co-determined by the kinds of people a person has been living with the longest, most intimately, and most regularly, and by incidental losses of such people. In short: new interpersonal relationships will be co-determined by old ones."[18]

According to Toman, it is the early intrafamily constellation that will be duplicated to some degree in the later, extrafamily relationships. The closer the new relationships come to the old relationships, other factors held constant, the better prepared the person will be for the new relationships and the greater the likelihood that these relationships will endure, be happy, and be successful.

Knowing only the variables of sex, age, and rank birth order or position in a family, such as first-born or second-born, and the absence or loss of parents and children in a family configuration, Toman has made numerous "blind diagnoses" that accurately fit the actual outcomes in interpersonal (familial) relations in four cases out of every five. Additional information, such as prolonged illness, financial difficulties, migration, drastic or unusual events, and constitutional peculiarities, account for the "fifth case."[19]

Elder's Adolescent Socialization and Personality Development

Glen H. Elder, Jr., takes a broader approach to socialization, seeing it as a transactional relationship, an exchange between the circumstances in which an individual exists and that which the individual puts in or takes out of his or her milieu.[20]

In adolescence, the individual is particularly active in this transaction; he is both acted upon by others and acts upon others to produce outcomes. It is a process that undoubtedly occurs in childhood, but not in as evident or dramatic a way as in adolescence. The meshing of *social timetables* and *organistic timetables* plays an important part in Elder's analysis. Elder is concerned with the expectations of a social system at particular intervals in a person's life and the physical-mental-emotional stages in which a person may actually exist. If the two cannot come together in some appropriate "fit," then the expected exchange cannot occur. It signals defeat and rejection for the individual and simply means that the society seeks some other individuals with whom it can deal.

Elder writes, "Encounters with increased requirements represent a potentially important stimulus of growth, but extreme discontinuity. or role demands which greatly exceed personal resources substantially increase the possibility of failure, loss of personal worth, and regression."[21]

Adolescence, then, is a crucial period in the life of a generation and requires recognition of what has already transpired in childhood and what lies ahead in adulthood. Depending upon how adolescence is handled, the transitions from childhood to adulthood can vary from encouragement and growth orientation to discouragement, rejection, and defeat. The "follow-through" from childhood is at the heart of Elder's analyses and suggests that family life is not sufficient, in itself, to override any other circumstances.

Brim and Associates: Socialization after Childhood

Brim and his associates[22] contend that socialization needs to go far beyond the adolescent stage that Elder has stressed—in fact, to consider the entire life cycle. Their contention supports the generational approach stressed throughout this text. Childhood represents only the starting point. Adolescence marks the connecting link between childhood and adulthood. But adulthood and later maturity stretch out for fifty or more years, and marriage, parenthood, work, and aging call for sustained role training. Other social institutions—schools, religions, government, and business—also play their part in this maturity training.

Alex Inkeles expressed it quite well when he wrote:

> Those who believe in the prime importance of infant and child experiences will argue that unless the disposition to act in a certain way, and some simple model or analogue of later behavior, are acquired during early childhood, the later development of appropriate social behavior will be impaired. They may or may not be right in all cases. Granting that the *disposition* and the basic model for the control of aggression, for obedience, and for the channeling of sexual energy may be laid down in infancy and early childhood, the acquisition of such dispositions and basic models is not in itself sufficient to qualify a person as properly or fully socialized. Society will judge him so only when he is able to *act* in the detailed ways specified by habit and custom for a person of his sex, age, and status.

Many students of socialization treat the acquisition of these secondary characteristics as if they were entirely unproblematic. They seem often to assume that if the proper ground is laid in early life, the rest of the necessary learning will take place more or less automatically. But the acquisition of the precise knowledge, skills, and behavioral details which go with significant social roles is anything but unproblematic. However successful the infant and child training, an individual's socialization may fail to meet society's standards because of inadequacies in social learning at later stages. Equally important, inadequacies in early socialization may be compensated for by effective social learning at later stages in the life cycle.[23]

According to Inkeles, there are three critical stages or "waves" in socialization. The first occurs within one's family. The second is concerned with heterosexual relationships, with work, and with political allegiance and action. This second wave, therefore, extends well beyond either childhood or adolescence. The third wave may require resocialization as changes in societal demands or in the adult and the aged necessitate a reformulization of appropriate behaviors. If familial socialization, extrafamilial socialization, and resocialization are resisted or inadequate, "deviant behavior, individual maladjustment, social tension, disruption, and perhaps creative change" occur.[24]

SUMMARY

The onset of parenthood marks the next critical stage for married couples as well as for generations. For parents, there is the time-consuming task of fulfilling their own adult lives. In this task, they attempt to work out a balance between their unique individuality and their couplehood. But their preparations for parenthood leave much to be desired. To most American parents, the anticipatory socialization has been minimal. The next generation is in the hands of parental amateurs.

Yet, the next generation's socialization processing begins promptly upon their entrance into the world. It begins in families, is sustained or reinforced in families, but ultimately moves out of families to embrace the whole of society. Socialization thus *works*, but the real question is with its *qualities*. What ends are to be reached? What does it do to personalities, careers, or the multitude of people it touches?

Without detailing the ways of achieving precise ends, parents inevitably function in terms of denaturalizing children, disciplining them, protecting their lives, interpreting the culture to them, developing their unique personalities, giving them some degree of negative and positive freedom, enriching family life, and solving problems. The reason precise details are not given is not that they are lacking but rather that there are various strategies from which to choose, depending upon personal or parental tastes or preferences. Pluralistic American society does not require, provide, or need a single formula for child rearing.

Family can be credited as one of the intervening variables in the socialization of children, but the degree of its impact and its primacy are still not quite evident. Available research and analyses are seemingly contradictory. On the one hand, studies such as those of Robins and Toman suggest that family is of primary and never-ending importance in the lives of individuals. On the other hand, the analyses of Brim and Elder suggest family as having incidental or even minimal effect upon life histories.

The place of families in the socialization process can best be seen and appraised through the multigenerational approach. This larger view indicates that prior studies and analyses were both correct and appropriate for the frameworks they used. Families do play a major role in the lives of the next generation, but they operate as initiators, as starting points, or as potentials. Their inputs are diluted, realigned, or minimized by the fortunes of time.

REFERENCES

1 Alice S. Rossi, "Transition to Parenthood," *Journal of Marriage and the Family*, vol. 30, no. 1, p. 31, February 1968. Used with permission.
2 Ibid., p. 32.
3 Ibid., pp. 35–36.
4 Hans Sebald, *Adolescence: A Sociological Analysis*, New York: Appleton-Century-Crofts, Inc., 1968, p. 56.
5 Some of the perspective of sociologists toward childhood can be deduced from such works as Francis J. Brown, *The Sociology of Childhood*, New York: Prentice-Hall, Inc., 1939; Oscar W. Ritchie and Marvin R. Koller, *Sociology of Childhood*, New York: Appleton-Century-Crofts, Inc., 1964; and James H. S. Bossard and Eleanor Stoker Boll, *The Sociology of Child Development*, 4th ed., New York: Harper & Row, Publishers, Incorporated 1966.
6 Ritchie and Koller, op. cit., p. 141.
7 *Conference Proceedings*, 1960 White House Conference on Children and Youth, p. 206.
8 Bossard and Boll, op. cit., pp. 133–146.
9 Lee N. Robins, *Deviant Children Grow Up: A Sociological and Psychiatric Study of Sociopathic Personality*, Baltimore: The Williams & Wilkins Company, 1966.
10 Walter Toman, *Family Constellation: Its Effect on Personality and Social Behavior*, 2d ed., New York: Springer Publishing Company, Inc., 1969.

11 Glen H. Elder, Jr., *Adolescent Socialization and Personality Development*, Chicago: Rand McNally & Company, 1968.
12 Orville G. Brim, Jr., and Stanton Wheeler, *Socialization After Childhood: Two Essays,* New York: John Wiley & Sons, Inc., 1966.
13 Robins, op. cit., p. 158.
14 Robins, op. cit., p. 167.
15 Robins, op. cit., p. 168.
16 Robins, op. cit., p. 172.
17 Robins, op. cit., p. 179.
18 Toman, op. cit., p. 6.
19 Toman, op. cit., p. 180.
20 Elder, op. cit., p. 3.
21 Elder, op. cit., p. 117.
22 Brim and Wheeler, op. cit.
23 John A. Clausen (ed.), *Socialization and Society*, Boston: Little, Brown and Company, 1968, p. 92. Used with permission.
24 Ibid., p. 93.

STUDY QUESTIONS AND ACTIVITIES

1 In what ways are parents amateurs at their tasks?
2 What does the author mean when he writes that "socialization works in *every instance*?"
3 Provide examples of interconnections between the maturation process and the socialization process in your own life or in the lives of others.
4 Is socialization tantamount to being "unnatural"? Why or why not?
5 What are the limits of negative freedom and positive freedom? In short, can parents err in "going too far" in either direction in socializing their children?
6 How does overprotection or underprotection produce so-called feminine or masculine cultural traits?
7 Is there a distinction between "interpretation" and "distortion" in the socialization of children?
8 What tasks are "child appropriate" and which are not?
9 How do you explain the fact that families are intervening variables in certain case histories and not in others?
10 Who can speak as "child advocates" if parents overstep their responsibilities toward children?
11 Discuss the "we-will-not-stand-in-your-way" approach of American families. What is its effect upon American children?
12 In what ways do families begin socialization and in what ways is their socialization function continuous for their children?

SUGGESTED ADDITIONAL READINGS

Benson, Leonard, *Fatherhood: A Sociological Perspective*, New York: Random House, Inc., 1968.

Burchinal, Lee G. (ed.), *Rural Youth in Crisis: Facts, Myths, and Social Change,* Washington, D.C.: U.S. Department of Health, Education, and Welfare, 1963.

Crosby, John F., *Illusion and Disillusion: The Self in Love and Marriage,* Belmont, Calif.: Wadsworth Publishing Company, Inc., 1973, Chap. 9, "A Marriage Legacy: Socialization for Tomorrow," pp. 133–148.

Frank, Lawrence K., *On the Importance of Infancy,* New York: Random House, Inc., 1966.

Goslin, David A. (ed.), *Handbook of Socialization Theory and Research,* Chicago: Rand McNally & Company, 1969.

Grollman, Earl A., *Explaining Death to Children,* Boston: Beacon Press, 1967.

Hentoff, Nat, *Our Children Are Dying,* New York: The Viking Press, Inc., 1966.

Hess, Robert D., and Judith V. Torney, *The Development of Political Attitudes in Children,* Chicago: Aldine Publishing Company, 1967.

King, Edith W., and August Kerber, *The Sociology of Early Childhood Education,* New York: American Book Company, 1968.

LeMasters, E. E., *Parents in Modern America,* Homewood, Ill.: The Dorsey Press, 1970.

Report to the Surgeon General, *Television and Growing Up: The Impact of Televised Violence,* Washington, D. C.: U.S. Health Service, 1972.

Skinner, B. F., *Beyond Freedom and Dignity,* New York: Alfred A. Knopf, Inc., 1971.

Chapter 14

Full Family Living

As Lillian Troll has pointed out, most discussion of generation gaps has dealt with the earlier end of the life cycle.[1] In this chapter, the middle and later phases of the life cycle are highlighted. It is understandable why so much study and publication have been concentrated upon children, adolescents, and newly married adults. In these oncoming generations, the foundations of the future are still being formed and there is still time to learn appropriate behavior. For generations at midcycle or in "the stage of the empty nest," there is far less time or margin for error. Further, those who study marriage and family in school are on the threshold of marriage and familial life, and their needs are paramount to family scholars. It is critical, however, to consider the whole multigenerational life cycle if people are to be fully informed of what lies ahead. To do otherwise would be like concentrating upon freshmen and sophomores while neglecting juniors, seniors, graduates, and alumni of successive classes.

In full family living, multigenerational relationships are fully developed: the youngest generations are well along in their socialization, the parental generations are experiencing the departure of their children, and the oldest generations are confronted with years of "roleless roles." A great deal of what parents and grandparents are experiencing is uncharted, but there is much to be learned from those who have gone ahead. No one generation is so cut off that other living generations cannot profit by its experiences. In multigenerational behavior, each generation can learn not only from its own experiences but from the experiences of other generations.

ONE-GENERATIONAL FAMILY LIFE

The normative pattern in the United States has been for men and women to marry within an age differential of approximately two or three years. Some 85 percent marry within this differential, which with the man usually being the senior, has held true for some thirty years (see Table 14-1).

These couples of similar ages may not have deliberately planned to remain childless, but their one-generational family style did become the essential pattern in their mutual lives. The number of families with no children of their own under eighteen years of age is surprisingly high (see Table 14-2). This table does not imply that families without children of their own under eighteen *never* had children, nor does it imply that they could not have adopted children to experience two-generational family living. Those families that are childless, however, do not necessarily adopt available or potentially adoptive children.

Most childless married couples do not adopt, but satisfy whatever longings they may have for intergenerational living through working with both the young and the old, either in families established by their relatives or in the course of their work or voluntary services. Childless couples of the same generation, however, do not necessarily have some innate need to be with, or frequently contact, persons of other age categories. Many are undoubtedly quite content with their life-style

Table 14-1   Median Age at First Marriage, Brides and Grooms in the United States, 1940 to 1970

Median age at first marriage	1940	1950	1960	1970
Bride	21.5	20.3	20.3	20.8
Groom	24.3	22.8	22.8	23.2

Source: U.S. Department of Commerce, Social and Economic Statistics Administration, Bureau of the Census, 1970, p. 60.

Table 14-2   Percent Distribution of Families with No Children under Eighteen Years of Age, United States, 1950 to 1969

Percent distribution of families with no children	1950	1960	1965	1969
Total	48.3	43.0	43.4	44.2
Nonfarm Families	49.0	42.9	43.1	43.8
Farm Families	44.4	45.2	47.7	51.3

Source: U.S. Department of Commerce, Social and Economic Statistics Administration, Bureau of the Census, 1970, p. 39.

and, indeed, count on the advantages of being free to do whatever they wish. Such couples can blend their personalities in satisfying ways and possess a harmony that many would like to emulate. Harried parents have to wait for many years before they can experience this one-generation couple pattern that contented and adjusted childless couples of the same generation have known all along. By chance or by choice, childless couples have often found maximal pleasure in associations with persons of their same generational backgrounds.

Middle-aged Parents Whose Children Have Grown Up

With the exception of the childless couples, one-generation family life comes sooner or later to parents whose children have left them to fulfill their adult lives. What remains in what has been said to be "a full family" are middle-aged parents who have mementoes of their children's growing up all around them. The formerly noisy rooms and hallways are now silent. The playful puppy for which the children once clamored is now approaching old age. The floor scratches, torn furniture, marred walls, or scuff marks are mute testimony of a home once "fully lived in." Now, pictures, toys, clothing, or treasured collections are stored away for occasional glances or sentimental examinations at some indefinite date.

The parents are alone together for the first time since the arrival of their first child, and they continue to think of each other in terms of "Mom" and "Dad," a habit left over from their many years of child rearing. Their husband-wife relationship can now be stressed, where before this relationship was muted in favor of parental responsibilities and interests.

Clark E. Vincent has written "An Open Letter to the 'Caught Generation' " in which he expresses, without hesitation, a strong empathy for parents whose children have embarked on lives of their own.[2] A few passages convey this spirit and this thinking:

Dear Parent:

If you are between 35 and 55 years old, you may belong to the *caught generation*—caught in between the demands of youth and the expectations of the elderly. The respect you were taught to give your parents may have been denied you by your children. You may have greatly appreciated what little your parents were able to give you during the depression, but received little appreciation for the much you sought to provide your children. Taught to accept and respect the authoritative (not authoritarian) wisdom and experience of your parents, you may find your own parental authority openly defied and your way of life derided.

You learned early the dignity of work, the necessity of saving. Now you are locked into the pattern of working and attempting to save—partly by habit but also by the two generations on either side of you. For the older generation, you may feel an obligation to backstop the dwindling resources of retired persons whose leisure time make your visits seem too infrequent and your work habits compulsive. For the younger generation, your children in their late teens and early twenties, you may continue to provide at least the necessities of life, while they criticize your work ethos that makes it possible for them to do their thing.

The threat of "love withdrawal," used by your parents to keep you in line as a child, may now be used by your children to keep you in line as a parent. As a child, you were to be seen and not heard, now as a parent you may feel you are to be neither seen nor heard.

Your age group, already thinned by the low birth-rate during the depression and further depleted by World War II, is insufficient in numbers to fill all of the leadership roles and administrative positions usually assumed by those in their 40s and 50s. And on each side of you are the elderly and the young whose needs and wants have increased markedly the demands on your generation for taxes, leadership, and administrative responsibility.

It is not surprising that some of you have stepped off the escalator—have declined the next "promotion" to yet additional administrative duties, higher taxes, and a heavier work load, thus depleting even more the ranks of those remaining.

Your generation is caught up in the painful and frequently bewildering side-effects of change, of a combination of historical factors that may never be repeated. Your empathic commensurating with youth confronted by a rapidity of social change that outpaces all but the swift is seldom reciprocated. Obscured or ignored is your own confrontation with change, attendant with the anxiety of having obsolete skills and knowledge, and insufficient time and energy to unlearn and relearn.

You hurt, and you are at least entitled to a better understanding of why you hurt. Knowing there are reasons for pain, real and not imaginary, makes it more bearable. In essence, yours is a scared generation, afraid even of its own children. Such fear is denied by some who may have resolved their anxiety about their children and their own adult-role ambivalence by joining, eulogizing, and subsidizing youth. Occasionally, they are the ones who "methinks doth protest too much" in defense of the hippy-types to cover their own secret fear of failure as parents of hippies. And some of them may be the ones who, stalled on the academic or business promotion ladder, encourage and use youth to attack the establishment they themselves fear. Some of them may even mimic the limited vocabulary and myopic historical view of militant youth by equating, for example, the actions of the Boston Tea Party with the destruction of property by a few of our militant youth. There is a difference: The youth of Colonial times defied taxation without representation; those few of today's youth who resort to violence and destruction want representation without taxation.[3]

Not only do parents return to their husband-wife roles with greater vigor when their children leave them, but as Clark Vincent has noted well, they have to evaluate their past performance as parents and decide what lies ahead for them. Having found status and meaning in parenthood, middle-aged parents typically extend their parenthood to the spouses of their married children. Looking even further ahead, grandparenthood is not too far away and may be particularly relished as a time for indulgence of yet another generation with far less responsibility or guilt feelings concerning their own children.

Relearning to be Husbands and Wives   As life-cycle data reveal, husbands and wives become parents fairly early in their married life and find their parental roles superseding their husband-wife roles. Many new parents have had to learn how to set aside their own self-interests or to abandon what used to be the undistracted attention of their spouses in favor of child-rearing functions for some twenty-odd years. Typically, the husband and father continues to support his expanding and growing family, while the wife and mother manages the domestic household.

With the children grown up and out of the home, however, there is realization that, aside from the two or three years before the arrival of the first child, there was minimal experience in having the total, undivided attention of one's wife or husband. Exclusive couplehood can now be experienced, but to the dismay of some couples, there seems to be little vitality left in being middle-aged husbands and wives.

Yet, husbands and wives who have anticipated the ebb and flow of generational life can be and have been ready to refocus their attention upon each other. They do need each other. They do understand each other. They are comfortable with each other. Or, they have learned the arts of developing self-interests and aid and abet each other in their separate, yet supportive, paths.

If not, the accumulated years have alienated them and frayed their tolerance of each other. Their personal integrity is at stake, and each may hold the other responsible for wasting their abilities, assets, and energies on unappreciative children and an unresponsive spouse. It is at this point that private rages can erupt. Manifestations of this type of pent-up hostility include noncommunication for prolonged periods, open criticism, public ridicule, separations, desertions, and divorce.

It is in middle age, then, that husband-wife relationships are *really* tested. The rosy promises of undying love prior to marriage are now to be fulfilled. As suggested, anticipation and constant practice, even during the childbearing and child-rearing years, can make the middle years satisfying. But, still, men and women are not teen-agers or young adults at this stage of family life. At ages forty and fifty, they must begin again to deal with their husband-wife roles. The new factor is the passage of time, what it has done to them, and what they have allowed it to do. Unguided, experimental, rather unprepared—just as they entered into marriage and parenthood—the newness of resuming husband and wife roles can be an attractive challenge for them.

There seem to be no magic formulas to be followed. All that husbands and wives can do is discover for themselves if their lifetime philosophies have been solidly built. It may well be too late for them to alter their course of action. In this event, their lives can instruct others in what not to do, in what attitudes to avoid. Or, they can become living examples of human ingenuity; they find their personal lives at this stage very rewarding.[4]

Elderly Couples, Alone Together, in the Stage of the Empty Nest[5]

Added years bring a married couple to the stage of the empty nest. Not only have children grown up and possibly had children of their own, but, normally, the husband has retired from his work or career. The elderly wife, however, has *not* retired from her domestic life. Her services and skills are still needed to maintain their home. She must learn, more than ever, to work around her husband as she continues her daily tasks of cleaning, preparing meals, washing clothes, or managing household affairs. Her "retirement" began years ago as her children grew up gradually, as her menstrual cycle ceased, and as she witnessed the developments in her husband and herself. His retirement was, by contrast, despite some forewarning, rather abrupt—employed one day and unemployed the next day. Such aged and retired husbands find themselves at loose ends, much like children who ask, "What is there to do?" when time hangs heavy in their hands.

Most reports indicate that elderly couples in the United States

Table 14-3   Self-assessments of Marital Roles, by Age of Married Couples, Percent Distributions

	Age categories					
	21–24	25–34	35–44	45–54	55–64	65 and older
Evaluation of marital happiness						
Very happy	52	48	48	43	40	46
Above average	20	22	23	22	20	18
Average	26	28	26	31	34	34
Not too happy	2	2	2	4	5	2
Not known			1		1	
Frequency of feeling adequate						
Often	15	14	11	8	8	11
Once in a while	51	47	42	38	37	24
Never	31	36	43	50	51	59
Not known	3	3	4	4	4	6
Marriage problems						
Had problems	45	50	42	38	31	19
No problems	53	44	51	54	58	71
Inapplicable	2	2	2	4	5	2
Not known		4	5	4		
Number in sample	(132)	(509)	(472)	(366)	(288)	(160)

Source: Excerpted from Chapter IV of *Americans View Their Mental Health*, by Gerald Gurin, Joseph Veroff, and Sheila Feld, © 1970 by Basic Books, Inc., Publishers, New York.

prefer to live independently in their own homes as long as possible. On the other hand, they do not seek to isolate themselves or to be isolated from their children and grandchildren. This is a state of what Leopold Rosenmayr and Eva Kockeis have described as "intimacy at a distance."[6]

Most grandparents are not too far away from relatives and are seen much more frequently by their children than stereotypic judgments would have persons believe. On the other hand, as with every stereotype, there is a grain of truth in the studied neglect of grandparents by some children and grandchildren.

For some years, gerontologists, students of the aging process and the aged, have debated two contrasting theories. On the one hand, there are the *disengagement* theorists who note the need for gradual withdrawal from society by the elderly.[7] On the other hand, *engagement* theorists support the contention that all generations, including the elderly, need to be active in society in order to live.[8] The middle ground, of course, contains elements of both positions. As generations come along, social displacements can and do occur. Indeed, they *must* occur if society is to endure. In this process, the persons in the later stages of maturity need to sever some of their former associations. But this does not mean a retreat from life itself. It means a reengagement along other lines, possibly those somewhat neglected or postponed in the past. Among these relationships are the friendships of long duration that persons may be fortunate enough to have acquired. Long-standing friendships are bonuses along life's way. Age peers share a common past and find this to be enough to maintain a lifelong comradeship. It is also quite possible to have had a relationship of unequal status, as between professor and student, military commander and soldier, or employer and employee. Because age is a great leveler, these social differences are minimized in favor of an abiding loyalty to each other as both have grown older.

One of the perennial themes concerning elderly couples is that their marriages deteriorate in time. Such appears not to be the case if self-reports from the elderly themselves can be taken at face value. Gerald Gurin and his associates in sample of 2,500 married adults in the United States, twenty-one years of age and older, reported for example, that elderly couples were just as prone as younger couples to maximize their marital assets and to minimize their marital difficulties[9] (see Table 14-3).

TWO-GENERATIONAL FAMILY LIFE

The Summer-Winter Married Couple

While some 85 percent of married couples belong to approximately the same generation, age differentials of greater variety do occur, particularly as persons enter into second and third marriages.[10] As first marriages are terminated by death or divorce, remarriages often become important to older generations. Charles Bowerman's study suggests that homogamy operates in remarriages in the sense that prior marital status helps determine who will marry whom. Thus, divorced persons tend to seek out other divorced persons and widowed persons seek out other widowed persons with greater than chance frequency.[11] Bowerman also suggests that greater variety is acceptable, as remarrying men often select women who are many years their junior. The converse is also possible, but rarer, given the tendency of women to marry their seniors and men to marry their juniors.

These *summer-winter* remarriages, usually of the husband, are two-generational in scope and so merit attention in a survey of full family living. Such marriages become the stimuli for gossip, particularly when the new husband is socially prominent. Little or no study exists concerning them, but they are added evidence that cross-generational love can and does exist.

Both generational representatives see values in such a marriage. It is flattering to the older man and easier for the younger woman to bring such a marriage into being. The woman has instant status that derives from an already established husband, and the older husband is judged, at least by his new wife, to be emotionally "young," a factor of considerable importance in youth-oriented American society. It is an altogether acceptable exchange.

Much humor is leveled at the sexual side of such a marriage, typically negative when applied to the elder marital partner.[12] But studies have shown that there is a sustained interest and active participation in sexual activity far into the advanced years.[13] Such findings come as no surprise to older men and women, who have known all along of their sexual behaviors. What is new is that family research has finally caught up with an area presumed to be nonexistent because of puritanical assessments.

Summer-winter marriages, by virtue of their participants, tend to emphasize the husband-wife relationship and not parent-child relationships. If there are children from previous marriages, these children have also married or are young adults who are far closer to emancipation than most children who acquire a second mother or father. To the adult offspring of prior marriages, the newer summer-winter marriages of their parents are welcomed. Not only are their parents finding a companionship that fills their lives, but their parents are far less likely to become the interfering in-laws of the more normal newly married couples of the same generation.

A final characteristic of summer-winter marriages is a time-consciousness that goes beyond that of marriages that may last as long as fifty years. For the elder partner, at least, time is running out, and summer-winter marriages of integrity seek to make the most of whatever limited time is available to them.

Parents and Children

A full family can minimally consist of two parents and an only child. But full families frequently include second, third, fourth, and fifth children. These siblings may be rather closely spaced so that they essentially belong to the same or similar generations. If the spacing is irregular, however, one set of children may be quite grown up while another set of children within the same family setting is immature. The menopausal child born to a woman supposedly past her childbearing years and the "unexpected" child who was conceived through some failure in contraception, as well as the wanted child deliberately conceived out of a love for children, are cases in point.

The birth order of a number of children and their sexual distribution set the structure for full family living. If the number of children is larger than usual, say, six to a dozen or more children, then generational differences come into even greater play, as James Bossard has outlined in his study of the large family system.[14]

The sharing of parental responsibilities among the older siblings is common to all these cases. The older girls are usually expected to act as the mother's assistants, and the older boys are expected to behave as extensions of paternal authority.

The larger the family, the greater the need for order of some kind. Timing of normal family activities, such as preparing meals, using the bathroom, making a trip, or going to bed, calls for careful planning and cooperation. Further, as Bossard has also noted, the petty details that upset the more intensive lives of small families—a spill of jam on the family tablecloth, a strong difference of opinion—are swept aside in order to get on with the more basic needs of eating, resting, and appropriate attention for each sibling.

Many members of large families have noted the lack of material things and the abundance of loving concern among siblings. A large family with minimal economic assets is no great blessing in disguise. There are diminishing returns as levels are reached wherein no single member can receive even minimal care. In the 1970s, at least, there is growing recognition that population pressures and overcrowding into finite spaces are reaching painful proportions. One symptom that is appearing with increasing frequency is the allegation among about-to-be-married young couples that they intend to have no children of their own but that they do intend to adopt orphaned or abandoned children. Time will reveal if these promises have any substance.[15]

As large families finally experience the full maturity of their children, there remains the problem of the aging parents. If two persons can rear six or a dozen children, can these children provide care and attention to the needs of their parents? The practical solution usually falls to the youngest child, who has not quite begun to establish his or her home. If the youngest happens to be the "baby sister," it is she who will devote greater portions of her time to the aging parents. All other siblings tend to offer some form of token support or care, but nothing approaching the devotion and service given parents by the one sibling who has taken the responsibility.[16]

Not only does role reversal occur in terms of dependence-independence between children and aging parents, but there is also "reverse socialization." In these circumstances, it falls to the younger generation to train and control their elders to cope with their physical decrements as well as with their losses in social position and power. It is quite a new experience for both generations, and the finesse needed to carry it off sorely tests the ingenuity of both children and parents.

Some years ago, Bossard reminded family specialists that they should pay far greater attention to a "neglected member of the family" than they were accustomed. This neglected member of the family was the family pet—most likely, a dog.[17] At least one of the invaluable services performed by the family pet is its function of prolonging the parental roles of middle-aged and elderly parents. The family pet *always* needs attention, and the pleasure it brings its keepers derives partially from the sustained dominance and importance of those who take care of it. The need to be needed is powerful, and parents whose children have grown up are gratified by this sustained dependence of their family pet over the years. Ideally, of course, the need to be needed extends to human relationships in which persons perform important functions by continuing to live as happily and effectively as possible.

THREE-GENERATIONAL FAMILY LIFE

As we have noted, most family units begin with husbands and wives of the same generation who, soon enough, produce children, the second generation. As we have also noted, two-generation family living can occur for childless couples who have entered marriage with extreme age differences, or children of a given couple can belong to two different generations by virtue of their uneven spacing. But the most frequent means of developing multigenerational family living has been for families to continue to live within the same households despite the arrival of new generations.

Instead of married children moving out to establish their own domiciles, they maintain their spouses and their offspring in the grandparental homes and three-generation families come into existence. In this additive process, the grandparents act as "hosts." If it is wiser to have aging parents leave their original homes for such reasons as failing health, too many rooms, costly maintenance, or sheer loneliness, then it is altogether possible that aging parents reside in the homes of their children as "guests."

Three-generation families have never been very popular in the United States and have numbered 5 percent or less for many years. The preference is to maintain independent residences for as long as possible.

However, preferences and practicality may not coincide, and three-generation households can and do exist.

Studies of three-generation households suggest that the middle generation, husbands and wives who are middle-aged, acts as a mediator between the grandparents and the grandchildren. Depending upon the middle generation's skills and understanding, the patterns of three-generation households are successes or failures.[18] Dorrian Sweetser confirms this theme with her cross-cultural studies of three-generation families in Finland, Sweden, and Great Britain.[19] Sweetser reports that the crucial relationship is between mothers and daughters or between mothers and daughters-in-law. Sweetser has observed that the more tension-free atmosphere occurs between mothers and daughters. In the case of daughters-in-law, a new accommodation must occur before it is clear how the two females will get along with each other in such close domestic proximity. The many years of experience that mothers and daughters have had go far in explaining why these two women can find some mutually acceptable system rather speedily.

GENERATIONAL REVERBERATIONS

If multigenerational family life has any social or personal significance, it is likely to be found in the impact representatives of one generation have had upon succeeding generations. This is the reasoning for focusing so much attention in this text on family traditions, vigencias, estates, and experiences.

A number of family-life educators have recognized this theme, and it is reflected in the manner in which they instruct their students. Shipman, for example, has relied heavily upon an autobiographical term paper as a device for students to pull together the myriad data of family life in some personal and meaningful way.[20] He cautions, however, that there are serious problems in dredging up family-life experiences that are characterized by traumas and discontinuity between and among generations. For those students whose family-life histories are filled with satisfying years, there is no problem. But for those students who have inherited some tragic or painful family backgrounds, the autobiographical sketches exacerbate an already sensitive situation.

Shipman does suggest that appropriate guidelines need to be formulated to handle these assignments. He will, for example, excuse certain students for whom the recall would be too traumatic. Such students can go on to do less emotionally loaded projects. One guarantee to prevent identification or embarrassment is to promise there will be no discussion of a specific family-life history until the persons concerned have graduated and are unknown to the present generation of undergraduates.

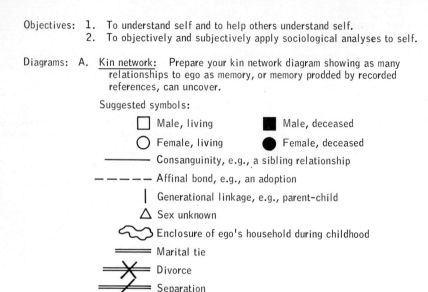

Objectives: 1. To understand self and to help others understand self.
             2. To objectively and subjectively apply sociological analyses to self.

Diagrams: A. Kin network: Prepare your kin network diagram showing as many
               relationships to ego as memory, or memory prodded by recorded
               references, can uncover.

               Suggested symbols:

                    ☐ Male, living   ■ Male, deceased

                    ○ Female, living   ● Female, deceased

               ───────── Consanguinity, e.g., a sibling relationship

               ───────── Affinal bond, e.g., an adoption

                    │ Generational linkage, e.g., parent-child

                    △ Sex unknown

                    ∿ Enclosure of ego's household during childhood

               ═════════ Marital tie

               ═══╳═══ Divorce

               ═══╱═══ Separation

           B. Significant others: Draw five concentric circles that represent the degree
               of closeness to ego and place within each symbols of persons ego holds
               as significant others in ego's life history.

               Innermost circle refers to ego and family of origin.
               Second circle refers to maternal and paternal kin.
               Third circle refers to close friends and associates.
               Fourth circle refers to functionaries (e.g., teachers, doctors).
               Fifth circle refers to distant personalities (movie stars,
               Presidents, fictional characters, etc.)

Figure 14–1 Class study assignment in sociology of childhood.

Shipman's experience is identical to that of the author in classes
concerned with the sociology of childhood. Students were asked to
prepare, aided or unaided, a kinship network tracing ascendent and
descendent generations in their families. Their own location within the
network was to be marked prominently with the term Ego. Further, they
were asked to prepare a diagram showing significant others in their lives.
(See Figure 14-1 setting forth the directions given students.) The assignment turned out to be a most unhappy experience for those students
whose generational backgrounds were filled with struggle, degradation,
anxiety, and other psychiatric dilemmas. One of the most dramatic and
unintentional results was the case of a young female student who literally
was tearing out her hair by the roots in her agonized recollection of
family incidents far back in her past.

Lewis Coser's materials suggest that much unwanted results can be
eliminated by removing personal identification by the assignment of

Example of kin network diagram:

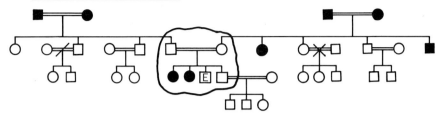

Example of significant others diagram: Accompany with an explanation of why
   individuals were selected as significant.
Identify heroes or heroines with an H; identify those ego strongly dislikes with a V.

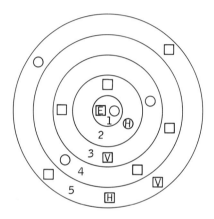

Objective background data: Provide the following information:
   Occupations of father and mother
   Family authority: patriarchal, matriarchal, equalitarian, other
   Religious preference, if any; ethnic backgrounds
   Placement in social class structure, size of childhood community, rating of ego's
      personal health

Subjective data: Provide brief but pointed essays on ego's childhood, adolescence,
   young adulthood, same-sex and cross-sex judgments, values, fears, goals, hopes,
   and plans, and finally, ego's philosophy of life

Figure 14-1   (Continued)

studies and analyses in pertinent literature.[21] Using episodes prepared by
skillful writers of literature, students can sharpen their abilities to trace
and to evaluate multigenerational impacts in families without becoming
emotionally enmeshed through personal identification. Even more effective is the study of biographies of famous or infamous persons who have
left their mark on human history in some large or small way. Students
start with full knowledge of outcomes and, by *ex post facto* analyses, can

trace generational antecedents with considerable interest. Most sociologists have left biographical material in the hands of nonsociologists, with the notable exceptions of the greats in sociological history. Few sociologists have taken the time to examine the multigenerational foundations of a person outside their field. One sociologist who has used the multigenerational approach with good effect is Paul Sites, a social theorist who has carefully examined the multigenerational background of the alleged assassin of the late President John Kennedy, Lee Harvey Oswald. His book entitled *Lee Harvey Oswald and the American Dream* comes very close to what can ideally be done by an insightful sociologist concerning the personal and social ramifications of a specific life history.[22] The point is that while many biographers are adept in eliciting background data and interpreting it, sociologists, too, can bring to bear their particular expertise on life histories and their societal impacts.[23]

SUMMARY

In full family living, students of marriage and family can go beyond their preoccupation with husband-wife adjustments, the arrival of children, and the socialization of their children. Husbands and wives may remain childless, voluntarily or involuntarily, and consequently find their relationships continuing as one-generation centered. Most, however, do have children and experience a renewed interest in themselves and their generational peers only after their children have departed from the home. Selected issues such as the status of middle-aged parents, in-law problems, and the need to relearn the roles of husbands and wives are typically viewed from the perspective of a youthful generation. In this chapter, these problems are viewed from the perspective of the middle-aged parents, themselves. Further, anticipatory socialization is begun by the middle-aged parents as they contemplate the conditions of the elderly grandparents.

Two-generational family life usually consists of the parents and their children. It can occur, however, in those marriages characterized by extreme age differentials between the spouses—marriages described as summer-winter in this chapter. But even alleged two-generation families may actually contain additional generational representatives due to uneven child spacing. In such instances, the oldest children are frequently required to assume parental authority and responsibilities earlier than normatively expected. In due time, role reversal and reverse socialization are experienced between aging parents and their mature children. In all these two-generation families, much depends upon the ability of generational representatives to work out cooperative patterns that both protect their interests and those of their adjacent generations.

Three-generational living is relatively infrequent in contemporary American society. Those three-generation families that have been successful depend heavily upon the middle generation to achieve some type of family harmony between the grandchildren and the grandparents.

Finally, generational reverberations are experienced within families and culminate in unique personalities and impacts upon the greater society. This applies to the nonfamous, the famous, and the infamous. Family-life educators have found the autobiographical sketch enables their students to pull together much marriage-and-family data and to apply these materials. Caution is needed, however, as this personalizing of data can trigger renewed anguish that may have been dormant up to and including entrance into college. One suggestion to avoid this possibility is to examine literature already "loaded" with familial experiences of fictional and nonfictional characters. Another suggestion is to reexamine the complete life histories of known personalities and by *ex post facto* analyses to discover just how multiple generations have left their marks upon individuals and the larger society.

REFERENCES

1 Lillian E. Troll, "The 'Generation Gap' in Later Life: An Introductory Discussion and Some Preliminary Findings," *Sociological Focus*, vol. 5, no. 1, pp. 18–28, Autumn 1971.

2 Clark E. Vincent, "An Open Letter to the 'Caught' Generation," *The Family Coordinator*, vol. 21, no. 2, pp. 143–150, April 1972. Used with permission.

3 Ibid., pp. 143–144.

4 See "The Sociology of the Elderly," *Sociological Symposium*, no. 2, Spring, 1969, and Supplement, 221 pages.

5 A most useful source is *The Family Coordinator*, vol. 21, no. 1, January 1972, special issue, "Aging and the Family." An interesting experiment in giving students "pre-experience" in what it means to be "old," is described in Robert Kastenbaum "Getting There Ahead of Time," *Psychology Today*, vol. 5, no. 7, pp. 53–54, 82–84, December 1971.

6 Leopold Rosenmayr and Eva Kockeis, "Propositions for Sociological Theory of Aging and the Family," *International Social Science Journal*, vol. 15, no. 3, p. 418, 1963.

7 Elaine Cumming and William E. Henry, *Growing Old: The Process of Disengagement*, New York: Basic Books, Inc., 1961.

8 Robert Kastenbaum, *New Thoughts on Old Age,* New York: Springer Publishing Co., Inc., 1964.

9 Gerald Gurin and Associates, *Americans View Their Mental Health: A Nationwide Interview Study*, New York: Basic Books, Inc., 1960, pp. 88–90.

10 Charles E. Bowerman, "Assortative Mating by Previous Marital Status: Seattle, 1939–1946, "*American Sociological Review*, vol. 18, no. 2, pp. 170–177, April 1953.

11   Ibid., pp. 176–177. See, also, Jessie Bernard, *Remarriage: A Study of Marriage*, New York: The Dryden Press, Inc., 1956.

12   See Erdman Palmore, "Attitudes toward Aging as Shown by Humor," *The Gerontologist*, vol. 11, no. 3, pp. 181–186, Autumn 1971.

13   One useful source is William H. Masters and Virginia E. Johnson, *Human Sexual Response*, chap. 15, "The Aging Female," and chap. 16, "The Aging Male," Boston: Little, Brown and Company, 1966, pp. 223–270. See, also, Harold I. Lief, "Interview: Sex in Older People," *Sexual Behavior*, vol. 1, no. 7, pp. 72–74, October 1971.

14   James H. S. Bossard and Eleanor Stoker Boll, *The Large Family System*, Philadelphia: University of Pennsylvania Press, 1956.

15   Of interest in this connection is Leslie Aldridge Westoff and Charles F. Westoff, *From Now to Zero: Fertility, Contraception, and Abortion in America*, Boston: Little, Brown and Company, 1971.

16   See *The Multi-Generation Family: Papers on Theory and Practice, Problems and Promise*, Division on Aging, New Jersey Department of State, June 1964. See, also, Paul H. Glaser and Lois N. Glaser, "Role Reversal and Conflict between Aged Parents and Their Children," *Marriage and Family Living*, vol. 24, no. 1, pp. 46–51, February, 1962; Irwin Deutscher, "The Quality of Postparental Life: Definitions of the Situation," *Journal of Marriage and the Family*, vol. 26, no. 1, pp. 52–59, February 1964.

17   James H. S. Bossard, "I Wrote about Dogs," *Mental Hygiene*, July 1950, pp. 385–390; James H. S. Bossard, "The Mental Hygiene of Owning a Dog," *Mental Hygiene*, July 1944, pp. 408–413, and Nelson Foote, "A Neglected Member of the Family," *Marriage and Family Living*, vol. 18, no. 3, pp. 213–218, August 1956.

18   Marvin R. Koller, "Studies of Three-Generation Households," *Marriage and Family Living*, vol. 16, no. 3, pp. 205–206, August 1954.

19   From a paper presented at the annual meeting of the Eastern Sociological Society, April 11, 1964, Boston, Mass., Dorrian Apple Sweetser, "Mother-Daughter Ties between Generations in Industrial Societies,"

20   Gordon Shipman, "The Use of Autobiographies in Marriage Education," *Marriage and Family Living*, vol. 24, no. 4, pp. 393–398, November 1962.

21   Lewis Coser, *Sociology Through Literature*, Englewood Cliffs, N. J.: Prentice-Hall, Inc., 1963.

22   Paul Sites, *Lee Harvey Oswald and the American Dream*, New York: Pageant Press, 1967.

23   A number of other articles concerning the later phases of family life cycles include the following: Arnold M. Rose, "Factors Associated with Life-Satisfaction of Middle-Class, Middle-Aged Persons, "*Marriage and Family Living*, vol. 17, no. 1, pp. 15–19, February 1955; Ruth S. Cavan, "Family Tensions between the Old and the Middle-Aged," *Marriage and Family Living*, vol. 18, no. 4, pp. 323–327, November 1956; A. Joseph Brayshaw, "Middle-Aged Marriage: Idealism, Realism and the Search for Meaning," *Marriage and Family Living*, vol. 24, no. 4, pp. 358–364, November 1962; Joan Aldous, "The Consequences of Intergenerational Continuity," *Journal of*

Marriage and the Family, vol. 27, no. 4, pp. 462–468, November 1965; Helene Borke, "A Family over Three Generations: The Transmission of Interacting and Relating Patterns," *Journal of Marriage and the Family*, vol. 29, no. 4, pp. 638–655, November 1967; Catherine S. Chilman, "Families in Development at Mid-Stage of the Family Life Cycle," *The Family Coordinator*, vol. 17, no. 4, pp. 297–312, October 1968; Mildred I. Morgan, "The Middle Life and the Aging Family," *The Family Coordinator*, vol. 18, no. 3, pp. 296–298, July 1969; Lillian E. Troll, "The Family of Later Life: A Decade Review," *Journal of Marriage and the Family*, vol. 33, no. 2, pp. 263–290, May 1971; and Donald Spence and Thomas Lonner, "The 'Empty Nest': A Transition within Motherhood," *The Family Coordinator*, vol. 20, no. 4, pp. 369–375, October 1971.

STUDY QUESTIONS AND ACTIVITIES

1 What are the contrasts between one-generational, two-generational, and three-generational family living?

2 How do age differentials between husbands and wives manifest themselves as couples age?

3 Suggest what would be the characteristics of "a sociology of the middle-aged."

4 In what sense does each generation owe the other compassion and understanding?

5 Is learning new roles a quality reserved only for the young? How does learning change with each generation as it moves along the life cycle?

6 Explain why some researches have uncovered progressive deterioration of marriage and family life while others have not.

7 Examine research and theory that attempt to appraise the dimensions of sexuality among the elderly.

8 Develop a paper explaining the nature of widowhood and widowerhood.

9 Contrast small-family systems with large-family systems.

10 What are the positive and negative features of pets in family contexts?

11 Use the suggested exercise in relating kin networks and significant others as they apply in your own life.

SUGGESTED ADDITIONAL READINGS

Atchley, Robert C., *The Social Forces in Later Life: An Introduction to Social Gerontology*, Belmont, Calif.: Wadsworth Publishing Company, Inc., 1972.

Carp, Frances M. (ed.), *The Retirement Process,* Washington, D.C.: U.S. Department of Health, Education, and Welfare, December 1966.

Cumming, Elaine, and William E. Henry, *Growing Old: The Process of Disengagement*, New York: Basic Books, Inc., Publishers, 1961.

Kastenbaum, Robert, *New Thoughts on Old Age*, New York: Springer Publishing Co., Inc., 1964.

Neugarten, Bernice L. (ed.), *Middle Age and Aging*, Chicago: The University of Chicago Press, 1968.

Riley, Matilda White, et al., *Aging and Society*, three vols., New York: Russell Sage Foundation, 1968 and 1969.

Rodman, Hyman, *Teaching about Families: Textbook Evaluations and Recommendations for Secondary Schools*, Cambridge, Mass.: Howard A. Doyle Publishing Company, 1970.

U.S. Public Health Service, *Patterns of Living and Housing of Middle-Aged and Older People*, Public Health Service Publication No. 1496, 1965.

White House Conference on Aging, 1971, Final Report, two vols., *Toward a National Policy on Aging*, U.S. Department of Health, Education, and Welfare, 1973.

Williams, Richard H., and Claudine G. Wirths, *Lives Through the Years*, New York: Atherton Press, 1965.

Part Three

Future Generations

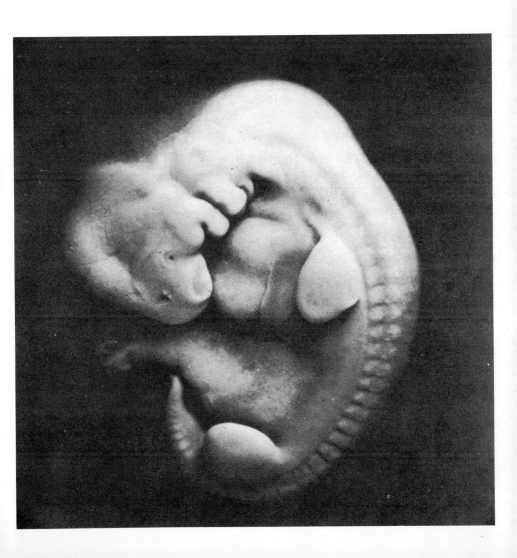

Chapter 15

Resources for Family Reorganization

There is nothing new about sex, marriage, and family systems being under attack. The polemics of David Cooper, for example, in his *The Death of the Family*[1] are stylistically bizarre but highly attractive to those who feel their selfhood is somehow stifled or denied by families as they have known them or as they understand them. This mood finds support in the provocative statements of Cooper when he writes, "When will parents allow themselves to be brought up by their children?"[2] Or, "Making love is good in itself, and the more it happens in any way possible or conceivable between as many people as possible, the better."[3]

In multigenerational terms, Cooper continues:

At this point I think one has to make a distinction between generations and their possibilities. I think that if we now, always in a first-world context, take the generation of people in early middle age, and also that of people now in their mid-teens to mid-twenties (the generation gap between these two groups now seems to be little more than twelve years) we find a common problem, albeit a problem that some of us might be grateful to have: the need for a strong, central two-person relationship that is inevitably felt by others to be somewhat excluding. Whether this need will apply, in the future, to the generation still in primary school is another matter, since the rate of break-down of the institutional fabric of bourgeois society may be rapid enough in the next decade to introduce, for them, the possibility of a less centric system of relationships. There may be a shifting system of dyads leading to a polycentric relationship structure, even though there will probably be a degree of hierarchization in the emotional significance of the various two-person relationships that each person has.[4]

In less esoteric or obscure language, family life has long been observed to be in a state of transition from one form to another, from one interactional pattern to another, and never quite in a fixed or stabilized posture. Social change is not a startling discovery for students of family life. It is a fact of life and is neither resented nor rejected by family scholars.[5]

The issue is not whether families as they are now known will continue to exist or disappear, but rather in what direction and in what form they will change. And, to those who see beyond form and direction, the consequences of such change are also critical.

At present, there are two major alternatives confronting family life: either family life is retained or it is rejected. If it is retained, there is need to consider in what ways it can be modified to meet social changes. Reorganization, reassessment, and realignment of generational traditions would follow this course of action. If family life as it is now known is rejected by future generations, something must be provided to fill the void. Our premise is that family life will continue into the foreseeable future. Accordingly, this chapter seeks to identify those resources that will help family life remain viable.

The second alternative, the rejection of the past and present, or in less dramatic terms, experimentation, is reserved for the next chapter, which deals with the future of the family as it is dimly seen from the perspective of the present.

THE CURRENT STRENGTH OF FAMILIES

Despite the grumblings and mumblings of malcontents concerning the sad state of American families and their inevitable demise, there is ample evidence that there still are contemporary families that are quite satisfying, resilient, and healthy as far as their participants are concerned. A sampling of 2,164 persons representing all persons eighteen years and older living in private households in the continental United States in 1971 found 60 percent of the husbands and 56 percent of the wives completely satisfied with their marriages.[6] That they never have wished to marry anyone other than their present spouse was reported by 71 percent of the married couples; 68 percent had never even thought of divorce as a solution to whatever marital problems they might have encountered. Attention, of course, is directed to those persons who have complaints because they are seeking some better way to satisfy their longings for "the better life." Extending their dissatisfaction to the total society, the same study revealed that 2 percent of the total population, 9 percent of the adult population, or 39 percent of the most critical elements in American society were willing to leave the United States if they had the chance.[7]

William Westley and Nathan Epstein have studied the families of emotionally healthy college students in Montreal, Canada, and confirm the ability of many families to produce college-age students quite prepared to deal with contemporary conditions realistically and effectively without self-recriminations, self-doubts, or self-hatreds that denigrate the larger society.[8] Westley and Epstein support the thesis that the husband-wife relationship needs to reflect respect and affection for each other and these feelings, in turn, are extended to their children who grow up to become emotionally healthy adults themselves.

Covering a period of some nine years, 170 students from 88 families were intensively studied by Westley and Epstein with the help of psychiatric-psychological specialists and sociological specialists. The families were divided into three categories: those that were the healthiest, those that were the most disturbed, and those families midway between the two extremes. The families represented were those of first-year McGill University students who were native-born Canadians, residents in Montreal, English Protestants, and emotionally well-balanced. The aspects of family life under investigation were power, psychodynamics, role, status, and work.

> [The] most important finding was that children's emotional health is closely related to the emotional relationships between their parents. When these relationships were warm and constructive, such that the husband and wife felt loved, admired, and encouraged to act in ways that they themselves admired, the children were healthy and happy. Couples who were emotionally close, meeting each other's needs and encouraging positive self-images in each other, became good parents. Since they met each other's needs, they did not use their children to live out their needs; since they were happy and satisfied, they could support and meet their children's needs; and since their

own identities were clarified, they saw their children as distinct from themselves. All this helped the children become emotionally healthy people.

This positive relationship between husband and wife did not depend upon their being emotionally healthy themselves, though quite clearly it was a great help. In some cases, the husband and wife were emotionally disturbed, but still managed to set up a good matrimonial relationship. When this happened, the children were emotionally healthy; it seemed as if the good marital relationship of the parents had insulated the children from the parents' emotional deficiencies.[9]

One of the most valuable findings was that the "father's care of daughters when they were babies and the mother's care of sons when they were children strongly influenced both the emotional health and personality of their children."[10] In short, "The child needs acceptance as a male or female by the parent of the opposite sex if he or she is to grow up to be emotionally healthy."[11]

At the opposite end of the spectrum from emotionally healthy families are "multiproblem" families.[12] They are familiar types to public welfare, correctional, and protective agencies throughout the country. They are known for their chronic need for assistance and services, their frequent crisis situations, their deviant behaviors, and their extensive generational histories and contacts with social-work agencies. Often they are antagonistic, alienated, or hostile to the very agencies that seek to help them. Relationships both inside and outside the families are negative in terms of hostility, health, economic strength, and existence as an ongoing unit.[13]

Fortunately, assessment of proportions of multiproblem families in various American communities varies from a high of about 8 percent to a low of 1 percent. The average is 2 to 3 percent, but their small proportions belie their reliance upon communal agencies. Well over half the combined services of many communities' dependency, health, and adjustment agencies are devoted to these same families.[14]

A profile of family functioning was developed by researchers and caseworkers in St. Paul, Minnesota, that could be used to evaluate at least three levels of family functioning: inadequate, marginal, and adequate. The three levels were described as follows:

Inadequate Functioning (Community has a right to intervene.) Laws and/or mores clearly violated. Behavior of family members a threat to the community. Family life characterized by extreme conflict, neglect, severe deprivation or very poor relationships resulting in physical and/or emotional suffering of family members; disruption of family life imminent, children in clear and present danger because of conditions above or other behavior inimical to their welfare.

Marginal Functioning (Behavior not sufficiently harmful to justify intervention.) No violation of major laws although behavior of family members is contrary to what is acceptable for status group. Family life is marked by conflict, apathy, or unstable relationships which are a potential threat to welfare of family members and community; each crisis poses the danger of family disruption, but children are not in imminent danger.

Adequate Functioning (Behavior in line with community expectations.) Laws and mores are observed; behavior is acceptable to status group. Family life is stable, members have a sense of belonging, family is able to handle problems without facing disruption, children are being raised in an atmosphere conducive to healthy physical and emotional development. Socialization process carried out affirmatively; adequate training in social skills.[15]

Applied to 150 of the most disorganized families in the St. Paul area, the scale revealed that the interpersonal relationships within the families were the most disturbed or disorganized, whereas there was greater ability to function cohesively in relationship to the external community.[16] The greatest accomplishment of these families, then, was to remain physically intact, despite a host of internal difficulties. The damage to personalities and needs, however, was almost incalculable.

The practical goal, of course, is to identify multiproblem families in the making as soon as possible and develop an effective program of prevention and intervention before family disorganization becomes full-blown. Most agree that poverty is one of the key factors in family disorganization, as it is in other social problems such as crime or inadequate educational systems. But enough is known to affirm that *economic* poverty is not sufficient to explain the host of difficulties that multiproblem families endure. Much more needs to be known and acted upon before family life can be improved for *all* levels of society. "Poverty" in a much broader sense is related to lack of knowledge and ability to meet human needs in a complex society. Intellectual and emotional poverty are the targets to attack, and family-life specialists seek to fill this void in people's lives.

THREE RESOURCES FOR FAMILY REORGANIZATION

There are three resources available to those who recognize the need to reorganize family life in more effective ways. These resources are *education, research*, and *counseling.* We begin with education because we can work only with what we currently know. We continue with research because we always need to know more. And we conclude with counseling because persons live in the present and cannot be helped by what may yet occur.

Education is often cited as a panacea, regardless of the problem. But, in the case of American family life, there is disagreement as to what data are relevant and what data are nonrelevant. Some would say that the data gathered so laboriously by past and present generations of family-life specialists are inapplicable today. Others are prone to sift through the wealth of information to determine that which is timeless, universal, or far-reaching.

Some would say that such data are available to all through mass media or mass education. Others would note that family-life data are unavailable to millions who require special help in obtaining it.

Finally, there is the unwarranted assumption that persons who may need education really desire it. Indeed, there are those who summarily reject or resist education for family life even when they encounter it. Or there are those who adopt countervalues. There are many students, however, who by choice or by chance have experienced family-life education at its best. These students are receptive and perceptive enough to recognize the complex nature of family life and realize the value of family-life education.

Education, of course, is not enough. Constant updating from research sources is needed. Valid, relevant, tested knowledge is "the growing edge" of a dynamic education that explores the unknown and that verifies, substantiates, or ascertains where generations are going. Family life may never be completely understood, but constant research efforts, at least, strengthen the knowledge of those who attempt to reduce the agonies of unnecessary distress among families.

Lastly, life goes on. People do meet, fall in love, or come together, in whatever way they deem appropriate, and establish families. They may or may not be exposed to family-life education. They may or may not know what new findings are being offered by family-life research. But they may, nevertheless, need help.

If it can be made available, counseling can be beneficial to those families in need of help. Those in "family trouble" can be helped, but much depends upon the presence of qualified family counselors and the willingness to work with them. What is interesting to note is that millions marry and create families with complete confidence in their own abilities to handle any and all problems that ensue from their marital or familial decisions. These same persons are convinced, for example, that medical, dental, or hospital care may become necessary at some point in their lives and would think twice about isolating themselves in communities that lack medical doctors, dentists, or hospital facilities.

Future generations may see a time when "doctors-at-marriage" or "doctors-at-family" will hang out their shingles. Such professionals will be consulted as regularly as the six-month interval between dental checkups or physical examinations recommended for most persons by the health professions. At present, the supply and quality of family counselors are limited, but there are many who have turned to family counselors in their desperation and have found relief or "cure" for their troubles.

Family-Life Education

Family-life education is a comparative newcomer on the educational scene in the United States. It developed in the late nineteenth and early twentieth centuries out of the ferment of the times that witnessed the decline of rural life, in which an agricultural base was the essential quality of life for most Americans. In its place came urban life based on industry. Family life could no longer be held in check by the older controls of primary groups, such as neighbors, relatives, fellow churchgoers, or friends. In addition, both descriptive and applied knowledge was growing in such specializations as pyschology, sociology, biology, economics, home economics, psychiatry, law, education, and medicine. Interest in mental, physical, and social health, childhood, home management, domestic-relations law, behavior problems, social work, teaching, and new-found relationships between males and females served to broaden interest in families themselves. Finally, national organizations, such as the American Home Economics Association, the American Social Hygiene Association, the National Council on Parent Education, and the Progressive Education Association, with the aid of large private and federal-government funding and the support of personnel from colleges and universities, came together to form the National Council on Family Relations in 1938.

The National Council on Family Relations is the leading organization in family-life education and publishes both the *Journal of Marriage and the Family* and *The Family Life Coordinator*, in which major research, education, and social services in behalf of family life are reported and shared among diverse professional and lay persons interested in marriage and family.

Most high schools, colleges, and universities throughout the country offer one or more courses in family life. Further, family-life education is being promoted at both ends of the formal educational process. At one end, more and more junior high and elementary schools are developing family-centered educational programs. At the other end, more and more graduate schools or specialized centers are trying to pull together the vast array of accumulating research and theory that deals with family-life education.

In brief, family life is no longer regarded as something that can be taken for granted. The variety, options, strategies, emphases, objectives, and social impacts of families are too involved to be passed over lightly. The well-educated person should know not only history, English, foreign language, and basic mathematics but also as much as possible about family life.

Family-life education does not lack opponents, however. Its critics and outspoken antagonists favor a return to the complete prerogative of parents to rear their children as they deem best. Further, opponents of family-life education vigorously object to sex education outside the home; to secular approaches that demean or negate religious philosophies; to the invasion of privacy of individuals, couples, or families; and to the permissive attitudes that accept a variety of ways to conduct human affairs. Many opponents question the ability of family-life education to achieve its objectives—a question, incidentally, that is rarely asked of other fields firmly established in schools throughout the nation. Finally, objections are raised about the integrity of family-life educators.

The sensitivity and hostility of those who are skeptical about the value, efficacy, or legitimacy of family-life educators run a high risk of offending both the general public and their clientele, the students themselves. Family-life education has been called the "graveyard" of some excellent teachers who might otherwise have been applauded for their enthusiasm, seriousness of purpose, and dedication. It is the unique subject matter of family-life education that seems to be at the heart of the matter. Most persons are convinced that they know little about such technical subjects as architecture, engineering, or medicine, but family-life education is "different." *Everyone* has experienced family life and regards himself or herself as highly qualified to judge how others should live. To the credit of most family-life students, they approach family-life study with the same respect they accord other subjects in which they have limited knowledge. They expect to learn, and they often report that they do.

There *are* internal problems within family-life education. One is the interdisciplinary nature of the field. It draws upon so many specializations as to tax the talents and attention of family-life educators. Another problem, the rapid expansion and proliferation of knowledge concerning such topics as psychosocial development, sexuality, political power, drugs, youth rebellion, minority rights, economic cycles, and comparative family life trouble family-life educators who seek to keep abreast of developments and to integrate their knowledge in some meaningful way for their students. Yet another problem is the presence of "empire builders" who wish to claim that family-life education is their exclusive territory. Such ambitious persons would oust all other educators from the field or subordinate them to their own perspectives. All students must come before them to be "educated," and all other fields are regarded as peripheral. Finally, those who teach family life and those who prepare family-life educators are products of their respective generational times. This they reflect in their susceptibility to normal human error, bias, or preferences that may cloud their thinking, scramble their ideas, and lead them to confuse their ideologies with ever-changing reality. They must constantly strive to be as open as possible to new ideas. The remark that the formula for failure is trying to please everyone is certainly applicable to family-life education and family-life educators.

Students want to know the state of our knowledge in family life. Most courses meet this desire by being as "functional" or practical as possible so that students may readily apply data to their own lives and situations. What is less popular is the synthesis of family-life data into some generalized, all-encompassing format. Yet this willingness to stand apart from immediacies provides the format that is needed to discover the thrust of family life. Much of this text has been concerned with the multigenerational approach which provides an ordering of family life phenomena which might otherwise be overlooked. Theories are the scaffolding that helps persons reach out to the details of a building. Otherwise they mistake a window, a door, or a decoration for the whole structure. There is more than one way to erect a scaffold, and the multigenerational approach is only one approach to family-life education. "Pure" courses in the sociology or the psychology of the family have been taught, and they have much to offer. But these theoretical courses tend to appeal to the already committed, the already convinced specialists. Most courses in family life, then, are a combination of theoretical and pragmatic sources.

Family-life education may or may not be a field that differs only in content from other courses. Good teaching in family-life education may or may not call for special skills. But there are teaching aids that are uniquely related to family-life education, and these have been increasing over the years.

Family Life Publications, under the leadership of Gelolo McHugh, has published, for example, one of the best series of inventories that deal directly with essential areas of family life. The inventories are subjected to rigorous tests of reliability and validity before they are placed on the market. They enable students and teachers to know what command they may have of the specific topic or area involved. The best known of these inventories are the Sex Knowledge Inventories, Form X and Form Y, but additional inventories have been developed that deal with dating, courtship, drugs, love, marital communication, marital prediction, marital stress, marital role expectation, parent-adolescent communication, religious attitudes, social competency, and venereal disease.[17]

A simulation game that deals with spouse selection is among the products offered by a Utah concern with the acronym of GAME, Games Aiding Motivation in Education.[18] The game, Compatibility, involves four to eight students who are provided sets of cards that offer a number of options that require open discussion among the participants. The rationale of choosing potential marital partners is, thus, exposed, and the students come away with a far better insight into how men and women think about each other than the usual classroom exchanges.

Family-Life Research

Family-life research, too, has grown enormously over the years and has been difficult to follow, even for professional family-life educators. Now and then the public hears about some spectacular breakthrough, particularly when the area of investigation is human sexuality. The Kinsey Reports on sexual behavior in the human male and female in the late 1940s and early 1950s made headlines.[19] More recently, most persons have heard about Masters and Johnson's studies, entitled *Human Sexual Response* and *Human Sexual Inadequacy*.[20] Many have judged these pioneering research efforts in human sexuality by the reactions of reviewers, essayists, journalists, or other shapers of public opinion. Far fewer have themselves read these works and grappled with the wealth of data they contain. What is missing is the training, experience, and active participation in family research on the part of many would-be critics or sympathizers. Instead, many have sought to use these studies to justify their own attitudes toward human sexuality. They can find such justification if they search hard enough, although these studies, as with most classic and pioneering efforts, raise more questions than they answer.

The diversity, abundance, and steady flow of family-life research require some means to bring the data together, lest they defeat the very purposes for which they were produced. Teams of scholars have begun to publish compendiums of family-life research, such as William Goode, Elizabeth Hopkins, and Helen McClure's *Social Systems and Family Patterns*.[21]

These inventories bring together the thousands of research articles scattered in professional journals and technical monographs. One result is to provide empirical ground upon which to base personal and social decisions pertaining to marriage and family. A proviso, of course, is needed to caution those who must act that "all" knowledge is not yet available.

For those who search for definite information concerning family life, there are the inevitable contradictions from multiple studies on the same topic. Further, there are gaps in the knowledge: key questions have been neither been asked nor answered. The best an inventory of research studies can offer is a wealth of hypotheses that have yet to be tied together in some macrotheory acceptable and useful for all.

Nevertheless, work in family-life research goes forward. If compendia are not readily available, yearly and decennial summaries in professional journals are useful. That the final truth has not been revealed in the 1970s is refreshingly honest—a quality that emerges when students find authorities saying quite simply that they do not know what the facts are or what they mean. What seems to be occurring in the present is the development of major research centers, such as the Institute of Family Research at the University of Minnesota, led by Reuben Hill and his associates. From such a center can come materials readily available to future generations. The organizational approach provides the necessary focus of hard data from which may come macrofamily theory and even family-life "laws." In the interim, men and women will try to live as best they can with less than complete information to guide them.

Family Counseling

It would seem presumptious to both teach and counsel with the sketchy information available to present generations. Yet, what data are available are ample enough to enable persons to expand their information horizons and cope with real-life problems. The latter is the function of family counseling.

One useful way to comprehend the nature of family counseling is to note the various ways it parallels the practice of medicine. Counseling grows out of the need for action, just as medicine does, despite any handicaps concerning the lack of tools, skills, or knowledge that might prevent, ease, or eradicate human suffering. A high order of medical or counseling know-how does exist, but professionals would be the first to admit that there is much yet that has to be done.

Persons do not wait upon education or research to enter into marriage and family life. They enter it as normally as they breathe. What they soon discover, however, are the *complexities* of marriage and family life, and it is at that point that they may cry out for help. Like the medical profession, family counselors are in a helping profession and seek to guide counselees as best they can.

By whatever means, whether education, reading research, retrospection, inspection, or introspection of real-life experiences, persons seek relief from their family troubles. Teachers, ministers, lawyers, medical doctors, or social workers are pressed into service whether they are prepared to do family counseling or not. Further, in desperation, persons in family distress turn to friends, roommates, relatives, neighbors, and age peers for solace. Few can resist such appeals, but, unfortunately, few are qualified to render the services needed.

Where such nonfamily counselors can be effective is by listening carefully to the distressed persons, providing them with an opportunity to express their emotions, to think out loud with them about their anxieties, and, where possible, to refer them to appropriate agencies or professionals. Such a service is called *consulting* and not counseling, a distinction made many years ago by Rex Skidmore and his colleagues.[22] To go beyond consulting is to court disaster, as many have found to their profound regret. The unwary find themselves caught up in the same troubles as those to whom they offer consultation and have merely compounded an already complex situation.

In an early work on marriage counseling, John Cuber outlined the basic similarities between family counseling and medical practices.[23] Essentially, three steps are taken by both medical doctors and family counselors: diagnosis, prognosis, and therapy.

As any well-trained doctor knows, diagnosis is the first step to take in patient care. Patients will complain about various symptoms, but the doctor needs to know what underlies the surface complaints. If causes are not found, the treatment of symptoms guarantees their reappearance.

In family counseling, a battery of diagnostic tests is often needed to uncover deeply set sources of external pain. Far too many have listened to the symptoms of marital or familial discord in terms of sexual incompatibility, financial inadequacy, or interference by relatives. Sex, money, and in-laws are *not* problems in themselves, but complaints concerning them lie far deeper in the psyche, as well as in social matrices, than amateur, would-be family counselors imagine.

Assuming that diagnosis is correct, that is, that the family counselor has indeed located the root of the symptomology, the next logical step is prognosis. Prognosis is the appraisal of the chances for success if therapy is applied. Prognosis for premarital counseling is usually very good; chances are that difficulties have not progressed too far and here is ample time for many alternative actions. Prognosis for marital counseling is a little less favorable because conditions have developed over time and have reduced the opportunities for positive action. Prognosis for postmarital counseling is the least favorable because even more time has elapsed and possibly created intolerable conditions that markedly limit options.

The reason why prognosis is an important step in counseling—one that is often neglected by untrained persons—is because prognosis indicates that efforts will be productive rather than counterproductive. Promising help to troubled persons without really knowing whether attempts will be truly effective is cruel. Time, itself, may be a healer, but delays may only serve to acerbate an already bitter situation.

In defense of those who are aware that their efforts may not yield the desired results, but who try to perform whatever therapies they can, there is something to be said for sustaining hope. Counselors work, as best they can, with limited resources and this may, in some cases, be more humane than destroying all hope for troubled persons.

Knowing what the targets for change are through diagnosis and knowing what the chances are for success if therapy is initiated through prognosis, family counselors move ahead to therapy. Fortunately, there are a number of therapies from which to choose. The therapies brought to bear on unique situations reflect the preferences, training, and aptitude of the counselor. Robert Harper has delineated some thirty-six systems of therapy that family counselors may elect.[24] All the "systems" work in the hands of skilled counselors, but some are obviously better for specific cases than for others. A number of excellent volumes on family counseling are also available for both practitioners and patients to aid them in the process of understanding their particular problems.[25]

Fundamental decisions on the part of the family counselor include decisions to use either *directive* or *nondirective* techniques, those that literally "direct" or "order" the counselee to behave in a specific manner or those that remove the counselor from providing clues to behavior and rely heavily upon the encouragement of insight on the part of the counselee to resolve his or her own dilemmas. Other strategic decisions involve seeing the client alone or with *conjoint* therapy in which both client and spouse are seen by the counselor in joint sessions. Widening the arena of personal interaction, some counselors prefer *family* counseling in which all those who constitute the actors in the real-life drama of the counselees are brought together to deal with whatever changes are possible to solve or modify the situation.

Marriage and family counseling, then, is not a field for amateurs. It is a field for professionals with the best credentials possible. The American Association of Marriage Counselors (AAMC) has been in existence for almost three decades to set the standards of the profession.

Entrance into the profession of marriage and family counseling begins with the achievement of a graduate or professional degree such as the Doctor of Philosophy degree, the Master of Social Work degree, or the Doctor of Medicine degree. These degrees are first achieved in related or "gateway" fields that bear upon marriage and family. Few family-life professionals enter their fields with family counseling as their ultimate objective. Most discover somewhere along the line that they do have an abiding interest in family counseling and so move on to postgraduate training in the specialization.

Postgraduate training in marriage and family counseling draws upon selected aspects of a wide variety of fields to fill in whatever may be missing in earlier or broader-based training. Essential ingredients in such postgraduate studies include knowledge of personality development, interpersonal relationships, sex anatomy and physiology, genetics and human growth, psychiatrics, sociological analysis of marriage and family, domestic relations law, and, above all, counseling theory and techniques from the field of guidance. Training includes a type of internship or clinical assistantship in which the trainee gains diagnostic skill, referral skill, attitudes of objectivity toward sex and sexual difficulties, and understanding of personal and social deviations under close supervision.

The needs exist. The supply of trained personnel is still too small to meet the national needs in the area of family counseling.

SUMMARY

Future generations will determine for themselves which way they will go. Either they will reorganize and strengthen familes as they are currently known, or they will destroy or abandon established forms and styles to create new forms and styles in family living. This chapter has focused upon those resources for family reorganization that are currently operative. The final chapter will concentrate upon more innovative, experimental, or more revolutionary family styles.

American families have been sorely criticized for their serious shortcomings, and yet there is evidence that the difficulties can be overestimated. Multiproblem families do exist, and while their proportions are small, their use of social services in communities is great. On the other hand, there are still a great many families that continue to produce healthy generations. This is not to cover up whatever troubles do exist in families throughout the nation. There is a wide difference between "problem families" and "families with problems." It is for the latter type that resources for family reorganization offer the best hope.

The three resources for family reorganization are education, research, and counseling. Education recognizes the level of current knowledge concerning families. Research extends the knowledge. And counseling serves those who may not know either research findings or education for marriage and family, but who have committed themselves to marriage and family responsibilities. All three resources are expanding in the United States, but not without external and internal critics. None of the resources is the epitome of perfection, but each represents the efforts of highly skilled and dedicated personnel who are doing whatever they can to raise the levels of family living for present and future generations.

REFERENCES

1 David Cooper, *The Death of the Family*, New York: Pantheon Books, a division of Random House, Inc., 1970.
2 Ibid., p. 5.
3 Ibid., p. 45.
4 Ibid., p. 50. Used with permission.
5 See, for examples, Arlene S. Skolnick and Jerome H. Skolnick, *Family in Transition: Rethinking Marriage, Sexuality, Child Rearing, and Family Organization*, Boston: Little, Brown and Company, 1971; Frank D. Cox, *American Marriage: A Changing Scene?*, Dubuque, Iowa: Wm. C. Brown Company Publishers, 1972; Gwen B. Carr (ed.), *Marriage and Family in a Decade of Change*, Reading, Mass.: Addison-Wesley Publishing Company, Inc., 1972; and Gail Putney Fullerton, *Survival in Marriage: Introduction to Family Interaction, Conflicts, and Alternatives*, New York: Holt, Rinehart and Winston, Inc., 1972.
6 John Lear, "Where Is Society Going?: The Search for Landmarks," *Saturday Review*, April 15, 1972, p. 38.
7 Ibid., p. 37.
8 William A. Westley and Nathan B. Epstein, *The Silent Majority: Families of Emotionally Healthy College Students*, San Francisco, Jossey-Bass, Inc., Publishers, 1969.
9 Ibid., p. 158. Used with permission.
10 Ibid., p. 164.
11 Ibid., p. 164.
12 L. L. Geismar and Michael A. La Sorte, *Understanding the Multi-Problem Family: A Conceptual Analysis and Exploration in Early Identification*, New York: Association Press, 1964.
13 Ibid., p. 17.
14 Ibid., p. 59.
15 Ibid., pp. 73–74. Used with permission.
16 Ibid., p. 81.
17 Family Life Publications, Inc., 219 Henderson Street, P. O. Box 427, Saluda, N. C. 28773.
18 Games Aiding Motivation in Education, P.O. Box 179, University Station, Provo, Utah 84601.Copyright by Jon M. Taylor, 1968.
19 Alfred C. Kinsey, Wardell B. Pomeroy, and Clyde E. Martin, *Sexual Behavior in the Human Male*, Philadelphia: W. B. Saunders Company, 1948, and Alfred C. Kinsey, Wardell B. Pomeroy, Clyde E. Martin, and Paul H. Gebhard, *Sexual Behavior in the Human Female*, Philadelphia: W. B. Saunders Company, 1953.
20 William H. Masters and Virginia E. Johnson, *Human Sexual Response*,

Boston: Little, Brown and Company, 1966, and William H. Masters and Virginia E. Johnson, *Human Sexual Inadequacy*, Boston: Little, Brown and Company, 1970.

21 William J. Goode, Elizabeth Hopkins, and Helen M. McClure, *Social Systems and Family Patterns: A Propositional Inventory*, Indianapolis: The Bobbs-Merrill Company, Inc., 1971.

22 Rex A. Skidmore, Hugh Van Steeter Garrett, and C. Jay Skidmore, *Marriage Consulting: An Introduction to Marriage Counseling*, New York: Harper & Brothers, 1956.

23 John F. Cuber, *Marriage Counseling Practice*, New York: Appleton-Century-Crofts, Inc., 1948.

24 Robert A. Harper, *Psychoanalysis and Pyschotherapy: 36 Systems*, Englewood Cliffs, N. J.: Spectrum Books, Prentice-Hall, Inc., 1959.

25 See Dean Johnson, *Marriage Counseling: Theory and Practice*, Englewood Cliffs, N. J.: Prentice-Hall, Inc., 1961; Richard H. Klemer, *Counseling in Marital and Sexual Problems: A Physician's Handbook*, Baltimore: The Williams & Wilkins Company, 1965; Ben N. Ard, Jr., and Constance C. Ard (eds.), *Handbook of Marriage Counseling*, Palo Alto, Calif.: Science and Behavior Books, Inc., 1969; and Bernard L. Greene, *A Clinical Approach to Marital Problems: Evaluation and Management*, Springfield, Ill.: Charles C Thomas, Publisher, 1970.

STUDY QUESTIONS AND ACTIVITIES

1 Are education, research, and counseling only ineffective "patchwork" of a defunct marriage and family system in the United States? Should such efforts be dropped in favor of some totally new forms of marriage and family in future generations?

2 Would family education be more effective if it were offered as a part of almost every educational effort rather than offered as a course or series of courses that focuses upon families alone?

3 Suggest research projects that are sorely needed in marriage and family life in the United States because, at present, there simply are no definitive answers to questions.

4 What is the difference between marriage "consulting" and marriage "counseling"?

5 What, in your opinion, are the qualities of an effective marriage and family counselor?

6 Is self-counseling or couple-counseling superior to seeking counseling from qualified family counselors?

7 Stage a counseling session or series of sessions and critique the procedures used.

8 Select what you consider the best piece of marriage and family research you have encountered and explain its value to the class.

9 Explain how future generations are helped by current work in family-life education, research, and counseling.

SUGGESTED ADDITIONAL READINGS

Broderick, Carlfred B. (ed.), *A Decade of Family Research and Action*, special issue of the National Council on Family Relations covering fourteen articles culled from the November 1970, February 1971, and May 1971 issues of the *Journal of Marriage and the Family.*

Brown, Muriel W., "Organizational Programs to Strengthen the Family," in Harold T. Christensen (ed.), *Handbook of Marriage and the Family*, Chicago: Rand McNally & Company, 1964, pp. 823–880.

Erickson, Gerald D., and Terrence P. Hogan, *Family Therapy: An Introduction to Theory and Technique*, Belmont, Calif.: Brookes/Cole Publishing Company, 1972.

Kerckhoff, Richard K., "Family Life Education in America," in Christensen, op. cit., pp. 881–911.

Leslie, Gerald R., "The Field of Marriage Counseling," in Christensen, op. cit., pp. 912–943.

Lief, Harold I., and Ernest van den Haag, "Debate: Is School an Appropriate Place for Sex Education?" *Sexual Behavior*, vol. 1, no. 5, pp. 64–73, August 1971.

Manley, Helen, "Sex Education," in Frank L. Steeves (ed.), *The Subjects in the Curriculum: Selected Readings*, New York: The Odyssey Press, Inc., 1968, pp. 377–387.

Nichols, William C. (ed.), *The Family Life Coordinator*, vol. 22, no. 1, January 1973, special issue, "The Field of Marriage Counseling."

Sager, Clifford J., and Helen S. Kaplan (eds.), *Progress in Group and Family Therapy*, New York: Brunner/Mazel, 1972.

Tate, George, *Strategy of Therapy: Toward the Engineering of Social Growth*, New York: Springer Publishing Co., Inc., 1967.

Walsh, Robert H., "The Generational Gap in Sexual Beliefs," *Sexual Behavior*, vol. 2, no. 1, pp. 5–10, January 1972.

Zuk, Gerald H., *Family Therapy: A Triadic Approach*, New York: Behavioral Publications, 1971.

Chapter 16

Families of the Future

Multigenerational study of families requires consideration of what future generations may encounter. There are enough critics of present conditions to counter the complacency of those who have reached some level of satisfaction. This has been particularly true of the past decade in a protesting, divided United States. A "brave new world" is possible by tearing down those systems that stifle people and building upon the ruins those that enhance the human condition. Families of the future will be among those systems, and we turn our attention to them. What can or should family life be like? What emerges may horrify some, interest others, and inspire still others.

Future orientation is fast becoming a new scientific specialization called *futurology.* Its practitioners call themselves *futurists* and have organized themselves into a World Future Society, An Association for the

Study of Alternative Futures. Chartered in Washington, D.C., in 1966, its membership has grown to over 8,000; it held its First General Assembly in 1971. Futurists have introduced university-level courses to gain even more converts in the future of such areas as technology, ideology, economy, and the conditions of mankind. In this concluding chapter, families of the future are singled out for discussion in the context of the futurology movement.

HOW FAR AHEAD IS THE FUTURE?

One determination is to specify just how far into the future one is looking. It makes a difference if one is describing possible events in 1984, 1990, or 2000. In the 1970s, the end of the twentieth century and the beginning of the twenty-first are well within sight and, accordingly, the year 2000 seems to be the most popular date that present generations want to consider. There is notably less concern and even less interest in some distant future, such as the year 4000 or 8000. The year 2000 holds the most appeal because *it will be experienced by present generations*, a temporo-centrism that is too strong to ignore.

Generations are primarily concerned about their *own futures* and far less concerned about what life might be like for unknown, untold numbers of generations yet to be born. The farther one projects the future, the greater become the chances for intervening variables to alter anticipated conditions. In addition, adoption of some humanitarian identification with infinite numbers of people over infinite periods of time is too much to ask of present generations.

Most of the reputable futurists of the 1970s are not particularly "youthful," except in outlook. Chronologically, futurists who have had their works widely publicized are middle-aged or older. The vast majority have spent a full lifetime gaining their expertise in specialized fields. As has been noted many times in multigenerational analysis, it is only after the traditions of the past and the trends of the present are understood that the future can begin to be dimly seen. The pattern is one of middle-aged persons developing ideologies that younger generations will accept, modify, or reject when they reach their majority.

HOW DOES THE FUTURE REVEAL ITSELF?

Perhaps the best summation of futuristic techniques may be found in Burnham Beckwith's book entitled *The Next 500 Years*.[1] Beckwith suggests at least a dozen different ways to delve systematically into the future. These are, in brief:[2]

1 Assume that conditions will continue and so study trends and project them.

2 Weigh both expert and public opinion concerning long-run trends.

3 Noting the difference between what experts and laymen hold to be true, follow the experts.

4 "Backward" societies will move in the direction of "advanced" societies; study this.

5 Distinguish between efficient and inefficient social organizations and predict that the inefficient will become efficient.

6 Observe the difference between the wealthy and the poor in various societies because the poor will begin to share in the wealth of the rich.

7 Ascertain the consumption of goods and services by the most intelligent or best educated in any class in any advanced country and these will become the objectives of those who are least intelligent or least educated.

8 Discover successful pioneering reforms in advanced states and other advanced states will make them state policy.

9 Study universal or global patterns because distinctive or unique localisms will be gradually displaced by them.

10 Study technological developments and anticipate their social consequences.

11 Examine feasible schemes offered in either utopian systems or in science fiction and these can be made real.

12 Engage in social engineering under the assumptions that pleasure-seeking and rational men and women will seek their own welfare.

Beckwith's twelve techniques involve at least three different ways to study the future. These are *projection, planning,* and *prediction.* Some distinctions concerning each of these can help clarify some of the problems of futurology.

Projection, for instance, consists of carrying out current trends to some logical conclusions. Projection amounts to saying that the future will consist of "more" of the present. To others, projection involves "catching up with reality," a reality that exists in the present for the few but which, in the future, could be extended to include the many.

Planning differs from projection in trying to achieve some consensus that certain conditions should prevail. Such agreement is followed by deliberate efforts to carry out the plan. Projection, then, is an exercise in logical thought. Planning is an exercise in action.

Prediction takes into account as many variables that could affect the future as possible. These factors are typically found in association with conditions. When they can be isolated, weighted, and tested for their causal connections, these factors, indicators, or items can be used to measure the chances that future results will occur. Prediction has been the objective of scientists schooled in the traditions of the scientific method. Unlike planning, prediction does not involve controlling variables or joining with others to bring about desired results. Nor does it rely upon qualitative judgments. It relies, instead, upon painstaking, quantitative analysis of the tangled skein of factors that produce specific results.

Undoubtedly, all three methods—projection, planning, and prediction—can be used to probe the future. Projection attracts attention because it is dramatic and imaginative. Planning appeals because it is creative. Prediction merits respect for its painstaking methods, but only the highly disciplined, the technically prepared, can participate in it and fully appreciate what it is trying to achieve.

Each futurist procedure, however, also has its unique problems. Many individuals or groups do not agree that the actions of the few should be extended to the actions of the many. Countermoves, popularized either as "backlash" or as "overreaction," can be and have been mounted, as, for example, the drive against sex education or the recent Supreme Court ruling on pornography.

Planning is criticized because there is serious doubt about the wisdom of moving too far ahead with plans without knowing their long-range consequences. For example, automobile transportation has promoted the development of superhighway systems, which may yet be judged to be a disastrous mistake because of damage to the ecology of the countryside. Our cities engage in short-range and long-range planning that has required constant building, rebuilding, and "renewals."

In prediction, *all* factors are not known or are not guaranteed as "surprise-free." Rather, those engaged in prediction are doing the best they can with increasing sophistication of the techniques of analysis and synthesis.

WHAT IS PROJECTED, PLANNED, OR PREDICTED FOR FAMILIES OF THE FUTURE?

A Variety of Family Forms

Family futurists are saying that in the future, a wide variety of family structures can coexist in American society. Indeed, these variations are already present. The only change will be one of wider acceptance that these forms have as much legitimacy as the familiar, exclusive, lifetime, monogamous marriages and mother-father-child families of the present. The manner of entering into marriage or terminating it, the length of time spent in a marriage, the number and identity of intimate marriage partners, the roles of parents, the treatment of reproduction control, and the relationships of the sexes with or without formal marriage are all projected changes of future families.

As explained earlier, progressive monogamy, or serial monogamy, is already current. Marriage is not necessarily entered into for a lifetime, but until the laws or the participants determine that a union should be dissolved. If a particular married or unmarried couple do not regard themselves as compatible, they divorce or move away from each other to decide if they wish to remain together or live with someone else. By changing partners freely, it is hoped that compatible partners will eventually be located. Persons will have distinctive "marriage careers" rather than "a marriage" within their lifetimes.

Monogamy would not be the exclusive form of marriage or the epainogamous* form of marriage that it is today. Polyandry, polygyny, and group marriage would be formally acknowledged as viable options. A woman would be allowed to have two or more husbands. A man would be allowed to have two or more wives. A number of men and women would form a group, "tribe," "nation," or commune and regard each participant as a husband or a wife.

In place of current kinship networks, "intimate networks of families" who mutually choose each other may evolve. Instead of fixed relationships with a set of relatives, individuals will search for those persons who can satisfy their needs. It is assumed that the individuals selected will also receive satisfaction from the initiating partner.

Variously titled trial marriages, student marriages, term marriages, or two-step marriages would become quite commonplace. Differing in some details, such as the use of contraceptives, the division of labor, and the amount of time involved, these marriages serve to test men and women who are inexperienced either with each other or with marriage itself. If they are mutually satisfying, couples can choose to continue their relationships. If not, there remains the option of not going forward and promoting any further period of mutual obligations.

Less Exclusiveness, Privacy, or Prudery Concerning Human Sexuality

Much of the above incorporates the expression of human sexuality within a framework of some sustained relationship of responsibility. Human sexuality, however, is currently being treated with increasing frankness. Family futurists, thus, can project a time when group sex, not group marriage, will be perfectly acceptable as an "outlet," in Kinseyan terms,

*Epainogami is marriage that is praised, sanctioned, supported, or approved—an innovative term credited to James. L. Gibbs.

for sexual drives. This wave of the future is presaged by what is now known as "swinging," "spouse sharing," or "swapping."

In brief, human sexuality is to be taken out of its present darkness into the light of day. Events normally hidden from the public will take place in full view, in public ceremonials, as they occur. Adolescence, signaled by a first menstrauation or a first seminal emission, will become family events or family rituals. Virginia Satir has suggested that there will be "loss-of-virginity" parties to mark the time when a person experiences his or her first coital act.[3]

College campuses house a youth-segregated community, and these youthful communities have already initiated coeducational dormitories in place of sex-cloistered cubicles. Visitation at any hour of the day or night is becoming established policy. Assignment of entering freshmen to dormitory rooms, regardless of sex, is the next logical step. Human sexuality is thus being treated as the normal part of life that it is and not to be circumscribed by sex norms that carry with them any onus of shame, degradation, or guilt. At least, this is the direction in which present generations seem to be steering future generations.

Reflecting the increasing frankness concerning human sexuality, more and more publications are appearing that attempt to answer the numerous questions left unresolved from earlier times. Notable among them has been David Reuben's book *Everything You Always Wanted to Know About Sex & Were Afraid To Ask*.[4] The title alone mirrors the trend to which we have been referring. Sometimes facetious, sometimes tongue-in-cheek, but sometimes very pointedly, Reuben pierces the armor of prudery with his directness and honesty. An example of Reuben's directness can be seen in his discussion of three forms of sexual intercourse: reprosex, love-sex, and funsex.[5] Reprosex is reproductive sex, or sexual intercourse for the purpose of conceiving children. It is, as he notes, "unpopular with teen-agers, unmarried lovers, gay young bachelors, single girls, and ladies with ten children."[6] Love-sex is favored by everyone, according to Reuben, "but not everyone has the chance to be exposed to it."[7] And funsex, Reuben says, is motivated by the pleasure it can bring, despite grave warnings to the contrary.

Greater Variety in Parenthood and in Reproduction

Parenthood will be quite different from that of the present. Carl Levett, for instance, has suggested that a "third parent" will become a career for well-trained, professional persons, most likely males, who would perform important socialization functions now normally assigned to natural fathers.[8] Such a career is already indicated in the efforts of the Big Brother, Big Sister, Adopt a Grandfather, or Parents without Partners programs in which empty family slots are filled with surrogates who are sympathetic to the needs of children for adult male and female models.

Natural parenthood will be controlled in future generations. Application for a license to have a child may become the accepted procedure. Training would be needed as evidence that persons could qualify for parenthood. Further, reproduction by AIH, AID, ETW, ETD, ETDD, and ET measures would increase. These acronyms are identified as follows: AIH indicates artificial insemination using the husband's sperm; AID indicates artificial insemination using a donor's sperm, ETW indicates egg transfer from the woman's ovaries to her uterus because her oviducts are blocked or occluded; ETD indicates transfering the eggs of another donor to the potential mother because ovulation has not been proceeding normally; ETDD indicates the practice of transfering both eggs and sperm from donors so that the potential mother acts as a host body; and ET indicates simply egg transfer alone. In ET or vitriparity, full term development of fertilized ova occurs outside the human body. Reproduction *in vitro*, the products of which are often referred to as "test-tube babies," has not yet been achieved, but remains a possibility for future generations. Table 16-1 summarizes these procedures and identifies the biological contributions of parents to their children.

Genetic research currently underway suggests that other control techniques could become routine. These include the ability to predetermine the sex of a fetus or to determine the sex of an unborn child. If the latter becomes common, so may the option to abort a child because of its sex. Other genetic studies indicate that *euphenics*, the ability to correct

Table 16-1 Biological Contribution of Parents to Offspring Acquired in Various Ways

Reproduction procedures	Biological contributions			
	Coitus	Paternal	Maternal	Maternal environment
Normal conception	X	X	X	X
AIH	—	X	X	X
AID	—	—	X	X
ETW	—	X	X	X
ETD	—	X	—	X
ETDD	—	—	—	X
Adoption	—	—	—	—
ET	—	X	X	—

Source: Adapted from Anne McLaren, "Biological Regulation of Reproduction," in Katherine Elliott (ed.), *The Family and Its Future*, London: J. & A. Churchill, 1970, p. 104. Used with permission.

genetic defects, and *eugenics*, the ability to produce genetic effects through breeding, can be perfected and applied to humans. Further, *algeny*, the biochemical alteration of genes themselves, is possible, as does nuclear cloning. *Nuclear cloning* consists of substituting the nucleus of a body cell for the nucleus of a fertilized egg. The result is that the qualities of the donor are inherited. Because there is an almost unlimited supply of body-cell nucleii, persons judged to have desirable genetic constitutions could be duplicated as many times as wished. Persons stamped with the same genetic features could be created to double, triple, or quadruple the reproduction of valued combinations.

Many of these procedures are now considered to be science fiction. However, because mankind has the capacity to use his intelligence, he may do so to his advantage or disadvantage. One of the most striking predictions has been made by the publication *The Immortality Newsletter*. This newsletter looks forward to the time when death will be conquered. Assuming that immortality is achieved for mankind, the newsletter notes that there will no longer be a *need* to have children, that is to bring children into the world to achieve immortality.[9] Such a prediction may seem absurd, but considered in the light of rapid changes that have already occurred, we hesitate to dismiss the idea.

New and Different Spouse-Selection Procedures

More and more persons are using computers to meet potential marriage partners. The huge population pools of the future may make it mandatory to find a spouse through a data bank. Each person may have his or her master card started at birth, and constantly updated to include all pertinent events or information. Either on a voluntary or an involuntary basis, individuals will seek out potential spouses through their master cards.

Sexual equality of the future will include the initiation and payment for dates by both sexes. Men will be asked to spend an evening, a month, or several months in the company of females. In either case, the cost of whatever entertainment or travel is involved will be borne by the initiating partner. The right of refusal, of course, will extend to either sex.

Mass Housing Changes for Families of the Future

Private housing in which a single family unit occupies a fairly extensive plot of ground may well be doomed in the future. Population pressures will require future generations to live closer together in high-rise apartments or cubicles with elaborate life-sustaining facilities in or near the same complex. Commuting to work would be a thing of the past because highly trained persons would "communicate" to work from their own cubicle.[10] Further, dome-covered cities would provide artificial external environments. Families would determine which specialized climate they preferred and could select from available lists cities that were tropical, semitropical, seasonal, or mainly "winterized" in their controlled atmospheres.

Cities of the future will be constructed not only vertically upward, but also vertically downward. Subterranean living will permit more persons to occupy less ground surface. "People storage" and "people containment" will be normal policy. Along with the abandonment of private housing will go private or personalized transportation. Mass transportation will supplant the automobile, and travel will be licensed or restricted to the privileged few.

New Sets of Future Values

The relationships between and among individuals and their families rest heavily upon the prevailing ethics or values of the times. Herbert Stroup has suggested that there are at least three options upon which to base familial forms and procedures of the future.[11]

The first is *prescriptive ethics*, such as are found in the Ten Commandments. "Rightness' or "wrongness" is predetermined, and all are to abide by the directives. If there is consensus, prescriptive ethics can work successfully. However, lacking popular support, directives may be honored in the breach or ignored altogether.

The second option is *purposeful ethics*. This option is said to be popular with educators, social workers, or "liberals" because goal-setting is done by groups of like-minded people. Not only are ways and means to achieve the goals set, but so are the goals themselves. Thus, in purposeful ethics, both objectives and procedures are mutually decided by special-interest groups.

In the third option, *situational ethics*, people determine what is "right" under specific circumstances. This is individualistic ethics or self-determination that fit well with the longings of individuals for freedom from traditional or group pressures.

Perhaps all three ethical prescriptions can be combined in the future. They may or may not work at cross purposes. If they could all be accommodated, the problems now visualized may vanish.

AN ABIDING FAITH IN FAMILIES

Interestingly enough, there is a sense of great faith in the worth of families. It seems to be based upon recognition that human beings are sensitive to the needs of each other. In a world that may be hostile, cold, or threatening, families seem safe harbors.

Richard Farson has observed that there is a crying need for genuineness, a demystification in Weberian terms, or a personal honesty that transcends all sham.[12] People are not going to be satisfied when they recognize that their present conditions can be changed. Emotions need to be expressed, and the best environment seems to be families. Emotions, however, need to be expressed without exploding into physical and mental pain for family participants or others.

Farson puts it very well when he notes that *"the greatest resource for the solution of any social problem is the very population that has the problem."*[13] He goes on to say, "Mental patients are better for each other than the hospital staff is for them. Students learn more from each other than they learn from professors. Addicts are better at helping addicts than psychiatrists are. Prisoners can run better rehabilitation programs for inmates than correctional officers."[14] Alcoholics, war veterans, the handicapped, elders, and racial, religious, or ethnic minorities find within their mutual experiences a comaraderie and understanding that can help them obtain the dignity and happiness they so desire. In familial terms, divorced persons, parents without partners, unmarried persons, widowed persons, and generations can understand, identify, and aid each other when they are together.

IT IS WITHIN OUR HANDS

For those who want direct answers in the present to the questions that veil the future, Daniel Bell refers to an old Talmudic (pertaining to the authoritative body of Jewish tradition) parable. Bell offered the parable during the deliberations of a Commission on the Year 2000, sponsored by the Academy of Arts and Sciences. It is as follows:

> There was once a rabbi who had the reputation of knowing what was in a man's mind by reading his thoughts. A wicked boy came to see him and said: "Rabbi, I have in my hand a small bird. Is it alive or is it dead?" And the boy thought to himself: If he says it is dead, I will open my hand and let it fly away; if he says it is alive, I will quickly squeeze it and show him it is dead. And the boy repeated the question, "Rabbi, I have in my hand a small bird. Is it alive or is it dead?" And the rabbi gazed steadily at him, and said quietly: "Whatever you will; whatever you will."[15]

SUMMARY

With the twenty-first century just ahead, the science of futurology is in its infancy. Marriage and family represents one of the most vital areas that futurists wish to consider. It seems easier to project the near future of the year 2000 than that of the years 4000, 8000, or beyond. Much of the interest in families of the future is generated by the fact that many persons alive today will actually experience some of the anticipated changes of the twenty-first century. Led currently by middle-aged or mature specialists, the youngest generations will be able to act upon whatever decisions concerning the future must be made.

Some dozen techniques are currently employed to penetrate the mysteries of the future, but they can be grouped under projection, planning, or prediction. Each can be criticized and each has unique problems, but the futurist techniques represent the work of some of the best minds and talents available to present generations.

The overall projections, plans, or predictions of future family life can be summarized into about six different trends: a variety of family forms; less exclusiveness, privacy, or prudery concerning human sexuality; greater variety in parenthood and reproduction; new and different spouse-selection procedures; mass housing changes; and new sets of future values.

Above all, there is abiding faith that families will survive in the future. In many ways, what *will happen* is in our collective hands.

REFERENCES

1 Burnham P. Beckwith, *The Next 500 Years*, Jericho, N. Y.; Exposition Press, 1968.
2 Ibid.
3 Virginia Satir, "Marriage as a Human-Actualizing Contract," in Herbert A. Otto (ed.), *The Family in Search of a Future: Alternate Models for Moderns*, New York: Appleton-Century-Crofts, Inc., 1970, p. 61.
4 David Reuben, *Everything You Always Wanted to Know about Sex & Were Afraid to Ask*, New York: David McKay Company, Inc., 1969.
5 Ibid., pp. 44–46.
6 Ibid., p. 45.
7 Ibid., p. 45.
8 Carl Levett, "A Parental Presence in Future Family Models," in Herbert A. Otto (ed.), *The Family in Search of a Future: Alternate Models for Moderns*, New York: Appleton-Century-Crofts, Inc., 1970, pp. 161–169.
9 *The Immortality Newsletter*, A. Stuart Otto (Ed.), vol. 2, no. 4, p. 4, April 1972, P.O. Box 696, San Marcos, Calif. 92069.
10 See "A Long Look Ahead," *Bell Telephone Magazine*, vol. 51, no. 1, pp. 3–7, January-February 1972.
11 Herbert Stroup, "Philosophy Predicts and Projects," in Richard E. Farson, Philip M. Hauser, Herbert Stroup, and Anthony J. Wiener, *The Future of*

the Family, New York: Family Service Association of America, 1969, pp. 52–54.
12 Farson et al., op. cit., p. 69.
13 Ibid.
14 Ibid.
15 Daniel Bell (ed.), *Toward the Year 2000: Work in Progress,* Boston: Beacon Press, 1967, p. 62.

STUDY QUESTIONS AND ACTIVITIES

1 Hypothesize situations in which representatives of young, middle-aged, and elderly generations will take respective positions of (1) favoring strongly, (2) moderately favoring, and (3) strongly opposing projections, planning, or predictions of future family life. Test these hypotheses with your own research design.
2 What are your personal reactions to what seems to lie ahead for families of the future?
3 Apply some of the techniques suggested by Beckwith to a study of families of the future. Divide the job among members of your class.
4 What "strains," if any, are imposed upon American society if multiple family structures and procedures coexist?
5 Can families of the future drastically change without parallel changes in other social systems in the United States?
6 Will radical changes have to occur in nonfamily systems before families of the future are possible?
7 What difference do you believe your own life will make in shaping the lives of future generations?
8 Critique Stroup's "prescriptive," "purposeful," and "situational" ethics. Must one or the other dominate, or is some combination feasible?

SUGGESTED ADDITIONAL READINGS

Bell, Daniel, *The End of Ideology: On the Exhaustion of Political Ideas in the Fifties,* rev. ed., New York: The Free Press, 1965, Chap. 13, "The Mood of Three Generations," pp. 299–314, paperback.
Davids, Leo, "North American Marriage: 1990," *The Futurist,* vol. V, no. 5, pp. 190–194, October 1971.
Dreikurs, Rudolf, "Equality: The Life-Style of Tomorrow," *The Futurist,* vol. VI, no. 4 pp. 153–155, August 1972.
Futurist, vol. IV, no. 2, April, 1970, special issue, "The Future of Women and Marriage."
Futurist, vol. VI, no. 5, October, 1972, special issue, "The Family as an Agent of Social Change."
Mead, Margaret, "The Future of Socialization," in Arlene S. and Jerome H.

Skolnick (eds.), *Family in Transition*, Boston: Little, Brown and Company, 1971, pp. 366–376.

Pierce, Chester M., "The Pre-Schooler and the Future," *The Futurist*, vol. VI, no. 1, pp. 13–15, February 1972.

Society, vol. 9, no. 4, February 1972, special issue, "New Life Styles for Americans."

Sussman, Marvin B. (ed.), *The Family Coordinator*, vol. 21, no. 4, October 1972, special issue, "Variant Marriage Styles and Family Forms."

Toffler, Alvin, *Future Shock*, New York: Random House, Inc., 1970.

Troll, Lillian E., "Is Parent-Child Conflict What We Mean by the Generation Gap?" *The Family Coordinator*, vol. 21, no. 3, pp. 347–349, July 1972.

Weigert, Andrew J., and Darwin L. Thomas, "Family as a Conditional Universal," *Journal of Marriage and the Family*, vol. 33, no. 1, pp. 188–194, February 1971.

Epilogue: Families in Multigenerational Retrospect

With this brief note, we continue to use the multigenerational approach. We look back over the labor of years to appreciate where we began, where we are now, and where we may hope to be. From one perspective, the state of our knowledge is pitifully small concerning families. Yet, even this is important to recognize lest we become self-satisfied and interested only in the problems of our times. From another perspective, the diversity of family life is impressive and challenges us to work even harder to grasp its nature.

Pages of print seem inadequate to express how men and women have sought to live together over the generations. Perhaps the unwritten words "between the lines," the spirit of what this text is trying to convey, has been grasped and savored by the reader. By using the multigenerational approach, we have taken a longer, and different, look at families than does the typical family text. Does this approach have merit? Can we benefit, and can others benefit, from it?

Some day, if not in the present, the labors of the many who have devoted themselves in love to making families truly satisfying can be appreciated. The little daily deeds, the accumulating years of experiences, the tireless efforts against all odds will be seen in perspective. In the meantime, families will endure because within them generations draw closer and sustain life itself.

Index

Bernard, Jessie, 139
Berne, Eric, 223
Billingsley, Andrew, 170–171
Birth control, 57, 82
Black families, 169–178
Blacks, 138–140
Blitsen, Dorothy R., 92–93
Blood, Robert O., Jr., 167, 250–251
Blood theory, 39
Blumel, C. S., 125
Boll, Eleanor, 270
Bossard, James H. S., 235, 270,
  287–288
Bowerman, Charles, 285
Bowman, Henry A., 14
Bride service, 54–55
Briffault, Robert, 51–52
Brim, Orville, 271, 273
Broken homes, 271–272
Budgeting, 254
Burgess, E. W., 3, 251

Cana conferences, 56
Cavan, Ruth, 190–193
Centers, Richard, 152
Chalitza, 57
Change:
  age grades, U.S., 117–120
  and challenge, 10
  occupational needs, U.S., 1960–
    1975, 156
  through revolution, 162
  social, 202–203
  and status of men and women,
    105–111
  youth as change agents, 164
Chicanos, 131–136
Children:
  deviant, 271–272
  and functions of parents, 265–270
  Greek, 60–61
  Hebrew, 57–58
  and parents, 286–288
  Plymouth Colony, 115–116
  Roman, 66
  Tungus and U.S., 89
  and WUMP families, 158, 161–163
Christ, Jesus, 56, 102
Christensen, Harold T., 3

Christians, early Western, 101–102
Cloning, nuclear, 325
Compadres, 134
Complementary needs, 238–239
Conflict resolution, 220–221
Confrontation, 221
Consensus:
  generational, 215–225
  individual, 237–238
Contraception, 57, 82
Cooper, David, 301–302
Coser, Lewis, 290
Cottrell, Leonard, 251
Counseling, family, 311–314
Cournot, Antoine, 200
Credibility gaps, 9, 199–212
Cross-cultural study of families,
  73–97
Cuber, John F., 39, 151, 312

Dating, 233–234
Democratization, 103
Demos, John, 117
Denaturalization of children, 265–266
Descent:
  bilateral, 40
  double, 43
  matrilineal, 43
  patrilineal, 43
Developmental stake, 224
Devos, George, 182
Disciplining of children, 266–267
Dissension, generational, 199–212
Divorce:
  American, 84
  entrances and exits in spouse selec-
    tion, 229
  Hebrew, 58–59
  no-fault, 204
  Tungus, 84
Double standard, sexual, 206
Driver, Harold, 137
Dromel, Justin, 199–202
Drugs, 210
Duvall, Evelyn, 238, 251–252

Education, family life, 305–310
Elder, Glen, 271–273

Frontierism, 104
Functions:
  family, 3–5, 74, 119
  parental, 265–270
Future families, 318–328

Gamble, Elizabeth, 101–102
GAME (Games Aiding Motivation in
    Education), 310
Games, 218, 222–223
Generations:
  in black families, 172–178
  common ground, 216–217
  conceptualization, 6–7
  conflict in Africa and Japan,
      123–125
  consensus, 215–225
  definition, 5
  dissension, 199–212
  dominant, 12–13
  Japanese-American, 179–182
  linkage, 8, 157–159
  middle, 121–122, 281–282
  needs, 218
  Nyakyusa, 80
  worth, 13–15
Gerontocracy, 13
Gibbs, James L., 322
Giddings, Franklin Henry, 236
Golden, Harry, 185
Goldscheider, Calvin, 186–188
Goldstein, Sidney, 186–188
Goode, William J., 92
Greeks, 99–100
Gurin, Gerald, 284–285

Harper, Robert, 313
Hebrew families, 52–59, 99
Heiskanen, Veronica, 189
Heritages, 17, 40–42
  (See also Vigencias)
Hetaerae, 61–62, 100
Heterogamy, 237
Hill, Reuben, 258, 311
Homogamy, 237
Homosexuality, Spartan, 62
Honeymoon, 240–241
Hopkins, Elizabeth, 310

Household, 35
Housing for families of future, 325–326
HRAF, 75–76
Human Relations Area Files (HRAF),
    75–76
Humanism, 103
Husbands and wives, 246–259, 282–283

Immortality, 325
Incest tabu, 63–64
Indians, American, 136–138, 221
Individualism, 104, 164
Inkeles, Alex, 273–274
In loco parentis, 12
Interpretation of culture, 268
Involvement process, 235–236

Japan, generational conflicts, 123–
    125
Japanese-American families, 178–184
Jews:
  American, 11
  contacts with blacks, 175
  families, 184–189
Johnson, Virginia F., 255, 310
Joint family, 35
Juvenocracy, 13

Kahl, Joseph, 152
Kalym, 86
Keniston, Kenneth, 207
Kenkel, William, 151
Kephart, William M., 41
Kiddushin, 55
Kinship network, 248–249
Kitano, Harry H. L., 183
Kockeis, Eva, 284
Koller, Marvin R., 39, 264
Kuypers, Joseph A., 224

Landis, Judson T., 252
Levir, 57
Lewis, Jerry, 169, 177
Lex Oppia, 101
Life cycle, 36–38
Linton, Ralph, 75